ETHNIC GROUPS OF INSULAR SOUTHEAST ASIA

VOLUME 2: PHILIPPINES AND FORMOSA

FRANK M. LEBAR, Editor and Compiler

Contributing Authors:

Eric S. Casino

William H. Geoghegan

Donn V. Hart

F. Landa Jocano

Thomas M. Kiefer

Marcelino N. Maceda

E. Arsenio Manuel

Melvin Mednick

Grace Wood Moore

Clifford Sather

Charles P. Warren

Aram A. Yengoyen

Renato and Michelle Rosaldo

HUMAN RELATIONS AREA FILES PRESS

New Haven

Compilation and publication of this volume has been financed in part by grants GS1763 and N3409 from the National Science Foundation.

Library of Congress Catalog Card Number: 74-19513
International Standard Book Number: 087536-405-5

[Cover design courtesy of BEE Cross-Media, Inc.]

PREFACE

This is the second of a two-volume survey of the peoples and cultures of insular Southeast Asia. The present volume covers the Philippine Islands and Formosa. Volume One (1972) includes Indonesia, the Andaman and Nicobar Islands, and the Malagasy-speaking peoples of Madagascar. Together with *Ethnic Groups of Mainland Southeast Asia*, by Frank M. LeBar, Gerald C. Hickey, and John K. Musgrave (HRAF Press, 1964), these volumes provide a series of descriptive ethnographic summaries, with accompanying bibliographies, synonymies, terminological indexes, and ethnolinguistic maps, covering the whole of what might be termed greater Southeast Asia, including the culturally-related regions of southern China and Assam. Summary formats and technical apparatus remain the same in all three volumes, the intent being a corpus of systematically arranged data, providing insofar as possible comparable descriptive categories and terminology for the entire area. For the original conception of the project and a discussion of earlier problems of ethnic group identification and classification with respect to the mainland, the reader is referred to the preface in LeBar et al. (1964). The identification of ethnic groups and the ordering of ethnic entries in the insular volumes follow closely the approach adopted by Raymond Kennedy in his various surveys of Indonesian peoples and cultures, i.e. a combination of geographic, linguistic, and cultural criteria. Thus the tribe, nation, or category subsumed under any one ethnic entry generally occupies a specifiable territory or habitat; the people do (or did) feel themselves to be one people or somehow historically related, and they did until the twentieth century, at least, have certain cultural and linguistic traits in common which served to set them off from neighboring groups. These criteria are purposely qualified as to tense, since much of the ethnographic literature dates from the turn of the century or earlier and thus ethnic entries, unless based on modern fieldwork, do not necessarily reflect recent change. A survey of this kind, focusing on the traditional culture, does have the advantage of complete coverage of an entire area according to a single format —thus providing a body of systematically arranged data for comparative use as well as a base from which to project studies of recent change. Considerable reliance has been placed on linguistic classification, since it is felt that demonstrated genetic relationships among languages remain the best indicators of present or past cultural ties among the speakers of those languages. The indigenous languages of the Philippines and Formosa belong to a single language family —Malayo-Polynesian. Extensive use has been made of Conklin's (1952) classification of Philippine languages and the recent lexicostatistical classification of MP languages by Dyen (1965, 1971). In most cases where it is given, Dyen's placement of a particular language or language group in his overall classificatory scheme has been noted; the scheme itself has not, however, been adopted as a basis for the ordering of ethnic entries, since it is felt that the lexicostatistical data alone, without testing or verification against other types of linguistic evidence, do not warrant their use in this way at present.

Technical notes. In general, groups are called by the name used most frequently in the literature. Each cultural summary is prefaced by a list of synonyms for the name of the group, wherever such are reported. Only generic synonyms are listed. All names, including variant spellings, names of local or restricted usage, subgroup names, etc. are included in an index at the back of the book, where each is keyed to the relevant group name as it appears in the table of contents. Pluralization of names in general follows popular usage as reflected in the literature. The summaries are, with some exceptions, written in the present tense. In each case, however, the reader should consult the historical section and also refer to the publication dates included in the documentation, in order to form his own judgment of the contemporaneousness of the data. A special effort has been made to document each summary section, and often each paragraph. References pertaining to an immediately preceding sentence or paragraph are enclosed in parentheses; those encompassing an entire section or several sentences or paragraphs are enclosed in brackets. The sources used for a particular entry are listed alphabetically by author in the bibliography section at the end of the entry, as well as in complete form in the master bibliography at the back of the book. Diacritical marks indicative of an author's transcription of native words have in general been omitted; the reader wishing to do so can easily find the relevant reference in the bibliography and proceed from there to consult a particular author's phonetic system. Anthropological terms for kin groups and descent rules have generally been reported as the original author uses them; where reference is made to Murdock's terminology, the reader should consult his *Social Structure* (New York, 1949). The authors of individual contributions are indicated in the table of contents, opposite the names of groups on which they have written summaries. Unless otherwise specified, all remaining entries and introductory materials have been compiled by the editor. Ethnolinguistic sketch maps for each of the major geographical divisions (e.g. Philippines, Formosa), as well as for individual islands (e.g. Mindanao, Luzon) will be found at the back of the book. In some cases, contributing authors submitted more data than could conveniently be included within the present volume, necessitating editorial abridgment. In cases where significant amounts of ethnographic data have been thus omitted, the Human Relations Area Files will make available to interested readers copies of the original manuscripts by future listing in its *Hraflex Books* series, a low-cost publishing program designed for descriptive ethnographic materials.

Acknowledgments. For aid in the identification of ethnic groups in the Philippines, special thanks go to Mario D. Zamora and his colleagues at the University of the Philippines; to Fr. Frank Lynch and his staff at the Ateneo de Manila; and to Professors Fred Eggan, Harold Conklin, and Donn Hart. A special debt of gratitude is owed Professor Eggan and the Philippine Studies Program at Chicago, without whose pioneering work in Philippine ethnography a work of this kind would have been doubly difficult. Professors Chen Chi-lu and Ruey Yih-fu, together with Raleigh Ferrell and Inez deBeauclair, at National Taiwan University, gave generously of their time in response to questions concerning the aboriginal groups on Taiwan. Special thanks go to Professor Toichi Mabuchi of Tokyo Metropolitan University, and to Kazuko Matsuzawa, presently a member of the faculty of Japan Lutheran Theological College, for their friendship and considerable help in the selection and translation of Japanese-language materials on the Formosan aborigines. For similar help with respect to Chinese-language materials on Formosa, thanks go to Hwei Li Chang, Cheng-ruey Ma, and May Cheng. Richard C. Fidler abstracted much of the literature on Luzon's mountain tribes, and Peter J. Wilson of Otago University aided in the preparation of draft manuscripts on these groups. I wish again to thank my colleagues at the Human Relations Area Files for help in the preparation, editing, and publication of the book, in particular Timothy J. O'Leary, who helped with bibliographic problems; Frank W. Moore, for his preparation of the ethnolinguistic sketch maps; and Elizabeth P. Swift, who edited the book with skill and patience. Finally, grateful acknowledgment is due the National Science Foundation for its generous support of both research and publication costs.

TABLE OF CONTENTS

PREFACE

PART I. SULU-SANGIHE

Introductory Statement 1

TAUSUG *by Thomas M. Kiefer* 2

SAMAL 5
    Introductory Statement 5

Balangingi *by William H. Geoghegan* 6
Bajau Laut *by Clifford Sather* 9
Jama Mapun *by Eric S. Casiño* 12
Yakan 13

SANGIR 13

PART II. PHILIPPINES

Introductory Statement 15

CHRISTIAN FILIPINOS *by Donn V. Hart.* 16

MUSLIMS 23

NEGRITOS 24
    Introductory Statement 24
    Northern Groups 25
        Introductory Statement 25
        Zambales Negritos 26
    Southern Groups 28
        Introductory Statement 28
        Mamanua *by Marcelino N. Maceda* 29

MINDANAO 31
    Introductory Statement 31
    Zamboanga 32
        Introductory Statement 32
        Subanun 32
    Lanao-Cotabato 34
        Introductory Statement 34
        Ilanon *by Melvin Mednick* 35
        Magindanao 35
        Maranao *by Melvin Mednick* 36
    Bukidnon Plateau 39
        Introductory Statement 39
        Bukidnon 39
    Southwest Highlands 40
        Introductory Statement 40
        Tiruray *by Grace Wood Moore* 41
        Cotabato Manobo *by Marcelino N. Maceda* 45
    Central Highlands 46
        Introductory Statement *by E. Arsenio Manuel* 46
        Upland Bagobo [Manuvu]
            by E. Arsenio Manuel 47

Davao Gulf 50
    Introductory Statement *by Aram A. Yengoyan* 50
    Mandaya *by Aram A. Yengoyan* 51
    Agusan Manobo 55
    Coastal Bagobo 58
    Bilaan 61
    Tagakaolo *by Aram A. Yengoyan* 62
    Kulaman *by Aram A. Yengoyan* 62
    Ata *by Aram A. Yengoyan* 63

PALAWAN 64
    Introductory Statement *by Charles P. Warren* 64
    Tagbanuwa *by Charles P. Warren* 64
    Batak *by Charles P. Warren* 68

BISAYAS 70
    Introductory Statement 70
    Sulod *by F. Landa Jocano* 71
    Magahat 72

MINDORO 73
    Introductory Statement 73
    Hanunóo 74

LUZON 76
    Introductory Statement 76
    Central Groups 78
        Introductory Statement 78
        Ifugao 78
        Bontok 82
        Lepanto (Sagada) 86
    Southern Groups 87
        Introductory Statement 87
        Ibaloi 88
        Kankanai 90

Northern Groups 91
    Introductory Statement 91
    Kalinga 92
    Tinggian 95
    Apayao 97

Pagan Gaddang 100
Southeastern Groups 102
    Introductory Statement 102
    Ilongot *by Renato and Michelle Rosaldo* 103

PART III. BATAN-BOTEL TOBAGO

Introductory Statement 107
YAMI 108

PART IV. FORMOSA

Introductory Statement 115

CHINESE 116

EASTERN LOWLAND GROUPS 116
    Introductory Statement 116
    Ami 117
    Puyuma 122

WESTERN LOWLAND GROUPS 126
    Introductory Statement 126
    Saisiat 127

CENTRAL MOUNTAIN GROUPS 128
    Introductory Statement 128
    Paiwan-Rukai 129
    Bunun 134
    Tsou 138
    Atayal 142

BIBLIOGRAPHY 149

INDEX OF ETHNIC NAMES 164

MAPS

PART I. SULU-SANGIHE

THE SULU-SANGIHE AREA includes the myriad islands in the Sulu and Celebes Seas that stretch south from Mindanao to Borneo and Celebes, serving as a cultural bridge between the Philippine Island world and Indonesia. This is an area of predominantly sea-oriented peoples, who through centuries of trading, slave raiding and piracy have spread widely to the surrounding coasts of Mindanao, Palawan, Borneo, Celebes, and Halmahera. That outside contacts were even wider in scope in former times is indicated by the fact that much of the pre-Spanish trade between China and Borneo was carried by boats plying out of Jolo in the Sulu Archipelago (Saleeby 1908.) The indigenous inhabitants of this extensive area speak languages whose ties are to the north, within the Philippine Islands; but Islamization, common throughout much of the area, has imposed a veneer of religious, social, and political institutions that tie these islands more to Indonesia and Malaya to the south and west. Islam was brought to the Sulu Archipelago by Peninsular and Sumatran Malays by at least the fourteenth century; and the Jolo Sultanate, founded in the mid-fifteenth century, gained ritual ascendency over the entire archipelago, surviving as a classic Malay trading and raiding state until partial pacification by the Spanish in the 1870s. [See under *Muslims*, elsewhere in this volume.] The Sangihe Archipelago, stretching north from Celebes, was traditionally claimed by the Ternate sultanate, which also claimed ritual hegemony over Banggai, Boalemo, and neighboring Muslim coastal principalities in eastern Celebes. [See under *Celebes*, Volume 1.] Both Spain and Holland contended for this area, and in 1677 the Sangihe Archipelago came under the authority of the Dutch East India Company. Christianity and Islam were both introduced at an early date, but today the Sangihe and Talaud islanders are for the most part Christian, with a strong substratum of indigenous animism. The islands of the Sulu Archipelago appear to have been inhabited indigenously by speakers of Samalan languages (Bajau, Balangingi, Jama Mapun, Yakan), related to those of the Central Philippines. Tausug, spoken by the politically dominant portion of the population, is most closely related to the Sugbuhanon spoken by lowland Christians in the Bisayas and northern Mindanao (Conklin 1955c; Chrétien 1963). Tausug appears to be intrusive in the Sulu area, possibly as late as 1200 A.D. Sangil (Sangir), a cluster of closely related languages spoken on the Sangihe and Talaud islands and on the nearby southern coast of Mindanao, has been grouped with Philippine languages (e.g. Esser 1938), although Dyen, on lexicostatistical grounds, prefers to leave it ungrouped within his Hesperonesian Linkage, with the comment that it may form a link between the languages of the Philippines and West Indonesia (Dyen 1965: 44).

BIBLIOGRAPHY. Arce 1963; Chrétien 1963; Conklin 1955c; Dyen 1965; Esser 1938; Saleeby 1908.

1

TAUSUG*

Synonyms. *Taw Sug, Suluk, Taw Suluk, Sulus,*
Joloanos, Jolo Moros

ORIENTATION. **Identification and location.** The
people call themselves *tausug* ("men of the current"), and this is the only ethnic group found on
the island of Jolo, southwest of Zamboanga in the
Sulu Archipelago. Heavy concentrations also occur
on the adjacent islands of Pata, Tapul, Lugus, and
Siasi, sometimes along with Samalan-speakers. While
Jolo Island is the demographic and political center
of the society, scattered Tausug settlements are
found throughout Sulu and North Borneo (primarily
around Tambisan and Lahad Datu, where they are
known as Suluk). Settlements of recent origin are
found in Zamboanga del Sur (Mindanao) and on the
northern and eastern coasts of Basilan Island. They
generally inhabit the larger volcanic islands (with
the exception of Tawi-tawi, which is sparsely populated) that are suited for intensive upland rice agriculture, leaving the smaller coral islands to Samalan-
speaking peoples. Geographic and cultural differentiation is minimal, and subgroups are not identified;
the distinction between coastal dwellers and inland
dwellers often found in the literature (Saleeby 1908,
Arce 1963: 3) is actually a native distinction relative
to the home of the speaker and does not reflect cultural differences. **Geography.** Jolo is a rugged volcanic island, about one-half of which is cultivated.
The remainder is either unusable mountain land, rain
forest, or former agricultural land which has turned
to imperata grass. The island is surrounded by coral
reefs, with mangrove swamps in some places. Rainfall tends to be very erratic, especially during the
relatively dry season in January. **Linguistic affiliation.**
The Tausug language is closely related to the Bisayan
subgroup of Philippine languages (Chrétien 1963),
especially to the Bisayan spoken around northeastern Mindanao. All evidence points to an intrusion
of Tausug from the north, probably during the last
millennium: it is not intelligible with the various
Samalan languages in Sulu, it is heavily concentrated
in a single locality, and it shows little dialectical
variation. A Malay-Arabic script is used for religious
and other writing (see Cameron 1917). **Demography.**
The number of persons speaking Tausug as their

first language may be estimated at about 325,000.
About 175,000 to 200,000 live on Jolo Island (Republic of the Philippines Census 1960). **History.** The intrusion of the Tausug language into Jolo may have
occurred as early as Sung times (A.D. 960-1279) as a
consequence of increasing Chinese trade. Islamic
influence began to be felt significantly by at least
the fourteenth century through the penetration of
three main groups: Arab traders and adventurers,
Sufi missionaries from Malaya and Sumatra, and
Chinese Muslims and traders from South China. The
establishment of the sultanate dates from the middle
of the fifteenth century (Majul 1966b). Islamization
was a continuous process lasting several centuries,
although there was a rapid development of sophistication in Islam during the nineteenth century. Trade
with Chinese junks was extensive until the Spanish
achieved naval superiority after 1840. Several official
trading missions were sent to the Celestial Throne
in the fifteenth and eighteenth centuries (Majul
1966c), and many Chinese cultural patterns have
permeated Jolo, including some culinary habits,
weights and measures, dress, and others. Malayan
cultural influence is also extensive, especially in the
formal features of the political system. Warfare with
the Spanish was almost continuous from 1578 to
1899, and the sultanate survived as a classic Malay
trading and raiding state until at least 1876, when
the Spanish were first able to establish a garrison
at Jolo. However, they never gained control over
the interior of the island, and the sultanate was
moved to Maimbung on the southern coast. Jolo
was a center of piracy and an entrepôt for slaves
taken in the Christian Philippines, although much
of the actual piracy and slaving was in the hands
of Ilanon retainers from Mindanao acting as privateers under commission by Tausug aristocrats.
American troops took control of the walled Spanish
city of Jolo in 1899, but control over the entire
island was achieved only in 1913. In 1915 Sultan
Jamal-ul-Kiram II abdicated all claims to secular
power, although maintaining his ritual position. Tausug acquired large numbers of weapons during World
War II, and Philippine government control in the
interior is minimal at present. **Cultural relations.**
The Tausug are the dominant ethnic group in Sulu
as a consequence of their numerical superiority,
rather warlike basic personality, and the previous
power and complexity of their political institutions.
The Tausug language is widely used for trade by

*The author of this entry, Thomas M. Kiefer, is Assistant
Professor of Anthropology at Brown University. His data
are based on field research in 1966-68 among the Tausug
in the Sulu Archipelago.

Samalan speakers, but few Tausug understand or would deign to speak Samal (Stone 1962). In areas where Tausug predominate, the pagan Samal Laut (Bajau) seek protection by establishing clientage relations with specific Tausug local groups. Traditionally, the entire Sulu Archipelago was under the ritual hegemony of the Tausug sultanate, and in Tausug theory the Samals were "owned" by the sultan.

SETTLEMENT PATTERN AND HOUSING. **Settlement pattern.** Interior homesteads are dispersed; concentrated fishing settlements occur along the coasts. The community may include from 20 to 100 or more houses, although corporate organization is minimal and the boundaries between communities vague and shifting. Clusters of several houses are typical. **Housing.** The house is normally a single rectangular room on 6- to 8-foot piles, with a thatched gable roof. It is surrounded by a series of elevated porches leading to a separate kitchen, and often is surrounded by a stockade for protection and to enclose animals. There are no rice barns; rice is stored in baskets placed on roof beams within the house.

ECONOMY. Subsistence is primarily through agriculture, fishing, and animal-keeping for meat (not milk), supplemented by production of coconuts and Manila hemp as cash crops. **Agriculture.** Dry-rice cultivation on permanent fields with plow and draught animals (cattle and water buffalo) is predominant. Irrigated and swampland wet-rice cultivation is practiced only in some interior valleys. Some sporadic shifting cultivation is found in the primary rainforests, although it is not important. Dry rice is usually intercropped with maize, millet, sorghum, sesame, and cassava, and fields of yams and peanuts are occasionally planted. Farms are left fallow every third year; fertilizers are not used. **Fishing.** Men within several kilometers of the coast engage in occasional fishing for subsistence, and full- and part-time fishermen are found in most coastal settlements. Fish are also bought from Samal Laut retainers. **Domestic animals.** Cattle, goats, and water buffalo are eaten on festive occasions. Chickens, geese, and ducks are abundant and are used for food; dogs and cats are largely parasitic, without economic significance. **Gathering.** Jolo has an abundance of wild fruits, which form a significant part of the diet: mangos, durian, jackfruit, oranges, and lanzones. Bananas are widely cultivated. **Industrial arts.** Most household and farm items are made of bamboo. Metal implements are locally forged, and the manufacture of bladed weapons and the decoration of scabbards with incised mother of pearl are important arts. Weaving is seldom done today except for the manufacture of woven headpieces, a characteristic Tausug feature of dress. Matweaving is done by women for home use and sale, although the best quality mats and simple ceramic objects are always purchased from Samals. There is no representational art, and decorative art traditions are weakly developed; in general Tausug prefer to import foreign wares. Most brass work found in Jolo is either Maranao or Brunei in origin. **Trade and markets.** Philippine currency is used to purchase a few imported items from Chinese shopkeepers. Traditionally, Spanish and other currencies were used in a very restricted domain, and external trade with the Chinese was in pearls, trepang, camphor, sandalwood, and birds' nests. Barter trade is conducted with Samal Laut at coastal markets by exchanging fruits and cassava for fish. **Property.** All land holdings are individual (through titular rights, rights of usufruct, and rights of tenancy). Holdings are usually dispersed, and a man may have farms in several locations in which he has variable rights. Traditionally, titular or ultimate rights resided in the sultan in the first instance and the regional and local headmen as his representatives, although for practical purposes this was a legal fiction. Houseland is jurally distinct from farmland. Water-holes, grazing land, mosque land, and beaches are not individually owned in traditional usage. Swampland and forest land is subject to individual ownership only with continuous use and improvement. Rights to trees are jurally distinct from rights to the land on which they are planted.

KIN GROUPS. **Descent.** In general, lineal descent has little functional or ideological importance; genealogies are seldom remembered farther than two or three generations back, and bilateral ties are paramount in most domains. In theory, children are filiated with the father and his kindred (called *usbaq*), but this rule only functions in relation to native reinterpretations of Shafi marriage law. **Kin groups.** The bilateral kindred extending to second cousins is the major recognized kinship category, although there is a slight unrecognized tendency for the effective kindred to be patrilaterally skewed, largely as an unanticipated result of norms of residence and land tenure. However, the kindred only acts as a group for the life crisis rites of Ego and his children; in other respects it is significant only as a source from which he can cement a series of particular dyadic ties. The bond between brothers and male first cousins is especially important for feud and political action, although there is no corporate responsibility of the kindred. Ritualized quasi-kinship (or friendship), involving dyadic alliances between males and sanctioned by an oath taken on the Koran, is a pervasive pattern motivated by desire for safety in travel and assistance in conflict.

Kin terminology. The basic reference kin terms are as follows:

Fa	*amaq*
Mo	*inaq*
So, Da	*anak*
Sibling	*taymanghud*
Younger sibling	*manghud*
Older sibling	*magulang*
FaBr, MoBr	*amaqun*
FaSi, MoSi	*inaqun*
Grandparent, grandchild (reciprocal)	*apuq*
First cousin (Ego's generation)	*(pang) tungud minsan*
Second cousin (Ego's generation)	*(pang) tungud makarua*
Third cousin (Ego's generation)	*(pang) tungud makatu*
Nephew or niece (descending generation at any degree of collaterality)	*anakun*
Wife	*asawa*
Husband	*bana*
Affine of Ego's generation (except spouse)	*ipag*
Parent-in-law, child-in-law (reciprocal)	*ugangan*

MARRIAGE AND FAMILY. **Mode.** Three alternative modes are found: elopement with girl's consent, abduction without consent, and arranged marriage. Marriage by negotiation between parents is the ideal, and payments of bridewealth are made in money, animals, rice, and heirlooms. The marriage ceremony itself follows Islamic law, phrased as a sacred contract between the young man and the bride's father. Occasionally marriages are arranged between prepubescent couples; in such cases the young man often works for his father-in-law until the girl's maturity. There is no institutionalized courtship; female virginity at marriage is valued; and premarital contact is difficult. **Form.** Polygyny is infrequent, although permitted. **Extension of incest taboos.** The taboo is extended to include persons of alternate generation of any degree of traceable kinship, half-siblings, and persons who have "sucked at the same breast." Prohibition of sexual relations is completely congruent with prohibition of marriage. Marriage within the extended kindred is preferential, especially with first cousins, due to the ease of marriage negotiations and the desire to avoid alienation of land and other property. About one-half of all marriages are endogamous within the kindred. **Residence.** Initial residence is prescribed for at least a year in the household of the girl's parents. Matrilocal residence may continue, or the couple may move back to the boy's household. Independent neolocal residence is a commonly occurring ideal, and eventual residence will nearly always be in the community of the boy, irrespective of household choice. **Domestic unit.** The nuclear family and stem family predominate. Extended families are rare and are always based on two sisters, with the household separating on the death of the parents. Other attached members of the household may include the kinsmen of either spouse, although there is a tendency for links with the wife to be more numerous. **Inheritance.** Islamic law respecting inheritance is not applied, although known by a few specialists. Customary law is ambiguous in most matters of inheritance, even though in theory it is bilateral, and actual decisions are reached after consultation among the heirs. In practice, land rights usually go to males, and esoteric knowledge and magic are usually given from father to eldest son. **Divorce.** Divorce is strongly condemned, and social pressures result in a low divorce rate (less than 10 per cent of all marriages). Property acquired during the marriage is equally divided, although the house usually goes to the wife. Arguments over property and children are rare. **Adoption.** Adoption by nonkinsmen is rare; fosterage of parentless children by kinsmen is more prevalent, although the child has no legal rights to the property of his foster parents except as such rights may be given him.

SOCIOPOLITICAL ORGANIZATION. The major cultural focus of Tausug society lies in political organization, law and litigation, conflict, and warfare. **Political organization (traditional).** Territorial subdivisions are of minimal importance in the Tausug polity; power is primarily over people and only secondarily over the territory they occupy. Political functions are not performed by corporate groups, but rather semicorporate offices legitimized in the hierarchy of the title system, headed by the sultan, and serving vaguely bounded publics. All political officials are by definition legal officials and derive their legitimacy from the fact that they represent the law (*saraq*, from Shari'a). Within the state there is no autonomous realm of administration which can be identified apart from the functions of adjudication. The power of community headmen is acquired through the leadership of conflict groups, and this de facto power is strengthened upon receipt of a title bestowed by the sultan. These titles are of Malayan origin (*panglima, ulangkayaq, maharaja*) and in theory are arranged in a chain of relative status, but in practice the configuration of titles at any time seldom reflects the actual balance of power, which is acquired through participation in a system of segmentary factions based upon the achievement of dyadic alliances with kinsmen and friends. The sultan is the head of all rank lines within the title system, and traditionally he or his close kinsmen were often leaders of alliance groups on the highest levels of segmentation. He was surrounded at the capital by a staff consisting of religious advisors and influential headmen who were often kinsmen. Succession was by election by this staff (Majul 1966a), although patrilineal succession was the ideal. Power was much greater at the center of the state than at its edges, shading off into mere ritual hegemony in Basilan and North Borneo. With the exception of rights of investiture and certain ritual functions, the political rights and functions of the sultan on the one hand and the various community and regional headmen on the other were largely the same. **Political organization (contemporary).** The basic ethos of the traditional political system is substantially the same as that found in contemporary Philippine national politics, with emphasis on dyadic ties and rapidly changing factions. Minimal and medial alliances still operate in the traditional manner, while the maximal alliance is led today by acculturated Tausug operating in the frame of Philippine electoral politics. The island is divided into eight municipalities, with elected officials in each, as well as a provincial governor for Sulu, and a national congressman; the major power of these officials stems from their ability to channel government largesse and secure immunity of their followers from government law. Although the political power of the sultanate is diminished, most ritual functions are still intact. Two persons currently claim the office as a consequence of a factional dispute over succession in the nineteenth century. Each has authority over roughly one-half of the island. **Social stratification.** The traditional estate system distinguished between the high ascribed status of *datu*, which was inherited patrilineally (comprising about 2 per cent of the population); commoners, including debt slaves, who had most of the jural rights of freemen; and permanent slaves (about 10 per cent of the population), consisting mostly of Filipino captives from the Bisayas. In theory all *datu* were descendants of a former sultan. Wealth and power were achieved independently of the mere possession of the title. **Social control and justice.** The concept of law is based on the Islamic notion of the primacy of divine commands as revealed in the Koran and subsequent commentary. Substantive law is divided into three categories: pure Koranic law, interpreted religious law, and customary law. Fines are typically imposed (of which a percentage is kept by the headman and sent to the sultan); blood money may be paid in cases of murder or injury, and ritual whipping is common for sexual crimes. Oaths on the Koran are used to determine truth; ordeals and wagers of combat are unknown. In theory, any titled official is empowered to adjudicate a case anywhere in the realm by virtue of his authority from the sultan. A headman whose legal authority is disregarded will either take direct action himself or give his sanction to private vengeance by the aggrieved party. **Warfare.** Feuds based on proliferating alliances are endemic, although there is no corporate responsibility of the kinsmen of the offender, and a system of purely individual and particular revenge prevails. A widely ramified feud may result in battles with several hundred participants (Kiefer 1969). External warfare was traditionally in the form of highly organized piracy raids for slaves and booty undertaken by Tausug and Ilanon retainers at the levels of the medial and maximal alliances, both with and without the permission of the sultan. External warfare was heavily sanctioned by the norms of Islam, and when Spanish hegemony was established in the nineteenth century a pattern of ritual suicide developed (*sabbil, juramentado*), in which a man enacted a personal jihad against a Christian settlement.

RELIGION. Muslim beliefs and rituals according to the school of Shafi are followed more or less closely, although regular daily prayers are practiced only by the elderly and pious. A basic distinction is made between revealed religion (*agama*) and the customary elements in religion (adat).

BIBLIOGRAPHY. Arce 1963; Cameron 1917; Chrétien 1963; Kiefer 1967, 1968, 1969; Majul 1966a, 1966b, 1966c; Reber 1966; Rogers 1959; Saleeby 1908; Stone 1962; Tarling 1963.

SAMAL*

SAMALAN SPEAKERS CAN BE divided into at least two major branches, distinguished from one another by language, culture, and recent geographical origin. The Western Samal predominate on the islands and coastal regions to the west of Jolo Island (121° E., 6° N.) and include the land-dwelling Bajau of Sabah, the Sama of the southwestern Sulu Archipelago, and the boat-dwelling Bajau (Pala'u or Orang Laut) of the Philippines, Sabah, and northern Celebes. The Eastern Samal trace their ancestry to points east of Jolo and divide themselves into subgroups (consistent with dialect variations) named after

*The major portion of this entry has been taken from data supplied by William H. Geoghegan for his summary of Balangingi Samal.

their respective islands of origin. The Balangingi (from Balanguingui Island) are politically and numerically dominant within the eastern branch. The Daundung (from Dongdong Island), Kabinga'an (Cabingaan Island), and Kaulungan (Kaulungan Island) should probably be assigned to this branch as well. Other Samalan groups, including the Yakan of Basilan Island and the Jama (Sama) Mapun of Cagayan Sulu, cannot easily be classified and may represent separate branches of the larger family. As a whole, Samalan languages are most closely tied to the various Bisayan groups (cf. Conklin 1955c), although the period of separation exceeds twenty centuries. According to the 1960 Census, there were 81,000 Samal (including Bajau) in Sulu Province. Nimmo (1968) estimates the total of all Samalan speakers in the Celebes Sea rim, including some 60,000 Bajau in Sabah, at around 200,000, which checks out well with Kuder's earlier estimate of 175,000, exclusive of North Borneo Bajau (Kuder 1945). Despite legendary accounts that place the Samal homeland in Johore (Sopher 1965), linguistic and cultural evidence shows them to be indigenous to the Sulu Archipelago. Maximum diversity within the Samalan dialects, for example, centers on the Jolo region; and the membership of Samal in the Central Philippine group of languages points to an origin in the Philippines rather than Malaysia. Separation between the Eastern and Western branches of Samal would appear to have occurred circa 1200 A.D., coincidental with the incursion of Tausug agriculturalists and traders into the area. The indigenous Samal probably divided their economy between agriculture and marine-based activities (fishing, trading, piracy). In those areas that fell under Tausug domination (including Jolo and most of the Western Samal region today), local Samal are totally dependent upon a marine economy; while in areas that stayed free of major Tausug settlement (including Cagayan de Sulu and all of the Yakan and Eastern Samal dispersion), a mixed economy remains dominant to this day. Early references to the Samal (Combés 1667 and Forrest 1780) attest to their warlike nature, their service as marine forces for the various sultanates of Sulu and Mindanao, and their willingness to engage in widespread piracy.

BIBLIOGRAPHY. Combés 1906; Conklin 1955c; Forrest 1779; Kuder 1945; Nimmo 1968; Sopher 1965.

BALANGINGI*

Synonyms. *Balangingi Samal, Balanguingui, Balanini, Samal, Sama*

ORIENTATION. **Location and identification.** The most widely dispersed of the Eastern Samal groups, with well-established communities ranging from the Samales Islands (including Balanguingui) in the southwest (122°20′E., 6°N.), throughout the eastern coast of Basilan, the southern and eastern coasts of the Zamboanga Peninsula, and the coastal interiors of Sibuguey and Dumanquilas bays. The Balangingi refer to themselves by this term or, occasionally, by the term Sama Balangingi. They recognize their linguistic ties to other Eastern Samal groups, but regard themselves as a distinct and internally homogeneous *bangsa* (or "people") within the larger group of Muslim Filipinos (*bangsa muslim*). Settlements are frequently located near coral reefs and large areas of mangrove swamp. **Linguistic affiliation.** A dialect of Eastern Samal, within the Central Philippine group of Malayo-Polynesian languages. **Demography.** Philippine census information on language affiliation is generally unreliable for the Muslims of Jolo and Zamboanga del Sur. Estimating from population figures for known Balangingi communities, there are probably around 5,000 (perhaps as many as 10,000) Balangingi within the region. **History.** The earliest references to the Balangingi as a separate group stem from the early 1800s (Mills 1925), when their activities as pirates and slavers posed a serious threat in the area of present-day Malaysia and western Indonesia. The advent of steam-powered gunboats severely curtailed their power, and a major blow was dealt when the Spanish destroyed their forts on Balanguingui Island in 1848 (Montero y Vidal 1888). Raiding within the Bisayan Islands and Sulu continued until after the turn of the century. With the eventual suppression of piracy and slave-trading by American military authorities, the Balangingi turned to coastal trading as a primary supplement to fishing and agriculture. With the effective solidification of international boundaries, however, most of the remaining trade has been redefined as smuggling. **Cultural relations.** For the Balangingi, the tra-

---

*The author of this entry, William H. Geoghegan, carried out fieldwork during 1966-67 in the region of southern Zamboanga and the Samales Islands. He is currently an Assistant Professor of Anthropology at the University of California, Berkeley.

ditional antipathy between Muslim and Christian has evolved into a workable, though sometimes uneasy, economic relationship. They maintain generally friendly relations with local Tausug and Yakan, and there is a relatively high degree of intermarriage with these groups. Among the Muslim inhabitants of their region, the Balangingi consistently represent themselves as the most powerful, followed by the Tausug, Ilanon, Yakan, other Eastern Samal groups (Daundung, Kabinga'an, etc.), Sama (land-dwelling Western Samal), and Pala'u (boat-dwelling Western Samal, or Bajau), in this order. The Pala'u are still referred to as *sali' 'aata-kami* ("like our slaves") and are treated with utter contempt.

SETTLEMENT PATTERN AND HOUSING. **Settlement pattern.** Small, compact communities of 100-500, often organized as wards (or "parishes") within larger villages and towns. Parishes are formed by households affiliating with a particular local mosque and its leader. Secondary affiliation is with a smaller group of adjacent households (up to about ten in number), whose members cooperate in day-to-day economic activities. Community membership is highly variable; seasonal and permanent migrations (of both individuals and households) are frequent. **Housing.** Houses consist of one or more small, rectangular rooms and an attached kitchen, located on a single level, and raised above ground on wooden pilings. Ideally, a house is located partially over water in such a manner as to allow the ground beneath it to be flooded only at high tide. Other houses may be built on dry land, raised approximately three to six feet above ground. This contrasts in both cases with Western Samal housing, which is customarily built completely over tidal mud flats or reefs.

ECONOMY. Fishing, agriculture, and marine trade. Other Eastern Samal groups rely almost totally on fishing as a source of income. **Fishing.** A variety of techniques, all of which are directed toward the production of a cash income through the local market system, are used almost exclusively by adult males. Among marine subsistence techniques oriented toward household consumption are spear-fishing, the use of small wicker traps, trolling for squid, and surf-casting with nylon hand lines. When necessary, two men may form a temporary partnership, or fishing "crew"; but the catch is generally divided and sold individually. Permanent crews, cooperatives, and so on, are nonexistent. **Agriculture.** Balangingi who have acquired the necessary financial resources to purchase land often give up fishing and take up agriculture. Copra production represents an important source of income. Fixed-field farming is also practiced in the lowland areas, with rice, corn, cassava, and bananas being the most important products.

Gathering. Coral reefs provide sea urchins, small octopi, several varieties of seaweed, and small marine mollusks, all of which are collected by women and children for household consumption. Mangrove swamps provide the major source of firewood. Forests supply many types of edible fruits, construction materials (principally bamboo), and plant products useful in native medicine. **Domestic animals.** Most households keep a few chickens, ducks, and geese as a source of eggs; and wealthier families may maintain a few goats as scavengers. All such animals may be used for food and sacrifice at important religious events. Pigs are entirely absent, owing to the Islamic prohibition, and a general avoidance of dogs is similarly justified. **Industrial arts.** There is an increasing tendency to rely on local markets for items of daily household use. The Balangingi no longer practice metal working or ceramics, and decorative art has all but disappeared. **Trade.** Most villages rely on local markets and the larger cities as outlets for fish and agricultural produce and as sources of food items, clothing, and tools. External trade, generally in the form of smuggling, is conducted on a wide scale. Participation is limited to a few wealthy and powerful individuals, however. **Property.** All items of human manufacture (e.g. houses and boats), and all items of natural origin subject to human use and improvement (e.g. farmland and swampland), are considered the personal property or under the direct control of a specific individual. For all practical purposes, the Balangingi do not maintain any form of corporate property. Fishing grounds on the open sea and unimproved forest land are open to common exploitation.

KIN GROUPS. **Descent.** Strictly bilateral in both theory and practice. Genealogies are normally shallow and have little importance to persons other than those who maintain large support groups. **Kin groups.** No permanent kin groups with consistent corporate functions. The bilateral personal kindred (*kaukampung*) technically consists of all persons with whom Ego shares a common ancestor, though the more significant segment contains only those with whom accurate genealogical links can be traced. The personal kindred (and that of one's spouse) is the major source of allies and supporters in crisis situations, disputes, ceremonial events, and economic activities. **Kin terminology.** In the Balangingi system of reference, sex distinctions are made only for parents and spouses:

PaPa, PaPaSb, PaPaCo, PaPaPa, etc. (and spouses of these)	mbo'
Fa	mma'
Mo	'ina'
PaSb, PaCo (and spouses of these)	si'it
Br, Si (Sb)	danakan

ElSb	siaka
YoSb	siali
Co (Cousin)	kaki
Ch	'anak
SbCh, CoCh (of Ego and spouse)	kamanakan
ChCh, SbChCh, CoChCh (of Ego and spouse)	'umpu
Hu	hella
Wi	henda
SpSb, SpCo, SbSp, CoSp	'ipal
SpSbSp, SpCoSp	bilas
SpPa	mato'a
ChSp, SbChSp, ChChSp, etc.	'ayuwan
ChSpPa	ba'i

When necessary, sex distinctions may be made by appending the markers *lella* ("male") or *denda* ("female"). Degree of cousinship may also be indicated when extreme specificity is desired: e.g. *kaki min tedda* ("first cousin"), *kaki min dua* ("second cousin"), etc.

MARRIAGE AND FAMILY. **Mode.** A couple is normally recognized as "married" if they have established residence and a sexual relationship with one another. Usually, however, the relationship is formalized through a religious ceremony conducted according to Islamic law, in which the husband enters into a formal contract with the bride's father and agrees to pay the latter a specified sum of money as bride-price. **Form.** Monogamy is almost universal, though nonsororal polygyny is permitted by Islamic law. **Extension of incest taboos.** Restrictions on sexual relationships, whether formalized by marriage or not, extend to an individual's siblings, all lineal relatives (parents, children, grandparents, etc.), siblings of lineal relatives, lineal descendants of siblings, and to all "milk siblings" (individuals who have been nursed by the same woman). Marriage is permitted between individuals of different generations (e.g. with a parent's cousin). Marriage within a person's kindred is encouraged, with cousins of all types being the preferred match. **Residence.** Independent residence is the stated ideal, and a couple will generally adopt this mode as soon after marriage as possible. Otherwise, there will customarily be a period of alternating residence between the households of the husband's and wife's closest kin, usually the parents. In cases where the closest kin of the husband and wife are of equal rank, preference goes to a location near the wife's relative. Over long periods of time, this practice tends to result in the formation of household clusters organized around a core of closely related women. **Domestic unit.** The primary domestic unit (or "family") is a commensal kin group: i.e. a group of kinsmen that consistently eat together, share cooking facilities, and maintain a common store of provisions (Geoghegan 1969). This unit is not necessarily identical to the group of people sharing a single house. A recognized family may occupy two adjacent dwellings (which share a single "kitchen"), and there are rare instances of two distinct families simultaneously occupying a single house. **Inheritance.** Formally bilateral, with fixed and movable property being equally divided among surviving offspring. **Divorce.** Divorce is not uncommon, with approximately 20 per cent of all marriages terminating in this fashion. **Secondary marriage.** Divorced or widowed individuals may remarry and generally attempt to do so. There are no strong preferences or prohibitions. **Adoption.** Adoption and fosterage are both practiced. No kin relation is necessary.

SOCIOPOLITICAL ORGANIZATION. **Political organization.** Parish membership is based simultaneously upon affiliation with a mosque and upon alliance with its recognized leader (*nakuda'*). The authority and power of the parish leader depends upon the size and prestige of his support group. In multiparish communities, one of the more powerful leaders may attempt to maintain a certain degree of communitywide political control. Regional authority was traditionally vested in the sultanate at Jolo, but the sultan's actual control over the activities of the Balangingi was usually rather tenuous. Today, the Balangingi nominally accord authority to a single individual who claims a majority of local parish leaders as supporters. Factionalism, however, is endemic within such large support groups. **Social stratification.** Formerly a three-level class system, including "lords" (*datu*), freemen, and slaves (*ata'*). Such class distinctions as currently exist are based more on power (*kawasa*) and wealth (*dayah*) within family lines, and there is relatively little individual mobility. **Social control and justice.** Each parish normally has its own legal official (*panglima*) and an assistant legal officer (*maharaja*), but the primary responsibility for dispute settlements generally rests with the parish leader himself. Disputes that cross parish lines, and those involving individuals from different villages, are difficult to settle, unless the parties involved happen to be fairly close kin or unless there is a village or regional leader with sufficient authority. Failing this, disputes may evolve into open violence, with sizable support groups being mustered on both sides. Nevertheless, there is relatively little tendency for the development of long-term blood feuds. **Warfare.** Raiding parties may be organized by a particular individual in retaliation for an act of piracy (usually perpetrated against smugglers), and personal vendettas may result in murder; but large-scale internal warfare is essentially absent.

RELIGION. **Religious systems.** The Balangingi are the most thoroughly Islamicized of the various Samalan ethnic groups, but Islam still represents only a rather thin veneer over more traditional beliefs. The degree of participation in Muslim religious activities is directly related to family wealth, and the maintenance of extensive religious knowledge and skills is an important source of prestige. Indigenous practices are principally concerned with obligations to remembered ancestors, and with the diagnosis and treatment of illness. **Supernaturals.** The term *'a'a* is used in reference to all sentient beings, whether visible or not. These include the "spirits" (*'umagad*) of people both living and dead; the partially visible and thoroughly malevolent animate bodies (*panyatta'* or *lutau*) of evil people; powerful spirits (*jin* or *kambo'an*) who dwell in large trees, rocks, sandy beaches, or imposing coral heads; discorporate voices or "ghosts"; bloodsucking, winged creatures of semi-human form (*balbalan*); and so forth. In accordance with Islamic belief, an all-powerful god (Tuhan or Allah) is recognized, as is a rather generalized "spirit of evil" (Saytan). **Practitioners.** Religious practitioners include those who occupy positions in a mosque (*masjid*), including the imam (priest), *hatib*, and *bilal* (other mosque functionaries). *Pakil* is a general term applied to any individual who has extensive skills in or knowledge of Islamic beliefs and practices. Traditional religious practitioners (*panday*) include midwives, herbalists, and more highly-skilled curers (generally older men) who have a personal *jin* (or *kambo'an*). **Ceremonies.** The major festivals of the Islamic lunar calendar are followed. Ritual acts performed during the life cycle include circumcision (*mag'islam*) performed on males at puberty and clitoridectomy on females at between one and two years of age. **Soul, death, and afterlife.** Islamic beliefs and practices are generally followed, though with a strong indigenous overlay. All persons have a soul (*'alua* or *ruu*) and a "spirit" (*'umagad*), the two sometimes being regarded as identical. The souls of "good" people go to heaven after a period of atonement, but it is uncertain what happens to the souls of "evil" individuals. The spirits of the dead remain in the vicinity of their graves, demand that their descendants remember and care for them, and may punish negligence and forgetfulness by causing disease. Funerary practices follow the Islamic ritual, including washing and perfuming, burial in a grave niche (with the head facing Mecca), and ceremonial readings, prayers, and meals during the first week and on the forty-fourth and one hundredth days after death. Graves are covered with sand or crushed coral, ringed by large stones and pieces of coral or concrete, and designated by a wooden marker.

BIBLIOGRAPHY. Geoghegan 1969; Mills 1925; Montero y Vidal 1888.

BAJAU LAUT*

Synonyms. *Badjo, Badjaw, Lua'an, Luwaqan, Orang Laut, Turijene, Sama, Palaqua, Pala'u*

ORIENTATION. **Identification.** The Bajau Laut are the most thoroughly sea-oriented of the various Bajau- or Samal-speaking peoples encircling the Sulu and Celebes Seas. Known as Badjo, Badjaw, or Sama, terms that also refer collectively to all Samal speakers, or as Turijene, Luwaqan (Lua'an), or Bajo, names given them by the Macassarese, Tausug, and Buginese, respectively, the Bajau Laut most often identify themselves as Sama Laut or Sama Mandelaut ("Sea Samal"), and are called Sama Palaqua by most other Samal speakers. [See Sather 1971 for a discussion of names and synonyms.] **Location.** Fragmented into widely scattered villages, interspersed with those of other coastal people, from Zamboanga Bay westward, through the Sulu Archipelago of the Philippines, to the Semporna District of Sabah (North Borneo), and southward along the adjacent coast of Kalimantan, through the islands of Macassar Strait, and eastward around the northern, western, and southern shores of Sulawesi (Celebes) and in the Togian Island Group of Tomini Bay. Additional, though much less numerous, settlements are reportedly present in the Banggai and Sula Island Groups, on Flores and Sumbawa, and in the Moluccas south of Halmahera. Settlements are situated directly along beaches, in estuaries, lagoons, or near the leeward edge of islands. [Heine-Geldern 1923: 701-04; Sopher 1965: 129-36, 143-57; van Verschuer 1883.] **Linguistic affiliation.** Within the Sabah-Sulu area, the Bajau Laut speak what is probably a single dialect of Samal. While divided into several regional variants, all are mutually intelligible and easily understood by Samal speakers west of Jolo. [Sather 1968.] The linguistic situation in eastern Indonesia is much less clear, although Cense and Uhlenbeck (1958: 27) report only minor dialectal differences. **Demography.** Maritime Bajau probably number between 20,000 and 30,000 persons. Somewhat more than 12,000 are present in the Sulu Archipelago, chiefly in the southern and central islands, and an additional 650 live in the Semporna District of Sabah. Between 10,000 and 15,000 are found in eastern Indonesia, mostly in coastal Sulawesi and on the surrounding islands. **History and cultural relations.** The Bajau

---

*The author of this entry, Clifford Sather, engaged in fieldwork among the Bajau Laut of Semporna District, Sabah, during 1964-65, visiting as well other Bajau communities in Sulu Province of the Philippines. For additional data on the Bajau or Laut (Sea) peoples of Indonesia, see Volume 1, under *Sea Nomads*.

Laut have long maintained ties with neighboring shore groups. Until the beginning of the twentieth century, most local communities in Sulu Province were under the personal protection of individual *datu*, and through a system of patron-client ties were linked in a peripheral way to the administrative structure of the Sulu state. From the perspective of the Bajau Laut, their former relations with surrounding groups have been largely exploitative, and they remain generally mistrustful of outsiders. Correspondingly, their neighbors tend to view them with considerable disdain, as social inferiors, and the local names used by the Tausug and Samal to refer to the Bajau Laut (*luwaqan* and *palaqua*, respectively) are both pejorative terms. During the last century, the Bajau Laut became increasingly sedentary. Only in the Tawi-tawi Island Group of Sulu Province (Arong 1962; Nimmo 1965), and possibly also in parts of eastern Indonesia, are they still predominantly boat-living. Elsewhere, boat communities have tended to coalesce into larger tidal settlements made up of pile-house villages close to market centers. In the Siasi area (Ducommun 1962), and perhaps in other parts of Sulu as well, the Bajau Laut are reportedly losing their separate identity and are being absorbed into the surrounding shore population. [Nimmo 1968; Sather 1971.]

SETTLEMENT PATTERN AND HOUSING. **Settlement pattern.** Local communities consist either of permanent villages built on piles over the sea or of groups of boat-living families who regularly moor their houseboats together at the same seasonal or permanent anchorage site. Most communities contain between 100 and 350 persons, although a few contain as many as 3,000. There are no communal structures, and most settlements are without property ashore. **Houses.** Most Bajau maintain pile houses in which they live for at least a part of every year. Houses are rectangular, generally 20 to 30 feet long and 15 feet wide, have gabled roofs, and are fronted by an open platform or boat-landing stage. The interior generally consists of a single large room. Houseboats are decked and provided with a living quarters consisting of a portable bamboo framework covered by a plaited nipah roof which can be removed. The family's food and water stores are kept near the stern, and here meals are prepared and eaten.

ECONOMY. Chief reliance on fishing, both as a source of subsistence and as a way of obtaining, through market activities, most other necessities. Nowadays some Bajau have begun to cultivate shore-side gardens. **Fishing.** Fishing is nearly everywhere a continuous activity, engaged in throughout the year. The seasonal organization of large fish drives, using nets and involving up to 60 boats, is highly fluid and is based essentially on day-to-day agreements entered into individually by the heads of each participating family. For the remainder of the year, these larger groups disband, and most fishing is done by smaller fleets, normally organized around relatively permanent sibling or sibling-in-law alliances. **Domestic animals.** Land animals are said to be "unclean" (*asabul*) and, with the exception of cats and fighting cocks, are rarely kept or eaten. **Industrial arts.** The Bajau Laut make most of their own fishing gear, although, in many cases, it is made from raw materials purchased in local shops or obtained through trade from neighboring shore people. Most adult men are skilled boatbuilders and make a variety of sailing craft. **Trade.** Although much trade has been rechanneled through local markets, the Bajau Laut still obtain agricultural produce, cooking hearths, metal utensils, and nipah matting from nearby shore communities in exchange for which they provide fish and other sea products. **Property.** The fishing areas of neighboring communities often overlap, and families from different villages in the same region frequently fish together during large-scale netting operations. Individual fishing grounds are an unowned resource, and neither the village as a whole nor its individual members enjoys exclusive rights to their use.

KIN GROUPS. **Descent.** Kinship is reckoned bilaterally. **Kin groups.** Close kindred are distinguished terminologically both from more distant relatives (*kampong* or *lawak*) and from nonkinsmen (*saddi*). The term *dampalanakan* (or *dampoqun*) is used to refer collectively to an individual's two sets of grandparents and their descendants down through Ego's generation. While circumscribed with reference to a set of truncal ancestors, *dampalanakan* relations are unique and always defined with respect to a particular individual or maximally a sibling set. The persons whom an individual refers to as his *dampalanakan* never form a discrete group; instead, they constitute a bounded social field, within which particular persons may be called upon for cooperation or assistance in a variety of specific situations. Most marriages occur between the children of *dampalanakan*. More distant cognatic ties are rarely traced laterally beyond third cousins. The village is not thought of as a kin group, although a high degree of interrelatedness exists in most communities. **Kin terminology.** Cousins may be referred to by sibling terms, if the speaker wishes to emphasize the closeness of their relationship, but the terminology permits their differentiation, and is essentially of Eskimo type. The basic terms of reference are as follows (Sather 1971):

10

Fa	*mmaq*
Mo	*nngoq, ina*
So, Da	*anak, ondeq*
Br, Si	*denakan*
ElBr, ElSi	*siaka*
YoBr, YoSi	*siali*
FaBr, MoBr	*bapaq*
FaSi, MoSi	*babuq*
Grandparents	*mboq*
Grandchild	*mpu*
Sibling's or cousin's child	*kamanakan*
Cousin (first, second, third)	*kaki (menteqdda, mendua, mentellu)*

MARRIAGE AND FAMILY. **Mode.** Marriage is arranged by the couple's parents, usually at the suggestion of the young man, and with the approval of the pair's *dampalanakan*. Once a proposal has been accepted, the bride's father designates a close agnatic kinsman, usually his brother, to act on his behalf as his daughter's guardian (*wakil*). The *wakil* gives the girl in marriage, receives the bride-price (*dalaham*) for her kinsmen, and acts on their behalf as an official witness to the pronouncement of the marriage formula by the bridegroom. **Form.** Marriage is monogamous. **Extension of incest taboos.** All cousins, except for the children of brothers, are favored as marriage partners. Disapproved unions include all intergenerational marriages, sororate unions, and in general any marriage between a man and a close kinswoman of his former wife. Similarly, a woman should avoid marriage with the brother or other close kinsman of a former husband. **Residence.** Among house-dwelling Bajau Laut, residence is generally uxorilocal for the first year or so of marriage, but is variable thereafter. Among boat-dwelling groups, a newly married couple usually establishes an independent household several months after marriage. **Domestic groups.** Among boat-living Bajau, the nuclear family constitutes the usual domestic unit (Nimmo 1965: 426). In house-living communities, the domestic group typically includes two or more siblings, together with their parents, spouses, and dependent children, all of whom live together under the headship of the house owner, who is normally the senior male member of the group. When partition of the original household takes place, each sibling, with the exception of the youngest, moves away to establish a separate household. New houses are usually erected close to the original dwelling. In this way, clusters of adjacent households are created whose core members are related by close ties of kinship and marriage. These clusters form an important unit of economic and ceremonial cooperation. **Inheritance.** The house is inherited by the married child residing with his or her parents at the time of their death. In practice, the heir is usually the youngest child. Traditionally, a man's boat was disassembled at his death and the pieces used to make

his coffin. Now, however, boats normally pass to the owner's son. Personal belongings are generally buried with the dead, while heirlooms are transmitted by homoparental inheritance, with the most valuable items going to the oldest children. **Divorce.** Most divorces occur within the first year or two of marriage. While most persons marry more than once during their lifetimes, few are married more than two or three times. Divorce is easily obtained, and dependent children accompany the mother.

SOCIOPOLITICAL ORGANIZATION. Every village has a headman, chosen by general consensus from among household heads. His principal task is that of calling a hearing whenever a dispute or breach of customary norms occurs. Neither he nor the village as a body can impose a judgment without the voluntary consent of the litigants. **Social stratification.** Wealthy men are respected and are usually able to maintain large households and extensive circles of supporters. Wealth is personally acquired, and there are no social classes based on inherited wealth. **Warfare.** The Bajau Laut view themselves as a nonviolent people. Despite a system of protective alliances, they were frequently harried in the past by their more powerful neighbors. Their response was generally flight, and most present-day communities have moved repeatedly.

RELIGION. Surrounding people consider the Bajau Laut pagans, although many, perhaps most, regard themselves as Muslims. However, there are seldom mosques in Bajau Laut communities, and their practice of Islam tends to be less orthodox than that of most neighboring groups. **Supernaturals.** Malevolent spirits (generically termed *saitan*) live in the jungle, along the beach, or in the sea. Other spirits are said to travel from place to place, often in the form of animals or fish, and hordes of wandering spirits may invade a village, causing an epidemic of illness. When this happens, the village spirit-mediums perform a major curative rite that involves the launching of a spirit boat (*pamatulikan*). **Practitioners.** Spirit-mediums (*jin*), both men and women, are able to commune directly with the supernatural through dreams and trance. These persons are called upon primarily for curing and divination. The imam, or village prayer leaders, are usually older men with some knowledge of the scriptures, who, in addition to leading prayers on ceremonial occasions, oversee all major life crisis rituals. **Ceremonies.** Several times each year the mediums perform a night-long public dance, during which each seeks to renew ties with a personal familiar through trance. This is said to benefit the community as a whole. Once each year the women and children of the village are bathed in the sea to protect them against spiritual attack. In addition, most Bajau Laut celebrate the major calendric rites associated with Islam, although few fast during Ramadan or observe daily prayers. **Soul, death, and afterlife.** Death rites follow Islamic practice. Several neighboring communities usually share the same cemetery. Individual grave sites are marked with wooden or stone markers, and burial plots are often surrounded by wooden enclosures. [Kiefer and Sather 1970.]

BIBLIOGRAPHY. Arong 1962; Cense and Uhlenbeck 1958; Ducommun 1962; Heine-Geldern 1923; Kiefer and Sather 1970; Nimmo 1965, 1968; Saleeby 1908; Sather 1968, 1971; Sopher 1965; Taylor 1933; van Verschuer 1883.

JAMA MAPUN*

Synonyms. *Bajau, Cagayano, Orang Cagayan, Samal Cagayan, Tao Cagayan*

ORIENTATION. The Jama Mapun are a subgroup of a Samalan-speaking population distributed throughout the border areas of the southern Philippines, northern Indonesia, and eastern Malaysia (Nimmo 1967). They are generally found in the southwestern sector of the Sulu Sea, particularly on the island of Cagayan de Sulu, in southern Palawan, northern Borneo, and in the score of small islands scattered between them, e.g. Turtle Islands, Bakungan, Banggi, Balabac, Pandanan, and Bugsuk. In this sector they are found mixed with other Samal and/or Bajau subgroups variously known as Banaran, Sibutu, and Ubian. Among them are also found Tausug speakers or Suluk from Jolo and Siasi. The Jama Mapun (*jama*, "men" of Mapun) economy was traditionally based on dry-field agriculture and maritime trading. It is impossible to judge, with the evidence presently at hand, whether their ancestors were "boat people" or sea nomads as described by Sopher (1965). Their total population is probably in the neighborhood of 25,000, almost one-half of whom live on Cagayan de Sulu. Historically, the Jama Mapun were variously subject to the vague, overlapping jurisdictions of the sultans of Brunei and Sulu (Majul 1964). At present, Cagayan de Sulu is an official municipality under the Province of Sulu, Republic of the Philippines.

SETTLEMENT PATTERN AND HOUSING. Local groups tend to form nucleated settlements around good anchorages; outside of these they show a scatter pattern, following the distribution of farms off the strand.

ECONOMY. Based on dry-rice agriculture, copra production, and trading. Fishing is little practiced except in the smaller islands. Traditional subsistence agriculture (*huma*) was in dry rice, corn, and cassava. After 1900, when copra came into demand on the world market, the islanders gradually shifted to copra production. Trading formerly consisted of barter between the natives of Palawan, who produced rice, rattan, and other forest products, and the natives and Chinese of Borneo, who supplied cloth, porcelain, brass gongs, and iron. The Jama Mapun acted as carriers or middlemen in this trade (Fox 1954). The post-World War II introduction of motorized boats has expanded this trade to Cotabato, Celebes, and the western Bisayas. [Casiño 1967a.]

KIN GROUPS. The kinship system shows both bilateral and unilineal features. There are Ego-centered cognatic categories, generally called *kampong*, which need not be localized. Patrilineal features appear in the inheritance of nobility status among the titled Datu and Salip class. Ancestor-centered kinship reckoning results in a category called *lungan*, which may be glossed as an ambilineal ramage inasmuch as it includes all descendants of an ancestor. **Kin terminology.** Some basic kin terms are:

GrPa	*bbo'*
Fa	*mma'*
Mo	*nne'*
MoBr, FaBr, MoSiHu, FaSiHu	*bapa'*
MoSi, FaSi, MoBrWi, FaBrWi	*dada'*
Siblings	*danganakan*
Cousins (cross and parallel)	*kaki*
Ch (Ego's Ch)	*anak*
SbCh, CoCh	*kamanakan*
GrCh	*mpu*

MARRIAGE AND FAMILY. Cousin marriage as near as the first degree is common. There is an indirect preference for MoBrDa, in the sense that marriage with a FaBrDa is under a vague proscription which, however, can be broken through payment of a ritual fine (*kapasu'an*). Marriage normally involves payment of a bride-price, which is geared to the relative social ranks of the bride and groom. Residence after marriage is initially uxorilocal, thereafter with whichever set of parents has the most to offer economically to the couple. The common domestic unit is the extended family, either through polygyny or the retention of married offspring in the same household, but separation of coresident married brothers usually occurs before the death of the family head. Divorce and inheritance in general follow folk Islamic rules.

---

*The author of this entry, Eric S. Casiño, carried out fieldwork among the Jama Mapun in 1963, 1966, and 1969-70. He is completing his Ph.D. degree in anthropology at the University of Sydney and is a member of the staff of the National Museum of the Philippines.

SOCIOPOLITICAL ORGANIZATION. Underlying the modern offices of barrio captain and town mayor is a set of traditional political notions and practices that cannot be understood apart from the historical institution of the sultanate and its religious adjunct represented by the *ulema* (cf. Mednick 1957; Majul 1964). Within the traditional polity, the Datu, personifying the secular order, and the Salip, representing the sacred order, shared between them the functions of social control and justice. Commoners were *tao marayao*, and "slaves" or nonfree dependents were *ata'* (*sinoho', ipun*). As a rule, members of traditional *nakura'* families (*nakura'* or *pame'an*, leader) occupy the modern political offices.

RELIGION. Islam, together with numerous folk beliefs and practices (Casiño 1967b).

BIBLIOGRAPHY. Arce 1963; Casiño 1966, 1967a, 1967b; Flores-Meiser 1969; Forrest 1779; Fox 1954, 1957; Majul 1964; Mednick 1957; Nimmo 1965, 1967; Sather 1967; Sopher 1965; Stone 1967.

YAKAN

Synonym. *Yacanes*

ORIENTATION. The Yakan, numbering some 60,000, constitute the indigenous population of the large island of Basilan, off the southern tip of Zamboanga Peninsula, western Mindanao. They are also found on the islands of Sakol, Malanipa, and Tumalutab, just east of Zamboanga city. Beyer (1917), citing older reports, characterized them as a semisedentary people in the mountainous interior, subsisting chiefly on sweet potatoes and the products of the hunt. Nowadays they are more widely dispersed, sometimes mixed with the coastal population. The Yakan are closely related linguistically to the seafaring Samal; they are, however, a land-oriented people, who subsist on agriculture (chiefly upland rice), together with copra production and cattle raising as commercial undertakings. Houses, occupied by economically independent nuclear families, are dispersed among the fields. Ancestral graves define the networks of cognatic kin ties that transcend parish boundaries. The concept of an Ego-centered kindred is present, but there are no corporate descent groups. The Yakan are nominally Muslims, but with a considerable admixture of older pagan beliefs and customs. [Beyer 1917; Frake 1969; Wulff 1964.]

BIBLIOGRAPHY. Beyer 1917; Frake 1969; Wulff 1964.

SANGIR

Synonyms. *Sangil, Sangirezen, Talaoerezen*

ORIENTATION. The inhabitants of the Sangihe (Sangir) and Talaud island chains between southern Mindanao and northern Celebes are referred to in Dutch publications as Sangirezen or Talaoerezen. They appear to be speakers of a single language or language group, Sangir or Sangil, also present on the southern Mindanao coast in the region of Sarangani Bay. Sangir is classed as a Philippine language by Esser (1938), and Conklin (1955c) places it within his Central Philippines group. The combined Sangihe-Talaud population in 1930 was approximately 160,000, resident for the most part in the Sangihe group (*Volkstelling 1930*). These islands were subject in the past to Muhammadan influence, stemming primarily from the Ternate sultanate to the east. Dutch administration, beginning in earnest in the 1890s, has, however, profoundly affected the indigenous culture, most noticeably perhaps in the widespread conversion to Christianity. Sangir (Sangil) speakers on the southern Mindanao coast appear to be undergoing a process of acculturation and absorption into coastal Moro society. Nowadays they are in all likelihood included within the category, Kalagan, by which the major Muslim groups refer to Islamized pagans (Mednick 1969).

ECONOMY. Traditional food crops include sweet potatoes, maize, bananas, and rice, grown in upland gardens by slash-and-burn methods. Sago is (or was) an important dietary staple (Frieswijk 1902). The Dutch encouraged the raising of commercial crops such as coconuts (copra) and nutmegs, with the result that the economy came to rely heavily on trade in these items, chiefly with Manado and Ternate, together with fishing and boatbuilding. The latter is (or was) a highly specialized craft, reportedly producing vessels capable of carrying up to 100 persons (Hickson 1889: 199).

SOCIOPOLITICAL ORGANIZATION. Chabot (1969) has partially reconstructed the traditional social structure at the local level for the island of

Siau in the Sangihe group. The coastal village, or *soa*, was an endogamous local group, the members of which were interrelated by kin and affinal ties. Houses were frequently arranged in opposing rows of four structures each. These "big houses" were inhabited by exogamous matrilineages, marriage ideally being with a member of another "big house" within the same *soa*. There was a marked social distinction between coastal inhabitants, *tau soa*, and those who lived in the hilly interior, *tau ruku* ("grass people"). The latter, of inferior social status, worked as retainers or "slaves" on lands owned by coastal lineages. Intermarriage was theoretically proscribed, but frequently took place between *soa* males and *ruku* females. The *soa* lineage houses derived their superior status in part because of their claims to perpetuating yearly ancestral rites and maintaining lineage prestige through bride-price payments. Hill people were said to "belong" to the various lineage houses, possibly indicating a ritual as well as an economic tie of some kind. According to Chabot, changes introduced by the Dutch subsequent to about 1900 altered this system to what is essentially a bilateral one. Dutch sources, e.g. Brilman (1937) and Miete (1938), describe a political system for Sangihe of principalities, each headed by a radja assisted by district and village chiefs. The Talaud islands were traditionally regarded as dependencies of these Sangihe principalities and Talaud islanders

as inferior and subject to enslavement. It is probable that this goes back to an earlier, pre-Dutch system of territorial domains ritually associated with royal or "founding" lineages, in a manner analogous to that found on Flores, Sumba, and elsewhere in eastern Indonesia. The traditional local structure described by Chabot also has obvious parallels elsewhere in Indonesia.

RELIGION. Kennedy (1935) mentions that although Islam and Christianity (in particular) have made great inroads, Sangirese religion still contains elements of an earlier, indigenous belief system. Ancestral spirits are (or were) important, as were annual lineage-sponsored feasts in their honor. Women (and occasionally men) served as intermediaries with the supernatural, through spirit possession, and conducted communal ceremonies and sacrifices, including human sacrifice. Disposal of the dead is normally by interment in a wooden coffin, frequently boat-shaped. Cave burial occurs occasionally. [Frieswijk 1902; Stokking 1923; van Dinter 1899.]

BIBLIOGRAPHY. Brilman 1937; Chabot 1969; Conklin 1955c; van Dinter 1899; Esser 1938; Frieswijk 1902; Hickson 1889; Kennedy 1935; Mednick 1969; Miete 1938; Stokking 1917, 1919, 1920, 1922a, 1922b, 1923; *Volkstelling 1930*.

PART II. PHILIPPINES

THE MYRIAD ISLANDS of the Philippine Archipelago extend for over 1,000 miles off the coast of Asia, from Formosa in the north to within a few miles of Borneo in the south, to form the western rim of the China Sea. Most of the more than 7,000 islands are small and uninhabited, the 12 largest accounting for some 95 percent of the total land area and population (Eggan et al. 1956: *1*, 11). The typical island is of volcanic origin, mountainous in the center, with narrow coastal lowlands intersected by short, swift streams. Only on Luzon and Mindanao are there major lowland plains or river valleys capable of supporting large, concentrated populations. The total population in 1960 came to some 27 million, of whom over 90 percent were Christians, 5 percent Muslims and somewhat less than 4 percent pagans. Christians, overwhelmingly lowland peasant farmers, are concentrated in the northern two-thirds of the Archipelago, on Luzon and the Bisayan islands, although rapidly moving into Mindanao and other traditionally Muslim areas in the south. The pagan peoples, ethnolinguistically less homogeneous than lowland Christians and Muslims, are found chiefly in the interior hills of Luzon, Mindoro, Palawan, and Mindanao. Overseas Chinese constitute an important, although numerically small (ca. 300,000), component of the population (cf. Amyot 1960; Laufer 1907; Reynolds 1964; Wickberg 1965; and see the selected bibliography in Saito 1972: 103-20). The indigenous peoples, with the exception of remnant Negrito and "mixed" groups, are racially of "southern Mongoloid" stock, similar in physical appearance to most other peoples of Southeast Asia; and the more than 75 distinct language groupings are all of Malayo-Polynesian affiliation, most closely related to the languages of Indonesia (Dyen 1965; Eggan et al. 1956: *1*, 323). The Archipelago has for millennia constituted a kind of outlying net for peoples and cultural influences moving out from mainland Asia. Settlement from the mainland goes back 15 to 30 thousand years to the existence of ancient land bridges, followed by a long period during which small (probably related family) groups—seafarers of diverse origins voyaging out from the Indo-Malayan and Indo-Chinese coasts—gradually populated the Philippine "island world" (Fox 1956, 1967; Yengoyan 1967). This view of events disagrees in some important respects with the earlier versions of prehistory, notably those of H. O. Beyer (1947, 1948), that invoked "waves" of migration with diagnostic racial and cultural characteristics in an effort to account for differences among contemporary pagan and other groups in the Philippines. In addition to their overly mechanistic character, Beyer's theories do not allow for local development of cultural forms, e.g. in response to changing ecological and demographic conditions (cf. Eggan 1963 on local development in Mountain Province, northern Luzon). The protohistoric period in Philippine history —roughly the five hundred or so years before Magellan—saw the entry into the area of Chinese, Hindu-Indonesian, and Arab traders, colonizers, and missionaries, with Islam gaining ascendancy in the southern islands in the 1400s, followed by Spanish conquest and Christianization commencing with the founding of Cebu in 1565.

Despite the seeming diversity of historic influences, it is possible to discern regularities that give meaning to Philippine culture history within the larger framework of Southeast Asia. Late pre-Spanish coastal society appears to have been relatively homogeneous, due in large measure to ease of interisland communication and the rapid spread in late protohistoric times of (predominately) Indian influences emanating from the Hinduized kingdoms of Java-Sumatra via Borneo (Fox 1956). This late protohistoric lowland culture appears, moreover, to have been linked to culture types in the interior mountains by similarities that presumably relate to an older base common to much of Southeast Asia (cf. Kroeber 1919, 1943). Thus, the student of Philippine ethnography must be struck by cultural similarities between, e.g. the Apayao of northern Luzon and the Bagobo of Mindanao, especially so in light of Laura Benedict's discussion of parallels between Bagobo-Manobo and pre-Spanish Tagal-Bisayan (Benedict 1916: 250ff.). Characteristics common to both uplanders and pre-Spanish lowlanders would appear to include the local settlement area made up of scattered hamlets and containing a population averaging something like 200-500 persons linked by cognatic and affinal kin ties —essentially an endogamous kin group corresponding to Murdock's "deme" (1949: 62-63). Relationships tend to be egalitarian and leadership diffuse, depending on bravery (headhunting or simply killing, associated with vengeance and feuding patterns) and personal charisma, signified by accumulated ritual wealth and attributed supernatural powers (cf. LeBar 1968). Renowned warriors gain influence over larger regions, but essentially each local settlement area is at enmity with all others. Men of renown sponsor major ceremonies, rites honoring the deities of blood, vengeance, and warfare, and the tutelary deities of warriors; and only they can participate in certain of the more esoteric rites. Sponsorship of ceremonies gives added prestige to such men, and also benefits the spiritual welfare of the entire community. The settlement area is in this sense not only a kin group but also a ritual community, having its own ritual peculiarities and speaking a common "ritual language." The similarity of all this to the basic socioreligious structure of longhouse communities in Borneo is striking. It was apparently this basic structure that characterized much of Borneo and the Philippines at one time. The medieval Chinese demand for "exotica" and the consequent expansion of trade into insular Southeast Asia (Schafer 1963, 1967; Wang Gung-wu 1958) created new markets and new sources of ritual wealth in the form of gongs, jars, and beads; while the introduction of wet rice, and its adaptation to terracing techniques as in Luzon's Mountain Province, wrought changes in settlement size and ultimately in community structure, introducing wealth in rice and land as the basis of political influence, prestige, and power. Later, Islamization in the south and Hispanization and Christianization in the north brought further changes to the coastal lowlands. The above outline, brief as it is, would seem to encompass the major historical processes that, in various combinations and permutations, have produced both the cultural amalgam of lowland peasant society and the cultural diversity among upland groups, two of the more important facets of contemporary Philippine life.

BIBLIOGRAPHY. Amyot 1960; Benedict 1916; Beyer 1947, 1948; Dyen 1965; Eggan 1963; Eggan et al. 1956; Fox 1956, 1967; Kroeber 1919, 1943; Laufer 1907; LeBar 1968; Murdock 1949; Reynolds 1964; Saito 1972; Schafer 1963, 1967; Wang Gung-wu 1958; Wickberg 1965; Yengoyan 1967.

CHRISTIAN FILIPINOS*

ORIENTATION. **Identification.** "Filipino," when used generically, refers not only to lowland Christians but also to highland primitive groups and the Islamized people of southern Mindanao and the Sulu Archipelago. In the past, Filipinos occupying the coastal lowlands and plains of Luzon and the central islands were subjected to similar ecological and acculturative influences, including Christianization. Considerable but not complete cultural leveling occurred among these lowland Filipinos, who are designated as cultural-linguistic groups (for their basic differentiation is not racial). Although considerable differences continue to distinguish the various Christian groups, "the use of a model called 'Filipino' is practicable, nevertheless, when attempting to obtain an *over-all* picture of the basic social

*The author of this entry, Donn V. Hart, is director of the Center for Southeast Asian Studies, Northern Illinois University, and has done extensive fieldwork in the Philippines, chiefly in the Bisayan area. He wishes to point out that his contribution has benefited from critical readings by Professor James Anderson, University of California, Berkeley; Professor Daniel Doeppers, University of Wisconsin, Madison; Mr. Morton J. Netzorg, Detroit, Michigan; and Professor Daniel Scheans, Portland State University.

characteristics of the dominant Philippine peoples, rather than specific knowledge of one or another group" (Eggan et al. 1956: *1*, 414). Finally, the more rural the milieu, the greater is the applicability of most of the following generalizations concerning Christian Filipino culture and society. The major Christian groups, ranked according to size, are: Cebuan (Sugbuhanon or Cebuano), Tagalog (Tagal), Ilokan (Ilocano), Panayan (Ilongo or Hiligaynon), Bikolan (Bicolano), Samaran (Samareño, Waray-waray or Samarnon), Pampangan (Kapampangan), and Pangasinan (Eggan et al. 1956: *1*). A generic name for Cebuans, Panayans, and Samarans is Bisayan (Visayan). Minor Christian groups are: Aklan and Hantik (Panay); Ibanag (Kagayan, Cagayanes), Itawes (Itavi), Sambal (Sambali), and Isinai (Isinay) all on Luzon; Ivatan (Batanes and Babuyan islands); Kuyonon (Cuyo and Calamian islands and Palawan); and Gaddang and Tinggian (Luzon: parts of these last two groups remain pagan). Christian Filipinos belong to a branch of the Mongoloid race characterized by such physical traits as brown skin, straight black hair, a flat face with a wide nose and medium-thick lips, slender build, and sparse body hair (Bailen 1967: 527-58; Kroeber 1943; Bean 1910). These characteristics have been modified in many cases through intermixture with Chinese, less so with Europeans (mainly Spaniards) and Americans. Persons with this mixed background are called *mestizos*. Differences among various lowland Filipino groups had been subjected to a cultural leveling process prior to the Spaniards' arrival, initiated mainly by the introduction of lowland wet-rice agriculture and coastal trade. The major consolidating forces in this process, however, were post-Hispanic: the overarching governmental and ecclesiastical systems; literacy; the rise of urban centers, money, and commerce; and the unifying effects of the anti-Spanish movements of the people (Keesing 1962a: 326). However, many Filipinos, based on stereotypes unsubstantiated by research, distinguish Christian Filipino groups according to prominent sociocultural traits. As would be expected, these "cultural folk caricatures" often are conflicting and imprecise (Tangco 1951; Eggan et al. 1956: *1*). Tagalogs (and sometimes differentiations are made between northern and southern Tagalogs) supposedly are proud, talkative, and boastful; they have a snobbish attitude toward other Filipino groups. Unlike Bisayans, Tagalogs are unusually fussy about their food. Bikolans are less adventurous than Tagalogs and Ilokans, more indolent and improvident. Few Bikolans live outside their home region except in Manila. Pampangans are noted gourmets, independent and self-centered, highly materialistic, and unusually loyal to their superiors. Ilokans, known as the "Yankees of the Pacific," are believed to be inordinately hard workers,

aggressive, hot-headed, willing to sacrifice present comforts for future benefits (Lewis 1971: 5-6). Perhaps because of these alleged traits, and certainly because of the relatively restricted agricultural potential of their region, Ilokans have settled throughout the Philippines (as well as Hawaii and mainland United States). In the Philippines, they are often itinerant traders. Ilokans are said to be both unusually religious and quick to resort to violence. They adjust easily to new environments. Pangasinans are supposedly one of the most conservative and sedentary of Christian Filipino groups: they are said to have a tendency toward fanaticism. As for the Bisayan:

> He is a happy-go-lucky man more interested in [the] here and the now than in the past or the future. He exceeds the Tagalog in his love of the finer things of life [including clothes and jewelry], so much so that, in contrast with the Samtoy [Ilokan], he is ready to spend his last peso to enjoy life to its last drop. . . . The Visayan is a hedonist . . . He is a lover like the Tagalog, but he expresses his consuming passion in music, not in poetry [Agoncillo and Alfonso 1960: 16].

Finally, Bisayans supposedly are the bravest of all groups; most Filipino professional fighters are Bisayans (Tangco 1951). **Location.** Christian Filipinos live mainly in coastal lowlands and valleys. Areas of heavy population are northwestern Luzon (the Ilokan region), the Cagayan Valley (north-central Luzon), and the alluvial Central Luzon Plain, the largest continuous Philippine lowland. Major groups inhabiting the densely settled Central Luzon Plain are Ilokans, Tagalogs, Pangasinans, and Pampangans. Tagalogs are the predominant population in metropolitan Manila. Southeast Luzon consists of one large, irregular peninsula, the Bikol. Here live the Bikolans, who also inhabit nearby Catanduanes Island and northeastern Masbate Island. Within the Bisayas, Samar and eastern Leyte are settled largely by Samarans, while western and most of southern Leyte are inhabited by Cebuans, who are also the dominant group on Cebu, Bohol, Siquijor, and eastern Negros. Panay and western Negros are occupied by Panayans. The Christian Filipino population of Mindanao, the second largest island in the nation, is composed mainly of Bisayan immigrants (mainly Cebuans and Boholans). **Linguistic affiliation.** Philippine languages are similar in grammatical and phonetic structure; all belong to the Malayo-Polynesian family of the Austronesian phylum of languages (Chrétien 1963; Fox et al. 1965). The mother tongue of most Christian Filipinos is either Cebuan, Panayan, Samaran, Ilokan, Tagalog, Bikolan, Pampangan, or Pangasinan. Until recently, more Filipinos spoke

English as a second language than any other tongue. Today a slightly larger percentage speak Filipino (the national language based on Tagalog) than English (Frei 1959; Corpuz 1966). Spanish was never extensively spoken, although many words and phrases have been incorporated into Philippine languages (Whinnom 1954). The 1960 census reported that Spanish was spoken by a little more than half a million Filipinos. Several "pidgin" languages have developed through the blending of Spanish with local speech forms, e.g. Chabakano (Spanish-Subanun-Cebuan) and Caviteño (Spanish-Tagalog) (McKaughan 1954; Panganiban 1961). **Demography.** Population figures for the eight major Christian Filipino groups, based on the last official census (1960), are given below (Philippine Islands (Republic) 1962-63):

Group	Population (in thousands)	Percent of total population
Cebuan	6,529.8	24.1
Tagalog	5,694.0	21.0
Ilokan	3,158.5	11.7
Panayan	2,817.3	10.4
Bikolan	2,108.8	7.8
Samaran	1,488.6	5.5
Pampangan	875.5	3.2
Pangasinan	666.0	2.5

In the late sixteenth century, the population of the Philippines was an estimated 500,000, which by the time of the 1960 census had increased to 27,087,685. Based on a projected decline of the fertility rate (to 2.8 births per woman of completed fertility by 1995-2000), the population of the Philippines at the start of the twenty-first century may be an estimated 73,000,000 (Concepcion 1966). As the result of improved sanitation and medical facilities, a better diet, and minimization of internal civil disorder, the life expectancy of Filipinos at birth has increased from 21 years (1902) to about 55 years (1965). Recent projections suggest a population rate increase of over 3 percent annually (Madigan 1968: 3-31). Unless this mounting overpopulation problem can be solved in the near future, the fabric of Filipino life is threatened. Luzon, Negros, Panay, and Cebu are the most densely settled islands. Not only has resettlement of Filipinos from densely to thinly populated regions failed to solve regional overcrowding but Mindanao, once regarded as a population "safety valve," can no longer provide significant agricultural land for new settlers without radical changes in transportation, land tenure, and agricultural methods (Wernstedt and Simkins 1965: 83-103). **History and cultural relations.** The Philippines were probably settled initially by myriad movements of small, often kin-related, groups, and factors such as local endogamy, intermarriage, ecological adjustment, trade lanes, and subsequent diffusion of culture probably explain the present biological and cultural differen-

tiation of Christian Filipino groups (Scott 1968). Chinese influence has been extensive (Wickberg 1965), but the Archipelago's geographic isolation from mainland Southeast Asia has minimized direct and extensive cultural donations from India (Francisco 1963). **Spanish Period (1521-1898).** Spain's greatest impact on the Philippines was to transform the Archipelago's population into the only Christian (Roman Catholic) nation in Asia. Additionally, slavery was officially outlawed in 1591; however, during the Spanish period, debt peonage became widespread. Among Spanish innovations were the introduction of the Roman alphabet, private ownership of land, the Spanish language, and the Gregorian calendar. Numerous plants from the New World (especially Mexico) were brought to the Philippines, among them maize, sweet potato, manioc, pineapple, tobacco, and peanuts. Although the people were extensively Hispanized, the process of acculturation was dual, involving the Hispanization of much of lowland Filipino culture and the Philippinization of diffused Spanish culture, e.g. the still prevalent folk Catholicism (Phelan 1959). Many aspects of indigenous lowland Filipino culture resisted modification, e.g. the relative equality of sexes (Alzona 1934). In pre-Hispanic societies women selected their mates, divorce was possible, and the wife, as today, usually managed the family's assets. Late in the centuries of the Spanish period a new sense of national identity was generated in lowland Filipinos, resulting in a Filipino revolution in 1896. Filipinos later made common cause with the United States in the Spanish-American war of 1898 (Agoncillo and Alfonso 1960). As a result of the complex events of 1898, the Philippines became America's sole possession in Southeast Asia. **American Period (1898-1946).** The United States, publicly announcing its intention of retaining the Philippines only until the people were ready for self-government, quickly shared political power with Filipino leaders. A national public educational system was established, with English the language of instruction. Agriculture and, to a lesser extent, industry were developed, although such developments were usually oriented toward American markets. Less successful were American efforts to help the poverty-stricken tenant farmer, control usury, and create a viable and independent economic system (Golay 1961). In 1935, after a plebescite voted overwhelmingly for independence, American withdrawal was planned to occur over a ten-year period. Before this period ended, World War II intervened, and the country suffered severely under Japanese invasion and occupation. **Independent Philippines.** In 1946, the Philippines became independent, and with technical assistance and financial aid from the United States, the immense task of rebuilding the war-ravaged nation began. Special efforts have been made to integrate more effectively the various segments of the nation, separated by insularity, distance, religion, and disparate general cultural development. On the whole, Christian Filipinos have minimal contacts with the highland groups and Muslim Filipinos (these two groups are now officially referred to as national cultural minorities), except where geographic propinquity and economic interest encourage or require such relationships (Abueva and de Guzman 1969: 30-34). With some exceptions, especially in the Baguio-Bontok areas of northern Luzon, primitive people remain outside the main stream of national life. In the Muslim regions, especially southern Mindanao and the Sulu Archipelago, relationships between Christian and Muslim Filipinos have been marked by mutual distrust and frequent conflict. The popular stereotype of the Moro, still held by many Christian Filipinos, is that of a warlike, violent, and ignorant person (Gowing 1964). Bisayan settlement of Mindanao, particularly during the postwar period, resulted in countless disputes—some bloody—between Christians and Muslims over land ownership. Several national government agencies, including the Commission on National Integration and a Tribal Research Centre, are working with modest success to improve the socioeconomic integration of these minorities.

SETTLEMENT PATTERNS. **Settlement pattern.** The typical rural Filipino may reside in a población (a large village or a small or middle-size town), but more likely in a barrio (village; a sitio is a segment of a village). The spatial arrangement of the buildings in many poblaciónes (especially in regions where Spanish influence was extensive) is in a semigrid system, with the plaza as a focal point. Usually near or facing the perimeter of the rectangular "plaza complex" are the church, public schools, market place, and the municipio, i.e. the municipal building housing local officials (Hart 1961). The rural elite (clergymen, schoolteachers, municipal officials, and more prosperous merchants) live in the población. Innovations often travel from the big cities to the poblaciónes, then radiate outward to the surrounding barrios and sitios. Village spatial characteristics differ, according to land utilization, terrain, proximity to roads, rivers, and cities. In the Central Luzon Plain, a region of intensive agriculture, villages usually are compact settlements; while in the rolling hills of Cebu, where dry upland farming is typical, most houses are scattered among the fields. **Cities and urbanization.** Although the Philippines is the second most urbanized Southeast Asian nation, only an estimated 14 percent of Filipinos live in cities over 10,000. More than one-half of these individuals reside in metropolitan Manila, the first truly "primate" city of Southeast Asia. In the mid-nineteenth

century, Manila was an old Spanish walled city with an estimated population of 150,000. By 1960, metropolitan Manila (Manila proper, Quezon, Caloocan and Pasay cities, and the districts of Makati, Mandaluyong, Paranaque, and San Juan) contained 8 percent (2,131,219) of the Philippine's total population. This metropole's estimated 1966 population was 3,075,000. "It is not only the political capital [Quezon City] but the capital of business, finance and commerce, of industry, of education [23 universities and 87 colleges], of the press and communications, of transportation, of medicine, of the arts and architecture, of fashion, fads and recreation" (McPhelin 1969: 782). Large cities other than metropolitan Manila have been classified broadly as either regional trade centers (e.g. Cebu city, Iloilo, and Davao) or provincial cities (e.g. Dumaguete, Tacloban, and Baguio) (Ullman 1960). These smaller cities, often ports, have fewer residing Euro-Americans and closer socioeconomic ties to their hinterlands. Many middle-sized towns are really urban cores surrounded by satellite villages (Pal 1964). Recently, however, some of these towns have developed highly urbanized suburbs, inhabited primarily by middle- and upper-class residents. Little detailed information is available on the lifestyles of urban Filipinos. Certainly the majority of the most Westernized Filipinos reside in the large cities. These Filipinos are fluent in English (sometimes in Spanish); many have been educated abroad. One study found for an urban community in Manila (Malate) that the composite, not the nuclear, family predominated (Eslao 1966). Fertility rates in the city are lower than in rural areas (Madigan 1968: 20). Research has shown that lower-class residents of Manila often retain the basic values associated with rural life (Hollnsteiner 1967). Some squatter settlements probably have such positive functions as preparing new rural emigrants for their later, and more complete, entry into the complexities of urban existence (Laquian 1968). **Housing.** Although house styles and building materials vary, the typical countryside dwelling is a two- or three-room structure, raised on piles. The house is built of bamboo (sometimes wood) and is cogon- or nipa-thatched, though increasingly commonly roofed with corrugated iron sheets (Hart 1959). Cooking is done indoors over a wood fire, and most occupants sleep on the floor on woven palm mats. Common farmyard animals are water buffalo, pigs, chickens, goats, dogs, and cats. The average village has a primary school, many through grade six; a *sari-sari* (a small general store) selling such basic items as matches, thread, lard, kerosene, and canned fish; and a small chapel (but no resident priest).

ECONOMY. Typical of its Southeast Asian setting, the Philippines is an agricultural nation (Sicat et al.

1964 and Spencer 1952). "One simple and significant fact is that Filipino agriculture is not very productive at best; its per-acre and per-capita yields are among the lowest in southern and eastern Asia, and rank low in world comparisons" (Wernstedt and Spencer 1967: 179). Rice occupies slightly less than half the total cultivated land and is the primary crop on nearly half of all Filipino farms. Coconuts, cultivated on more land than any other crop except rice, are found throughout the Archipelago. Copra (dried coconut meat) is a major export. Next to rice and coconuts, the most farm land is used to raise maize. One out of every five Filipinos eats as his daily staple food maize that is milled and then boiled like rice. Other important crops, grown largely for export after processing, are abaca (Manila hemp) and sugarcane. The major sugar-producing areas are central Luzon and northern Negros. Philippine industry, expanding since a slow start around 1900, made its greatest advance during the last decade (Huke et al. 1963). Most of this industry (largely agroprocessing) is concentrated in the general Manila area, and more than 50 percent of all Filipino industrial workers are employed in factories there. Two-thirds of the rapidly diminishing Philippine forests are classified as being of commercial value. Fish are a major source of protein in the Filipino diet, yet present production is inadequate for local needs. Fish are caught not only in the surrounding seas but also in the rivers and lakes, and are also raised in fish ponds. Subsistence fishing involves the use of many different types of nets, bamboo traps, hooks and lines, explosives, and piscicides. Shrimp, crabs, and snails are also caught in the paddies, rivers, lakes, and swamps. A typical rural diet consists of boiled rice (in much of the Bisayas, maize is a rice substitute), vegetables (tomatoes, eggplant, taro, onions, garlic, and stringbeans), chicken, fresh and dried fish, and a fish sauce (patis) to flavor the cooked rice or maize. For many families, the consumption of beef and pork is limited to festive occasions, e.g. the fiesta or a wedding. Some popular fruits are bananas (fresh, boiled, and fried), pineapples, chicos, lanzones, and mangoes. Stimulants consist mainly of alcoholic beverages: tuba made from the sap of the coconut, nipa, and buri palms; basi, from sugarcane juice; and, increasingly, bottled beer. Cigarettes and cigars, often made of locally grown tobacco, are smoked; betel nut chewing is still widespread but of declining popularity among younger Filipinos.

KIN GROUPS. Descent is bilateral (cognatic), with membership in descent groups traced through both male and female links (Eggan 1968, Jocano 1969). The structure of the referential terminology is Eskimo, with cousins equated and differentiated from siblings; vocatively, the kinship terminology type is Hawaiian. The basic kinship vocabulary stresses the generational principle. Other than parents, all kinsmen in the first ascending generation from Ego are termed either uncles or aunts. All relatives in the second and succeeding ascending generations are called grandparents, with exact generation indicated by modifiers. In one's own generation, all kinsmen except siblings are termed cousins, with the relationship degree indicated by a numeral modifier. No distinction is made between cross and parallel cousins. In the first descending generation from Ego, all relatives, except children, are called nephews and nieces, and in the second and succeeding generations, grandchildren. Basic referential kinship terms for three major Filipino groups are given below:

	Cebuan	Ilokan	Tagalog
Mother	ihahan	ina	ina
Father	amahan	ama	ama
Sibling	igsoon†	kabsat†	kapatid†
Child	anak†	anak†	anak†
Uncle	uyoan	uliteg	amain
Aunt	iyaan	ikit	ale
Cousin	igagaw°	kasinsin°	pinsan°
Grandparent	apohan†	apo†	apo†
Grandchild	apo†	apo†	apo†

†Sex is indicated by a modifier, e.g. Ceb. igsoon nga lalake (sibling male = brother) or Ceb. anak nga babaye (child female = daughter). Sometimes vocatives are also used as referentials, e.g. Tagalog, tiyo (uncle) or lolo (grandfather).
°Degree is indicated by numeral modifier, as in English, e.g. Ceb. igagaw igtagsa (first cousin); for Ilokan, kapidua (second cousin) and kapitlo (third cousin).

The nuclear family is of extreme importance among all Christian Filipinos. The Philippines has been described as a "familial" society, because so many social activities in the community focus on this group. One explanation for the private and public nepotism of Filipino society is the superordination of the family over the individual. Various attempts have been made to classify household types, but the data are not sufficient for comparative use (Nurge 1965). Possibly various types are merely examples of different phases in a household development cycle (Davis and Hollnsteiner 1969). Available data on the nature of the personal kindred, i.e. Ego's personal kinship group, are limited; potential cognate members of the kindred cluster along a lineal axis linking the fifth ascending and descending generations, but only those within four degrees of cousinhood collaterally. Similarly, it is not clear whether or not all Filipino groups include affines as members of the kindred. Another key concept of Filipino social structure is the personal alliance that is differentiated primarily from the personal kindred because the former includes nonkinsmen (Hollnsteiner 1963). The membership of an individual's personal alliance is integrated through kinship (real and ritual), reciprocal obligations, associational ties, and proven friendship. Such personal alliances form a crucial link between the average citizen and the country's elites. Some regard the personal alliance concept as the *"sine qua non* to discussions of Filipino interpersonal relations" (Davis and Hollnsteiner 1969: 68). A definitive statement on Christian Filipino residence rules awaits additional research. Generally, however, residence is initially optiolocal, with secondary neolocal residence. An important and neglected aspect of Filipino social organization is the variety of ritual kinship based on the Roman Catholic concept of godparenthood (Hollnsteiner 1963 and Eggan et al. 1956: *1*). In the Philippines, compadrazgo, or ritual coparenthood, is emphasized. Major stress is placed on social bonds between godparents and parents. The major occasions for the creation of ritual kinship ties are baptism, confirmation, and marriage. Ritual relationships (often called *kumpari* = compadre = godfather) based on baptism are regarded as the most important.

MARRIAGE AND FAMILY. Most boys are voluntarily circumcized shortly before or at puberty; imitative magic practices often are associated with a girl's first menses. Courting begins in the late teens, and often is kept a secret, especially from the girl's parents. Since most teen-age girls are chaperoned, the most favorable occasions for meeting and courting are such community affairs as the fiesta, harvest, and the social activities associated with the rites of passage. The "double standard" in sexual behavior is a generally accepted code of conduct for most males, particularly prior to marriage (Pal 1956). Generally, Filipinos are married by the time they are in their late teens or early twenties. Marriage is monogamous; divorce (but not legal separation) is virtually impossible in the Catholic Philippines. Marriage of cousins closer than third or fourth degree is generally regarded as incestuous. Bride service rarely occurs today; when it does, it is in a mild form, in which the young man voluntarily "helps around the house." On the whole, sororate and levirate second marriages are uncommon and generally disapproved when they occur. Marriage negotiations, especially in the rural areas, are often complicated, sometimes long, and frequently anxiety-laden (Pal 1956). In the past, most marriages were parentally arranged. Today the boy often courts and wins the girl, and then informs his parents he wants to marry. Although parental approval is most important, and the procedures for negotiation of the marriage often remain traditional, effective authority in the selection of a spouse largely has passed from the parents to the young folks. Common-law marriages occur, but are less frequent today than in the past. Inheritance

is equal among heirs, with no restrictions based on age or sex. Adoption occurs, but rarely in its legal form; Filipinos frequently "adopt" a relative, often a sibling's child.

VALUE SYSTEMS. Socialization processes early inculcate in children, and enculturation reinforces, the fundamental values of Christian Filipino society. *Utang na loob* (an unpayable "debt of gratitude"), an aspect of the pervasive reciprocity of Filipino social life, defines the lasting moral obligation created when one accepts a voluntary gift or service (Kaut 1961). Another crucial value is the concept of shame (Tag. *hiya*). If an individual fails to repay his "debt of gratitude," he is said to be a shameless person (*walang hiya*): he dishonors himself and his family. This complex of values helps explain the massive indirection characterizing Christian Filipino behavior. As a result, another major value is the avoidance of conflict, or *pakikisama* (getting along) (Lynch 1964). The exact nature, operation, and spread of these values among various Christian Filipino groups is imperfectly known; in fact their relative importance has been challenged (Jocano 1966; Davis and Hollnsteiner 1969). In summary, social existence among most Christian Filipinos is much concerned with intragroup cohesion; the individual receives sustenance and security within this system in return for its defense. The nuclear family is the most secure and highly integrative unit, and supposedly the one Filipino value that occupies the "largest area in the total field of values" is the emotional closeness and security generated within the nuclear family (Bulatao 1962). Research on the Filipino's basic (or modal) personality configuration is too limited and controversial to be utilized for summary comments (Lawless 1969; Guthrie and Jacobs 1966).

SOCIOPOLITICAL ORGANIZATION. The largest Philippine geopolitical unit, excepting the nation, is the province (Wurfel 1959). Most large islands are divided into several provinces, whereas some (e.g. Cebu) are all one province. The provincial governor and board members are elected, but some provincial officials are appointed by national officials. The province is politically subdivided into municipalities, each of whose electorates votes for a mayor and other local officials. Until 1956, the official village leader was appointed by the municipal council. In that year, formal political democracy was extended to the village level; the barrio capitan and council members now are elected. Their taxing and political powers, however, are very limited. National executive power is vested in the office of the President, whose powers are greater than those of its American counterpart. The bicameral Congress consists of a Senate and a House of Representatives. Today the two major political parties, separated more by the personalities of their leaders than by substantive issues, are the Nacionalista and Liberal. Since independence, Filipinos have changed their office holders by democratic procedures, although election violence does occur (Landé 1965; Grossholtz 1964). **Social differentiation.** Although existing knowledge on Filipino social classes is imprecise, and its exact nature is disputed, the great majority of the people fall into two classes: upper ("Big People") and lower ("Little People") (Lynch 1965). Social class is based mainly, but not solely, on land and inherited wealth. In most barrios the residents belong to a single class, with social differentiation primarily as gradations from prosperous small holders to poor tenants. A symbiotic relationship, often exploitative but sometimes mutually beneficial, exists between the upper and lower classes. The "Big People" own land, possess political power, lend money, and provide other essential services to the "Little People," who serve as their tenants and political supporters and are recipients of their favors or aid during personal emergencies. In large urban centers, a middle class is emerging, composed mainly of professional and government personnel. For the middle class, education is a major factor, facilitating social mobility.

RELIGION. Many Filipinos retain the pre-Hispanic belief that normally invisible spirits of the land and their deceased ancestors' souls influence their lives for good or ill (Hart 1966: 65-71). As a result, Philippine folk Catholicism is an intricate and unique blend of the faith of the Spanish conquistadores and the viable animism of the ancient past. For administrative purposes, the Catholic church divides the Philippines into six ecclesiastical provinces, with each province subdivided into smaller units down to the parish. In rural areas, the parish priest, usually an individual of considerable local importance, resides in the población (Anderson 1969; Gowing 1967). The religious calendar lists an elaborate and colorful complex of activities, with a mixture of ritual, recreational, and sociopolitical functions. Some of these events are a festive Christmas; the rich drama of the Lenten season; All Souls' Day, when the cemetery is visited to pray for the dead; and the patron saint's fiesta. Nearly all communities have adopted a patron saint, who watches over the residents' welfare. The annual fiesta, usually held on the saint's feast day, is a gala event of religious services, feasting, athletic contests, games of chance, cock fights, and social dancing. Extensive Protestant missionary activities in the Philippines did not begin until the American period. Although the record

is uncertain, probably the first Protestant service of worship in the Philippines occurred in August 1898 (Gowing 1967). The first American Protestants to arrive were the Presbyterians, Methodists, and Baptists. Today there are several hundred different Protestant denominations in the Philippines, although the Protestant Filipino group remains a significant if slow-growing minority (Elwood 1968). Major Filipino Christian religious affiliations, according to the 1960 census, are given below:

Religion	Membership (in thousands)
Roman Catholic	22,686.1
Aglipayan (Philippine Independent Church)	1,414.4
Protestant	785.4
Eglesia ni Kristo	270.1

The Philippine Independent Church (Iglesia Filipina Independiente), known popularly as the Aglipayan Church, was founded in 1902 (Achutegui and Bernad 1961-69). The ritual is largely of Catholic derivation, although each congregation is self-governing, and priests do marry. It is now allied with the Episcopal Church. The Iglesia ni Kristo, established in 1913 by Felix Manalo, a Catholic converted to Protestantism, rejects the mass, the primacy of the Pope, confession, and saints. Its doctrine is derived largely from American Protestantism (Clifford 1969; Kavanagh 1955).

BIBLIOGRAPHY. Abueva and de Guzman 1969; de Achutegui and Bernad 1961-69; Agoncillo and Alfonso 1960; Agoncillo 1965; Alzona 1934; Anderson 1969; Bailen 1967; Bean 1910; Bulatao 1962; Carson 1961; Chrétien 1963; Clifford 1969; Concepcion 1966; Corpuz 1966; Davis and Hollnsteiner 1969; Demetrio 1966; Eggan et al. 1956; Eggan 1968; Elwood 1968; Eslao 1966; Fox et al. 1965; Francisco 1963; Frei 1959; Fresnoza 1957; Friend 1965; Golay 1961; Gowing 1964, 1967; Grossholtz 1964; Guthrie and Jacobs 1966; Guthrie 1968; Hart 1959, 1961, 1965, 1966, 1969; Hayden 1942; Hollnsteiner 1963, 1967; Huke et al. 1963; Jocano 1966, 1969; Kaut 1961; Kavanagh 1955; Keesing 1962a; Kroeber 1943; Landé 1965; Laquian 1966, 1968; Lawless 1969; Lewis 1971; Lieban 1967; Lynch 1964, 1965; McGee 1967; McKaughan 1954; McPhelin 1969; Madigan 1968; Nurge 1965; Nydegger and Nydegger 1963; Pal 1956, 1964; Panganiban 1961; Phelan 1959; Philippine Islands (Republic) 1962-63; Reyes 1966; Scheans 1963; Scott 1968; Sicat et al. 1964; Spencer 1952; Stone and Marsella 1968; Tangco 1951; Ullman 1960; Wernstedt and Simkins 1965; Wernstedt and Spencer 1967; Whinnom 1954; Wickberg 1965; Wurfel 1959; Yengoyan 1967; Zaide 1957; Zamora 1967.

MUSLIMS

INHABITANTS OF THE Philippine Islands who have converted to Muhammadanism are generally referred to as Moros, a term dating back to the Spanish conquest. The peoples so designated, located for the most part in Mindanao and the Sulu Archipelago, are racially and linguistically similar to other Filipinos. The difference lies in the fact that the southern Philippines were Islamized from Borneo and Malaya prior to the Spanish conquest and the subsequent Christianization of the central and northern islands. Spain never achieved effective control of the southern Moro areas—a task finally accomplished by American forces by about 1915. These areas identified with Muslim Malaysia to the south and west, joining Malacca, Brunei, Goa, and Java in resisting the growing trade monopoly of Westerners—Dutch, Spanish, and Portuguese. For almost three hundred years, Moros terrorized the seas from Brunei to Manila, while the Sultanate of Sulu expanded its territory and waxed rich from the spoils of piracy and pillage. There is thus a long legacy of conflict, fear, and mistrust between Christian and Muslim in this area of the world. The term Moro encompasses at least ten recognized ethnolinguistic groups or categories, including Maranao, Magindanao, Ilanon, and Sangir in western and southern Mindanao; Tausug, Samal, Yakan, and Bajau in the islands of the Sulu Archipelago and the coasts of Zamboanga; Jama Mapun on Cagayan Sulu Island; and Melebuganon (Melebugnan) on Balabac Island and the adjacent coast of Palawan. These groups totaled over one and one-quarter million in 1960; a major part of this total was identified as either Magindanao, Maranao, Tausug, or Samal. [See elsewhere in this volume for entries under these names.] The languages spoken by the various Moro groups belong, with minor exceptions, to Conklin's Central Philippine language group (Dyen's Sulic Hesion); a few, such as Maranao and Magindanao, are mutually intelligible. Most

Moros observe the Islamic taboo on consumption of pork, although the degree of orthodoxy varies widely, the Yakan and Bajau being relatively more lax in these respects. The Tausug, by virtue of their early conversion and their historical identification with the once-powerful Sulu Sultanate, regard themselves as superior to other Moro groups. Perhaps the most characteristic feature of Moro society, aside from religion, has been the so-called "*dato* system," whereby all persons in a district considered themselves allied to a local *dato* (*datu*), sultan, or similarly titled individual. Under this system, the Moros were organized into innumerable petty states or principalities, in a manner not unlike the early coastal Malay sultanates of Sumatra, Java, Borneo, and Celebes. Leadership was largely restricted to members of aristocratic family lines, whose claim to authority rested ultimately on Koranic scripture; actual power was a matter of individual charisma backed by the number and strength of one's entourage. Intermarriage among aristocratic families was a favorite way of gaining allies and building power. This system, particularly where it has coincided with the rise of powerful sultanates, has given a cohesiveness to Moro society that is lacking among most of the pagan peoples of the Philippines. Although pacification and extension of centralized government has removed the actual power of the old sultanates, the basic patterns of organization persist within the context of modern political life; nowadays when Moro leaders seek political office the local principality often becomes the basis for a party organization (cf. Hunt 1954). It is only relatively recently that Moros have begun to operate within the national political structure. During the American period and throughout the early years of the Republic, the Islamized areas in the south were administered as "special provinces," and integration, political or otherwise, is still far from complete. The Moros occupy some of the best agricultural land in Mindanao, a major "frontier area" designated for resettlement from more populous areas in central and northern Philippines. Resultant land disputes, aggravated by the fact that the settlers are overwhelmingly Christian, has exacerbated the traditional alienation of the Moros. Consciousness of religion and cultural distinctiveness remains strong, and con-

tinued resistance to absorption into the national culture makes this relatively large and militant minority a major problem in terms of contemporary government planning.

BIBLIOGRAPHY. Arce 1963; Conklin 1955c; Dyen 1965; Hunt 1954; Kuder 1945; Mednick 1956; Saleeby 1905, 1908.

NEGRITOS

REMNANT GROUPS OF SHORT-STATURED, dark-skinned forest dwellers are found in many parts of the Philippines. These groups vary considerably, however, with respect to physical features as well as their degree of cultural development. What might be thought of as the "classic" Southeast Asian Negrito stock, as represented among the Andaman Islanders and the Semang of the Malay Peninsula, is restricted in the main to a few regions of Luzon Island, most notably the province of Zambales. Elsewhere in the Philippines, the situation becomes much less clear-cut. In the interior mountains of Panay and Negros Islands (Bisayas group) and northeastern Mindanao are peoples that can perhaps best be characterized as "Negrito-like." They are, however, regarded by Schebesta (1952-57: 1, 118-19) as of basically Negrito stock, although racially "mixed" and heavily acculturated. The Batak of Palawan are excluded by Schebesta from his consideration of Philippine Negritos, on the grounds that they represent a basically Veddoid element similar to that found among the Senoi of the Malay Peninsula, a view concurred in by Estel (1953). Beyer likewise classified the Batak as a non-Negrito people (1917: 59). On the other hand, Cole (1945) and Kroeber (1943: end map) both regarded the Batak as Negritos, possibly following Barrows (1910b). The question turns partly on the significance of hair form. Barrows rejected the conceptual differentiation of a wavy-haired (Veddoid) strain from a kinky or woolly-haired (Negrito) strain in Southeast Asia. He thus classified the Batak, along with other short-statured, dark-skinned, wavy-haired peoples as basically

Negrito—a procedure that has occasioned some confusion in the subsequent literature.

It is generally assumed that people of Negritic stock were once widespread in the Philippines, existing as small, scattered bands of hunters and gatherers in lowland and coastal areas. Subsequent incursions of more numerous peoples of Indonesian (Proto-Malay, Early Asiatic) and later Deutero-Malay (Southern Mongoloid) stock mixed with these earlier arrivals, driving remnant groups into isolated pockets in the mountains, where they are occasionally found in more or less pure form today. Extensive intermixture of Negroid Negritos with Mongoloid Malays (together with alleged "Veddoid," "Australoid," "Papuan," and other increments) has produced a range of physical types throughout the Philippines, such that occasional individuals appear "Negrito-like," others "Veddoid-like," etc. Thus the problem of characterizing whole populations as Negrito or non-Negrito becomes, outside of limited areas on Luzon, extremely difficult. Language and culture are of little help in this respect. An original non-Austronesian language, if it existed, disappeared long ago; all Philippine Negritos nowadays speak the language of their nearest non-Negrito neighbors. Practically all Negritos today practice some measure of shifting cultivation and are in some kind of symbiotic trade relation with neighboring hill tribes and lowland peoples. Acculturation has in all cases proceeded to the point where it is virtually impossible to demonstrate other than bits and pieces of any "original" Negrito culture.

The most common generic exonyms for Philip-

pine Negritos or Negrito-like peoples consist supposedly of variations on the word for "black"
Malay and related languages such as Tagalo...
Aeta, Ayta, Aita, Ati, Ata, Agta, Ita, Eta. S...
ta's adoption of Aeta as the preferred...
given this term more or less general...
manner similar to the usage of S...
Negrito peoples of Malaya. Th...
gritos or Negrito-like people...
is impossible to state wit...
ance. It is generally recko...
and 30,000, the great majority...
on the island of Luzon (Scheb...
173; Garvan 1963: 10; Beyer 1917:

BIBLIOGRAPHY. Barrows 1910b; Bey...
Cole 1945; Estel 1953; Garvan 1963; Kr...
1943; Newton 1920; Schebesta 1952-57.

NORTHERN GROUPS

ALTHOUGH NEGRITOS WERE recorded in all the
foothill margins of the northern Luzon highlands
in Spanish times (cf. Rahmann 1963), pure Negrito types are today restricted to the mountains
of southern Zambales Province, northwest of
Manila. Negrito-like populations of mixed blood
are (or were) present along the west coast in the
Ilokos Mountains, along the swampy Apayao-
Cagayan border in the far north, in the mountains of eastern Luzon from Cape Engano south
to the Tayabas Isthmus, and in the mountainous,
peninsular Tayabas, Camarines, and Albay portions of extreme southern Luzon (Beyer 1917:
56ff.). Schebesta (1952-57: 1) divided the Luzon
Negritos into (1) western Aeta or Hambal (2)
northern Aeta or Ata (3) eastern Aeta or Baluga
(4) southeastern Aeta or Manidé. Acceptance of
a term such as Baluga (meaning "mixed" or
"hybrid") depends on the degree to which the
people concerned wish to be identified with
lowland Filipinos. More common are names, such
as Ita (Aita, Eta, Ata, Ati, Agta), that have been
derived from the lowland Filipino for "black."
Names such as these are exonyms of lowlander
origin; local ethnonyms may be based upon such
age, but are more often associated with some
ture of the local landscape. Depending on

tio...
pino...
in return...
ments whic...
lationships, on...
unscrupulous low...
and otherwise, poin...
between Negritos and...
the past (Garvan 1963: 1...
gritos in the early Spanish...
summarized by Rahmann (196...,
sis of relevant sources in Blair...
1903-09). The H. Otley Beyer collec...
grito manuscripts and other source...
(Beyer 1912-23: Section A, Set 17, Vols...
includes many first-hand observations by prie...
government officials, teachers, and travelers, most
notably John Garvan, who lived and traveled
with Negrito groups in all parts of the Philippines
off and on for a period of 20 years, beginning in
about 1903. His valuable manuscript notes were
published posthumously, on microfilm in 1955
and in book form in 1963. Fr. Paul Schebesta
made brief visits to various Philippine Negrito
groups in 1938-39, incorporating these data in his
monumental survey of Asiatic Negritos (Schebesta 1952-57). Fr. Morice Vanoverbergh has published several papers based on first-hand obser-

vation among the Negritos of northe...
ern Luzon in the years 1924-36. W...
preliminary account of a trip thro...
(Reed 1904) has been supersed...
Fox's ethnobotanical study of t...
gritos of southern Zambales (...
remains the only ethnically...
study of a northern Philipp...
Beyer (1917: 59) is of the...
called Negrito populations...
offlying islands, particula...
Baler Bay south to Ca...
Papuan than Negrito,...
tain rather striking c...
Guinea. The name D...
applied to these e...
Fox (1953a: 174) v...
'Negroids' [that...
taller, 'Papuan-...
resenting a ra...
distinct from...

BIBLIOGR...
Robertson...
mann 19...
overber...

ZA...

S...

n and east-
. A. Reed's
gh Zambales
ed by Robert
e Pinatubo Ne-
ox 1953a). This
focused, scientific
ne Negrito group.
opinion that the so-
of the east coast and
ly from the region of
arines Norte, are more
nd calls attention to cer-
ltural affinities with New
umaga or Dumagat is often
st coast populations, whom
as characterized as "not pygmy
Negritos], but remnants of a
ke,' sea-migrating 'Negroid,' rep-
ial intrusion into the Philippines
he pygmies."

APHY. Beyer 1912-23, 1917; Blair and
1903-09; Fox 1953a; Garvan 1963; Rah-
3; Reed 1904; Schebesta 1952-57; Van-
h 1925, 1929-30, 1937-38.

MBALES NEGRITOS

nonyms. *Aeta, Ayta, Hambal, Pinatubo Negritos, Sambal, Western Aeta*

ORIENTATION. An estimated 6,000 Negritos are found in scattered groups throughout the Zambales Mountains, a range paralleling the southwest Luzon coast and occupying most of Zambales Province, together with contiguous portions of Tarlac, Pampangan, and Bataan. Those in the Mt. Pinatubo region of southern Zambales have been studied intensively by Fox (1953a). Here the inhabitants call themselves Paan Pinatubo Ayta, i.e. the "people (*ayta*) on the thigh (*paa*) of Mt. Pinatubo." These and other Negrito groups within the Zambales Range have also been described by Reed (1904) and Garvan (1963), both based on first-hand observation in the early years of this century. The Negritos generally occupy the lower slopes, rarely above 1,500 feet, and are surrounded by lowland Christian populations—Tagalog, Pampangan, Ilocano, and Sambal. Virtually all speak a dialect of Sambal and, according to Garvan (1963: 107), call themselves Sambal. Lowlanders

refer to Negritos generally as Ayta (Aeta) or variations thereof. Schebesta (1952-57: *1*) classified the Zambales Range Negritos as Western Aeta or Hambal.

Despite considerable mixing with Sambali and other Filipino groups, the Zambales Negritos retain to a considerable extent the physical characteristics of the Asiatic Negrito—short stature, woolly hair, low-bridged, widely flared nose, wide-set eyes, and moderate to very dark brown skin color. All have been heavily acculturated as a result of prolonged contact and intermarriage with coastal Filipinos. The Mt. Pinatubo groups appear to have borrowed much of their cultural inventory, including language, from their Sambali neighbors; and Schebesta went so far as to suppose that they are basically Sambali-Malays mixed with Negritos (Schebesta 1952-57: *2*, 309, cited in footnote annotations to Garvan 1963: 254). Their greater degree of cultural sophistication relative to other Luzon Negritos may support this view. The possibility of intensive Sambal-Negrito intercourse at some time in the past is raised also by Reed (1904: 28-29), reasoning from the virtually universal presence of Sambal throughout the southern Zambales Range, to the exclusion of other (neighboring) lowland languages. In connection with these speculations, Fox notes that the plants known to the Pinatubo are not those of the original high tropical forests, indicative of a former habitat at relatively low altitudes, probably in open areas adjacent to the primeval forests. [Fox 1953a; Garvan 1963; Reed 1904.]

SETTLEMENT PATTERN AND HOUSING. **Settlement pattern.** Scattered settlements or encampments, rarely containing more than three or four households, totaling 20-40 individuals (Fox 1953a: 188). The average settlement size in less acculturated areas farther from the coast is considerably less than this. Encampments are semipermanent, being moved on the average of every year or so, coincident with exhaustion of local resources, epidemic illness, inauspicious omens, and the like. It is probable that [related?] groups or bands exploit a geographically defined territory, although information on this point is lacking. According to Fox (1953a: 346), there is no discernible pattern in the arrangement of dwellings. Garvan, on the other hand, reported that houses were almost always arranged in a circle about a central dance place (1963: 29). Schebesta, who also failed to find an arrangement of this kind, thinks that it w: characteristic of the ancient culture of Asiatic N gritos (cited in footnote annotation to Garvan] 241). **Housing.** Traditional style houses are permanent affairs of bamboo, banana stalks, and grass. Crude, floorless lean-tos serve porary protection while the people are tr hunting. Encampment dwellings are usua tent-shaped, with one side, containing a

platform, walled; on the opposite side is a hearth placed on the ground beneath a long, sloping roof. House styles vary considerably, however; Negritos living a more settled existence in contact with coastal Filipinos build houses more similar to those of their lowland neighbors. [Fox 1953a: 346ff.]

ECONOMY. All Zambales Range Negritos nowadays engage in highly inefficient shifting agriculture, although their remarkably encyclopedic knowledge of local plant and animal life, combined with the evidence of tradition and folklore, indicate former reliance on a basically nomadic hunting and gathering economy (Fox 1953a). Sweet potatoes, cassava, and maize, grown in swiddens, along with semicultivated taros, yams and bananas, supply upward of 85 percent of the diet at present. A great variety of wild foods—fruits, nuts, berries, roots, honey, larvae—make up an additional 7 percent, while meat accounts for only about 8 percent (Fox 1953a: 245-46). Upland rice is grown by some acculturated groups. Millet is absent, while the seeds of *Coix lachryma-jobi* are used for necklaces, but never as food. **Hunting and fishing.** Dogs and fire are used to drive deer and wild pig, which are then dispatched with bow and arrow (increasingly nowadays with guns). A great variety of traps are known for smaller game, and birds are occasionally taken with the use of blinds and liming. Arrow poisons are known, but rarely used. It is evident that hunting has declined in importance as a source of food, as has fishing—although the recent introduction of rubber-propelled spears for underwater fishing has revolutionized that activity. Fish were traditionally taken by damming, poisoning, trapping, and shooting with bow and arrow. [Fox 1953a: 276ff.] **Domestic animals.** Chiefly dogs, used in hunting. Young wild pigs are occasionally captured and kept as pets. **Industrial arts.** Ceramic wares and cloth are obtained by trade with lowlanders; apparently neither pottery making nor weaving were practiced aboriginally. The techniques of bark cloth manufacture are, however, well known although little utilized at present. Among the Pinatubo, blacksmithing is easily the major craft specialty. A great variety of arrow points, bolos, and even crude shotguns are made locally, utilizing the "Malayan" bellows. Smiths and smithing are subject to taboos and ritual behavior not found among the lowland Sambal. [Fox 1953a.] **Trade.** Forest products, beeswax, and tobacco are traded to lowlanders for cloth, salt, pots, metal, and rice. Metal arrow points, manufactured by Pinatubo smiths, are traded to Negrito groups throughout the Zambales Range. **Division of labor.** According to Fox (1953a), women have most of the responsibility for agriculture, food collecting, and small-scale fishing. Men do some hunting, and young men, especially, engage in fishing with underwater spear and goggles. Males, however, spend much of their time away from home—visiting, trading, negotiating marriages, and generally maintaining contact with relatives in other encampments. **Property.** Items of personal property are limited in number, and in general of relatively little value. Ceremonial property, chiefly in finely made arrows and red cloth, serves as gifts to the spirits, as bride-price, and as hereditary gifts to children (Fox 1953a).

MARRIAGE AND FAMILY. Among the Pinatubo, parents often contract the marriages of their children when the latter are still young, and disputes over bride-price payments, consisting of arrows, bolos, cloth, and money, are a major source of intergroup conflict (Fox 1953a). According to Garvan (1963: 107), bride capture is (or was) a common alternative avenue to marriage in the Pinatubo area. Incest prohibitions vary considerably, but according to Fox (1953a), the Pinatubo groups allow cousin marriage even within the first degree, provided a "cleansing" rite is performed. Residence following marriage appears to be generally patrilocal. Although there appears to be no exclusive preference for marriage either within or without the local settlement, it would seem from Garvan's account that marriage is more often village-exogamous. Polygynous marriages are allowed, but in practice are rare. In case of divorce, it is expected that the bride-price will be returned if the woman is at fault; in practice, relatives prevent divorce wherever possible, and divorce is relatively uncommon among Luzon Negritos as a whole. In the Zambales area, however, it tends to run about 10 percent (Garvan 1963: 82).

Decorative disfigurement, e.g. teeth chipping or pointing, teeth blackening, and cicatrization, are present among some, but not all, Luzon Negrito groups. In some cases they appear to be a symbol of maturity and a necessary preliminary to marriage or (in the case of cicatrization) a preventative against disease. Tight boars'-hair arm and leg bands are for men a sign of bravery and provide magical protection against injury. In some areas, as among the Mt. Pinatubo Negritos, these customs are dying out or have disappeared entirely. [Fox 1953a: 374; Garvan 1963: 45-46, 82.]

SOCIOPOLITICAL ORGANIZATION. **The local group.** According to Garvan (1963: 155), the Negritos live in groups (encampments) of from three to ten families totaling ten to fifty persons. Each such group is bound together by family ties, with the oldest male acting as leader, assisted by other elders "who are his brothers, uncles and other kin." Fox (1953a: 188) adds that each village or extended family is an independent communal grouping. Thus the local group is composed of what would appear to approximate a patrilocal extended family. Kinship is by inference reckoned bilaterally, but probably with a patrilineal emphasis. Fox calls attention to the markedly communal and noncompetitive nature of Negrito society; authority is diffuse, group composition fluid, and the people themselves highly mobile. **Social control.** Serious disputes are brought before an informal council of older men, with the eldest acting as primus inter pares. Decisions are enforced chiefly by appeal and persuasion; there is no concept of abstract political authority. Day-to-day relationships are governed by pressures of public opinion, operating through belief in the threat of supernatural sanctions. Thus violation of a property right, without subsequent acknowledgment and compensatory gifts to the owner, can cause the latter to become ill. Such behavior is regarded as a heinous crime, and the person thus offended can, by public announcement, threaten the person or family of the offender. This in turn activates powerful group pressure on both parties to settle the affair amicably, since intra-group conflict is to be avoided at all cost. [Fox 1953a: 319ff.]

RELIGION. **Supernaturals.** Most spirits (*anito, kamana*) are well disposed to man unless provoked. Nature spirits "own" property, e.g. bamboo groves, game animals such as deer and pig, and medicinal plants. Violation of such "property rights" can be a major cause of misfortune and illness unless compensating gifts of tobacco, wine, and red cloth are made in the form of spirit offerings. Certain plants, when burned, give off smoke which can drive away evil spirits; and talismans, such as neolithic stone tools, are worn as protection against such spirits. [Fox 1953a.] **Practitioners.** According to Fox (1953a: 186), male and female mediums (*manganito*) obtain personal tutelaries from the spirit inhabitants of tabooed forest clearings. Mediums hold curing séances (*anituwan*) at which, by dancing, they enter what appear to be trance states during which they are possessed by their spirit familiars. Diagnosis and treatment are aided by assistants who question these tutelaries. Cure may be effected by spirit capture, i.e. capture of the offending spirit within the patient. Garvan (1963: 218-19) adds that mediums and séances are more characteristic of groups influenced by lowland culture. Among less acculturated Negritos, it is more usual to find simply a few individuals more skilled than others in the knowledge of medicinal plants and their magical properties. The great elaboration of ethnobotanical lore and practice, including that related to medicinal plants, is well documented by Fox (1953a: 315-45), who adds that lowland Filipinos frequently have great respect and/or fear of the better-known Negrito practitioners. Illness is generally thought to be due to supernatural causes, most often the unrecompensed violation of

the property rights of spirits or fellow villagers. Another common theory is that of *timbi*, a condition brought on by thunder (*kilat*) and lightning. The Negritos fear these phenomena and possess many medicines to ward off "thunder attacks," caused when *kilat* becomes angered at behavior such as teasing earthworms or laughing at the sexual intercourse of animals (Fox 1953a: 338-39). **Ceremonies.** Fox mentions the gathering of large numbers of Negritos for a "fiesta of the spirits" (*iwi*), held annually in December or January when food is plentiful. Another ceremony, *talbung*, is held in a wallless, shedlike ceremonial structure when illness is being caused by the spirits of enemies killed by the participants—or by ancestors of the participants. On such occasions, males may wear the *bagudi*, a decorated neck band, said to have been worn formerly by a man who had killed a person (Fox 1953a: 373). **Soul, death, and afterlife.** According to Fox (1953a: 186), the Pinatubo formerly abandoned the dwelling where a death had occurred. Garvan (1963: 165ff.) notes that burial customs vary widely, but that generally the Negritos practice inhumation, with the corpse wrapped in a mat or cloth. Burial may be in a horizontal or vertical grave, either beneath the house or at a distance. Mourning customs, treatment of the grave, and the like vary according to degree of cultural borrowing from neighboring groups. In southern Zambales, it is generally believed that the souls of the dead journey to a home on Mt. Pinatubo. Garvan likewise reports the same tradition among the Pinatubo groups of former headhunting expeditions, *mangayau*, in association with ceremonies at the time of death (Garvan 1963: 170). These, he believes, may date from Spanish times, when Sambali lowlanders fled to the hills and allied themselves with Negritos against the Spanish (Garvan 1963: 235).

BIBLIOGRAPHY. Fox 1953a; Garvan 1963; Reed 1904; Schebesta 1952-57.

SOUTHERN GROUPS*

THE BISAYAN ISLANDS, in particular Negros and Panay, are in their interior mountainous regions inhabited by scattered groups of "Negrito-like" people who until recent times appear to have relied on a primarily hunting and gathering economy, depending on trade with lowlanders for certain essentials, such as salt and metal. In southern

---

*Compiled by the editor from the available literature and from manuscript notes on the present condition of Panay and Negros Negritos contributed by Marcelino Maceda. For the Mamanua of northeast Mindanao, see the entry following, also contributed by Professor Maceda.

Negros, they are located nowadays chiefly within the Bais Forest Preserve, north of coastal Bayawan; and in the north, chiefly around Bago, Toyanan, Obang, and Talave. On Panay, so-called Negritos are found in Antique Province, barrios of Tina, Arobo, Igkasul, Pantad, Igtunarum, and Villafont; and in Iloilo Province, barrios of Balud and Sianon. On Negros, these peoples are known as Agta or Ata ("black") and on Panay as Ati or Antiqueño. The latter term ("one who comes from Antique") is commonly used throughout the Bisayas to mean Negrito (Rahmann and Maceda 1962). Relatively few data of a systematic nature are available on any of these groups— with respect either to their customs or physical characteristics. Beyer (1917: 60-64) was of the opinion that they were racially mixed and that, with the possible exception of those in northern Negros, they could not be said to contain much if any of an Asiatic Negrito component. All nowadays rely on inefficient shifting agriculture, together with fishing, hunting, and collecting. On Panay, where they hire themselves out as timber cutters or as workers in the sugarcane fields, the Ati are gradually merging with the poorer rural peasantry. Here the term Ati connotes a social rather than racial distinction (Rahmann and Maceda 1962). The Ati of the Bais Forest Preserve in southern Negros are still pagan; their rituals and ceremonies appear, however, to contain mostly elements common to surrounding groups (cf. Oracion 1967a). The Negrito component in the population of Mindanao is discussed in the entry following, i.e. *Mamanua*, and in the Mindanao section, elsewhere in this volume, under the entry for *Ata* (Davao Gulf region).

BIBLIOGRAPHY. Beyer 1917; Gloria 1939; Oracion 1960, 1963, 1967a; Rahmann and Maceda 1955, 1958, 1962.

MAMANUA*

Synonyms. *Amamanua, Congking, Kongking, Mamaw, Manmanua, Mamanwa, Mamaua*

---

*The author of this entry, Marcelino N. Maceda, is Professor of Anthropology and Economics in the University of San Carlos. His data are based on continuing fieldwork among the Mamanua, beginning in 1953.

ORIENTATION. **Location and identification.** Chiefly the Diuata Mountains in northern Surigao and adjacent portions of Agusan Province in northeastern Mindanao. Semipermanent local groups nowadays exploit the headwaters of the Bacuag, Tandag, and Tago rivers; and the Mamanua have for a long time lived in the Lake Mainit area (environs of San Roque, San Pablo, Mayag, Kitcharao, Ipil, Sibahay, Badiang, Kantugas, and Mahayahay). The people refer to themselves as Mamanua or Amamanua, terms of reference also used by Christian settlers. The latter in addition refer to Christianized Manobo and Mamanua as Conquista, which in its corrupted form—Congking or Kongking—carries a pejorative connotation. The Mamanua can be classed racially as Asiatic Negroids —although very much mixed, so that only a few individuals resemble the pure Negrito type. The hair tends to be kinky, individuals with wavy hair being hybrids. Many of the older generation are less than five feet tall. The mestizo or hybrid type is met with more frequently in the lowlands; the "purer" types tend to remain in the mountains. **Linguistic affiliation.** The Mamanua speak a language of their own, although they also speak Surigueño, a Bisayan language related to Cebuano. [Both Conklin (1955c) and Dyen (1965) classify "Mamanua" as a member of the Central Philippines language group, closely related to Sugbuhanon (Cebuano)—Ed.] **Demography.** Estimated at around 1,000. **History and cultural relations.** Garvan in 1910 heard reports of Negritos or "Negrito-like" peoples in various parts of eastern Mindanao, including the upper tributaries of the Libaganon and Salug in the vicinity of Mt. Panombaian, as well as in other parts of the island (Garvan 1931: 4-5). The present-day Mamanua of northeastern Mindanao are in a transitional stage, heavily influenced by Christian settlers from the lowlands (Cebuano, Waray, etc.) and by neighboring Manobo tribesmen, with whom they frequently intermarry. Their former seminomadic hunting and gathering economy is giving way to shifting agriculture and, in some cases, the planting of permanent money crops, such as coconuts.

SETTLEMENT PATTERN AND HOUSING. Local groups of from three to twenty households form semipermanent settlements or encampments, sometimes on a mountain ridge, e.g. those in the environs of Kitcharao, or in a valley, e.g. Kantugas. The groups move from place to place, however, seeking locations where food gathering and a little agriculture can be practiced. The arrangement of dwellings in a settlement usually assumes a circular form. Distinctive structures are lacking, except that in settlements where monthly full-moon prayer ceremonies are held the shaman's house is larger than average. Houses are raised on piles, rectangular in shape, and gable-roofed, but without walls. A shaman's house may measure up to 20 meters in length, although the average is around four meters. When on hunting or collecting expeditions, use is made of a simple lean-to or a handy cave.

ECONOMY. **Subsistence.** Mainly inefficient shifting agriculture, with sweet potato the staple, backed by maize, taro, yams, and some rice. Supplementary sources of food include hunting, fishing, and gathering. Men go every day to trap and hunt, aided by dogs and guns, although increasing scarcity of game has diminished the importance of this activity. The bow and arrow, once the favored weapon, has virtually disappeared from use. Wild pig and deer are the prime game animals but pythons and monkeys are also taken. Fishing has become increasingly important, and techniques include damming, torching, poisoning, and spearing with a rubber-propelled underwater spear. Some cash income is derived by working for Christian settlers as loggers and hunting guides and by selling or trading forest products, such as rattan. **Property.** Hunting and fishing grounds are community-owned, while cultivated pieces of land belong to individual families. Food, from whatever source, is considered communal property and must be shared with all members of the local community. Songs and prayers belong to the shaman, and can only be transmitted if taught to another person by him. As the Mamanua become more agricultural, private ownership of land is assuming more importance.

KIN GROUPS. The local group is composed principally of blood relations; affinal relatives rarely join the group permanently. While authority is male oriented, the reckoning of relationships is bilateral. One's father is called *ama* and his mother *ina*; brothers, sisters, and cousins are lumped under the term *lumon*; uncles and aunts on both sides are called *ama* and *ina* respectively; grandparents are called *popoy*, a term probably of Surigueño rather than Mamanua origin; brothers-in-law and sisters-in-law are called *bayao*.

MARRIAGE AND FAMILY. **Mode.** A young man who wants to get married will seek out a bride from another group, i.e. exogamy. A go-between is engaged by the boy's parents, and a bride-price (*bogay*) fixed. This may consist of 50 or more pesos cash, several sacks of rice, cooking utensils, cultivated fields, etc. A simple mutual feeding ceremony is performed on the date of marriage. Bride service is sometimes demanded, and couples occasionally elope if no formal arrangement can be made. **Form.** Monogamy predominates, although polygyny is tolerated. **Marriage rules.** Close relatives are forbidden to marry; in-laws are sometimes considered within this prohibition. **Residence.** After marriage, the young couple may choose to stay for a time with the bride's relatives. Ultimately they settle permanently in the husband's local group, i.e. patrilocal residence. Upon the death of their parents, it is rare that married male siblings will separate from one another. They continue to stay in the same locale, as members of one local group. During times of economic difficulty the local group may break up into individual families, but as soon as times are better they come together again. **Divorce.** Relatively easy if no children. A man can easily seek separation from his wife; on the other hand, if a woman wishes to divorce her husband, her family must return the entire bride-price. Divorcées can remarry.

SOCIOPOLITICAL ORGANIZATION. Maximum sociopolitical organization is at the level of the local group, composed mainly of related families. Its leader is the oldest and wisest male, who must at the same time be generous, a good hunter, a good negotiator, a good speech maker, and a brave man. The status is earned, not inherited, and the powers attached to it are persuasive rather than absolute. Shamans and medicine men can also hold this influential position. **Social control.** Punishment of a crime is traditionally left to the aggrieved party. In the past, a person judged guilty of rape, for instance, could be killed, but now the perpetrator is either fined or made to marry the victim. Very few cases of vendetta are reported nowadays. Ostracism is the most common form of punishment for offenses against the group, although more serious cases are likely to go before the elected barrio captain of the nearest Christian community.

RELIGION. **Supernaturals.** The Mamanua believe in a supreme being, Magbabaya, the creator of the world and everything in it. Spirits, *diwata*, include evil, witchlike *encantos*, a frequent cause of illness, and the mythological Kabang, who was shot down by Mamanua archers; his hair turned into gnats and his chopped-up flesh became leeches. **Practitioners.** The shaman, *sukdan*, performs curing séances, during which he or she may go into a trance. One becomes *sukdan* by training, meeting a good *diwata* in the forest, dreaming that one has been called to the profession, or by inheriting curing powers from either parent. The medicine man, *tambayon*, is the expert in curing with the use of plants. A *tambayon* may also at the same time be a *sukdan*. **Ceremonies.** Every full moon, the *pagdiwatahan* ceremony attracts many people from afar. This is essentially a prayer meeting to request the spirits to cure sick people and purify the participants. The ceremony is led by the *sukdan*, and prayers are alternated with dances to the beating of gongs. *Bayakag* is mainly a thanksgiving ritual, consisting of prayers, dancing, and feasting. In planting small fields, the *hongod* is performed, in order that the harvest may be bountiful; and while preparing a certain poisonous root (*kuyot*) for consumption, a part of the treated root is offered to the dead ancestors. **Death.** The corpse is wrapped in a pandanus mat and placed in a crude coffin, after which it is either buried in the nearby forest or left to decay in the house where death occurred. Food and implements of the departed are left on the grave. Following disposal of the corpse, the entire settlement moves out to a new location.

BIBLIOGRAPHY. Blumentritt 1896; Bornemann 1955; Conklin 1955c; Cooper 1940; Dyen 1965; Garvan 1931, 1963; Maceda 1954, 1956, 1957, 1963, 1964a; Rahmann 1955, 1956.

MINDANAO

PROTOHISTORIC MINDANAO appears to have been inhabited by peoples of a primarily generalized Malayan stock, speaking languages related to those found elsewhere in Insular Southeast Asia. There is some evidence of an earlier Negrito strain among modern hilltribesmen, most pronounced in groups such as the Mamanua, but this population must have been relatively small and rapidly absorbed by later arrivals who drifted in, probably via Borneo and the Sulu Archipelago. The indigenous cultures would seem to have been characterized by a relatively high degree of homogeneity, in part due to earlier Hindu influences, and in general conforming to the reconstructed lowland cultures of Tagalog and Bisayan peoples at the time of first Spanish contact (cf. Benedict 1916). On Mindanao, this basic pattern was altered most noticeably in areas dominated by Muslims subsequent to the early fifteenth century, where essentially kin-based, *barangay*-type, social structures were converted into hierarchically ordered *datu* systems with relatively complex political overtones (Mednick 1965). This development occurred initially in western Mindanao, but apparently diffused to other areas, most notably into the Davao Gulf region. Although cultural parallels do exist between Mindanao and groups such as Dusun-Murut and even Kenyah on Borneo, these appear for the most part to be of a generalized Malayan type, common to much of Southeast Asia. Thus, despite a supposedly close linguistic connection between the southern Philippines and northern Borneo and Celebes, known cultural similarities do not appear to be of the type that would reflect protohistoric migrations of a specific people or peoples in either direction (cf. Cole 1913). Nowadays, the majority of indigenous cultures on Mindanao are virtually extinct or fast disappearing, under the impact, first, of Moro institutions, but, most profoundly, as a result of the wholesale immigration of Christian Filipinos that has accompanied the proliferation of government-sponsored resettlement schemes and economic development programs, beginning as early as 1913. Today, peoples of immigrant Filipino stock constitute the major ethnolinguistic group in all but two of the provinces of Mindanao.

Conventional tribal nomenclature most often consists of generic-type exonyms of lowlander origin, compounds such as Mandaya, from *man*, "people," and *daya*, "upriver"; Banuaon, from *banua*, "back country"; Bukidnon, from *bukit*, "hill"; Tagakaolo, from *taga*, "inhabitant of," and *ulu*, "headwaters." The most widely occurring of these generic exonyms is Manobo, which most probably was originally a lowland Moro term meaning "hillman" (from *man*, "people," and *obo*, "hill" or "mountain"). The term appears to have been adopted by Spanish officials and missionaries and applied widely throughout Mindanao as a tribal designation. During Spanish times it acquired the additional connotation of pagan, i.e. nonbaptized. [Cf. Garvan 1931.] Manobos are the most widely dispersed of Mindanao's indigenous inhabitants (Agusan, Surigao, Bukidnon, Davao, and Cotabato provinces). Whereas the 1939 Census reported 73,000 Manobos (making them among the most populous of the pagan groups), the 1960 Census recorded only 47,000—reflecting either an absolute increase in mortality rates or a process of absorption into dominant lowland groups—or simply the difficulty of accurate census-taking in interior rural areas. The linguistic unity of the various Manobo groups has been affirmed by the setting up of a Manobo family of languages, to include Agusan Manobo, Ata, Bagobo, Binokid (Bukidnon Manobo), Cotabato Manobo, Dibabawon, Kulamanen, Ilianen, Sarangani Manobo, Tigwa-Salug (Central Manobo), and Western Bukidnon Manobo (Elkins et al. 1969-70). Manobo is, in turn, most closely related to the central and northern Philippine languages, along with most other languages of Mindanao. The exceptions are Bilaan, Tagabili, and Tiruray, classed together by Conklin (1955c) in a less closely related Southern Philippine group. Regardless, however, of differences in linguistic affiliation, the indigenous cultures of Mindanao, with the exception of the Moros on the west coast, appear remarkably similar in general outline. The present volume has accordingly adopted the device of ordering ethnic entries by geographic regions within Mindanao, a procedure reflecting as much as anything common ecological and historical factors, which, it is felt lend some degree of cohesiveness to the presentation. Lowland Christians are discussed elsewhere in this volume under *Christian Filipinos;* the Negritos of Surigao Province (the Mamanua) are described under the general heading of *Negritos.*

BIBLIOGRAPHY. Benedict 1916; Cole 1913; Conklin 1955c; Elkins et al. 1969-70; Garvan 1931; Mednick 1965.

ZAMBOANGA

THE MOUNTAINOUS ZAMBOANGA PENINSULA extends west and south of the main body of Mindanao, forming a natural link with the island world of the Sulu Archipelago. Its port city, Zamboanga, has long been the principal trade center within a southern Philippine Muslim world stretching from Tawi-tawi in the west to Davao Gulf in the east. Much of the Peninsula was formerly claimed by the sultans of Magindanao and Sulu, and the area was for over two centuries the scene of protracted fighting between Spanish and Moro forces. Despite partial pacification by Spanish and later American governments, and the early immigration into the area of Bisayan settlers, coastal Muslim *datus* continued to wield much power locally. In recent decades, however, Muslim dominance has declined with the influx of large numbers of Christian Filipinos. In these respects, the history of Zamboanga closely parallels that of the northern coast of Mindanao. Christians (chiefly Cebuano-speaking Bisayans) now outnumber Muslims (Tausug, Yakan, Samal, Magindanao) by a ratio of nearly four to one (Wernstedt and Spencer 1967: 570). Both groups are concentrated along the narrow coastal lowlands; the indigenous pagan peoples, collectively termed *subanen* by Christians and Muslims, are scattered throughout the interior uplands. Economic development of the area, particularly logging and pioneer farming schemes, has begun to affect lands traditionally claimed by the hill tribes, a process analogous to that taking place elsewhere in Mindanao. Subanun culture is summarized in the entry immediately following; the various Samal-speaking populations of Zamboanga and nearby Basilan Island are described elsewhere in this volume under the general heading of *Sulu-Sangihe.*

BIBLIOGRAPHY. Wernstedt and Spencer 1967.

SUBANUN

Synonyms. *Subanen, Suban'on*

ORIENTATION. **Location and identification.** Pagan shifting cultivators in the interior of Zamboanga, the large mountainous peninsula of western Mindanao. Christians, Muslims, and pagans of Zamboanga use words such as *suban'on* or *subanen* to designate any interior-dwelling pagan. These terms have the common meaning of "up-stream people." The peoples so designated represent a distinctive cultural and linguistic group, descended from an original common language and culture (Frake 1957). Coastal populations of mixed Subanun and Moro blood are called locally Kalibugan, and the term can by extension refer to any Subanun who has moved to the coast and adopted Islam (Christie 1909: 13). **Linguistic affiliation.** According to Frake, Eastern and Western Subanun form a subgroup of the Central Philippine language group (cf. Eggan et al. 1956). Dialect diversity within Subanun is nowhere of a magnitude to interfere with communication between adjacent areas. (Frake 1957). **Demography.** About 70,000 (Frake 1960: 51). **History and cultural relations.** There is a long history of exploitation of Subanun by Muslims from Mindanao and Sulu. The weakening of Muslim power in recent decades has seen the influx into coastal Zamboanga of large numbers of Christian Bisayans, and the Subanun are now faced with the threat of wholesale land appropriations. In some areas they have already been forced to replace swidden farming with permanent field agriculture. [Frake 1960, 1967: 14ff.]

SETTLEMENT PATTERN AND HOUSING. **Settlement pattern.**
The typical settlement is an unnamed, impermanent cluster of three to twelve dispersed households, usually on a prominence overlooking the swiddens. The pattern appears to be a compromise between the value placed on household isolation and the need to cluster fields, in order to reduce the perimeter exposed to faunal enemies (Frake 1960). **Housing.** Impermanent, rectangular, thatched, pile dwellings, usually housing a single nuclear or polygynous family. The interior is a single room, but living and sleeping areas are clearly delimited. Granaries, also on piles, are constructed near the dwellings (Frake 1960).

ECONOMY.
Primarily shifting agriculture, with some fishing in inland streams. Rice is the preferred food, but consumption is uneven; much rice is consumed in fermented form or traded to lowlanders. Secondary crops include maize, Job's tears, sweet potato, and manioc. Fish, shrimps, snails, and vegetables are eaten as side dishes. Bananas and papayas are the principal fruits. Chickens and pigs (the latter both domesticated and wild) are eaten only on ceremonial occasions. Trade iron is forged locally to make knives and other tools. Women do the weaving and (formerly) pottery making. Armlets and anklets of brass wire were once popular. Teeth are filed and blackened, especially among women. Traditional wealth, formerly traded in from the coast, consists of old Chinese jars, gongs, brass cannon, and cloth (Christie 1909: 40). Property rights to land are not recognized among the Subanun (Frake 1960: 57).

KINSHIP.
Corporate kin groups other than the family are absent. The bilateral personal kindred does not extend beyond second cousins (Frake 1967: 128ff.). Both kindred and settlement are agamous with respect to marriage rules (Frake 1960: 55). **Kin terminology.** Basic categories of kin terms include the following (Frake 1960: 63-64):

GrPa	*gapu*
Fa	*gama*
Mo	*gina*
PaBr	*kia*
PaSi	*dara*
Sib, Cousin	*pated*
So, Da	*bata*
SibCh	*manak*
GrCh	*gapu*

MARRIAGE AND FAMILY. **Mode.**
Marriage involves complex legal negotiations between families, conducted by go-betweens, and often begun before a couple reach puberty. Much emphasis on negotiation of bride-price, calculated in terms of traditional wealth. Bride service for a period of three to four years is common (Frake 1960, 1967). **Form.** The nuclear family is the rule; polygyny occurs in less than 10 percent of recorded cases (Frake 1960: 54). **Extension of incest taboos.** Marriage with siblings or parents' siblings is prohibited. First-cousin marriage, accompanied by payment of a token fine, is common. **Residence.** Initially matrilocal until fulfillment of bride service. Thereafter neolocal but (alternatively) in the vicinity of the household of either the husband's or wife's parents (Frake 1960). **Domestic unit.** Typically a nuclear or polygynous family, strictly limited to two generations. Members of a family jointly cultivate a single annual swidden and hold joint title to all (movable) property attributable to any one member. All corporate characteristics of the family cease upon the death of either parent or in case of divorce (Frake 1960, 1967). **Inheritance.** Following the death of a parental member, the corporately-owned movable property of a full family is inherited equally by all offspring of both sexes (Frake 1960). **Divorce and secondary marriage.** Divorce is relatively rare and is accompanied by prolonged litigation between the families involved in the original bride-price negotiations. Sororate and levirate rules pertain with respect to secondary marriages (Frake 1960, 1967).

SOCIOPOLITICAL ORGANIZATION.
The Subanun are characterized by an overlapping network of politically unorganized communities of neighbors and kin. These exhibit little stability or continuity over time. Neighboring communities do tend to form regional groups, whose members interact from time to time in trade, feasting, and litigation (Frake 1967: 19). Communities and regions extend informal recognition to individuals skilled in litigation, whose

legal decisions and imposed fines insure a degree of social control at the indigenous level. Litigation is a major preoccupation, and skill in manipulating interpersonal relations by legal debate is highly valued. Much of Zamboanga was formerly claimed by the sultans of Magindanao, whose agents, Muslim *datus* in the coastal settlements, extracted tribute from the inland Subanun. Nowadays the provinces of Zamboanga are divided into municipalities charged with administrative and policing functions. Until recently, these have had relatively little effect on Subanun in the interior. [Christie 1909; Frake 1967.] **Warfare.** Present-day Subanun consider any kind of violent behavior highly undesirable. It is not clear whether this was the case prior to Spanish and Moro pacification. There is some evidence that the death of a highly regarded individual formerly required the killing of a victim by the relatives, in order to provide a soul companion for the deceased (Frake 1967: 22ff.).

RELIGION. With the exception of death ceremonies, religion plays a minor role in the life cycle. The dominant concern is with the prevention and cure of illness. **Supernaturals.** Deities, *diwata*, with human-like attributes, and lesser beings, generally of a malignant nature. **Practitioners.** Male and female religious specialists, *belian,* attain their status by training or, involuntarily, by revelation. As mediums they hold séances with personal deities or with souls of the dead; as shamans they may be expert in the magical or medical curing of illness; and as priests they conduct religious offerings during festivals. [Christie 1909: 71ff.; Frake 1964, 1967: 26ff.] **Ceremonies.** A festival may be sponsored by an individual in fulfillment of a vow, e.g. following recovery from illness or after a good harvest. Festivals are marked by competitive singing, drinking of rice beer, and dancing on a raised, flexibile platform connected by an upright pole to a resonator in the ground; they may continue for three days or more, with as many as 200 people present. Ritual acts by *belian* during the festivities include the placing of offerings of rice, betel, and tobacco on multitiered altars; the burning of incense and striking of gongs; and the dancing by participants in prescribed patterns while brandishing bunches of long leaves in either hand. [Christie 1909: 73ff.; Frake 1964, 1967.] **Soul, death, and afterlife.** A kind of soul substance resides in the joints of the body. There is also a soul proper, which goes to an afterworld following death. The deceased is buried as soon after death as possible, nowadays in a cemetery outside the village. Christie (1909: 59-60) describes the use of a coffin made from a hollowed log, the two halves sealed and tightly bound. The same source cites reports of former burials in or near dwellings, in caves on rock shelves, or (for children) in jars. A ceremony, held soon after death, has as its primary purpose the lifting of such mourning restrictions as the prohibition of litigation. Among wealthy families, a second ceremony at a later date takes the form of a festival, with feasting, drinking, and dancing on the sprung platform. Religious specialists (usually several) carry out ritual acts, including the ceremonial killing of a cock, said by some to be a substitute for human sacrifice. [Christie 1909: 77, 79ff.; Frake 1967.]

BIBLIOGRAPHY. Christie 1909; Eggan et al. 1956; Frake 1957, 1960, 1964, 1967.

LANAO-COTABATO

THE COASTS OF southwestern Mindanao, together with the Lake Lanao uplands and the extensive inland drainage area of the Rio Grande de Mindanao—the modern provinces of Lanao del Sur and Cotabato—constitute the homeland of the Mindanao Moros, a congeries of closely related groups, the most populous nowadays being the Maranao and Magindanao. The term Ilanon (Iranon) has been used historically for all Mindanao Muslims, although today the people who so designate themselves are limited to a relatively small coastal population around Polloc Harbor, facing Illana Bay. Ilanon may be regarded as a subdialect of Maranao, which in turn is closely related linguistically to Magindanao. Both Maranao and Magindanao are grouped in the Central Philippine subgroup of the Philippine stock of Indonesian languages (Conklin 1955c). According to the 1960 Census, Muslims in Lanao del Sur and Cotabato provinces numbered slightly more than 700,000; subtotals by speech community are, however, likely to be inexact. The Mindanao Muslims appear to share their basic culture with the Christian coastal, lowland groups who dominate the Philippines (Fox 1968). They are, however, linked by religious ties to Islamic peoples in Zamboanga and the Sulu Archipelago, with whom they formerly combined in intermittent alliances against the common enemy—the Spanish and their Christianized Filipino converts.

BIBLIOGRAPHY. Conklin 1955c; Fox 1968.

ILANON*

Synonyms. *Iranon, Ilanum, Ilano, Illanun Ilanun, Lanon*

ORIENTATION. **Location and identification.** The Ilanon are historically the most famous Mindanao group, particularly outside the Philippines, where their raiding and piracy brought terror to all of Insular Southeast Asia. As a result, the name came to stand for all of the Muslim groups of Mindanao. The name is best understood today as denoting a relatively small group, which is in some ways distinct but in other ways a variation of the language and culture of the Maranao and Magindanao. The Ilanon are concentrated nowadays in the area surrounding and inland from Polloc Harbor—most particularly in the North Cotabato Province municipalities of Parang, Bugasan, Buldon, and Barira—but reports deriving from the Spanish period (Saleeby 1905: 13; Forrest 1780) indicate that there were once Ilanon settlements across Illana Bay on the eastern side of the Zamboanga Peninsula, and that there was competition with Magindanao for dominance of these shores. The Ilanon are also credited with having established communities and/or bases of operation as far away as Sumatra (Hall 1968) as well as in Jolo (Forrest 1780) and North Borneo. All of these have disappeared with the exception of the North Borneo settlement, which survives as an ethnolinguistic community (Illanun) in modern Sabah, numbering some 4,000 persons and located mainly on the western coastal plain, from the lower reaches of the Tempasuk north to the Kudat Peninsula (Sather 1967; Appell n.d.). The region historically associated with the Ilanon is comprised mainly of the southwestern portion of the Lanao-Bukidnon plateau, plus the adjoining coast down to the lower valley of the Cotabato River. In the Nuling area and on the northern slopes of the Cotabato Valley, the Ilanon are mainly a memory, and the people emphasize their connection to the Magindanao. But in places such as Malabang, Balabagan, in the portions of Lanao del Sur south of the lake, and along the coast surrounding Polloc Harbor there are those who not only think of themselves as "Iranon" but claim to be *ndurunan* "in-between," a distinct people having their own society with a status equal to that of their neighbors. **Demography.** An estimated total population of about 65,000, based upon census figures for districts where Ilanon are known or said to reside. **History.** The Ilanon are historically best understood as a development out of a protohistoric population distributed along the eastern and northern sides of Ilana Bay, south to

the beginnings of the Tiruray highlands. Although elements of the population were also inland, major concentrations were probably along the coast, particularly the lower reaches of rivers. As the Philippines moved more firmly into the orbit of greater Malaysian contact and commerce (around 1000-1200 A.D.), these rivers became important as avenues into the interior, with the strategic location of the Ilanon making them both carriers and major recipients of trade and contact. The southern part of this population, focused around the Cotabato River and its distributaries, evolved into the Magindanao, mainly on the basis of social and political criteria, e.g. the organization of political units such as the Sultanate of Magindanao. The rest of the population remained distributed along minor rivers and in back of the numerous mangrove swamps, with a major center of development in the area between Balabagan and Malabang. This differentiation may have taken place before the process of Islamization began sometime in the fifteenth century. The spread of wet-rice cultivation and, later, the introduction of corn encouraged the growth of populations on the Lanao-Bukidnon plateau and emphasized another differentiation on the basis of ecology and dialect, with the gradual emergence of the Maranao as a distinct ethnolinguistic group. The Ilanon appear in recorded history as the most feared pirates in greater Malaysia (Hall 1968: 339). Alone or in combination with the Samal and Magindanao, fleets of Ilanon boats rowed by slaves and armed with brass cannon raided islands and shipping from Sumatra to New Guinea (Tarling 1963). There were also raids into the Central Philippines. Spanish efforts at retaliation resulted in the inland areas, particularly around Lake Lanao, becoming both a sanctuary and a base for operations. So important did the lake area become that it led to the notion that the Ilanon were originally, if not solely, people coming from the lake. The decline of piracy in the nineteenth century eroded the basis of interaction between the lake and coastal peoples and intensified what may have already existed, the tendency for people around the lake to think of themselves as Maranao rather than Iranon or Ilanon. Moreover, the distinctive sociopolitical system which they developed, the "Encampment of the Lake" (Mednick 1965) spread out to involve inland areas beyond the lake, including those down toward the coast.

BIBLIOGRAPHY. Appell n.d.; Forrest 1779; Hall 1968; Kuder 1945; Mednick 1965; Saleeby 1905; Sather 1967; Tarling 1963.

MAGINDANAO

ORIENTATION. The town of Cotabato on Mindanao's west coast is the site of the old Magindanao Sul-

---
*The author of this section, Melvin Mednick, also contributed the entry on Maranao.

tanate, founded, according to legend, by Sarip Kabongsoan, descendant of an Arabian Sharif, who with his brothers emigrated from Johore to found Islamic communities in Mindanao, Sulu, and Brunei. The Magindanao Sultanate at one time claimed ritual hegemony over all of western and southern Mindanao, and its fleets, with those of Ilanon and Sulu, terrorized the seas until its final submission to Spain in 1884 (Saleeby 1905). The Magindanao (Maguindanao) nowadays occupy much of coastal Cotabato Province, with large concentrations in the lowland valleys of the Cotabato River system. They are found also in sizable numbers in Zamboanga and in the city and province of Davao. Speakers of Magindanao, a language closely related to Maranao, number some 359,000, according to the 1960 Census. The majority grow wet rice by capturing flood waters of the Cotabato, although some Magindanao are dry-field agriculturists and only semisedentary. The sociopolitical system appears to be considerably more complex than that of the Maranao, the hierarchical structuring of relationships approaching more closely that of the (Tausug) Sulu Sultanate (Mednick 1965). Magindanao *datus* have traditionally exercised tenuous political control within portions of the southwestern Cotabato uplands inhabited by Tiruray and Manobos, an extension of long-standing trading relations between coastal Muslims and their pagan upland neighbors.

BIBLIOGRAPHY. Kuder 1945; Mednick 1965; Saleeby 1905.

MARANAO*

Synonyms. *Maranaw, Ilanon, Iranon, Ranao, Lanon, Hiloona*

ORIENTATION. **Location and identification.** The Maranao are traditionally centered around Lake Lanao, the largest deep-water lake in the Philippines, at an elevation of 2,200 feet within the western segment of the fertile Bukidnon-Lanao Plateau, western Mindanao. It is this location that gives them their name, which connotes "residing near a lake." The Maranao's own version of their origin is recounted as part of an epic folk tale, many of whose themes and elements are of Indic origin. The beginnings of Maranao culture and society are traced to a mythological civilization, Bumbaran. When this civilization collapsed, survivors wandered to Lanao. Later,

Sarip Kabongsoan of Johore, a descendant of the Prophet and a wonder worker, found his way to the mouth of Cotabato River, where he married into the highest ranking families and converted the Magindanao to Islam. Descendants of these marriages went to Lanao, where they married descendants of the Bumbaran people. Although nominally Muslims, there are few institutions in Maranao culture of obvious Islamic origin, especially as compared with Magindanao and Tausug. **Demography.** The Maranao ethnolinguistic community numbers around 400,000, making it the largest cultural minority in the Philippines. About 350,000 Maranao live in the province of Lanao del Sur, which they dominate (except for a few thousand Bisayan-speakers on the coast). The balance are mainly in the province of Lanao del Norte, where they are a minority among Bisayan-speakers. There are increasing movements of Maranao into the mountainous areas south of the lake in the province of Cotabato, and small communities of Maranao are found in almost every major population center in Western Mindanao, in Davao, and in the Sulu Archipelago. **History.** The Maranao appear to have been a mainly inland, agricultural, population since protohistoric times, most likely an inland development of a population once centered south and west around Ilana Bay and the mouth and lower valley of the Cotabato River. Glottochronology (Conklin 1955c) suggests a separation from this population beginning around the thirteenth or fourteenth century. Initial concentrations appear to have been around the southern and southeastern parts of the lake and are perhaps associated with the spread of wet-rice cultivation. Communities southwest of the lake maintained contact with the coastal Ilanon into historic times and cooperated with them in their raiding and trading expeditions. For this reason, the Maranao are often identified with the much-feared Ilanon pirates of Mindanao (Tarling 1963). The Maranao were the last major Philippine group to become Muslim, and were also the most successful in their resistance to Spain. They were administered separately from the rest of the Philippines until the establishment of the Republic, and provincial officials continued to be appointed from Manila until 1959. The Maranao area is now a regular province in all regards. Mutual fears and hostilities formerly restricted immigration into the lake area, where only a few thousand Christian Filipinos and a handful of Chinese were able to establish themselves. World War II, Independence, contact with Bisayan speakers on the coast, and communication with the Muslim world have, however, set the stage for changes which became manifest during the 1960s. Education has become an accepted avenue to mobility, and awareness of national government and party politics a pervasive feature of social life (Mednick 1961).

---

*The author, Melvin Mednick, spent the years 1956-58 in field research among the Maranao. He is presently Professor of Anthropology at Virginia Commonwealth University.

Though agriculture remains basically oriented toward subsistence, there is increasing production, particularly of rice, for a national market. A striking development of recent years is a religious revival, with a thousand or more Maranaos making the pilgrimage to Mecca each year.

SETTLEMENT PATTERN AND HOUSING. **Settlement pattern.** Basically one of hamlets, containing from three to thirty multifamily dwellings. In wet-rice areas, houses are usually in a lineal pattern, following the course of a river or road. In hilly, dry-rice areas, hamlets are smaller, and houses cluster irregularly in the vicinity of a water source. The politically defining feature of a hamlet is a mosque, and its socially defining feature is at least one substantially built "great house," belonging to the leading kin group in the community, which serves as a place for community gatherings. Today there are likely to be several such houses in a hamlet. Until American times, a hamlet was also likely to contain one or more "fortresses," areas enclosed by earthen walls reinforced by thorny plants and trees. They served as places of retreat and protection in time of hostilities. **Housing.** Houses are usually of lumber, raised from one to seven feet above the ground. The main body of the house is a rectangle, up to 25x60 feet. The interior is usually undivided. At least two families, and sometimes as many as ten, occupy a house, though the average is between three and four. The roof is usually high, steeply sloped, and of galvanized iron. In the ideal great house, internal and external beams and posts have prow-shaped carvings jutting from the eaves and outside walls. Attached to the end of the house is a kitchen shed, dominated by a large earthen hearth. Traditionally there is sometimes an additional room at the top or side of the house used as a chamber for unmarried women.

ECONOMY. **Agriculture.** Plateau areas grow one crop of wet rice a year, relying mainly on captured rainfall. Some corn and camotes are grown on marginal lands. Garden crops (taro, squash, cassava, chili peppers, sugarcane) and tree crops (betel nuts, papayas, bananas) are mainly for household use. Hilly areas utilize permanent fields to grow a variety of cash crops (corn, camotes, coffee, cassava, peanuts) although dry rice is grown to the extent possible. **Fishing.** Formerly important to the domestic economy. Fish populations in Lake Lanao have now declined to a point, however, where most fish must be brought in from the coast. **Domestic animals.** Water buffalo, goats, dogs, chickens, and ducks. Only buffalo are given significant care. Cattle and a few horses are present in upland areas. **Industrial arts.** The lost wax process is used to produce brass jars, containers, and musical instruments. Iron is forged, and gold and silver are worked. There is no marked social advantage or disadvantage attached to metal work, although there are remnants of associated taboos. **Trade.** With the decline of local markets, peddlers have extended their activities, and small groups of itinerant Maranao are to be found in almost every major market in Mindanao, either buying, selling, or both. This is a continuation of an old tradition, wherein traders moved between the pagan hill peoples and the coast, which was the source of valued objects (metal, porcelains, weapons) coming from greater Malaysia. **Property.** The most valued forms of property are residential and agricultural land (especially wet-rice lands), houses (especially the "great houses") animals (particularly water buffalo), weapons (today mainly guns and rifles, but formerly brass cannon, swords, and daggers), and prestige-giving objects (decorated swords, jars and containers of brass, gold coins, trays, and gongs). Productive resources, especially land, are usually individually owned by either sex. Landholdings are mostly small, and share tenancy low, though increasing.

KIN GROUPS. Maranao society is formally organized on the basis of ambilineal ramages having as their major function the allocation of status relative to each other. Each ramage is a line of descent termed a *bangsa*. There are a limited number of such lines, each derived from an ancestor conceived as the founder of the line and the source of hereditary rights and status. The lines are broken up into segments stemming from more recent ancestors identified with particular locales and communities. The most significant and effective portion of a line is the segment descended from an ancestor so recent that individuals are linked to each other by ties of bilateral kinship as well as ambilineal descent. Several such segments linked through a mutual ancestor formally organize a community. Individuals reckon ambilineally from founding ancestors in order to claim and participate in rights with them. Antecedents who were not founders of hereditable rights are ignored for purposes of descent, or are treated only as links to a founding ancestor. The number of descent lines that individuals can inherit is restricted by the limited number of ancestors recognized for descent purposes. Inheritance of descent lines is cumulative, but unevenly distributed. All persons inherit at least two descent lines, some claim as many as fifteen, while the average appears to be about six.

Overlapping with descent, but conceptually different from it, are bilateral kin groupings. The largest of such groupings, the bilateral kindred, is comprised of the kin circle of each of the four grandparents, and ultimately includes all relatives within the fourth degree of consanguinity. The bilateral kindred is never known in its entirety and functions mainly in regard to bride-price. The most important bilateral kin grouping is a kin circle made up of all kin to the second degree of consanguinity. This is the group of relatives toward whom Ego will most consistently orient and among whom kinship usages and sentiments will most strongly prevail. **Kinship terminology.** Eskimo, with suggestions of an underlying Hawaiian system.

MARRIAGE AND FAMILY. **Mode.** All marriage arrangements are accompanied by a bride-price (traditionally in land, animals, weapons, and slaves), whose size is determined by the kinds and number of descent lines of the parties involved. The size of the bride-price is of special significance because of its effect on descent line inheritance. Families which can raise large bride-prices are able, over the years, to contract marriages to a variety of descent lines, especially the more important ones. Since the inheritance of descent lines is cumulative, descent line differences between individuals become, in significant part, an expression of bride-prices paid in previous generations. **Form.** Polygyny is generally permitted. Usually, however, only wealthy and powerful persons are able to practice it. **Marriage rules.** Sororal polygyny and the sororate are strongly discouraged. Marriages with first cousins, nieces, or nephews, are frowned upon but can take place. Matrilateral cross-cousin marriage is sanctioned on religious grounds, but is rare. Marriages within the larger bilateral kindred, especially between persons related at the third and fourth degree of consanguinity, are encouraged for reasons of kinship solidarity. **Residence.** Usually uxorilocal in the case of young couples. When the final portion of the bride-price is paid, a couple may live in a community of their own choosing. However choice is constrained by factors such as availability of farmland, the need to have descent line rights in order to reside within a community, and the importance of having a number of kinsmen in the community of residence. **Domestic unit.** The domestic unit occupies a portion of a multifamily dwelling and is defined as those who eat together and/or share a sleeping area. Normally this is a married couple and their immature offspring. Multiple wives are usually housed separately. A sibling group does not necessarily remain attached residentially to the parental domestic unit, but it is considered desirable that at least one married child live in the same house or community as do the parents. **Inheritance.** In theory, all siblings inherit equally. Residential land and houses are often jointly owned, with effective control and use in the hands of one sibling, usually a male. Both sexes may inherit agricultural land, but the tendency is for women to inherit less and/or give up immediate use of such lands to male siblings. Other items of tangible nature are mostly inherited by the sex that uses them.

SOCIOPOLITICAL ORGANIZATION. **Political Organization.** Every Maranao hamlet is organized in terms of two or more ambilineal descent lines, or *bangsa*. Each descent line owns at least one title, which is inherited by all descendants of the founding ancestor. The person who actually holds the major title is the representative and symbol of the rights and status of the descent line. Within each hamlet one, and occasionally more than one, descent line and its title-holder are declared superordinate. This person, whose title is often "Sultan," is the chief political figure in the hamlet. Neighboring hamlets group together on the same principle; within such a group there is one hamlet, represented by its leading descent line and title-holder, considered to be superordinate by the rest. This larger organization of hamlets and descent lines is the effective sociological and political community, and the leading title-holder the most important political figure. Another "level" of political organization associates the groupings of hamlets within a region on the same principles of sub- and superordination. This regional grouping is mainly symbolic and ceremonial. Finally, there are four territorial divisions, which enclose the groupings and subgroupings of descent lines and hamlets. These are the traditional *pongampong* or "encampments" of the *pat a pongampong a ranao* ("the four encampments of the lake"), i.e. the Maranao considered as a total society. The *pongampong* are frequently referred to in the older literature as "tribes" or "clans." Political and armed conflict was formerly endemic at all levels of society (Mednick 1965). **Social differentiation.** In the folk conception of Maranao society, a three-rank system of stratification cross-cuts descent line organization: (1) persons having hereditary claim to titles (2) free men having no claim to titles, and (3) bond slaves. Stratification nowadays, however, is based mainly upon differences in wealth and power and continues to be expressed through the descent line system. Political and economic power gravitates toward higher ranking descent lines and prestigious titles. **Social control.** Persons of prominent descent, especially title-holders, are responsible for maintaining order in their communities, judging disputes, and guaranteeing decisions with their own power and wealth. Some kinds of litigation (e.g. land transfer, marriage problems, and division of property) are influenced by Koranic law, and in these matters the help of devout and learned men is sought. Ordeals (e.g. by fire) and oaths upon the Koran were used in the past, but are no longer important. The Philippine court and police system are also available, but tend to be used in order to gain advantage or as a last resort.

RELIGION. The Maranao are Sunni Muslims with evidence of minor Shi'ite and Sufi influence. Alongside Islam is belief in local spirits and beings. Each individual is born with a companion spirit, whose disappearance or displeasure brings illness or death. *Diwata* are associated with air, water, earth, etc. The most important class of spirits is the *tonong*, including the unquiet dead, especially important at times of life crises, such as birth or illness. Religious roles such as prayer leader (imam) or religious judge (*kali*) are attached to descent line titles. Practitioners involved with non-Islamic spirits include the *pandarpa'an*, often an old woman skilled at contacting the spirits, and the *pamamantok*, who can engender or counter black magic (Isidro 1968b: 84 ff.). The ceremonial calendar follows that of Islam. Death rites are the most important life crisis ceremonial and are celebrated over a period of 104 days with distributions of food and money.

BIBLIOGRAPHY. Conklin 1955c; Gowing 1964; Isidro 1968a, 1968b; Kuder 1945; McAmis 1966; McKaughan and Macaraya 1967; Mednick 1956, 1961, 1965; Saber 1961, 1963; Tarling 1963; Villaluz 1966; Warriner 1964.

BUKIDNON PLATEAU

THE MODERN ADMINISTRATIVE province of Bukidnon lies almost wholly within the interior uplands of northern Mindanao, between Lake Lanao and the high central cordillera, a region of broad, grass-covered plateaus, intersected by steep-sided river valleys. The indigenous population, estimated in 1960 to number somewhat over 70,000, is made up chiefly of speakers of Bukidnon, a member of the widespread Manobo family of languages. Rugged mountain barriers have served to some extent to isolate the indigenous Bukidnon from neighboring Moro and Manobo populations to the west, east, and south. In recent decades, however, the area has experienced a period of relatively intense settlement of Christian Filipinos, immigrants from the coastal lowlands to the north, together with the spread of commercialized farming and cattle raising. The Bukidnon now comprise less than one-third of the total population of the province, and are rapidly being absorbed into the dominant lowland Filipino culture pattern.

BUKIDNON

Synonyms. *Higaonan, Higaunen*

ORIENTATION. **Identification.** The people usually refer to themselves as Higaonan, "mountain dwellers," but are more widely known as Bukidnon, a lowland Bisayan term meaning mountain people (Cole 1956: 5). The indigenous culture has been profoundly affected by the large-scale immigration of Christian Filipinos, and Christian missionaries have been active in the interior since about 1880. Fay-Cooper Cole carried out fieldwork among the Bukidnon in 1910, and his brief monograph summarizes the little that is known concerning the indigenous culture (Cole 1956). The acculturative changes that have occurred since the turn of the century are described in Lynch (1955). Beyer (1917: 41) regarded Bukidnon culture as probably similar to that of the pre-Spanish Bisayans of the northern Mindanao coast, and Cole (1956: 134) concurs in this view. **Linguistic affiliation.** Bukidnon (Binokid, Binukid) is classified by the Summer Institute of Linguistics (SIL) as a member of the Manobo family of languages. The latter, in turn, includes most of the indigenous languages spoken on Mindanao. There are several dialects of Binokid, including Banuaon (Banuanon), spoken along the Agusan border. Southern Bukidnon Manobo (Central Mindanao Manobo) appears on SIL maps as Tigwa-Salug. [Elkins et al. 1969-70.] **Demography.** Estimated by Beyer (1917) at 48,500 and by Lynch (1955) at around 35,000. The 1960 Census gives a total of 70,000 persons who claim Bukidnon as their mother tongue.

SETTLEMENT PATTERN AND HOUSING. Settlements appear formerly to have been located for defensive purposes, chiefly in forested foothills and mountain passes. These "settlements" apparently centered around a local or petty *datu*. Families within the territory dominated by a *datu* lived in impermanent, low-walled, thatch and bamboo houses near their shifting fields. "Tree houses," raised high for defensive purposes, seem to have been used on occasion. Government officials and missionaries have consistently encouraged resettlement in permanent towns along major avenues of communication.

SOCIOPOLITICAL ORGANIZATION. Cole (1956: 79ff.), drawing on memories of informants and on early reports (e.g. Clotet 1889), describes the central

Bukidnon area as having been organized under a superior or ruling *datu*, with local areas or "districts" dominated by petty *datus*. The latter lived in large pile dwellings with their multiple wives, retainers, and fighting men. Their followers occupied scattered homesteads, repairing to the compounds of the *datus* on ceremonial occasions and in times of danger. A *datu's* followers worked his fields, and in return he afforded them protection. *Datus* owned prestige wealth, such as jars and gongs, and some, at least, were entitled to wear the distinctive headdress of a distinguished warrior. They claimed the protection of a special group of spirits, by whom they were aided in performing ceremonial duties, judging disputes, and arbitrating bride-price settlements. Disputes were settled most often by fines (plates, jars, animals) and/or by the use of ordeals. **Warfare.** Warfare, for prestige and slaves, was common until recent decades. Although headhunting does not appear to have been practiced, Cole was told of the former existence of human sacrifice in connection with funerary practices, whereby an enemy captive was ceremonially speared to death by the relatives of the deceased, to the accompaniment of animal sacrifice and the drinking of rice beer (Cole 1956: 86). Warriors wore padded hemp-cloth coats, together with colorful embroidered sashes and kilts. Weapons included spears, knives, and wooden shields.

RELIGION. **Supernaturals.** Ancestral spirits are invoked on occasion, and food is offered them, but there are no major ceremonies in their honor. The most powerful spirits are named deities (*magbabaya*) of the upper world, underworld, and four cardinal points. These are held in great awe, but are not as intimately concerned with the affairs of men as are the innumerable members of a complex pantheon of named nature spirits, patron deities, mountain gods, and the like (Cole 1956: 91-98). Names and attributes of spirits and details of ritual procedure appear to have been highly consistent throughout the various Bukidnon areas visited by Cole in 1910. The Bukidnon share the taboo, widespread in Mindanao and Borneo, against mocking animals, lest such behavior offend the spirits, resulting in thunder, lightning, and floods. In the case of the Bukidnon, it is the supernatural force or deity, *anit*, who is thus offended (Elkins 1964). **Practitioners.** Persons of both sexes may become *baylan*, religious specialists who divine the cause of illnesses, recover lost souls, and officiate at major events where the spirits are summoned. One becomes *baylan* by personal choice and subsequent apprenticeship to an established practitioner. Cole found no evidence of spirit possession, although all *baylan* are (or were) considered under the protection of a pair of spirit patrons. [Cole 1956: 89ff.] **Soul, death, and afterlife.** Belief in multiple "souls," *gimokod*, some of which

can leave the body temporarily, causing illness. At death, the body is wrapped in a mat and carried on a bier to the place of burial, where it is interred in a bamboo-lined grave. The spirit of the deceased is fed for a few days after burial, after which it goes to live on Mount Balatocan. The mourning period for a widow may last for a year or more. [Cole 1956: 76.]

BIBLIOGRAPHY. Beyer 1917; Clotet 1889; Cole 1956; Elkins 1964, 1968b; Elkins et al. 1969-70; Lynch 1955.

SOUTHWEST HIGHLANDS

THE SOUTHWESTERN Mindanao highlands extend for more than 125 miles along the southern coast of Cotabato Province, where ranges with elevations up to 4,000 feet, facing directly on the Celebes Sea, have traditionally served to isolate the pagan, swidden-farming tribespeople of the interior uplands from all but intermittent trading and slaving relations with coastal Muslim populations. Beginning in 1913, but particularly in the years since 1948, government-sponsored resettlement projects have resulted in the movement into Cotabato of large numbers of Christian Filipinos (Pelzer 1945; Hunt 1954; Wernstedt and Spencer 1967). Although resettlement and economic development have been chiefly in the large interior valley lowlands (e.g. Cotabato, Koronadal), settlers have in recent decades started moving into the more accessible upland valleys and plateaus (cf. Maceda 1964b), and the tribal peoples, estimated at less than 10 percent of the total 1960 provincial population of one million, are increasingly being drawn into an expanding lowland economy. This situation has been dramatized by the recent "discovery" of a band of cave-dwelling hunters and gatherers, the Tasaday, deep in the rugged forested area inland from the coastal town of Kiamba. Although they appear to be linguistically related to speakers of Manobo-type languages—swidden agriculturists in the hills to the west and north—they were apparently living an isolated "stone age" existence until contacted by nearby settled tribes in 1966 (MacLeish 1972; Llamzon 1971).

The southwestern Cotabato hill tribe languages include Tiruray and Tagabili, members of a

"Southern Philippine" language group which also includes Bilaan, spoken by peoples farther east in the mountainous Sarangani Peninsula (Conklin 1955c). Speakers of Cotabato Manobo, although scattered throughout the area under such local names as Ubo, are concentrated on the Kulaman Plateau, between the Tiruray to the north and the Tagabili to the southeast. There is considerable cultural similarity among all these peoples, and in broad outline they conform to what might be called a generalized Manobo culture type. The influence of lowland Moro culture is everywhere evident; the so-called *datu* system has penetrated the uplands to varying degrees, but most notably among the Manobo in the Kulaman Plateau area. Legendary accounts of hill tribe origins commonly mention former residence in coastal or lowland valley areas, with a history of having been driven into the hills by Muslim and (later) Christian expansion. Tales to the effect that the ancestors of present day hill tribesmen and coastal Moros were once "brothers" are common. Relatively little has been published concerning any of these groups, least of all on the Tagabili (Taboli, T'boli), who may turn out to be simply a westward extension of a basically Bilaan population into the vicinity of Lake Sebu and the upper Allah River system (Cole [1913: 129-48] records speculations concerning the former identification of Bilaan with the Lake Buluan area and the Tagabili).

BIBLIOGRAPHY. Cole 1913; Conklin 1955c; Hunt 1954; Llamzon 1971; Maceda 1964b; MacLeish 1972; Pelzer 1945; Wernstedt and Spencer 1967.

TIRURAY*

Synonyms. *Teduray, Teguray, Tidulay*

ORIENTATION. **Identification.** The Tiruray or Teduray (called "Tidulay" by the Magindanao) of Cotabato Province differ physically, linguistically, and culturally from the Magindanao of the Cotabato Valley to the north and east and from the Manobo, who live beyond the Tran River to the south. There are slight differences in these respects among the Tiruray themselves, who differentiate three subgroups, the river people, the coast people, and the mountain people. These groups speak slightly different dialects and in racial characteristics probably represent a Proto-Malay and Malay mixture, with the latter strain stronger in the first two groups. Some individuals among the mountain people have characteristics suggesting Negrito influence. Culturally, in contrast to the lowland-dwelling Muslim Magindanao, the Tiruray, like the Manobo, are an upland people who have in large part retained their own religion. **Location.** Bounded by the Tamontaca River on the north and the Tran River on the south, the coast on the west, and the southward-curving Cotabato Valley on the east (6° 45'-7° 12' N.; 123° 58'-124° 25' E.), generally at an altitude of 1,000 to 2,500 feet. There is gradual migration to the more ruggedly mountainous country to the south as the Tiruray district becomes deforested and more densely settled by colonists. There is little external migration otherwise; a few young people leave to work in Cotabato City or to go to school. **Linguistic affiliation.** Malayo-Polynesian. Classed by Conklin (1955c) in a Southern Philippines group of languages, along with Tagabili and Bilaan. A ritual language is used for negotiations and ceremonies. Records are kept by means of pieces of bamboo and knotted rattan. **Demography.** The 1960 Census listed 26,000 persons who claimed Tiruray as their native tongue. Schlegel (1970: 9) estimates that only about 10,000 still live the traditional tribal life. **History and cultural relations.** The Tiruray say that they and the Magindanao are the descendants of two brothers, the elder of whom refused to be Islamized and went into the mountains, subsequently entering into a trading pact with his Moro brother. Historically, institutionalized trading pacts did exist between the Tiruray headsmen and Magindanao *datus* of the coast and valley, until they were broken up by the Spaniards and Americans. During the centuries of fighting between the Spaniards and the Moros, some of the latter fled to the neighboring heights and perhaps joined the Tiruray there. The Spanish, and later the Americans, sought to contain Moro influence by making the Tiruray Christian and sedentary through missions and schools (cf. Tenorio 1892) and protected them with soldiery. They also established plantations along the coast and used Tiruray labor on them. Since 1900, Christian Filipino colonists, land speculators, and lumbering interests have entered the Tiruray uplands, along with Chinese storekeepers. Today the Tiruray around Tamontaca on the northern edge of the district, now settled by Magindanao, profess Islam; while some on the coast and in the vicinity of

The author of this entry, Grace Wood Moore, is a member of the staff of the Human Relations Area Files. Her data are based on anthropological fieldwork among the Tiruray in 1950-51, under the auspices of the Fulbright program.

the largely Christian town of Upi-Nuro in the center of the district profess Christianity. The mountain Tiruray have been little affected by these religions. With Independence, the government of Cotabato Province was largely put in the hands of Magindanao officials, from whom the Tiruray were no longer protected; the courts were presided over by Christian Filipino judges. The Tiruray are now either adopting the way of life of the Moros or Christian Filipinos or they are retreating to the south, into Manobo country. Relations with the Manobo, some of whom are called Dulangan by the Tiruray, are generally peaceful. Where the peoples are in contact, there is some intermarriage, and there is visiting on the occasion of celebrations. Tiruray men around the Tran River not uncommonly take Manobo wives.

SETTLEMENT PATTERN AND HOUSING. **Settlement pattern.** Local groups ranging in size from a few families to 20 or more live in the vicinity of a headman, whose house is frequently on a height above the smaller houses of his followers. During the agricultural season, there is further dispersion to houses nearer the crop clearings. As more distant clearings are made the community gradually shifts to a new area. The size and stability of a given group depends in large part on the strength of its leader; a weak leader may control only his extended family, a strong leader up to 20 or more families in a large extent of forest for the making of clearings. Such a "country" with its inhabitants is known as an *inged.* **Housing.** The rectangular, gable-roofed house is built on posts four to six feet above the ground. Floors and walls are of bamboo or bark, and the roof is covered with shingles of grass or leaves. Cooking may be done on a framed-in dirt hearth just inside the door or on a kind of porch or lean-to. The inner part of the house, away from the door, is used for sleeping, storing possessions, and consultations. In a headman's larger house, this part may be raised a few inches or even bench high to form a sitting or sleeping platform, and the interior may be partitioned into two rooms.

ECONOMY. Traditional economy based on swidden agriculture with some hunting, fishing, and gathering; in times of scarcity there is considerable dependence on gathering. **Agriculture.** Dry rice, including glutinous varieties, maize, sweet potatoes, squash, and sugarcane are the principal crops in the forest clearings. Other crops, such an manioc, taro, bananas, onions, and tobacco, are important in areas where market produce is sold. The chief agricultural implements are the ax and machete, the planting stick, weeder, and crescent-shaped harvesting knife for rice. Noise devices are used to scare birds and ani-

mals. The agricultural calendar is based on the stars and the phases of the moon (cf. Schlegel 1967). **Fishing and hunting.** Shallow mountain streams provide small fish, eels, and shellfish, caught mostly in traps of bamboo and rattan. On larger streams the water is dammed, and the fish are caught with the hands or baskets, or pools may be poisoned. Blowguns are used for birds, bows and small arrows for monkeys (darts and arrows may be poisoned). Deer and wild pigs are taken with larger arrows or with spears. Sharpened bamboo sticks and spring traps are also used for game, while wild chickens are caught with decoys and snares. Hunting expeditions, undertaken at night with guns, spears, and dogs, are organized on rare occasions. **Gathering.** Wild products are constantly sought by the Tiruray for food, the ingredients of chews, medicines, charms, and raw materials for manufactures. Bamboo, rattan, timber, and bark are gathered on special expeditions when the need arises. In times of drought or pest invasions, and annually before the harvest, the gathering of wild tubers is an important means of subsistence. **Domestic animals.** Dogs for hunting and chickens for food and sacrifices. Water buffalo are sometimes used in farming the deforested areas. **Industrial arts.** Basketry and woodworking are the principal crafts. There is some working of shell, and scrap pieces of metal are fashioned into implements. **Trade.** In return for rice, baskets, rattan, and beeswax, the Tiruray obtain salt, cloth, and metal goods from Chinese storekeepers or Magindanao or Christian Filipino traders. Magindanao trader-gamblers sometimes make trips to Tiruray settlements, where they sell coastal food products. Internal trade is accomplished largely through gift-giving, bride-price exchanges, and fines. **Property.** Primarily communal, and of two types: that produced by communal labor (mainly houses and food) and the largely imperishable symbolic property called *tamuk,* used for bride-price and fines, and made up chiefly of metal and glass bead necklaces, gongs, spears, swords, fighting bolos, metal belts, betel boxes, and porcelain bowls. This property is always on call, so to speak, to help a kinsman out of trouble or to provide a bride for him. Personal property is limited to everyday clothing, homemade implements, charms, and ornaments, and is insignificant.

KINSHIP. **Descent.** Bilateral. **Kin groups.** Bilateral kindreds. **Kin terminology.** Hawaiian, in Murdock's usage:

GrPa	*bebe*
Mo	*ideng* (familiar: *iday*)
Fa	*boh* (familiar: *abay*)
FaSi, MoSi	*ina*
FaBr, MoBr	*momo*
Sibling relationship	*setuare*

YoSib	*tuare*
ElSib	*ofo*
Br	*lageay* ("man")
Si	*libun* ("woman")
Cousin (1st)	*setiman bebe* ("same grandparent")

(The children of first cousins call each other by a term that means "separate grandparents once," their children in turn, "separate grandparents twice," etc.)

Ch	*nga*
GrCh	*bebe*
Spouse	*baowag*
Pa-in-law	*terima*
Ch-in-law	*awas*
Br-in-law (between men)	*efel*
Si-in-law (between women and cross-sex)	*ibo*

MARRIAGE AND FAMILY. **Mode.** Bride-price, consisting of *tamuk* property, which may also represent animals (buffalo or horses, rarely cattle). **Form.** Polygyny is common, and may be sororal. **Extension of incest taboos.** If first counsins or aunt-nephew/uncle-niece marry, fines are imposed. Cousins with one set of different grandparents may marry, but a special article is required in the bride-price. **Residence.** Tends to be patrilocal if the bride-price is paid, but there is considerable shifting of residence. **Domestic unit.** The household, consisting of a man, his wife or wives, and children. Relatives of either spouse, but particularly the husband's, may join the household at times, or more or less permanently. Average size of household is five to ten members. Because of quarrels, divorce, incapacitating illnesses, and a high mortality rate, the household unit is relatively unstable as compared to the extended family grouping of which it is a part. **Inheritance.** A deceased man's brother takes over the family (levirate), even if there are adult sons, and he determines whether or not any division of property is made among the sons. If the widow has a small child, she may get some token for it. If there are no brothers and there are adult sons, the eldest will get most of the property and distribute some to the younger sons. Should there be no brothers or sons, the property would fall to the adult male most closely associated with the household (cousin or nephew of the deceased). **Divorce.** Divorce is negotiated by the headmen representing the spouses and their kin; disposition of bride-price and children depends on adjudged relative guilt of each spouse. If the husband offers enough *tamuk*, he can demand all the children (his group "owns" them by virtue of having paid bride-price for the mother), but very young children usually remain with the mother. **Secondary marriage.** Both the levirate and sororate are practiced. **Adoption.** Rights over a person are acquired by the payment of *tamuk*, the goods used for the payment of bride-price and fines (bride-price is a kind of fine for "stealing" one's

child). The children of a woman for whom *tamuk* has been paid belong to the kin group who paid it; if another group were to claim rights over such a "child" (even when the child is an adult), *tamuk* would have to be paid to the original group before such a claim would be recognized.

SOCIOPOLITICAL ORGANIZATION. **Political organization.** Tiruray society is organized essentially on the basis of kinship ties, with the oldest capable man acting as head of an extended family group. A man may acquire followers beyond his extended family if he knows and is fluent in the esoteric language that is used for ceremonies and for negotiations involving *tamuk*. Such negotiations are called *tiawan* (cf. Schlegel 1970). If a group lacks a man skilled in *tiawan*, called a *kefeduan*, one may be brought in. A fluent speaker who is also healthy, strong, brave, and aggressive (attributes indicating supernatural power) holds his own group together, attracts other followers, and is thus in a position to acquire more goods and to wield more influence at gatherings. An active headman must travel a great deal and maintain a network of communication so as to keep informed of events and to negotiate in the interests of his group. Families are in a sense "owned" by the headman who represents them in legal matters. Should another headman act for them, especially if he were to collect *tamuk* for them, it would be claimed that he had "stolen" them. Nowadays the Tiruray district as a whole is governed by Magindanao and Christian Filipino officials; Tiruray have served under them in minor capacities. **Social control and justice.** The male head of the household governs its members, and the headman of the extended family group governs the affairs of the group. To settle problems between different groups, the headmen meet with the interested parties and negotiate a settlement in fines. Women cannot be held responsible for the payment of fines; their kin, or more immediately their fathers or brothers, are responsible for them. One is guilty both before his fellows and before the spirits and ancestors, the fines being symbolic of just punishment. The aim of justice is to make the two sides equal. If one side feels unjustly treated, it may seek vengeance, and therefore every effort is made during the negotiations to prevent this. [See Schlegel 1970 on Tiruray law and justice in relation to morality.] If a fine cannot be raised immediately by the group representing the guilty party, it may be allowed as a debt for a certain length of time, after which vengeance is sought. Or a third party, a powerful headman, may offer the goods necessary to keep the peace, and he thus acquires certain rights over the person for whom he has paid *tamuk*.

Respect is important in social control. The universe is viewed in terms of hierarchies of power (earthly and supernatural); inferiors should show deference to superiors, who in turn should be kind (show pity) to those beneath them. Thus punishment must be tempered by kindness and pity; a wrongdoer overly shamed may attempt to regain respect by blindly attacking with a sword anyone in his vicinity. Tiruray legends portray the hero as having been shamed and subsequently going through the forest killing everyone he meets, emerging with great supernatural power. It is believed that such a leader will eventually arise and lead all the Tiruray to the upper world. **Warfare.** Disputes, unless negotiated, may lead to vengeance killings, accomplished by a few men lying in ambush or creeping under a house to kill the occupants. There is no evidence of headhunting or cannibalism.

RELIGION. The native religion presents the universe as multilayered, with the earth in the center. The beings above the earth help human beings to reach the upper regions or to acquire supernatural power on earth. When a human being acquires sufficient power, he may go to the highest being, Tulus, to ask for pity for other human beings. If he becomes truly powerful, his entire body, not just his spirit, goes on such a quest. At each place along the way, the person acquires more power to make him strong enough to continue. Stories of such journeys and the adventures along the way are popular. The spirits of the upper world, including the ancestors, punish human beings for disrespect toward the elders, the ancestors, and tradition. For example, the spirit of thunder and lightning strikes human beings with lightning for putting animals on a human level by talking to them or dressing them up. To be struck by lightning is also a punishment for disrespect toward old people. Another spirit punishes people for disrespect by making the earth sink and become water, causing whole *inged* to disappear. On this earth various classes of natural phenomena are represented by a spirit owner or guardian, who punishes human beings with sickness, accidents, or death for disrespect toward the phenomena they represent (water, trees, grass, caves, deer, etc.). **Supernaturals.** The major classes of supernatural beings are: Tulus, the highest being; the *maginalao*, powerful beings of the upper worlds; *segoyong*, nature spirits on this earth; malevolent giants and dwarfs, including the *busao*, giants who eat the livers of persons; *bolbol*, who may come to a man who has demonstrated his bravery and give him whatever he desires, including evil power over other persons. **Supernatural objects.** Bamboo containers for offerings, magic sticks of especially hard wood, magic stones or peculiarly shaped objects for charms and curing. A miniature shield and sword represent power (invulnerability) in battle. The color red represents bravery; white, curing power. **Practitioners.** Supernatural power is acquired by suffering to gain the pity of the spirits —e.g. staying alone in the forest overnight—or by demonstrating great bravery to earn rewards from the spirits, who give power or tell one what he must do to get it by means of medicines, charms, etc. A person with such power is a *belian*, who maintains contact with the spirits, makes offerings to them, and interprets the supernatural world for human beings. He works primarily through magic to cure, to cause storms to pass, to paralyze enemies, and the like. Another type of practitioner, the *getuan*, acquires his knowledge from the elders and cures illness with herbs and charms, reads palms and omens, knows the rites for good crops, etc. **Ceremonies.** Ceremonial gatherings occur in connnection with crisis rites and at the time of the parting of the years, when the headman makes arrangements with his followers for the coming agricultural season. **Illness.** Illness is caused primarily by the spirits as punishment for disrespect. Some bad spirits, and human beings in league with them, eat the livers of human beings, causing them to sicken and die. Death also occurs when a person's spirit leaves his body and does not return. Therapeutic practices include the use of magic, sacrifices to the spirits, blowing on and fanning the affected parts, and the laying on of hands. **Soul, death, and afterlife.** The soul or spirit is in one's head and leaves the body during sleep; dreams are the experiences of the spirit outside the body. At death, when the breath "breaks," the spirit leaves this earth for an abode in the upper world, from which it can see this earth, but cannot return to it. There are various abodes for the dead, according to the manner of death. **Funeral practices.** Close relatives sit by the corpse, while others make noise to keep the spirits away. In a day or two, when the relatives have gathered, the body is put in a coffin, which is tied shut and carried to the burial ground, followed by relatives who beat gongs. Before burial, the ties of the coffin are cut to allow the spirit to depart. Food and articles useful to the spirit are left on the grave. After the party returns to the house, the ground is carefully swept and a chew is put on a stone near the trail to the cemetery, as an offering to Tulus to provide an easy way to the upper world for the spirit. On the eighth night, the spirit returns to the dwelling for the last time, when a final ceremony is held, with general merrymaking to show in the presence of the spirit that there are no "bad minds" over the death. The next morning the spirit is escorted with food offerings toward the burial ground, from which it is supposed to proceed to the abode of the dead.

BIBLIOGRAPHY. Conklin 1955c; Schlegel 1967, 1970; Tenorio 1892; Wood 1957.

COTABATO MANOBO*

Synonyms. *Dulangan, Tudag*

ORIENTATION. **Location and identification.** The central portion of Cotabato's southwestern highlands, behind the coastal towns of Kalamansig, Lebak, and Kraan, is occupied by scattered settlements of pagan hilltribesmen—referred to as Manobo or Tudag by Magindanao in the surrounding lowlands and as Dulangan by the Tiruray, their highland neighbors to the north. The Manobo say that they moved into their present habitat during the last century, having been driven from the coastal portions of Tran and the great plains of Cotabato to the east by incursions of Muslim Magindanao and (more recently) pioneering Christian Filipinos. Intermarriage with both groups, and with Tiruray, has produced a variety of physical types. In addition, Negrito and Veddoid traits (broad noses, wavy to curly hair) are noticeable. **Linguistic affiliation.** The language is identified on Summer Institute of Linguistics maps as Cotabato Manobo, which, despite some features characteristic of Tiruray-Tagabili-Bilaan, is classified as a member of the Manobo family of languages (Elkins et al. 1969-70). The latter family appears to have its greatest degree of differentiation in the central Mindanao area. Tagalog serves as a lingua franca in trade with lowlanders. **Geography.** Access to the Kulaman Plateau, a large tract of rolling terrain surrounded by high mountains, is via the Tran River Valley from the coast or, from the east, via the Kulaman River, a tributary of the Cotabato (Rio Grande de Mindanao). At some 2,500 feet, the climate of the Plateau is moderately cool, with no pronounced variations in rainfall. Virgin tropical rain forest is still found on the higher ranges. **Cultural relations.** The Manobo in this part of Cotabato have undergone considerable culture contact. Much of their sociopolitical organization appears modeled on that of the lowland Magindanao, with whom many Manobo now seek to identify. More recently, pioneering Christian Filipinos (Ilongos, Cebuanos, Warays) have moved into the area, where they live in close proximity to Manobo settlements. The Christians, bringing with them schools, constabulary, and other agencies of the national government, have introduced changes that will have a decided effect on indigenous Manobo culture.

SETTLEMENT PATTERN AND HOUSING. **Settlement pattern.** Scattered, named settlements, separated by natural boundaries. Each settlement composed of an average five to eight (range one to twenty-one) households, located within shouting distance. Traditionally located on a hill top as protection from surprise attack. With an average household size of 8.5 persons, the typical settlement contains from 40 to 70 inhabitants. No specialized religious or other structures. **Housing.** Permanency of house construction depends on accessibility of swiddens. Houses are ordinarily of bamboo and thatch, rectangular in shape, low-walled, and raised 3-6 feet on piles. Multilevel houses are occasionally met with (Reynolds 1966); the fireplace is lowest, whereas the sala, for eating, sleeping, and rituals, is much higher. Rice is stored within the house in large bark containers. Gongs, spears, and trophies of the hunt are prominently displayed.

ECONOMY. Semisedentary, marginal agriculture (an integrated *kaingin* system), supplemented by fishing, hunting, and trade. Cash income from contract clearing of *kaingin* for Christian settlers and selling rattan, hardwood houseposts, and other forest products to lowlanders. Both sexes hire themselves out as porters. **Agriculture.** The appearance of the constellation Balatik (Orion) in January signals the start of cutting and felling in preparation for burning. Intercropping of maize and rice is common; other cultigens include bananas, sweet potatoes, taro, and vegetables. Fields are fallowed after two or three harvests. Implements include axe, bolo, and digging stick. **Domestic animals.** Chickens, pigs, dogs, cats, horses, water buffalo—the latter two as prestige wealth and for paying bride-price and fines. **Industrial arts.** Blacksmiths make blades and spear points. Anklets and bracelets of silver and bronze, made by the cire perdue process, are items of trade with other Manobos and with lowlanders. **Trade.** Goods and labor commonly exchanged or paid for in terms of their equivalent value in prestige goods and heirlooms, i.e. horses, gongs, beads. Those Manobo who have been in long contact with lowlanders understand the use of money, although they are frequently cheated in such transactions. **Property.** Hunting grounds are reserved for the common use of members of the local settlement; whereas fields under cultivation and those in fallow belong to the family cultivating them. Harvested cereals, although belonging to individual seed owners within the family, are under the general disposal of the housefather, also the owner of prestige goods such as gongs, beads, and horses.

---

*The author of this entry, Marcelino N. Maceda, is head of the Department of Economics in the University of San Carlos. His data are based on fieldwork in the Kulaman Plateau-Upper Tran River area of Cotabato in 1962-64. A few linguistic and comparative notes have been added by the editor.

KINSHIP. Kinship is reckoned bilaterally to include second degree cousins. Kin groups include nuclear and extended patrilocal families, with the local settlement comprised mainly of male consanguineal relatives, e.g. brothers and first and second degree cousins and their inmarrying spouses (Maceda 1968: 23). This, plus the general avoidance of marriage with close kinsmen, tends to make the local group exogamous, although not rigidly so. Kin terms of reference, male speaking, are as follows:

GrPa	bebe
Fa	ma
Mo	ina
FaBr, MoBr	momo
FaSi, MoSi	ina
Sibling	kakay
Cousin (male)	haddi
Cousin (female)	tabay
Wi	sawa
WiFa, WiMo	nugangan
WiBr	ufol
WiSi	ibu
WiFaBr, WiMoBr	momo uloy
WiFaSi, WiMoSi	ina uloy

MARRIAGE AND FAMILY. Families tend to form paired reciprocal relations with respect to exchange of women in marriage. First-cousin marriage is not common, but is practiced. Arranged marriages or betrothals may occur at an early age in order to reduce the amount of the bride-price, since under this arrangement the boy may go to work for the girl's family while she is still quite young. A bride-price in prestige goods (gongs, blades, horses) is a necessary part of the marriage contract and is fixed by family heads or *datus* in protracted negotiating sessions, *antang*. Permanent residence subsequent to marriage is jurally patrilocal, although extended visits may be made to the girl's family. Polygyny is practiced by men of wealth and/or influence for reasons of economic and sociopolitical gain. Divorce is possible for both sexes, although if initiated by the wife, her family must return the bride-price.

SOCIOPOLITICAL ORGANIZATION. **Political organization.** An average five to eight households, related by blood and affinal ties, comprise the local settlement. The eldest among the male family heads serves as *datu* (leader, spokesman, and judge) and in return receives filial loyalty from the group (Maceda 1968). Several such settlements occupy a territory or domain under a leading *datu*, whose influence depends in part on kin ties with his followers. A loose confederation of several such territories may be under the authority of a rajah or sultan—titles modeled on those of the Muslim Magindanao and in some cases purchased from coastal Magindanao sultans. Such offices carry relatively little authority per se; Manobo *datus* can only persuade, not command. There are stories, however, of the former absolute authority

of such figures (Maceda 1964b). **Social differentiation.** Weakly developed at the local level. Leadership in Manobo society is achieved, not ascribed at birth. *Datus* are men who have demonstrated abilities as fighters and skilled negotiators and who, through astute trading and strategic marriages, have accumulated material goods and a loyal following of kinsmen. The more property a man owns, the higher his prestige. Old gongs, krises, spears, beads, silver and bronze ornaments, old Chinese bowls and plates, horses, water buffalo, and wives are all important in this respect. **Social control and warfare.** Vengeance and blood feuding are recurrent themes in Manobo culture. Disputes are most often settled by an institutionalized pattern of negotiation, *antang*. Skilled arbitrators (*datus*, or those aspiring to this coveted office) bring the parties together, determine guilt, and assess damages. Successful negotiators are given a portion of the fine as compensation. Although individual vendettas are (or were) common, organized warfare seems to be foreign to Manobo concepts. There are no reports of headhunting (Maceda 1964b).

RELIGION. There is belief in a supreme being, Namola, and rituals honoring the spirit or soul of rice. These, and curing rites, are performed by shamans, *beliyan*. Corpses are kept in sealed, split-log coffins until after a good harvest, when the relatives can afford the necessary mortuary feasting. The coffin is interred in a shallow grave or, according to Reynolds (1966), half-buried so that the deceased's spirit is free to come and go. After this interment the deceased's former abode is abandoned or burned by the near relatives. Clay or stone burial jars, some seeming to date from the eighteenth century, have been found in caves in the Kulaman Plateau area—possibly the remains of ancestors of present-day Manobos (Maceda 1964b).

BIBLIOGRAPHY. Elkins et al. 1969-70; Lopez 1964, 1965, 1968; Maceda 1964b, 1966, 1967b, 1968; Reynolds 1966.

CENTRAL HIGHLANDS*

THE CENTRAL Mindanao highlands—the region of intersection of the provincial boundaries of Davao, Bukidnon, and Cotabato—are drained on the east, to Davao Gulf, by the upper tributaries of the Libuganon and Davao rivers and on the west by the Kabacan, Arakan, Tinanan, and Kulaman—tributaries of the upper Pulangi, itself a part of the

*The data contained in this entry were contributed by E. Arsenio Manuel, who also wrote the entry that follows, on Upland Bagobo (Manuvu). Comparative linguistic notes have been added by the editor.

vast Cotabato (Rio Grande de Mindanao) River system, which empties ultimately into the Moro Gulf. Trade and cultural contacts in this hitherto underdeveloped and remote region are oriented chiefly to the southeast, to trading centers such as Calinan, or to Kidapawan on the Cotabato side. The peoples throughout much of this area are in popular usage termed Bagobo, derived probably from *bago* ("new") and *obo* ("man"), applied by Bisayan, Spanish, or Muslim missionaries to newly converted natives along the Davao coast. The term has since acquired the added meaning of "native" or "hill tribesman," and is, like Manobo, a generic one of lowlander origin, encompassing in this case at least four distinct but interrelated groups—Manuvu, Matigsalug (Matidsa'ug), Attaw (Jangan or Guianga), and Tagabawa (Tahavawa). The Attaw and Tagabawa were the "Bagobo" of the Davao coast at the time of Spanish and later American occupation (see under *Coastal Bagobo,* below). They now live in scattered hamlets around Mount Apo and southwestern Davao City. The Manuvu and Matigsalug, on the upper courses of the Davao (Salug), Tinanan, and Kulaman rivers, are closely related linguistically to one another and to neighboring Ata; and, as among the latter, dark-skinned, curly-haired individuals are a common element in the population. The Matigsalug, in particular, retain much of their aboriginal culture. The languages of this tri-province area are shown provisionally on Summer Institute of Linguistics (SIL) maps as Bagobo, Kulamanen, Tigwa-Salug, and Ata—all classed, along with neighboring Binokid and Ilianen, as members of a Manobo family of languages. Bagobo, in turn, appears at present to consist of at least three languages—Tagabawa, Obo (Manuvu), and Guiangan (Attaw) (Elkins et al. 1969-70).

BIBLIOGRAPHY. Elkins et al. 1969-70.

*UPLAND BAGOBO (MANUVU)**

Synonyms. *Manobo, Obo, Obbo*

*The author of this entry, E. Arsenio Manuel, is Professor of Anthropology in the University of the Philippines. He has done extensive fieldwork in the central highlands, in both Cotabato and Davao, as well as elsewhere in the Philippines. A few linguistic notes have been added by the editor.

ORIENTATION. **Location and identification.** The Manuvu occupy an extensive region between the upper Pulangi and Davao rivers, roughly 124°55'-125°20'E., 7°-7°35' N. Manuvu is derived from the wordbase *tuvu* meaning "grow, grown"; the prefix *man*—or *mang*—is an obsolete morpheme connoting "people." Manuvu would mean, then, "aboriginal people." Actually, however, the Manuvu have vague ideas about the meaning of the term (cf. Garvan 1931: 1-2). *Taha*— is used instead to designate "native or resident of," the suffix —*on* denoting "people or language of." The Manuvu are not homogeneous, a fact indicative of their mixed ancestry. The Taha'urug subgroup occupies a mountainous area immediately west of the Davao River in its middle course; their number is estimated at over 1,000. The Tinananon inhabit uplands drained by tributaries of the Tinanan, an eastern tributary of the Pulangi. The Pu'angi'on are found on the northern stretches of the Pulangi River up to the village of Punti'an in southeastern Bukidnon. Lastly, the Kuamanon inhabit the Kuaman (Kulaman) River area between the Pulangi and upper Davao (Salug) rivers. These subgroups have developed special occupational and artistic skills as well as dialect differences; the latter are, however, no barrier to communication. **Geography.** The Davao side of Manuvu land is rugged mountainous terrain; westward, toward Cotabato, the topography opens up to gentler slopes and wider valleys. Rainfall is moderate, with no marked seasonal variations. The forests teem with wild pigs, deer, birds, lizards, snakes, and monkeys. **Demography.** An estimated 30,000, based on surveys in the pilot barrio of Dallag in 1962. **Linguistic affiliation.** The Manuvu occupy an area provisionally marked on Summer Institute of Linguistics maps as Obo (Obbo'), one of a group of Bagobo languages. The Bagobo language group is in turn classed within a larger Manobo language family, which includes a considerable proportion of the languages indigenous to Mindanao (Elkins et al. 1969-70). **History and cultural relations.** According to tradition, Moro warriors penetrated the uplands in the nineteenth century or even earlier, provoking armed retaliation by the Manuvu, who, in a rare instance of such cooperation, combined forces with the neighboring Matigsalug. More commonly, the Manuvu carried on regular trade relations with the neighboring Matigsalug, Attaw, and Ilianen, interrupted by sporadic, small-scale feuding and raiding. Trade with coastal Attaw (Guianga) dates from the midnineteenth century if not earlier. Older informants state that their ancestors were still wearing barkcloth at that time, and that they acquired the costumes of the Attaw in exchange for venison and wild pig meat, an indication that game in the coastal areas was becoming scarce. The capture of children and women introduced weavers into Manuvu communities and the start of local production of (abaca) cloth. Traders brought home gongs from the Attaw and Tagabawa (see under Coastal Bagobo), as well as horses and water buffalo. The latter were in turn traded to Matigsalug for long-bladed knives. The Matigsalug areas were until recently prime sources for slaves, whom the Manuvu traded to Attaw for ornaments, jewelry, gongs, and gong music. During the first decades of the American regime, the Manuvu learned the cultivation of abaca from the Attaw, whose lands Japanese and American planters were buying and renting. Following World War II, hog raising was introduced by Bisayans. The movement of the latter into Manuvu land has increased greatly in recent decades, facilitated by the construction of logging roads into the mountains.

SETTLEMENT PATTERN AND HOUSING. **Settlement pattern.** In more rugged terrain, dispersed neighborhoods of a few houses, located on mountain spurs or the banks of deep ravines. Sometimes a hilltop is selected for a small village site. These settlements tend to be impermanent, due to the demands of shifting agriculture, although the inhabitants tend to return to the same sites in a cyclical pattern. Tree houses, clustered closely together for defense, were present formerly. Where the terrain opens up into broader valleys, villages tend to be larger (up to 100 families) and more or less permanent. **Housing.** The contemporary house is raised on piles, rectangular in shape, with a gable roof of bamboo, grass, or bark. The walls, without windows, are of bark. A sleeping room is provided for unmarried daughters, and boards are suspended beneath the gable for the use of boys and unmarried men. An annex may be added for a married daughter. Floors may be of different elevations, raised from one and a half to three feet. Granaries are small, separate structures, raised on piles.

ECONOMY. Prior to World War II, subsistence was approximately 75 percent from agriculture and 25 percent from hunting, fishing, and gathering. The contribution of the latter three activities has now declined to around 5 percent. **Agriculture.** Families have two or more swidden sites, which they rotate every two or three years. Maize, rice, and sweet potatoes are the staples, supplemented by squash, beans, sugarcane, bananas, and various tubers. Millet was formerly planted around the edges of the fields. Intercropping, seed selection, and fallowing are practiced; fertilizing and irrigation are unknown. Chief tools are the bolo, wooden spade, and digging and dibbling sticks. The use of plows is still rare. Abaca and coffee have in recent decades been introduced as cash crops in some areas. **Hunting and fishing.** Formerly important, but commercial logging has depleted the supply of game. Wild pig and deer were speared or trapped. Monkeys and other small game were taken with bow and arrow or (an older method) with traps. Birds were caught by liming or with traps, blowguns, or bows and arrows. Fishing techniques included damming and poisoning, trapping, and (more rarely) the use of spears and bows and arrows. **Domestic animals.** Traditionally limited to dogs and cats (as pets, not eaten) and chickens (as food and ritual sacrifice). Hog raising is recent. Horses, water buffalo, and (recently) cattle, obtained by trade with coastal tribes, are important as wealth and figure in marriage exchange and in payment of fines and debts. Households keep caged *limukon* doves for augury. **Industrial arts.** Potters, blacksmiths, and weavers, along with medicinemen, midwives, and epic singers, were held in high esteem in the aboriginal culture. Pottery making and weaving have largely disappeared in recent decades. **Trade.** During Spanish times, the Attaw and Tagabawa were the intermediaries in trade between the Davao coast and the interior uplands, meeting hill tribesmen at designated centers such as Calinan. Internal trade was limited to exchange (ten knives = one small gong; one large gong = one horse); these traditional equivalencies continued in the hills until about 1950. **Property.** Although the *datus* exercise ultimate authority to dispose of land, effective ownership is in the hands of villagers. Land tenure may appear cyclical, but in fact ownership (symbolized by the presence of betel, coconut, and fruit trees and by graves) is never lost by temporary disuse. Old porcelains and gongs used on offering stands and heirloom pieces, such as old spears and the headdress of the *bahani* (knight-errant), are sacred and may not be bartered or sold. Rice was formerly included in this category. Separation of property rights as between husband and wife is recognized: a part of her bridewealth goes directly to the wife and she also claims any damages or fines that may accrue to her after marriage; and a man, especially a trader, is the owner of any goods or animals acquired in his bartering activities. Above all, it is the goal of a housefather to endow his eldest son with all possible wealth so that he may carry on the name, support his siblings, marry them off, and answer for fines, damages, or other financial claims brought against any one of them.

KINSHIP. Bilateral kindreds share in the raising of bridewealth, the payment of wergild, and in the recruitment of vengeance parties. Since villages are in general small, the inhabitants tend for the most part to be interrelated by ties of blood and marriage. This fact, plus the rigid enforcement of incest prohibitions, makes the local group statistically, if not jurally, exogamous. The Manuvu use a single term (*ama*) for father and uncle and a single term (*ina*) for mother and aunt. Siblings are terminologically equated with cousins, and there is a single term for grandparents and grandchildren.

MARRIAGE AND FAMILY. **Marriage rules.** Any relationship (traced bilaterally) is considered a bar to marriage. Incest prohibitions are rigidly enforced lest the deity, Anit, visit sickness and death on the perpetrators and their kinsmen. Additionally, lightning may strike them, or they may be turned to stone (cf. Manuel 1961, Elkins 1964). **Mode.** Boys are supercised prior to marriage, and both sexes undergo teeth filing and tattooing during adolescence. Parental arrangement is considered the modal form, although the degree of choice allowed may vary widely. A brideprice, consisting nowadays partly of livestock, is an essential part of the marriage contract. **Form.** Polygyny is practiced, largely for economic or sociopolitical gain. **Residence.** Initially the husband becomes a member of his wife's parents' household. In later stages of matrilocality, the couple may live elsewhere within the village, but the son-in-law is still obligated to help support his wife's parents. **Household unit.** The modal domestic unit is the nuclear family, augmented at times by a married daughter with husband in matrilocal residence. **Inheritance.** The greater portion of a man's property (including family heirlooms) goes to his eldest son, who may also partition inherited land among his siblings, especially sisters who continue to reside within the village. The first-born is obligated to support his younger siblings, and to raise bridewealth for outmarrying brothers, receiving in turn part of the bridewealth when sisters marry. **Divorce and secondary marriage.** Divorce may be accomplished by formal complaint by either party, followed by a hearing and a decision by the *datu*. Both the levirate and sororate are practiced (a male or female cousin may be substituted for a brother or sister of a deceased spouse). Family continuity is thus assured and interkin-group relations maintained. Furthermore, the occurrence of intervillage and intertribal blood feuds is thereby lessened, since the man in matrilocal residence is for all practical purposes a hostage.

SOCIOPOLITICAL ORGANIZATION. **Political organization.** Traditionally no political integration above the level of the village. Multiple *datus* (e.g. three or more in a large village of 100 families) maintain peace, chiefly in the roles of judges and "fixers," i.e. collecting wergild and delivering same to the aggrieved party. A successful *datu* must have wealth (surpluses of rice, maize, and cloth, plus accumulated trade goods such as gongs, blades, water buffalo, and horses) and must also be a skilled negotiator. *Datus* usually train one of their sons to succeed them, although any man with the necessary qualifications can achieve the

position. Subsequent to World War II, and in response to the encroachment of loggers and Christian Filipinos, a single *datu* has been recognized as pre-eminent in the tri-province area of Manuvu land. This individual is also a celebrated priest-shaman (*tamanuron*) and is reputed to have a powerful protective spirit—charismatic qualities which have aided his rise to power. **Social differentiation.** No social classes. The social and ceremonial importance of warriors, so important among coastal Bagobo, disappeared long ago in the uplands. Ownership of wealth is highly fluid, due to the demands of kinsmen and the system of wergild. "Slaves," i.e. those captured in raids, are ordinarily treated well and eventually marry into their captors' villages. **Social control.** Vengeance and honor are important themes in Manuvu life. A wide range of behaviors may, under appropriate circumstances, be interpreted as insulting or worse, and damages demanded. Insults and property disputes (e.g. over bridewealth) easily lead to feuds involving the obligatory participation of kinsmen on both sides. Disputes that cannot be settled at the family or kin level are taken to the *datus*, who judge the case, determine damages to be paid (in rice, gongs, horses, cloth, etc.), and see that these are collected and handed over to the aggrieved party. If damages cannot be raised by the defendant and his kinsmen, the *datus* may make up the difference themselves in the interest of keeping the peace. [The *datus* receive, as compensation, a percentage of such fines among the Cotabato Manobo described by Maceda elsewhere in this volume.] Ordeals and oaths are resorted to in fixing guilt; serious cases are concluded by *pagkitan*, ceremonial sharing of food by both parties under supervision of the *datus*. **Warfare.** Intervillage and intertribal blood feuds were endemic prior to World War II. Vengeance parties were composed of members of the local kin group, or a *bahani* (knight-errant) might be engaged to wreak vengeance. A vengeance party, of ten or more, might include scouts, advanced and rear guards, killers (*tahavunu*), and porters. If serious enough, neutral *datus* functioned as arbitrators. Intervillage feuds were concluded by a peace-making ritual, *pakang*, which included blood drinking and the spearing to death of a slave to even the score of slain. Headhunting was absent.

RELIGION. The Manuvu have a rich folk literature. Singers of long epic poems, *tuwaang*, perform at most gatherings, recounting the exploits of heroes in the time of the mythical ancestors. There are elements in these epic myth cycles of flooding, brother-sister incest, and petrifaction (Manuel 1958, 1961). **Supernaturals.** A supreme deity, Manama, inhabits the topmost of a nine-layered skyworld. He has little to do with earthly affairs, however, entrusting these to a host of paired male-female lesser deities, *diwata*. A husband-wife team and their children are the keepers of an underworld abode of the dead. **Practitioners.** No professional priesthood. Female practitioners are absent, and séances are not practiced. A hierarchy of male priest-shamans includes *pohohana*, prophet-diviners capable of performing miracles such as rainmaking; *tamanuron*, who claim the protection of guardian spirits; and *walian*. *Datus* may at times assume the role of priest-shaman, i.e. in connection with harvest and marriage ceremonies. Simple offerings and prayers can be made by housefathers, artisans, and hunters at prayer stands in the house, yard, or swidden. Sickness is caused by evil spirits, *busaw*, and is treated by a *walian* or *tamanuron*. Physical deformities are the work of Anit, who becomes angry should mortals mock animals such as dogs, cats, or frogs. **Ceremonies.** Major rituals, involving the participation of priest-shamans and in some instances held at the house of a leading *datu*, occur at the start of the clearing season, first harvest, thanksgiving (*sahakaan*), illness, and marriage. There is also an annual bellows-blessing ceremony for smiths —but nothing of the kind for potters or weavers. **Death.** Tree burial was at one time common practice. More recently, the corpse remained in the house, which was then abandoned by near kinsmen. Burial in the house yard has become the accepted practice in those areas converted to the cash cropping of abaca and coffee. A thatched hut is raised over the grave, but once the departed spirit has been taken by Manama from the underworld up into the skyworld, little attention is paid to it.

BIBLIOGRAPHY. Barnard et al. 1955; Benedict 1913, 1916; Cole 1913; Combés 1906; Elkins 1964, 1968a; Elkins et al. 1969-70; Garvan 1931; Gisbert 1892, 1902; Manuel 1958, 1961, 1963, 1969a, 1969b; Montano 1886; Schadenberg 1855; Svelmoe and Abrams 1955; Walkup 1919.

DAVAO GULF*

THE CLASSIFICATION OF ethnic groups or tribes in the southeastern (Davao Gulf) region of Mindanao is most difficult, since tribal lines and cultural practices cannot be analyzed as distinctive patterns. Classifications such as that by Cole (1913) suffered from the difficulty of devising an adequate tribal taxonomy. The presence of intertribal and extratribal marriages, the taking of slaves, the importance of long-distance trade, and the movement of populations from the interior to the coast and more recently from the coast to the interior have obliterated tribal lines. Despite these reservations, the various ethnic groups all share numerous similarities, both in cultural traits and social structure. Shifting cultivation, dispersed settlement patterns, art styles, clothing, and religious orientations are fairly uniform throughout the area. With respect to level of basic socioeconomic structure and degree of political integration, these groups manifest a number of similarities which set them off from other groups in Mindanao. The tribal population of eastern Mindanao was characterized as warlike, in that headhunting was a major cultural focus, which in turn was the basis of political leadership. Among all these groups—Mandaya, Bagobo, Manobo, Bilaan, Tagakaolo—the *magani* (*bagani*) held positions of great social and ceremonial importance (Benedict 1916: 254). In western Mindanao, on the other hand, ethnic groups such as the Subanun are devoid of any headhunting practices, and warfare was not a cultural institution.

At least three levels of political integration may be differentiated prior to intensive Bisayan contact. The greatest political complexity existed in the *datu* system of the coastal and lowland Bagobo. The *datu* that Cole describes for the Bagobo is found nowhere else in the area. The existence along the coast of permanent lowland villages with rice cultivation and the commercial production of hemp in foothills behind the coast were imperative to the solidification of power and authority among the Bagobo *datus*. The elaborate dwellings, the maintenance of vast households, and the extensiveness of slavery supported *datu* rule over numerous minor leaders. The hierarchy of petty leaders who were subordinate to a single paramount *datu* provided the channels of support for the political hierarchy through taxation, corvée labor, and intensive regional trade. This political development might also have been in response to Spanish contact and Moro trade. The presence of these foreign elements provided more wealth in goods and cash, and in turn Spanish and Muslim demands were carried out through the *datu* leadership. The scale of *datu* activities reached new proportions externally, while power and authority solidi-

---
*Contributed by Aram A. Yengoyan.

fied internally through extensive controls over the populace.

This elaboration of political authority is absent in the second level of political integration, which includes the Mandaya and upper Agusan Manobo, the Bilaan, and probably the Tagakaolo and Kulaman. Political authority and leadership among these groups was not extensive, and the right to rule was more fragile. The Mandaya *bagani* had to continuously meet internal demands through external conflicts for land, slaves, and tribute. Furthermore, the sedentary aspects of lowland Bagobo social organization were absent, thus the ability to maintain continuous firm control over the population was always a problem. Charisma is a very important factor in keeping one's political position among the Mandaya, while with the lowland Bagobo *datu* the right to rule was inherent in the office and was seldom challenged.

A third level of political integration is found among the Ata, where no political leaders emerged beyond the male household head. Each household was an autonomous unit, and links between households were only through labor exchanges and kinship. This pattern is now typical of the upland Mandaya after the collapse of the *bagani*.

Presently, lowland-upland contacts have altered many aspects of tribal life. Missionaries, churches, and occasionally mosques dot the countryside and have quasi-converted most of the tribal peoples to Christianity or Islam. The Philippine educational system has made an impact—both positive and negative—through the proliferation of small barrio schools throughout Davao, Agusan, and Cotabato. But the major problem for the ethnic groups is their inability to hold their traditional lands from loggers, Bisayan farmers, and other commercial interests. The dispossession of land by outside elements has now assumed vast and serious proportions. The ethnic groups have no legal claim in the Western sense to their property, and through force and violence lands are being taken away from them. The conflict over land again reflects the clash of two cultural traditions. For tribal people, land is a free good, maintained only by usufruct; while for lowland Filipinos and commercial interests, land is a capital good, which is owned as abso-lute private property. The Western-style courts of agrarian relations recognize the latter as the basis of ownership, resulting in legal support for commercial interests. At times this conflict becomes violent, but gradually the ethnic groups have lost and have retreated into the barren interior mountainsides. Contemporary economic changes are radically altering and destroying the socioreligious basis of ethnic life. In the long run, the ethnic groups will gradually be absorbed into a way of life which is Bisayan culture.

BIBLIOGRAPHY. Benedict 1916; Cole 1913.

MANDAYA*

Synonyms. *Mansaka, Mangwanga, Mangrangan, Managosan, Magosan, Pagsupan, Divavaoan, Dibabaon*

ORIENTATION. **Identification.** The Mandaya are the largest ethnic group in southeastern Mindanao. Although the term Mandaya, meaning "inhabitant of the uplands," is widely used, Cole (1913) noted five synonyms for this designation. These are as follows:

1. *Mansaka.* "Inhabitants of the mountain clearings." Presently this includes those Mandaya who formerly inhabited the interior areas and have recently moved into the coastal areas of Kingking, Mabini, and Lupon on the north and east side of Davao Gulf.
2. *Pagsupan.* Mandaya living near the Tagum or Hijo Rivers.
3. *Mangwanga* or *Mangrangan.* "Dwellers of the Forest." Mandaya populations living in the heavily forested interiors. Sometimes this group is designated as Mangguangan, and it may be a distinctive group from the Mandaya.
4. *Managosan* or *Magosan.* Mandaya who live on the headwaters of the Agusan River. This area is now called the Maragosan Valley. Presently most of the inhabitants are Mansaka speakers, while Mandaya is found in the more mountainous regions to the east.
5. *Divavaoan* [*Dibabaon*]. A division which inhabited a small district to the south and west of Compostela.

---

*The author, Aram A. Yengoyan, is Associate Professor of Anthropology, University of Michigan. He has done fieldwork among the Mandaya in 1960-62, and again in 1965.

By the middle 1960s these divisions were no longer utilized in all regions, though particular categories are occasionally recognized. Racially the Mandaya as well as the other Davao groups are quite uniform, representative of the basic Malayan type and overall culture area affiliation noted by Cole (1945). **Location and geography.** The Mandaya occupy eastern Davao Province, between 7°-8° N. and 126° to 126° 75′, E., including the southern ranges of the Pacific Cordillera. Coastal plains give way rapidly to rolling grasslands, which reach an elevation of 1,500 feet. The grasslands, or *cogonales*, are not uniformly flat, but are dissected by numerous small rivers and streams. Beyond the grasslands one finds secondary and primary forests, which extend up to 4,000 feet. In this area the Mandaya have retained their swidden agricultural practices, while in the foothills they have changed to a cash economy with the cultivation of abaca. The largest mammal is the wild pig, though at one time wild deer were also present; other mammals are bats, rodents, and monkeys. Domestic animals are chickens, pigs, goats, dogs, horses, cows, carabaos, and zebus. Horses, cows, and carabaos are rarely found in the mountainous, rice-growing areas, but are present in the grasslands, where they are utilized for transporting abaca to the coastal settlements. No domestic livestock is utilized for rice agriculture. Birds, reptiles, fish, and shellfish are present and are systematically obtained by spears and traps. **Demography.** Cole (1913) estimated the Mandaya as numbering between 25,000 to 35,000 and thus representing the largest tribal unit in southeastern Mindanao. Many contemporary coastal peoples are actually Mandaya who have been baptized, symbolic of a change in reference group from Mandaya (i.e. pagan, backward) to Bisayan (i.e. Christian, progressive) (Yengoyan 1966a). It is estimated that there are from 3,000 to 5,000 Mandaya still oriented toward the traditional way of life, with another 15,000 to 20,000 presently inhabiting coastal settlements and fully involved in a lowland Bisayan cultural pattern. **Cultural relations.** Cultural relations are mainly with coastal lowland Bisayan populations, although there is contact with Muslim villages in the Mati area and inland from the Davao Gulf Coast. Muslim teachers are occasionally encountered among the interior groups, where conversion to Islam is still an important issue. Historically, the Mandaya had contact with the Spanish through missionary and military activities and, after 1900, with American planters around Mati, Kingking, and Lupon.

ECONOMY. **Agriculture.** Upland Mandaya agriculture is based on the cultivation of rice, tubers, and other cultigens by swiddening techniques, both primary and supplementary. Rice is the most important food item, although tubers and cultigens provide the bulk of the daily diet. Millet (*dawa*) and oats (*ceba-da*) are usually planted on the edges of a swidden along with a variety of tubers, which at times may gain primacy if the rice harvest fails. The swidden cycle is typical of other shifting agricultural populations, except that the burning phase is absent due to the high and evenly distributed rainfall. **Diet.** Folklore, myth, ceremonies, status in the neighborhood group, and daily conversation usually revolve around rice (*umay*) and its various aspects. Although rice represents the ideal food for daily consumption, such is not the case and probably was never completely fulfilled within the agricultural cycle. Root crops and bananas, along with vegetables, constitute the bulk of the diet; however, rituals or other beliefs associated with root crops are totally absent. Meat in the form of chicken and fresh fish is seldom consumed, due to the scarcity of poultry and the slight interest in fishing. Pigs are eaten only on festive occasions. **Property.** Land tenure rules reflect the economic demands of shifting cultivation. With no important capital goods to be inherited and with land as a free good which is only held by usufruct, land tenure rules are such that no one is limited to the continual working of selected agricultural sites. Any field with productive cultigens belongs to the original cultivator as long as the cultigens, fruit trees, etc. are still productive. If one desires to cultivate a swidden which was formerly cultivated, and fruit trees are still productive, an exchange of rights is initiated through the transfer of pigs for the right to cultivate. No formal socio-kin groups possess tenure rights to land and other private property. The nuclear family is the only unit that maintains claims and rights to land (Yengoyan 1971).

SETTLEMENT PATTERN. Villages of compact populations are absent. The most common settlement type consists of a clearing containing a single roofed structure, occupied by a single nuclear or polygynous family under one male head. Each such settlement is located adjacent to a swidden, and in the uplands this type is the ideal and normal residence pattern. Dual household settlements consist of a clearing containing a single roofed structure inhabited by two or more male family heads and their nuclear or polygynous families. The link between family heads is either father/son or father/son-in-law. This type only occurs in special changes in residence arrangements, e.g. to inherit special claims to productive rice lands. The distance between households varies from one-half to two kilometers, but new households are always relocated in sight of a neighbor. Residential changes occur following each cultivation cycle, usually 12-14 months, thus informal networks of labor exchange, visiting, and mutual help continually vary. Dispersed simple settlements are grouped into larger

MINDANAO

units, which may be termed "neighborhoods." A number of neighborhoods are combined into "domains," which represent the largest recognized discrete entity. The neighborhood and the domain are not groups in the sense that individuals within these units combine for certain purposes. As larger groupings of households, each entity is cross-cut by local and extended group affiliations and kindred networks. The occurrence of exogamy and endogamy at various levels binds settlement to settlement and neighborhood to neighborhood. As geographical units, which are spatially and temporally impermanent, larger social groupings provide a means of classifying kinsmen and non-kin by location rather than by genealogical relationships, which are frequently forgotten. In the uplands the whole of Mandaya society as seen by each family unit is circumscribed by the domain one inhabits, and adjacent domains are considered traditional enemies.

KINSHIP. Social organization reflects the economic imperatives of shifting cultivation. With the necessity of maintaining mobile social units, which must continuously exploit new forest growth, the absence of permanent kin groups beyond a single generation is expected. Like many other Philippine upland groups, descent is cognatic in that each person traces relationships through both parents. Genealogical knowledge seldom extends to second cousins, however. Descent is important only for maintaining status, prestige, associations, and certain rights, but no formal descent groups exist. All groups are Ego-based, thus resulting in numerous overlapping personal kindreds which link one kinsman to another. Kindreds form groups only when certain jobs or tasks must be accomplished, and once the ends are realized the kindred-based group dissolves. Among the uplanders, the kindred (*kalumonan*) includes grandparents, second cousins, and all descending generations. The number of individuals within a kindred varies from 75 to 120 persons, though important people and *bagani* (warrior chief) descendants may have far more than the average range. Affines are included in one's *kalumonan* through the occasional extension of consanguineal kin terms to include in-laws and through reciprocal bonds, which are also extended to certain affines. The kindred does not regulate marriage preference, thus it cannot be considered as an exogamous unit. Ideally, one marries a distant cousin, but second-cousin marriages are permitted after a nominal fine is imposed on the groom's side. Bilateral kindreds never combine into localized kin groups, and in general one's kindred is widely dispersed due to economic activities which require mobility. **Kin terminology.** Kinship terminology is of the Eskimo type, but the terminology of address is commonly Hawaiian. Behaviorally, collateral kin are treated in a similar manner as lineal kin. [See Yengoyan 1964.]

MARRIAGE AND FAMILY. The Mandaya family (*kabanayan*) is the basic social unit and the only autonomous economic group. Since the dissolution of the family means economic collapse for its members, a number of positive social patterns, such as the levirate, sororate, polygyny, and adoption, maintain the family after death or divorce has dissolved the original unit. Divorce is exceedingly rare and highly impractical, since each individual fully realizes all of the difficulties involved in separation, especially in repaying in-laws the amounts of cash and food used in the marriage feast. **Form.** Two types of families are recognized. The most common is the nuclear family, composed of a single spouse of each sex and their unmarried children. Polygynous families, composed of a single male and two or more wives and their children, account for less than 10 percent of all families. Polyandrous and communal family units were not encountered, nor were they recorded in genealogies. **Mode.** The selection of a spouse is based on kinship considerations, domain affiliation, and personal characteristics. All marriages are within one's generation; intergenerational marriages are not socially sanctioned. Bride-price and bride service are common, and numerous arrangements are present to suit the various parties. During the courting period, the boy will provide small gifts to the girl. When the girl's parents feel he is sincere, they ask him to introduce himself in a formal manner. The boy then asks his father to accompany him to the girl's parents. If the girl's parents agree, a long period of haggling over an appropriate bride-price ensues. Go-betweens (*kunama*) are utilized. Bride-price is made in cash, carabaos, cows, pigs, and *pinggan* (Chinese porcelain plates). **Residence.** After marriage, the young people may move to their own household or with one of the in-laws, depending on the bride-price and bride service arrangements. Post-marital residence is highly flexible, depending on what the groom owes his in-laws and on considerations for future cultivation plots. While neolocality is considered as the ideal both among the upland rice cultivators and the abaca cultivators in the foothills, this pattern represents only one possible phase of residential change. At least five residential cycles are possible:

(1) Marriage to permanent matrilocality, when a man's spouse is the last remaining unmarried offspring.

(2) Marriage to temporary matrilocality to neolocality, when an individual is unable to pay the bride-price and obligates himself to bride service.

(3) Marriage to temporary matrilocality to patrilocality, similar to (2), except that after bride

53

service is finished, the married couple return to the husband's parents' residence.

(4) Marriage to patrilocality, same as above but no required bride service.

(5) Marriage to neolocality.

SOCIOPOLITICAL ORGANIZATION. Political authority was vested in the headman (*bagani*). The requirements for becoming a *bagani* consisted of personal valor, fortitude, physical strength, and being the son of a former *bagani*, but above all a certain amount of charisma. Each *bagani*, before assuming the title, had to kill seven to nine men in battle and in surprise raids. *Bagani* succession among the Mandaya was semistructured on a genealogical basis, although one was required to fulfill the necessary prerequisites before assuming the title. Each *bagani* had his domain of political authority where his rule was law, but the sphere of influence was always in flux. The acquiring and possessing of suitable primary forest for a *bagani* following was important, thus borders gradually shifted; however the territory that a *bagani* controlled was recognized as the collective historical area of its inhabitants. The *bagani* were distinguished from other warriors and commoners by their clothing and turban-like headpieces. Although each *bagani* had autonomous rule, his behavior was curtailed by an advisory council (*angtutukay*), whose judgment and integrity were respected by commoners. The council was consulted by the *bagani* on the following matters:

(1) To review petitions from commoners concerning the desire to redress a wrong or take revenge against another outside the domain by means of warfare.

(2) The size and strength of a war party into another area for captives, valuables, or to acquire additional choice areas of forest.

(3) To hear, arbitrate, and settle all intradomain disputes arising from theft, adultery, violence, rape, murder, etc.

(4) To select a *bagani* successor among the sons of the *bagani*'s first wife if the present warrior chief was unable to rule or had passed away.

(5) To transmit the demands, needs, and grievances of commoners in a domain to their ruling *bagani*.

With the demise of the *bagani* complex in the middle 1920s, political leadership and authority have been circumscribed to smaller socioeconomic units. In the abaca areas, the *bagani* was replaced by the *tenyente*. Each *tenyente* of a barrio or sitio is chosen by the elders, and he acts as a nominal leader with very limited authority and power. Among the upland rice cultivators there is virtually no type of leadership beyond the family/household head. **Social differentiation.** Unlike the longhouses of Borneo or the elaborate *datu* dwellings of the Bagobo, the *bagani* quarters were not much larger than ordinary dwellings. The only diagnostic mark of the *bagani* settlement was the number of compartments, which were divided by split bamboo walls. Each apartment was the living quarters of a wife or concubine, ranging from nine to twelve women per warrior chief. *Bagani* settlements were usually in the center of the domain and in easy access to the commoners. Each *bagani* had his lands cultivated by slaves or labor service from his followers, who furnished subsistence needs for the *bagani* and his families. **Warfare.** In addition to the protection of individual rights, maintaining intraterritorial order, and carrying out intra- and interterritorial revenge raids, a *bagani* was also under pressure to acquire new areas of primary forest for exploitation by his followers. The encroachment on neighboring areas resulted in numerous skirmishes and thus in continuous feuding and warfare. If a petitioner's claims for vengeance were justified by the council of elders, or if a *bagani* desired to lead a raid, the warriors (*maniklad*) were called together. A commoner of extraordinary valor could become a *maniklad* by taking three lives. The average size of warrior forces was from 40 to 50. Individuals sought for crimes were killed, and their wife or wives, children, and property taken by the *bagani* to be divided up among his *maniklad*. *Bagani* were thought to be immune to death by killing, due to their possession of powerful charms (*anting-anting*).

RELIGION. The Mandaya religious structure centers on an elaborate hierarchy of spirits (*anito*) and a group of female shamans (*ballyan*), whose general function is the interpretation of the supernatural and how it relates to man and nature. Besides various creation legends and death spirits, the majority of Mandaya supernatural beliefs are related to some aspect of man's compromise with the environment. The *ballyan* influence is paramount in all matters pertaining to the religious side of life, as well as in maintaining the core of tribal custom and beliefs. Although *ballyan* political influence is nil, they have the power to interpret supernatural implications of a *bagani*'s action, and such an interpretation may produce negative effects. At present the Mandaya, especially those inhabiting the foothills and participating in a market economy, are in various degrees of religious conversion to Catholicism. But the pattern of religious change is one in which baptism to Catholicism means not only a rebirth of the soul but the opportunity to take part in the basic lowland Bisayan cultural pattern (cf. Yengoyan 1966a). **Supernaturals.** The major class of supernatural beings are spirits. Many of these, such as the *diwata* and the *asuang*, have been described by Cole (1913) and Benedict (1916).

Spirits are recognized as being of ultimate importance in insuring that crops succeed, and thus their role in everyday life is critical. In none of the spirit pantheon does one find witchcraft, for spirits are both benevolent and malevolent in action and never take the form of human beings. The Mandaya *asuang* is generically similar to the Hiligaynon *aswang* and the Bicol *asuwang;* however, in the latter two regions the *aswang* or *asuwang* implies the existence of witches, a phenomenon which is absent among the Mandaya. Lynch (1949: 401-27), citing Castaño, notes that *asuwang* beliefs in Bicol during the late sixteenth century were limited to spirits and not witches, but that presently they imply witchcraft. The attributing of witchcraft to the *asuwang* among lowland Christians may be the result of replacement of aboriginal beliefs with Western European folk beliefs during the era of Spanish missionizing, i.e. utilizing witchcraft as a means of social control by placing sanctions on various types of anti-Spanish behavior. **Practitioners.** As shaman, the *ballyan* acts as mediator with the spirit world, though certain *ballyan* are considered closer to certain spirits than others. At the time of planting, harvesting, birth, death, sickness, curing, calamities, etc., *ballyan* are requested to apply their special powers for a smooth transition through periods of crisis. Garvan (1931: 200-03) describes the Manobo *bailan* as a priest of either sex whose role is the interpretation of the *diwata* (spirits). The Mandaya *ballyan* is always a woman, since the predilection in becoming a *ballyan* is fit behavior only for females. Furthermore, to describe a *ballyan* as a priest is not justified, since the role does not involve a full-time participation with the supernatural, and, in fact, a *ballyan* must support herself in working in her spouse's *kaingin*. Most *ballyan* inherit their role by learning the practices, dances, and interpretations from a kinsman (i.e. mother, MoSi, FaSi), however, about one-fifth of those who attain *ballyan* status obtain it through birth or through "divine" inheritance without previous aspirations or premonitions. Others become *ballyan* at any time in their life cycles if they are struck by *tulanang,* a condition of violent physical trances and temporary mental disorders, which may last from a few hours to a week. Physically the state resembles an epileptic fit. Mentally, the individual talks and shouts in a disorganized, incoherent manner; however, in these vocal outbursts, other *ballyan* note which spirit is manifesting itself in the individual. When the convulsions end, the new *ballyan* is taught the dances and rituals from other shamans. After learning the rituals, the other *ballyan* consider her as the leading mediator of the spirit that possessed her. Thus the *ballyan* hierarchy consists of two groups: "divine" *ballyan,* by ascription, and *ballyan* who acquired the status through learning the rituals. Contrary to the custom among the Manobo, where the *ballyan* are not designated by distinctive apparel (Garvan 1931: 202), the Mandaya *ballyan* is clad in a dark red, maroon, and black abaca skirt and blouse.

Garvan (1931: 203) notes that the Manobo *bagani* is a war priest, whose main role is the sacrifice of captives in war. The Mandaya *bagani* appears not to have religious or supernatural functions and cannot be described as a warrior priest. Captives taken during headhunting raids were sacrificed by the *bagani,* but this behavior is not part of the supernatural, since sacrifice was primarily to avenge deaths. Although a *bagani* may be assisted by certain spirits, the primary aim in taking captives was not to fulfill the dictums of his supernatural guides.

BIBLIOGRAPHY. Benedict 1916; Cole 1913, 1945; Garvan 1931; Lynch 1949; Yengoyan 1964, 1965, 1966a, 1966b, 1966c, 1971.

AGUSAN MANOBO*

ORIENTATION. The extensive Agusan River system drains much of eastern Mindanao, between the central highlands and the Pacific Cordillera. Batuan Bay, together with the lower valley of the Agusan, for centuries provided a natural corridor into the interior for Spanish missionaries as well as for Christianized lowland Bisayans. The indigenous inhabitants, swidden farming pagans on the upper reaches of the Agusan and its many tributary streams, were, as elsewhere in Mindanao, referred to by these lowlanders as Manobo, a term connoting, variously, "hillman" or "unbaptized." It was these scattered hill Manobo settlements, particularly those on the upper Baobo, Simulao, Ihawan, etc., tributary streams of the upper Agusan in the region of the Agusan-Davao border, that were visited by John Garvan in 1905-10 and described by him in a well-documented monograph (Garvan 1931). In this upper Agusan area, Manobo intermeshed with Mandaya, Ata, Dibabaon (a mixed Manobo-Mandaya group on the Agusan-Davao border), and Mangguangan ("people of the forest," scattered settlements in the hills north of Compostela, markedly primitive with some Negrito characteristics, the prime target of slave raids by surrounding Manobo and Mandaya peoples). Contact with these and other groups to the west, including Banuaon (Bukidnon), is mentioned frequently by Garvan, and it is evident that the upper Agusan Manobo share many cultural similarities with Bagobo, Mandaya, and other southeastern Mindanao peoples.

Christianization of the Agusan began in earnest in

---

*This summary of traditional Agusan Manobo culture is taken entirely from *The Manobos of Mindanao,* by the gifted ethnographer, John M. Garvan. Garvan's manuscript notes, based on observations throughout the Agusan Valley during the years 1905-10, remained unpublished until 1931.

the late 1870s; it was well along by the first decade of the twentieth century and has continued to the present, along with the influx of Cebuano-speaking Bisayans. Relative to the Cotabato and Davao Gulf regions, however, the Agusan Valley is still sparsely populated (Wernstedt and Spencer 1967: 537ff.). The Manobo population, estimated at somewhat less than 40,000 by Beyer (1917: 55), has in all probability decreased with the merging of acculturated individuals into the predominant lowland population. Matildo (1953: 42), using figures derived from the 1948 Census, reports a total of 25,000 native Manobo speakers for Agusan Province. Matildo's survey of the Wawa-Ojot, Gibung, Umayan, and Simulao provincial subdivisions documents the effect of Christianity, government schooling, modern electoral procedures, and resettlement projects on the aboriginal culture. The old warrior chiefs have disappeared, along with their vital roles in the political and ceremonial life, and it is evident that the pagan, hill Manobo culture described by Garvan has all but disappeared from the modern scene.

SETTLEMENT PATTERN. Under ordinary, i.e. peaceful, conditions, people lived in "settlements" of one or more houses, each house containing from one to four nuclear families. Settlement size, which varied from as few as 20 to up to 200 persons, depended on the reputation of the local headman, many of whom combined the status of chief with that of *bagani*, renowned warrior. Houses appear to have been located near the fields, probably in a scattered hamlet or "neighborhood" pattern, although in time of warfare the people moved in close to the chief's house, where they constructed tree houses for defense.

ECONOMY. Subsistence based on swidden agriculture. Staples, in order of importance, were sweet potato, rice, taro, sago, and maize, supplemented by wild pig, deer, fish, birds, monkey, and python. Domesticated pigs and chickens were sacrificed and consumed at festivals. **Industrial arts.** Women wove hemp clothing and manufactured simple earthern pots, while men made canoes, baskets, and traps. Metal working appears to have been virtually unknown in Garvan's time. **Stimulants and bodily deformations.** Betel and fermented drinks (palm sap, sugarcane and honey) were widely used and had important social and ceremonial connotations. The liquor, set out in sacred jars for ritual use, was consumed from cups rather than through straws. Teeth were filed and blackened, both sexes tattooed, and adolescent males underwent supercision.

KINSHIP AND MARRIAGE. Inferentially bilateral. Cousin marriage theoretically proscribed, but possible by payment of ritual fines. The local settlement appears to have been agamous with respect to marriage.

Exchange of wealth (weapons, jars, pigs, slaves) was vitally important to the marriage contract and the subject of much negotiation. A period of bride service usually preceded the setting up of an independent household. Polygyny was allowed but in practice limited to wealthy chiefs.

SOCIOPOLITICAL ORGANIZATION. The region of the upper Agusan was in 1910 divided into mutually hostile domains or districts, dominated by warrior chiefs, *bagani*, noted for their bravery, generosity, skills in arbitration, and magic powers of invulnerability. [*Datu*, according to Garvan, was a lowland Bisayan term not used by hill Manobo.] The position was not hereditary, although eldest sons often succeeded their fathers. Authority was tempered by custom and the collective voice of older men. The inhabitants of a domain, living in scattered hamlets near the fields except in time of war, tended to be related to the warrior chief [probably through cognatic and affinal kin ties]. The territory of a domain was regarded as the collective ancestral property of this quasi-localized kin group, which constituted, as well, a ritual community in that "each settlement, as represented by its priests and shamans, has its own set of deities to whom they and their relatives have recourse" (Garvan 1931: 190). **Social differentiation.** Garvan mentions a "warrior class" and "slaves" [and, by inference, those in between, i.e. "commoners"]. However, Manobo society appears to have been markedly egalitarian in nature. The authority of the *bagani* chiefs rested mainly on demonstrated ability and personal charisma, although they were entitled to wear distinctive clothing and were generally wealthier in terms of wives and slaves than their compatriots. The *bagani* acted in the role of defender and avenger on behalf of his community, and as a trusted arbiter in disputes over property. With respect to the powerful spirits of blood and war, the *bagani* functioned as priest (Garvan 1931: 144ff.), and in fact one might speculate that a community was spiritually incomplete without a resident *bagani*. **Justice, vengeance, and property.** Preoccupation with vengeance, which Garvan names as the chief theme of Manobo life, seems to have been embedded in a culturally elaborated complex that included arbitration of disputes over property, in which warrior chiefs played an important role. Garvan's account of Manobo life conveys the impression of a virtual obsession with property and debts, particularly the evaluation of goods on occasions such as marriages, where, by protracted bargaining, each side sought to outmaneuver the other. Concepts of contract, loans, interest, and liability were apparently well developed, and all property, whether freely given or under contract, had eventually to be paid for. Debts could be inherited, and one function of a good arbitrator was the ability to manipulate genealogical reckonings and remembered debts to

56

the advantage of his client. Property transactions were mostly in terms of lives (blood debts), or in goods (slaves, cloth, jars, rice, pigs) having agreed-on equivalency values. It is not clear, however, whether goods actually changed hands on all occasions or whether financial transactions remained largely "on paper." Disputes were settled if possible by arbitration, a powerful incentive to this end being the ever-present threat of private blood vengeance and the possible involvement of relatives of the disputants. Public threats by an aggrieved party usually led to pressure by relatives to arbitrate, with both sides careful to appear indifferent to the outcome. Well-known warrior chiefs might be retained as arbitrators, meeting privately or in a public gathering to agree on payment of a fine by one or the other of the disputants. Such meetings, attended by crowds of relatives and friends, might last for days. Famous arbitrators displayed their powers of oratory, persuasion, and cunning in driving hard bargains on behalf of their respective clients, aided by the evidence of witnesses and recourse to oaths and ordeals. Should arbitration fail, a man was free to take private blood vengeance, in which case he might hire a neutral *bagani* to do this for him. Or, by recourse to *tawagan* ("seizure") he might, by public announcement, threaten to kill or seize the property of a neutral party—thus enlisting the aid of the threatened man's relatives against his original opponent. **Warfare.** As of 1910 the entire upper Agusan region was rife with inter-domain blood feuds, arising for the most part from disputes over violation of property rights. Raids were led by warriors, whose *bagani* status was enhanced according to the number of killings they could lay claim to. Although high-ranking *bagani* were expected to eat the hearts and livers of slain victims, heads were apparently not taken. Captives were, however, prized as potential slaves and/or human sacrifice. For this purpose the Manobo most often raided Mangguangan settlements; the Manobo, in turn, were preyed upon by Mandaya war parties.

RELIGION. **Supernaturals.** The higher deities, *umli*, dwelt in the upper heavens and were unconcerned with the affairs of men. Lesser gods, *diuata*, the deified spirits of legendary Manobo, interested themselves in earthly happenings by becoming familiars of the *bailan*, through whom they communicated their desires for the good things of earth, such as betel, and in addition advised on the problems and questions of mortals. Demons, *busau*, were hostile to man and a major cause of illness. The *tagbanua* were the spirit owners of forests and hills. *Tagbusau*, patron deities of violence and warfare, demanded blood; their propitiation was the sole prerogative of *bagani* warriors. Although Garvan makes no mention of animals as messengers of the gods, he does report frequent recourse to omen birds, as well as the prohibi-

tion of mocking behavior toward animals, sanctioned by the threat of petrifaction. Offerings to spirits of the recent dead were made at major ceremonies, but the dead were not invited to be present on such occasions. **Practitioners.** Man was thought to have two spirit companions, or "souls," one on either shoulder. Should one of these be devoured by demons, the other, grieving, would wander off to the spirit world, thus causing illness. It was the task of the *bailan* to recover the wandering soul by sending his own spirit familiar in quest of it. A person of either sex could become *bailan* by displaying an epileptic-like state, a sign that he or she had been entered by a spirit familiar. In the combined role of medium and shaman, *bailan* officiated at a variety of ceremonies, making offerings and, while in a trance state, divining illness, prophesying, and stating the desires of the spirits. **Ceremonies.** Ceremonies in connection with illness, agricultural pursuits, and death were most often conducted by *bailan*, although housefathers performed minor rituals on behalf of a household. Betel, liquor, food, and blood figured prominently in most offerings, although the deities were also fond of sweet-smelling substances, e.g. perfumes. Prophylactic fowl waving was common, as was the smearing of blood, usually that of a sacrificed pig. Ritual paraphernalia included palm fronds, sacrificial bowls, stands and racks, and crude wooden images representative of various deities. Garvan makes no mention of major, communitywide renewal festivals on the order of the all-important Bagobo *ginum*. The *bagani* chiefs did, however, officiate at bloody sacrifices to the powerful *tagbusau* spirits prior to setting out on military expeditions (Garvan 1931: 213). On these occasions, the *bagani* made food offerings and drank the blood of a sacrificed pig while in something resembling a trance state, said to be induced by spirit possession. These Manobo war rituals appear in some respects similar to parts of the Bagobo *ginum;* and Garvan's meager data on human sacrifice likewise recall Bagobo practices. In fact, Garvan is inclined to attribute human sacrifice to Bagobo and/or Mandaya influence (1931: 214). **Death.** A deceased person was buried beneath the ground in a wooden coffin on the day following death. The burial site was normally deep within the forest, although burial beneath the house occurred. In any event, the house was abandoned by the living. A mourning period of seven days was ideally terminated by a death feast, although a year might elapse before the family could accumulate the necessary food and drink for a major feast. Following the death feast the deceased had no more claims on the living. Funeral customs for chiefs apparently differed little from those of commoners, although Garvan did gather some evidence of more elaborate funerary practices formerly, including the use of boat coffins and jar burial—possibly in caves (1931: 126).

BIBLIOGRAPHY. Beyer 1917; Garvan 1931; Matildo 1953; Wernstedt and Spencer 1967.

COASTAL BAGOBO

ORIENTATION. Bagobo in a linguistic sense refers to a language group (Bagobo) within a larger family of languages (Manobo), which has its greatest degree of differentiation within the central Mindanao highlands (see under *Central Highlands*). Bagobo, in turn, according to Summer Institute of Linguistics surveys, appears to consist of at least three languages —Obo, Tagabawa, and Guiangan (Elkins et al. 1969-70). Laura Benedict and Fay-Cooper Cole, in 1906-10, used the term Bagobo in a tribal sense for pagan settlements in the hills east and south of Mount Apo, behind the Davao Gulf coast towns of Daliao, Santa Cruz, and Digos. This area appears on SIL maps as largely Tagabawa, a term not mentioned by either Benedict (1916) or Cole (1913), although the latter does remark that the "neighboring Obo and Guianga" are probably to be considered part of his Bagobo "tribe" (1913: 128). While terms such as Manobo and Bagobo have been adopted and applied in a precise sense by linguists, the term Bagobo as used by Cole and Benedict for the people they studied is of little help in fixing ethnic identity. The unit of identification for the people themselves appears to have been an upland valley or hill top, and the usual ethnonym "people of such and such a river valley" (e.g. Sibulan or Cibolan) or "such and such a hill top" (e.g. Talun). It is commonly the case in Southeast Asia that local groups of this kind more or less contiguous within a larger area recognize similarities in such things as language and dress and, in addition, subscribe to a ritual unity supported by legends of common origin— which may have been the case with the domains southeast of Mount Apo that made up the "Bagobo tribe" of Cole and Benedict. According to Cole (1913), the several domains, each with its *datu* or warrior-chief, recognized the political authority of the *datu* of Cibolan. A political hierarchy of this kind may, however, have been the result of Moro influence, although evidence on this point is inconclusive. The acquisition of a generic name such as Bagobo can be seen as the result of attempts by lowlanders and Westerners to label an ethnic reality which lacked a convenient tag in the form of a "tribal" ethnonym.

The culture described by Cole and Benedict has for all intents disappeared from the area in which they found it functioning in 1906-10. The further spread of Christianity, the introduction of a plantation economy, and resettlement among coastal Bisayans have all contributed to a fundamental cultural reorientation. Presently most Bagobo populations are scattered in the interior ranges beyond Davao City (see under *Upland Bagobo*), while those on the coastal plains have fully adapted to a lowland, Bisayan way of life. The *datu*, as the dominant political leader, is no longer operative, although descendants of former *datus* consciously claim relationship. In most areas, the scattered upland Bagobo populations are involved in market relationships with the coastal Bisayans. Abaca (hemp), corn, and upland rice are sold and exchanged for commercial items such as cloth, kerosene, and other household goods. At present most of the aboriginal Bagobo and Guianga groups are found to the northwest of Mount Apo and in eastern Cotabato.

SETTLEMENT PATTERN AND HOUSING. According to Cole (1913), the houses—gable-roofed, single-room, bamboo and thatch affairs raised on piles— were scattered on or near the swiddens. The house of the "local ruler" or *datu*, in some cases capable of accommodating several hundred people, constituted the ceremonial and defense center for a "district." Here, according to Cole, was a sleeping platform for warriors and illustrious guests, rooms for the *datu* and his wives, symbols of wealth such as gongs and old jars, hanging spirit altars, and decorated poles sacred to the patron deities of warfare. [In the mountain settlements studied by Benedict (1916), a separate ceremonial structure, the *dakul bale* ("big house"), was erected in the home village of the local ruler for celebration of the major festival, *ginum*.] By all accounts, a *datu* functioned as temporal and ecclesiastical head of a district—of what might be termed a ritual domain—consisting probably of scattered hamlets or neighborhoods in close proximity to the upland swiddens. The house or localized establishment of the *datu* then functioned as the focal point for the people—possibly interrelated by ties of kinship and marriage—within his domain. Benedict (1916: 186) states that the village was agamous with regard to marriage; she neglected, however, to obtain this kind of information for the "cluster of villages" (presumably the district or domain).

ECONOMY. Subsistence was primarily from upland rice, grown on swiddens. Supplementary crops included sweet potatoes, maize, bananas, sago, and coconut. Meat was obtained by hunting and fishing; domestic animals, including chickens (for sacrifice), water buffalo (for dragging loads and riding), and horses (for ritual fighting or racing?) were relatively little used as food. **Industrial arts.** The Bagobo were the "most extensively ornamented" people in the whole of the Philippine Archipelago (Beyer 1917: 38). Woven hemp cloth and items of clothing decorated with embroidery and beadwork were made by the women and were widely traded. Smithies, hidden from public sight among the fields, produced fine work in brass, bronze, and iron. Bagobo knives were famous, as were small bells cast by the lost wax process by melting down pieces of old bronze gongs of Chinese origin. **Trade and wealth.** Well-established trade with neighboring Bilaan, Tagakaolo, and Ata peoples. Hemp, knives, and bells were traded to the coast in return for beads, shell discs, and salt. Wealth was calculated in such things as rice, sugarcane liquor, gongs, jars, antique spears and swords, finely woven and decorated textiles, and girdles and arm and leg bands of brass and copper. These goods were likewise pleasing to the deities; thus textiles, brass girdles, etc. were offered or "dedicated" at major ceremonies such as *ginum*. Gongs, especially old ones, were named and highly valued, serving as a standard unit of barter in trading valuable objects and calculating large debts and marriage payments (Benedict 1916: 84). There is evidence in the literature of what was probably a well-developed pattern of financial manipulation involving the accumulation of ritual wealth to be displayed, consumed, or dedicated to the gods by participants in, or sponsors of, periodic religious festivals.

KINSHIP AND MARRIAGE. Cole (1913) mentions the [presumably bilateral] reckoning of kinship to the second degree of consanguinity, with marriage prohibited within this degree of relationship. The choice of a marriage partner was relatively free, and infant betrothal was lacking (Benedict 1916: 185). Parents customarily negotiated the marriage settlement, which consisted of a bride-price of bronze gongs [or of goods valued in units of gongs?], with a return gift by the girl's side equal to one-half the value of the bride-price. A boy usually spent a year or so in the home of the girl's parents, in what amounted to a period of trial marriage (Benedict 1916: 181). The establishment of a separate residence, and the marriage ceremony itself, were customarily deferred until the birth of the first child. Marriage rites, including the exchange of wealth between the families of the bride and groom, were presided over by an older woman in the role of priestess. They included the application of lustral water to the heads and joints of the young couple, the drinking of sacred sugarcane liquor, and, formerly, in the case of noted or wealthy families, the sacrifice of a slave. Polygyny was permitted but in practice limited to men of wealth, i.e. the *datus*.

SOCIOPOLITICAL ORGANIZATION. **Political Organization.** The "Bagobo tribe," as described by Cole and Benedict, appears to have consisted of a number of districts and domains, each with a *datu* ("man of renown") as its temporal and ecclesiastical head. His large house and surrounding entourage constituted a focal point on occasions of major ceremonies, and, according to Cole (1913), his followers maintained his house and fields, in return for which he supported a body of warriors for the common defense. In addi-

tion, he adjudicated disputes in concert with a council of older men, with authority to impose fines, enslavement, or the death penalty. According to Cole, the position was hereditary, with an eldest son favored to succeed his father. The same source mentions a "Chief of all the Bagobo" with his seat at Cibolan, south of Mt. Apo; it is unclear, however, whether this position was indigenous, the result of Moro influence, or possibly a political position created by the American administration, building on the probable ritual priority of Cibolan in the indigenous culture. The role, if any, of kinship in the definition of domains is unknown. They did, however, function as ritual units, and "tribal" identity was, in fact, defined in terms of those qualified or allowed to participate in the most sacred parts of the *ginum* festivals (Benedict 1916: 150). **Social differentiation.** Cole and Benedict discuss Bagobo society in terms of *datus*, commoners and slaves, the latter prisoners of war or those unable to pay their debts. The *datus* (from Malay, *dato'*, head of family, elder, grandfather, chief) were "men of renown," who, possibly as a result of coastal Moro influence, appear to have achieved a considerable degree of juridical and political power within limited domains. The institution of "men of renown," associated with what might be termed ritual domains, appears, however, to be rooted in older ideas widely diffused throughout insular Southeast Asia, having to do with the spiritual welfare of the local (probably kin-based) community. It is likely that the *datu* complex, as observed by Benedict and Cole in 1910, was historically related to the institution of *magani* or *bagani* ("brave men," "warriors")—a status of considerable prestige achieved by the taking of human life under culturally prescribed conditions, with the individual entitled to wear special headgear and other accouterments graded according to the number of persons killed. *Magani* were under the protection of powerful deities of violence and bloodshed; only they could eat the sacred omen bird, *limoken;* and only they were allowed to participate in certain critical stages of the important *ginum* ceremony (Benedict 1916: 241). The head *datus* mentioned by Cole and Benedict appear to have been also high-ranking *magani*, i.e. men who had taken many lives and thus men of great bravery (also "potent," "renowned"). With regard to their secular roles, they might be termed "warrior-chiefs," while with regard to their ecclesiastical roles during *ginum*, they might best be termed "warrior-priests." Although "any man of wealth" was entitled to sponsor the all-important *ginum* ceremony, in practice it was "most often conducted in the home village of a head *datu* who presides over a group of rancherias" (Benedict 1916: 94-95). The sponsor of *ginum* was granted supernatural assurance of prosperity and increase in wealth, as were all participants "who make gifts to the gods in the prescribed manner" (Benedict 1916: 94-95).

Although the literature is unclear on this point, it appears that much of the dynamic of Bagobo culture may have been provided by a pattern of accumulation of ritual wealth through financial manipulation; the display and ritual dedication of such wealth at periodic festivals sponsored by individuals and their families; and the fact that sponsorship of such festivals not only brought prestige and spiritual rewards to the sponsor but also benefited, through religious renewal and spiritual cleansing, the entire community. **Warfare.** Feuding and open hostilities were evidently endemic, both among Bagobo groups and with neighboring Bilaan, Ata, and Tagakaola (Cole 1913). Noted *magani* warriors undertook killing expeditions alone, under commission from a *datu,* or as leaders of parties sent out to avenge the death of a member of the community. In addition to the renown to be gained by killing, the capture of prisoners of war (to be used or sold as slaves or human sacrifice) was a motivating factor. Heads, hands, and scalps were occasionally taken as trophies, and Benedict (1916: 158ff.) suspects that headhunting was at one time a necessary part of the *ginum* ceremony. [*Magani* participated in the ritual eating of the liver of a slain enemy.] Spears, knives, and shields were used as were protective wrappings of hemp cloth, and, formerly, buffalo hide and rattan armor.

RELIGION. Benedict comments on the highly sacrificial nature of Bagobo ceremonial, in which bloody sacrifice was blended with offerings of food and manufactured goods. The dead were not present at major ceremonies and in fact were encouraged to stay away; it thus appears that ancestral spirits lacked the vital role in affairs of the living characteristic of many Indonesian societies—unless the many named protective and patron gods can be regarded as deified ancestral spirits, a point which is unclear in the literature. **Supernaturals.** The general term for gods was *diwata.* Benedict (1916) divided the world of supernaturals into: (1) A pantheon of myth gods, dwelling in nine heavens, and of little concern to man. (2) Various named divine beings, closely associated with man's interests, e.g. nature deities, war gods, and protectors of home, field, and industries such as smithing and weaving. These included a creator god, Pamulak Manobo; a god of thunder, Kilat, who punished those who mocked animals by breaking their necks; and Tigyama, guardian of the home. An embodiment of goodness and purity, Malaki t'Olu k'Waig, was the beloved culture hero and great healer. To Mandarangan, a class of war gods and protective spirits of warriors, many of the rites of the *ginum* were directed, as also to Tolus ka Balekat, associated with healing and detection of disease-causing spirits. (3) A host of evil spirits or demons, *buso,* the cause of illness and misfortune and the subject of numerous propitiatory and exorcistic rites. According to Benedict, the term *anito* referred to any of the deities in the aspect of communicating directly with mortals through the oracles of mediums, although Cole adds that the spirits could communicate their desires to man through calls of omen birds, particularly a kind of dove, *limoken.* **Practitioners.** There was no full-time priesthood, and the roles of those who did function as religious practitioners were flexible. Benedict (1916) classifies religious functionaries to include: (1) the *datu,* in his role as master of ceremonies and chief officiant at major ceremonies such as *ginum* (2) the *magani* ("brave men" or warriors), who alone cut the sacred bamboo poles and who alone approached the poles during the most awesome portions of the *ginum* ceremony (3) priest-doctors, usually old women, skilled in herbal and magical curing, who also officiated at séances, where the divinities spoke to the people through mediums, and as priestesses at marriage and harvest ceremonies (4) mediums, *mabalian,* usually older women, through whom messages from the divinities were received. The *mabalian* appear to have gone into a trance state, during which time they had to be in total darkness, i.e. invisible to those in the audience. Mediums also functioned as priestesses during portions of the *ginum* ceremony. **Ceremonies.** The major ceremony was the *ginum* (*ginEm*) festival, an occasion for community renewal, general welfare, health, and thanksgiving. According to Benedict, it could be sponsored by any wealthy man, but in practice was conducted by a head *datu,* in his home village, on behalf, apparently, of all the hamlets or neighborhoods within the domain of which he was ritual and temporal leader. It was not given in the same village more than once every year or so, although a *ginum* was likely to occur somewhere in Bagoboland once every few months (Benedict 1916: 94-95). The three- or four-day ceremony included the sacrifice of a slave (or a substitute in the form of a chicken); the drinking of sacred sugarcane liquor; ritual bathing and anointing with lustral water to expel disease; the ritual dedication of fine woven and embroidered garments, brass ornaments, and antique weapons to gain increased wealth; and antiphonal chanting of tales of the mythical ancestors. The central liturgies and most important sacrifices were made by the *datu,* assisted (in the cases recorded by Benedict) chiefly by his son and wife, the latter in the combined roles of priestess, medium, and director of women's activities. When not actively engaged as an officiant, the *datu* (or sponsor) sat on a raised ceremonial seat, *dega-dega.* The focal point of *ginum* was a hanging altar fronted by two upright shaved and decorated bamboo poles within the *dakul bale* ("big house"), the ceremonial structure or temple erected expressly for the purpose. The procuring of the poles and their erection in the *dakul bale* by young, specially chosen *magani,* the ensuing sharing of sacrificial food and drink by all *magani,* together with the recounting of military prowess while grasping the bamboo poles and the generally high level of emotional affect throughout this portion of the ceremony led Benedict to conclude that it was formerly associated with headhunting and/or human sacrifice (Benedict 1916: 158ff.). The account by Cole (1913) of *ginum*, which generally agrees with that of Benedict, states that the festival was held during the period following harvest, coinciding with the appearance of the constellation, Balatik. It was in former times preceded by a headhunt, the trophies of which were hung on specially decorated poles during the ceremony. As of 1910, the Bagobo sacrificed a chicken, the blood of which was sprinkled on the decorated poles—evidence, in Cole's view, of former human sacrifice. According to Cole's informants, a human sacrifice was formerly required at least once a year, to thank the gods for abundant crops and good health; this could and frequently did coincide with *ginum*, but was not a necessary accompaniment. The sacrifice of a slave (e.g. a Bilaan, captured or purchased) was also required of a family following the death of one of its members. **Soul, death, and afterlife.** Benedict reports belief in a left-hand (evil) and right-hand (good) soul, the adventures of the former while absent from the body being a cause of illness. At death, the left-hand soul became a *buso* (evil spirit, demon), while the good soul went to a Land of the Dead in the underworld, there to lead a life much as it did on earth. Before finally "crossing over," it had to undergo ritual bathing in a mythical River of the Dead. A watch was kept by relatives for one or two nights after death, after which the corpse was buried. Chiefs were formerly buried in wooden coffins decorated with carved crocodile heads, while the bodies of commoners were simply wrapped in mats for burial. According to a longstanding custom, burial was normally beneath the house; alternatively the dead body was left in the house, which was then abandoned. According to Cole (1913), the family remained in mourning until the death taboos could be lifted by performance of a human sacrifice. Families unable to bear the full cost of a slave normally purchased a share in the annual human sacrifice that coincided with *ginum*.

BIBLIOGRAPHY. Benedict 1913, 1916; Beyer 1917; Cole 1913; Elkins et al. 1969-70; Raats 1969.

BILAAN*

Synonyms. *Balud, Baraan, Biraan, Bilanes, Blann, Buluan, Buluanes, Tagalagad, Takogan, Tumanao, Vilanes*

*This outline of Bilaan culture was prepared by the editor, utilizing the earlier work of Cole (1913), together with a summary statement of modern conditions among the Bilaan contributed by Aram A. Yengoyan and based on his fieldwork in the Davao Gulf area in 1960-65.

ORIENTATION. **Location.** Prior to American occupation, the Bilaan occupied the hills behind the west coast of Davao Gulf, extending north to Bagobo territory and west into the Davao-Cotabato watershed. Although Cole's (1913: 129-48) account notes a population of 10,000, the Bilaan now probably number close to 25,000, making them one of the largest groups in southeastern Mindanao. Their present distribution ranges from the Davao towns of Sulop, Hagonoy, Malita, Malalag, Matanao, and Jose Abad Santos, west to Lake Buluan and Allah, south to Dadiangas and Kiamba, and north to Kabacan and Midsayap. Only in very recent times have they migrated to the coastal areas. In Davao, most Bilaan still reside in the interior, while the Kulaman, Tagakaolo, and Bisayans inhabit the coastal plains and foothills. In Cotabato, the Bilaan are flanked by the Magindanao Moro, Sangil (Sangir), and Tagabili to the west and south. **Linguistic affiliation.** Bilaan, together with Tagabili and Tiruray, are classed by Conklin (1955c) as Southern Philippine languages, distinct from his Central Philippines group, which encompasses the remaining languages of Mindanao. This distinctiveness of Bilaan-Tagabili-Tiruray vis-à-vis the other Mindanao languages is also noted by Thomas and Healey (1962) and by Dyen (1965). Despite their linguistic position, Cole was able to state with some confidence that the Bilaan were culturally quite similar to their Bagobo neighbors to the north (Cole 1913: 148).

SETTLEMENT PATTERN AND ECONOMY. In 1910, houses stood adjacent to swiddens (*kaingin*), dispersed but in sight of one another. This dispersed pattern still holds for upland Bilaan in the interior, where the house type is similar to that among Mandaya (except that the houses of the *datus* tend to be larger—up to five rooms, with scattered huts within the compound for laborers). Sugarcane, bananas, and root crops are grown in kitchen gardens, while rice, maize, and millet (*dawa*) are cultivated in the *kaingin*. Maize, usually harvested twice yearly, is replacing rice as the staple food. Fishing and hunting provide important supplements to the diet. Domestic livestock, such as chickens, pigs, and dogs, are universal, while a horse or cow is commonly owned by the *datu*.

SOCIOPOLITICAL ORGANIZATION. Each upland river valley or highland plain was the district or domain of a ruling *datu*, a position which Cole says was hereditary and by primogeniture. The *datu* was both judge and defender vis-à-vis his followers, who in turn worked his fields. A wealthy *datu* could have as many wives as he could secure, either by capture or purchase. The status of "renowned warrior," *lebe*, appears to have been similar to that of the Bagobo *magani*. Warrior parties went on avenging raids seeking to kill and gain *lebe* status; they also took captives as slaves and/or for human sacrifice. Nowadays *lebe* are no longer found, according to the *datu* of Molmol, who claims that they went out of existence early in the American period. Each *datu* is the autonomous chief over an area as far as his personal influence will reach, having authority to conscript labor for agricultural needs as well as administering justice and conducting negotiations with other *datus*. On his death, he is succeeded by the eldest son of his first wife, with the approval of the elders. Bilateral emphasis, single nuclear households, and the extension of sibling terminology over generational collaterals are characteristic of contemporary Molmol Bilaan.

RELIGION. Categories of Bilaan supernaturals, as described by Cole (1913), parallel those of the Bagobo, although specific names differ in many instances. The patron deities of warriors appear to have been identical in both societies. A class of *almo-os*, consisting of older women, functioned as combined priestesses-shamans-mediums in a manner similar to *mabalian* among the Bagobo. Although human sacrifice occurred at the death of a great chief, Cole makes no mention of this practice, nor of headhunting, in connection with anything like the major recurrent renewal festivals (*ginum*) of the Bagobo. The method of performing the sacrifice was, however, very similar in both tribes.

BIBLIOGRAPHY. Cole 1913; Conklin 1955c; Dyen 1965; Thomas and Healey 1962.

TAGAKAOLO*

Synonyms. *Calaganes, Kalagan, Kagan, Laoc, Saka*

ORIENTATION. According to Cole (1913: 159), *tagakaolo* means "those who dwell at the head of the river," a name applied to an estimated 6,000 hill tribesmen in the intermediate area between the western Davao Gulf coast (largely occupied by Kulaman and Moro groups) and the interior uplands (Bilaan territory). At present they are found in the coastal towns of Malita and Lais, employed as plantation labor, although aboriginal Tagakaolo still reside in the interior—on the upper tributaries of the Malita, Lais, and Talaguton rivers. Cole (1913: 158) reported a "degraded division" of Tagakaolo, called Laoc, in the Haguimitan Mountains of San Agustin Peninsula, on the east side of the Gulf. A survey of the Haguimitan area in 1961, however, found the region inhabited by Mandaya, with little or no evidence of a former Tagakaolo population. Tagakaolo, together with most

other languages of Mindanao, is classed by Conklin (1955c) within his Central Philippines language group. The aboriginal culture pattern was apparently similar to that of Kulaman and Bilaan with respect to the special status of warriors and its association with patron deities and human sacrifice. Swidden agriculture is still practiced nowadays in the interior, but corn has supplanted rice as the major staple. With the harvesting of corn two or three times per year, the settlement pattern among the upland Tagakaolo is more clustered than in regions where a single rice crop is grown. Most upland settlements are composed of from eight to ten households in close proximity. Metalwork comes from the Moro or the Mandaya—still recognized as the best metalworkers in Davao. Trade objects are obtained directly from itinerant Muslim merchants.

BIBLIOGRAPHY. Cole 1913; Conklin 1955c.

KULAMAN*

Synonyms. *Culaman, Culamanes, Manobo, Sarangani Manobo*

ORIENTATION. Cole located the Kulaman along the Davao Gulf coast and adjacent foothills of the Sarangani Peninsula, extending north as far as the Padada River, just south of Digos. A few had migrated, in post-Spanish times, to the eastern side of the Gulf, along the coast of San Agustin Peninsula (Cole 1913: 149). They are now, however, less widespread; surveys carried out in 1962 found Kulaman most numerous in the coastal barrios in the southern half of the municipality of Jose Abad Santos and on adjacent Sarangani Island. Earlier estimates placed the total of Kulaman at around 3,500, but they now number over 6,000. Although they are referred to by coastal Bisayans as Manobo, they do not consider themselves related to other so-called Manobo. Kulaman is, however, classed (as Sarangani Manobo) among the Manobo family of languages by linguists of the Summer Institute of Linguistics (Elkins et al. 1969-70). In earlier times, they were probably a more sea-oriented people, but the acceptance of a sedentary existence was forced on them by the Moros, who controlled the Davao Gulf during the latter half of the nineteenth century. According to Cole (1913), intercourse with Moros favored the development of a hierarchy of ruling *datus*, with the result that the Kulaman were able for a time to claim tribute from

---

*The data for this entry were contributed by Aram A. Yengoyan, based on fieldwork in the Davao Gulf area in 1960-65. A few additional notes from Cole (1913) have been added by the editor.

*The data for this entry were contributed by Aram A. Yengoyan, based on fieldwork in the Davao Gulf area in 1960-65. Additional notes from Cole (1913), together with a statement on the linguistic position of Kulaman, have been added by the editor.

upland groups such as Tagakaolo. Kulaman culture appears to have been similar to that of Bilaan and Bagobo with respect to the special status accorded warriors, including human sacrifice to the patron deities of bloodshed and war, and raids to obtain captives for sacrifice and/or as slaves were formerly common (Cole 1913). The Kulaman around Caburan, in the southern Sarangani Peninsula, are now sedentary, living in small barrios and farming coconuts, corn, and abaca, along with fishing in the shallow bays. Rice was abandoned in the early post-World War II period and has been supplanted by increasing abaca cultivation. Bisayan and Kulaman populations live side by side and have intermarried in many areas. In comparison with other tribal groups, intermarriage between Kulaman and Americans or Spaniards is relatively frequent, and has provided the basis for the wealthy families in Caburan. Aboriginal religious and ceremonial practices are no longer present, since most Kulaman have converted to Christianity.

BIBLIOGRAPHY. Cole 1913; Elkins et al. 1969-70.

A T A*

Synonyms. *Atag, Dugbatang, Dugbatung, Tugauanum*

ORIENTATION. Ata is classed as a member of the Manobo family of languages by linguists of the Summer Institute of Linguistics (Elkins et al. 1969-70). Ata (Atag) speakers are found nowadays primarily in northwestern Davao Province, on the upper reaches of the Lasang (Lasan) and Libuganon rivers (Mapula, Palma Gil, Asuncion, Kapalong and Santo Tomas), although they extend across provincial boundaries into parts of southeastern Bukidnon and southwestern Agusan. The dominant economic activity is still swidden cultivation of rice and tubers, with corn now becoming popular. In 1961, the Ata around the Kapalong, Maguinon, and Kapugi, tributaries of the upper Libuganon, were producing a surplus rice harvest, which is presently quite rare. Any food surplus

---

*The data for this entry were contributed by Aram A. Yengoyan, based on fieldwork in the Davao Gulf area in 1960-65. Additional notes from Cole (1913) and Garvan (1931), together with a statement on the linguistic position of Ata, have been added by the editor.

is traded to the lowland Christians for clothing, bolos, knives, and canned fish. Hunting and fishing occupy most important roles among the Ata, and of all of the Davao groups, their aboriginal subsistence patterns are the least unchanged. Wild pigs, monkeys, and reptiles are taken with the use of bows and arrows, spears, and wicker traps. Fish are caught by the damming and draining of creeks or with bamboo fish traps. Beyond the nuclear family household, the political coordination and leadership found among the Bagobo and Mandaya is absent among the Ata. Polygynous family households are also absent. The exchange of material goods as part of the bride-price is usually absent, since objects of value are very scarce. Ata material culture, except for simple subsistence tools, is noted for its paucity. The elaborate abaca weaving and silversmithing found among other Davao groups is also totally absent. Western-style clothing is worn and obtained through trade. Although Ata as a dialect remains as a household and interhousehold language, Cebuano-Bisayan is used as a lingua franca in interacting with the Bisayans.

Cole (1913: 162ff.) located the people whom he called Ata in a broad area stretching from the Libuganon and Lasang (where they were known as Dugbatang or Dugbatung; also Tugauanum) to the headwaters of the Davao and Pulangi rivers, north and west of Mount Apo. Garvan (1931: 5), quoting older Spanish sources to the effect that *ata* was a Bisayan term applied in southern Mindanao to Negritos in the interior northwest of the Davao Gulf, implied the use of the term in a generic sense for dispersed groups of mixed Negrito-Manobo ancestry. Garvan further cautioned against confusion of the term Ata in the above sense, and Atas (Hataas, Ataas), meaning "high" or "those who dwell on the heights," referring to a people of advanced culture located by older Spanish sources on the northwestern slopes of Mount Apo. It is evident, as implied by Cole, that the term Ata has been used in a variety of meanings, and that groups referred to by that name may differ culturally. Thus Ata-speakers in the Lasang River area show strong Bagobo influence and, in other than a linguistic sense, might be classed as Bagobo; on the other hand, Ata-speakers on the upper tributaries of the Libuganon evidence few Bagobo cultural traits (Elkins et al. 1969-70).

BIBLIOGRAPHY. Cole 1913; Elkins et al. 1969-70; Garvan 1931.

PALAWAN*

PALAWAN IS THE fifth largest and the westernmost of the major islands of the Philippines, and, as such, comprises nearly 80 percent of the land area of modern Palawan Province. The mountainous, coral-fringed, main island constitutes a partial land bridge between the Sunda Shelf and the Philippine Archipelago. The considerable antiquity of human occupation of this region is demonstrated by recent excavations at Tabon Cave on the southwestern coast of Palawan (Fox 1967). The principal island groups associated with the main island are (1) the Calamian islands to the north between Palawan and Mindoro (2) the Dumaron-Cuyo group off the northeastern coast, and (3) the Balabac-Bugsuk group off the southern coast. Most of Palawan is densely forested, and its total area of 4,550 square miles is the most sparsely populated of the larger islands of the Philippines. Fox (1954) estimated the 1950 population at around 60,000, with roughly equal proportions of Christians, Muslims, and pagans. At the time of first Spanish contact, the indigenous population of Palawan (Paragua) and its outlying islands probably consisted of: Tagbanuwa (Tagbanua, Tagbanwa, Tagbanoua); Batak (Batac); Palawan (Palawano, Paluanes, Palawanin, Palaweño); Kenoy (Queney, Kanay, Kenne, Kenei); Moro or Molbog (Muslims, including the Melebuganon on Balabac Island); Kalamian (Calamian); Agutayano (Agutaynon); Kuyono (Kuyonon, Cuyono); and Kagayano (Cagayano). All of these groups, with the probable exception of the Batak, are basic Malayan in physical type. The Tagbanuwa are located in central and northern Palawan. The Batak are found in scattered areas north of Puerto Princesa in northeastern Palawan, chiefly in the interior regions of Babuyan, Tanabog, and Tinitian. The Palawan are located in southern Palawan, mainly in interior regions south of Apurauan on the west coast and south of Aboabo on the east coast. A few Palawan are distributed among the Moro groups in the Balabac-

Bugsuk islands. The Kenoy are deep in the interior of southern Palawan (Conklin 1949a: 272), occupying an inaccessible mountainous area northwest of Brooke's Point. Moro or Molbog groups are found on Balabac and adjacent islands, on the east coast of Palawan as far north as Panakan, and on the west coast as far north as Alfonso XIII. Kalamian peoples originally occupied Coron Island and coastal settlements on Busuanga Island and adjacent smaller islands. The Kalamian are closely related linguistically to the Tagbanuwa. The Agutayano (on Agutaya Island of the Cuyo group), the Kuyono (on Cuyo Island), and the Kagayano (on Cagayan Island) presently show no vestiges of their aboriginal culture. [See also elsewhere in this volume under *Jama Mapun*, the Samal-speaking inhabitants of Cagayan Sulu.] Anthropological field studies are available on only two of these groups, the Tagbanuwa (Fox 1954) and the Batak (Warren 1964). In addition, much has been written on the ancient Indic script of Palawan and neighboring regions of the Philippines (cf. Conklin 1949a; Francisco 1966; Gardner and Maliwanag 1939-41).

BIBLIOGRAPHY. Conklin 1949a; Fox 1954, 1967; Francisco 1966; Gardner and Maliwanag 1939-41; Warren 1964.

TAGBANUWA*

Synonyms. *Tagbanwa, Tagbanua, Tagbanoua*

ORIENTATION. **Identification.** Shifting cultivators of generalized Malayan physical type. Fox (1954) has described the Tagbanuwa (from *tiga* or *taga banuwa*, "people of the village") as a sophisticated pagan group, organized into relatively autonomous villages. They practice matrilocal residence, the social structure is bilateral and stratified, the society is extremely ritually oriented, and the cult of the dead forms the

---

*Contributed by Charles P. Warren.

*Contributed by Charles P. Warren, based on Fox (1954). Some additional notes, taken from the same source, have been added by the editor.

nucleus of their religious practices. Much of Tagbanuwa culture is of general pan-Malayan type, with numerous specific resemblances to North Borneo. Political and juridical institutions, however, show considerable evidence of Muslim (Philippine Moro) influence. **Location.** The central regions of Palawan Island, midway between Mindoro in the Philippines and the Sabah coast of northern Borneo. Primarily coastal, or near-coastal, riverine dwellers. Prior to 1910, there existed a few mountain villages, but these were apparently formed during the eighteenth century. The central Tagbanuwa appear traditionally to have occupied the area between Puerto Princesa and Panakan on the east coast and between Napsaan and Birung on the west coast. It is probable that the settlements north of Napsaan were formed recently. **Geography.** Mountains averaging 2,500 to 3,000 feet divide the island into two narrow watersheds, one of which drains to the east into the Sulu Sea and the other to the west into the China Sea. The greatest concentration of people, including the Tagbanuwa, is on the eastern side of the island, where there are more extensive lowlands. The climate is tropical, the soils fertile, and the tropical vegetation heavy. **Linguistic affiliation.** Malayo-Polynesian. A member of the Central Philippine language group (Dyen 1965; Conklin 1952). There are two subdialects, Tangdulanen and Silanganen. The Tagbanuwa are one of the three groups in the Philippines who still employ an ancient syllabic script of Indic origin (Conklin 1949a). **Demography.** Approximately 7,000 (Fox 1954: 21). **History and cultural relations.** There is some evidence of early Hindu influence via Brunei. Moro traders and petty *datus,* chiefly of Tausug (Jolo) origin, dominated the island throughout all but the last few years of the Spanish period. Intensive contact with Spanish culture did not occur until Puerto Princesa was established as the politico-military capital in 1872. American, and later Filipino, influence began about 1904, when a penal colony was established at Iwahig. Despite these influences, Tagbanuwa culture has remained largely intact and, in particular with respect to religious practices, has undergone only superficial acculturation. Indigenous traits such as ear plugs, teeth blackening and filing, copper and brass wire anklets, blowpipes, and bark cloth have, however, virtually disappeared from the modern scene.

SETTLEMENT PATTERN AND HOUSING. **Settlement pattern.** Relatively compact villages of from 45 to 500 persons, the median size being around 150. Large villages may be divided into subresidential areas, often formed by a group of matrilineal siblings and their families. Villages are defined on the ground by a rule of matrilocal residence and by village rituals in which each family must participate. **Housing.** Rectangular, raised on piles five or six feet above the ground. Floor, sides, and roof are of bamboo, rattan, and palm fronds in various combinations, and the roof is gabled.

ECONOMY. Primarily shifting cultivators of dry rice. Some cash income from the sale of forest products. **Agriculture.** Rice (*paray*) is considered a divine gift, the perfect food. It yields, moreover, the ritually important rice wine (*tabad*), the perfect drink. Rice is intercropped with corn, millet, and minor food plants such as sweet potato, cassava, and taro. Vegetables are planted near the dwellings in house-lot gardens. **Fishing and hunting.** Fishing techniques include pole and line or hand lines; shrimping by hand or with a small jig; poisoning; drying and damming streams for placement of weirs; night fishing with torches. The recent introduction of fishing guns has supplanted many of these methods. Wild pigs are hunted with spears and dogs. **Domestic animals.** Nowadays many water buffalo, as well as a few cattle. The primary use of the former is for hauling sled loads of gum (see under *Trade*). Both buffalo and cattle are ridden. Although the Tagbanuwa are familiar with the native plow used by neighboring Christians, they do not and will not employ this implement. Despite a marked interest in water buffalo, it is unlikely that these animals were known prior to the present century. **Industrial arts.** Some smiths still use the old "Malay forge" to make spears, knives, writing implements, and branding irons. **Trade.** Palawan is one of the primary sources of "Manila copal," and the Tagbanuwa are the only gatherers in the central regions of the island. The gum is obtained in the mountains from the bark of a tree belonging to the Pine family (*Agathis philippinensis* Warb). The sale of gum, split rattan, and local rice provides a major source of income for the Tagbanuwa. Forest hives yield honey and edible young bees, as well as the ritually important wax, formerly a basic item of external trade. Moros still trade in the Aborlan area, but not directly with the Tagbanuwa. Gongs, betel boxes, and stoneware are consigned by the Moros to Christian and Chinese storekeepers, and the Tagbanuwa buy them from the latter. **Property.** Few things are owned by the Tagbanuwa, the most valuable being the Chinese jars that are important in ritual activities. Brass betel boxes, gongs, trays, knives, and spears are other items of property.

KIN GROUPS. **Descent.** Bilateral. **Kin groups.** The network of consanguineal relationship includes all descendants of Ego's eight great-grandparents; hence, blood relationship extends laterally to include third cousins. Theoretically, marriage should not take place within this extended kinship group, the bilateral family. The bilateral pattern is in practice distorted by a lineal emphasis, whereby individuals tend to think of themselves as descendants of a single prominent ancestor or of a particular patrilateral or matrilateral kindred. These factors necessitate a distinction between the bilateral family and the bilateral kindred. The former includes consanguineal kin as defined by the rule of incest and those who normally interact in everyday life. The latter group includes additional individuals who are regarded under specific circumstances as kinsmen but who are not actually members of the bilateral family. **Kin terminology.** The kinship system, terminologically and behaviorally, is generational:

GrPa	apu
Fa	ama
Mo	ina
FaSi, MoSi	minan
FaBr, MoBr	amayan
Sib	sulsug
ElSib	aka
YoSib	ari
Cousin	tagsa
Ch	anak
Nephew, niece	kamanakon
GrCh	apu

Residential groups and most other associations are built around sibling relationships; economic, juridical, and political activities all reflect sibling solidarity. Affinal ties are tenuous, and a variety of social mechanisms attempt to stabilize these relationships. Custom law demands that formal respect be shown affines at all times, even during drinking orgies. Affinal kin older than the speaker may only be addressed by the appropriate kinship term, and affinal relatives assume a dominant and often critical attitude toward sons-in-law, facilitated by the rule of matrilocal residence.

MARRIAGE AND FAMILY. **Mode.** Aristocratic families formerly arranged marriages, often between cousins, for political and economic gain. A payment in goods by the boy's family formalized the contract. Nowadays payment of a "bride fee" in money constitutes the marriage ceremony. **Form.** Polygynous marriages (preferably sororal) are favored, but in practice are rare and limited to the wealthy. **Marriage rules.** All members of Ego's bilateral family are taboo as marriage partners. **Residence.** If the couple come from different villages, residence is initially in the household of the girl's parents until the couple build their own dwelling. This is characteristically in the maternal residential area of the village —always, if the girl's parents insist upon it. The Tagbanuwa are ever-fearful of *ratyun*, or "poison," and it is always other villagers, particularly the more distant ones, who are the "poisoners." Consequently, the rule of matrilocal residence could create a hazardous situation for the in-marrying male from another village. Matrilocal residence works, however, because most marriages are actually village endogamous, and most villages are large enough to support this arrangement. **Domestic unit.** The affinal

relationship is tenuous until a child is born. The birth of a child formalizes the two-generational elementary family (father-mother-child) and activates the four-generational bilateral family, the exogamic unit. The elementary family is the basic social, economic, and household unit, and the cult of the dead is centered here. The elementary family and the sibling group are the only social units that show corporate features. **Inheritance.** Ideally, children, regardless of sex, share equally. This pattern is somewhat modified by the tendency in some families toward primogeniture and by the system in which priority is established by ritual needs. Jars used by a female medium must, if possible, pass to a female medium. If the bilateral kindred does not have succeeding *babalyan*, the jars will normally be held jointly by the sibling unit or, if possible, divided among the siblings and ultimately passed to their respective children. Jars and other ritual objects are almost never sold, for they are constantly needed in the rituals associated with the family-oriented cult of the dead. Families take great pride in and derive prestige from the ownership of heirlooms. These objects are now rare, jars having been used in the past for secondary burials, and the bowls and plates for grave furniture. **Divorce.** Among childless couples, the least incompatibility leads to divorce. Hereditary leaders attempt to settle difficulties by a marriage council before agreeing to a separation of a couple with children, however.

SOCIOPOLITICAL ORGANIZATION. **Political organization.** The Tagbanuwa think of themselves as belonging to a "nation-state" with a supreme leader, the Masikampu. However, the social and political structure remains basically oriented toward village autonomy. The basic units of the social structure— the elementary family, the bilateral family/bilateral kindred, the village, and the "nation-state"—are each coexistent with a ritual subsystem. Jural and political leadership is confined to hereditary leaders (*ginu'u*), descendants of a titled aristocracy created by Jolo Muslims some centuries ago in an effort to structure their trading relations with the Palawan tribes. Nowadays the Tagbanuwa are theoretically responsible to officials of the national government. Hereditary leaders continue, however, to exercise jural and ritual responsibilities at the local level. **Social differentiation.** Tagbanuwa society is roughly stratified on the basis of "high bloods"—the hereditary leaders (*ginu'u*) and their relatives, as well as most *babalyan* or "mediums" and their kin. The rest of the population (a minority) form a class of "low bloods." There was formerly a small class of servile debtors, the *uripen*, who had a slavelike status. The inherited social position of the "low blood" spouse is not altered in an interclass marriage. The children of such a marriage, however, are considered "high bloods," and, based upon individual ability, a male child of an interclass marriage can become a hereditary leader. Concern with social status, particularly in interclass marriages, has led to a marked lineal emphasis, either patrilateral or matrilateral. Hereditary leaders enjoy the distinction of prestigeful titles (of Moro origin), the highest of which is that of Masikampu. Sons normally succeed to their fathers' titles, although relative age and ability do enter in. A *ginu'u* is one who is thoroughly versed in tradition and custom law, is able to speak well in council, and has the reputation of supernatural power attributable to possession of some magic object, such as a particularly famous and ancient Chinese jar. Hereditary leaders often combine the status of religious functionary, i.e. "priest," with their more usual functions as judges and arbitrators. In the latter capacity they may be thought of as the legal guardians of their respective bilateral kindreds. Holders of the Masikampu and higher *ginu'u* titles formerly exercised considerable power and enjoyed such privileges as having their fields tilled by followers and/or debt slaves. **Social control and justice.** Among the Tagbanuwa, custom law is enforced by the decisions of an imposed aristocracy, rather than by recourse to threatened or actual violence and blood feud, as among some Philippine groups. Interpersonal relationships are regulated by kinship obligations and by a complex system of custom law with fines and fees determined in councils (*surugidin*), in which hereditary leaders function as arbitrators and judges. The system has the characteristics of a self-enforcing moral order, involving linked obligations and rights requiring satisfaction through payment of fees and fines if an individual is to maintain the position of a "legal being."

RELIGION. The Tagbanuwa make no distinction between a social world and a "natural" environment. They see in the environment countless deities and malign spirits, as well as a class of spirit-relatives who are subject to social control. In treating the environment as social, they are provided with an ordered explanation of "natural" phenomena. In short, one social and moral order encompasses the living, the dead, the deities, and the total environment. This ritually defined universe is a conservative one. The Tagbanuwa think and speak of the past, not of the future, and it is the cult of the dead that is the key to this ethical system. This is not a system of "ancestor worship," for the depth of this cult is consistent with the shallow range of the bilateral kinship system. Those invoked are generally fathers, mothers, brothers, or sisters—members of the elementary family. **Supernaturals.** Multilayered sky worlds are inhabited by named deities, the highest of which, Mangindusa, is the "punisher of crime," most specifically incest. The mythical *salakep* are small, dark, kinky-haired beings who once lived among the Tagbanuwa and are now the cause of epidemic illness.

Numerous environmental, guardian, and patron spirits are important to man's welfare, but the greatest attention is given to the spirits of the ancestral dead, *tiladmanin*, who are the principal cause of common illnesses. The possession by adult men of magic charms and objects, *mutya*, gives them supernatural powers and is associated with belief in witchcraftlike "poisoning." **Practitioners.** Religious specialists are the *babalyan*, the *maglambay*, and the *katungkulan*, the latter being "priests" or "priestesses" in the traditional sense. It is these individuals who converse with environmental spirits, who are "possessed" by deities and ancestors in ceremonies, and who keep alive the full range of religious beliefs. *Babalyan* is the common term for "medium" or "shaman," usually female. They participate in a variety of rituals and may enter a trance state induced by swinging. **Ceremonies.** Fox (1954) records a large inventory of ceremonial and ritual occasions. Many have to do with the cult of the dead, i.e. interaction with the spirits of the ancestral dead, performed at all levels, from those carried out by members of the family to those performed by the Masikampu on behalf of the "nation-state." Ritual acts include the drinking of rice wine through straws inserted in jars; offerings of rice, chickens, and betel; and the construction of ceremonial platforms and rafts, decorated with leaf streamers attached to high, upright poles. The post-harvest season is the period of ritual-social drinkfests, the focal point of Tagbanuwa life. Rice wine lures the dead to participate in rituals with the living and disposes them to help their relatives achieve full and healthful lives. These are likewise occasions for singing and dancing, forming blood pacts, and courting. They are never purely secular affairs, however, for the wine is a ritual drink, the product of the divine food, rice. **Soul, death, and afterlife.** A person has a single "true" soul as well as five "secondary" souls, the latter acquired in early infancy at a special *lambay* ceremony. Death occurs when the "true" soul leaves the body. The souls of those who have died natural deaths go to an underworld, *basad*. Death may also occur as a result of "poisoning," violence, epidemic illness, or the "eating" of the soul by evil spirits. The souls of the epidemic dead are transported to a special afterworld in spirit canoes. Disposal of the corpse is nowadays by burial in the ground. The soul's connection with the living is severed by a death rite seven days after burial, and during this period the surviving spouse is under strict taboos and is rigidly secluded. The dwelling of the deceased is subsequently abandoned. Funerary rites were formerly more elaborate, at least for prominent religious functionaries, and included secondary jar burial.

BIBLIOGRAPHY. Conklin 1949a, 1952; Dyen 1965; Fox 1953b, 1954; Marche 1884; Venturello 1907; Warren 1956.

BATAK*

Synonyms. *Batac, Tinitianes*

ORIENTATION. **Identification and location.** Hunters, gatherers, and (nowadays) quasi-shifting cultivators, loosely organized into bands distributed sporadically in the mountains and along the seacoast of the northeastern portion of Palawan Island, from the Babuyan River on the south to the vicinity of Malcampo on the north. Regarded by some as Negritos (cf. Miller 1905), although Beyer (1917: 59) called them an almost pure Papuan type. Recently characterized as "Veddoid" by Estel (1952). There is considerable physical variation among subgroups, and the problem of how best to characterize the population as a whole has not been settled [see under *Negritos* elsewhere in this volume]. **Geography.** The entire Batak region is mountainous or hilly and is covered mostly by second growth tropical forest and heavy undergrowth. There is a narrow coastal plain, with the mountains reaching into the sea at many places. **Linguistic affiliation.** Malayo-Polynesian, with strong affinities to the Central Bisayan group of Philippine languages, especially Tagbanuwa and Palawano. Most men are bilingual in both Batak and Tagbanuwa. No indigenous writing system. **Demography.** Approximately 800 to 1,000. **History.** Toward the end of the Spanish period, the Batak bands were gradually organized into groups, which eventually developed into the larger subgroupings as they are known today. Tanabag, the first Batak coastal settlement to be organized, was reportedly established about 1870 by a Christian Filipino. Before this, the people were scattered throughout the mountains nearby. The Batak were presumably seminomadic hunters and gatherers, who, in the past hundred years, have undergone considerable acculturation in contact with Moro, Spanish, and Christian Filipino officials and traders. This is most evident in respect to the introduction of dry-rice agriculture and the resultant effects on settlement pattern and political leadership. Similarities in these respects to neighboring Tagbanuwa are evident. **Cultural relations.** The territory of the Bataks is bounded on three sides by Tagbanuwa-speaking peoples, and the coast is occupied at several points by settlements of Christian Filipinos, principally Tagalog and Cuyonon speakers. The policy of the government, which encourages both the Batak and Tagbanuwa to live on the same reservation, is contributing to the amalgamation of the two groups in this area. Bataks and Christians come into contact in the barrios and coconut plantations which dot the shoreline of northeastern Palawan. In such instances, the

former not infrequently work for the latter, while continuing the collection and sale of beeswax, resins, and rattan.

SETTLEMENT PATTERN AND HOUSING. **Settlement pattern.** The total Batak population is divided into local subgroups, composed of an indefinite number of small, semimigratory bands. The band is a transitory social grouping of related and nonrelated individuals who have common interests in economic activities and who comprise the work group whenever communal enterprise is performed. The settlement, or temporary village (barrio), is merely a cluster of houses located near the seacoast and astraddle a major path leading from the coast into the forest. It (as well, probably, as the phenomenon of subgroups) has developed in direct response to government demands that the Batak establish a relatively permanent place of residence. The settlement serves as a geographic focal point and a rainy season residence for those bands who roam the nearby area, although there are no formal bonds uniting such transitory groups. It is also the hub of the paths leading to the fields under cultivation and is marked by the domesticated flora that abound along the paths and between the houses. **Housing.** Houses in the settlements are modeled after those of nearby Christian homesteaders, i.e. built on piles, with rectangular floor plans and nipa palm roofs. The temporary shelters utilized during their nomadic activities are only lean-tos of sticks and leaves, with leaves also used to cushion the ground.

ECONOMY. **Agriculture.** The Batak appear to have learned the shifting cultivation of dry rice in upland swiddens quite recently. Their coastal settlements are characterized by haphazard growths of coconut palms and fruit trees and by occasional small gardens planted to vegetables and to recently acquired root crops, such as sweet potatoes and cassava. **Fishing and hunting.** Fishing techniques include bow and arrow, basketry traps, and damming and poisoning, but fishing appears to be only an occasional pastime. The men are ardent hunters and spend considerable time in this activity, but the return in game is small. Wild pigs are hunted with dogs, spears, and bows and arrows, and the latter are also used for monkeys and other small game. The blowgun is rarely used nowadays. There is no ritual distribution of the meat of slain animals, and no association of discrete hunting territories with specific groups of hunters. **Gathering.** Wild yams, nuts, ferns, insects, grubs, and eggs are collected for use as food, but they constitute only a small proportion of any meal, since the obtaining of this type of food is unreliable. Groups inland from the coast obtain salt from the ashes of certain plants. **Domestic animals.** Limited to dogs, for hunting, and semidomes-

---

*The author of this entry, Charles P. Warren, is Assistant Professor of Anthropology, University of Illinois, Chicago Circle Campus. His data are from fieldwork on Palawan in 1950-51.

ticated cocks, for fighting. **Industrial arts.** Pottery-making, weaving, and metal working absent. Mats and baskets are made by women, and barkcloth was formerly manufactured. **Trade.** Food, cloth, salt, and knives are obtained from Christian Filipino traders in exchange for forest products, such as rattan, resins, and gums, in particular copal. **Property.** Movable property is minimal, limited to a few items such as spears. Property rights to land (in the vicinity of the coastal barrios) can be inherited by both sexes.

KIN GROUPS. **Descent.** Bilateral. **Kin groups.** There are only three easily discerned, discrete, social groups in Batak society: family, band, and settlement. The family is based on kin ties, the band on subsistence activities, and the settlement on geographic locality. Other social groupings are not discrete entities and must be described separately relative to each individual in the kinship web—e.g. personal kindreds—or to each position in the spatially organized network of inhabited localities—e.g. the territory. Sites and areas are culturally recognized but geographically defined localities. **Kin terminology.** The kinship system, terminologically and behaviorally, is generational:

GrPa	*apo*
Fa	*ama*
Mo	*ina*
FaSi, MoSi	*dudu*
FaBr, MoBr	*tata*
ElSib	*owa*
YoBr	*oyag*
YoSi	*manaw*
Cousin	*rogud*
GrCh	*apo*

Special terminology is used to address or refer to affinal relatives.

MARRIAGE AND FAMILY. **Mode.** If a woman agrees to marriage, the man approaches her parents, offering them the customary bride-price, a money gift which varies in amount from locality to locality. Bride service may be performed if the girl's father demands it. **Form.** Monogamy is the most frequent form of marriage. Polygyny, though rare, is practiced. Polyandry, even rarer, is reported to have occurred. **Marriage rules.** Incest is rigidly defined. Intergenerational marriage is prohibited, as is marriage between a woman and her husband's brothers and a man and his wife's sisters. Cousin marriage is restricted to fourth and third cousins, the latter only after a blood purification ceremony. **Residence.** Customarily near the girl's parents. **Domestic unit.** The nuclear family is the basic social and corporate unit. Each family has its own shelter, both while on hunting and collecting expeditions and during seasonal occupation of the temporary coastal settlement. The normative nuclear family may be extended horizontally by permitted, but infrequent, polygyny or poly-

andry. **Inheritance.** When a man dies, the wife inherits until the children marry, at which time sons, daughters, and the mother receive equal shares. If both parents die, the children and near relatives inherit equally. Relatives perpetuate necessary inheritance information by means of stories, *surubli'in*, and division of property is supervised by an elder. When two or more persons inherit property, e.g. a spear or agricultural land, it will sometimes be used in rotation. **Divorce.** Severe marital conflict usually culminates in divorce. Complaints on both sides are aired at a conference presided over by an elder, the divorce being finalized by both sides contributing a small amount of money. The bride-price is returned only if proceedings were initiated by the wife.

SOCIOPOLITICAL ORGANIZATION. **Political organization.** The present-day leader of all the Batak is an elder, *kapitan*, residing in the coastal settlement of Sumurod. He functions as nominal leader and advisor to other *kapitan*, heads of aggregates of bands in the local areas in which they reside, with respect to such matters as placement of settlements, timing of economic pursuits, organization of copal collecting activities, etc. The *kapitan* is chosen by the adult members of the local group from among those men considered the best hunters and fighters. These positions appear to have evolved as the result of Moro, Spanish, and Christian Filipino contacts, particularly with respect to attempts to organize the copal trade. **Social control and justice.** The *masikampo* is the local group expert on customary law and conducts all important meetings of elders, *surugiden*. There is only one *masikampo* for each settlement or local group, elected to the position from and by a group of elders, men of demonstrated wisdom in decisions relating to customary law. One of the principal duties of the *masikampo* is the levying of fines against persons found by a *surugiden* to be guilty of a breach of customary law. The presiding elder, *kaliwagan*, does the fining, *kaliwagan* being another name for the *masikampo*, or leader, of the *surugiden* at which the amount of the fine was decided. No decisions are legal without the presence of the *karinpasan* or witness to all official acts. **Warfare.** Organized warfare is absent.

RELIGION. **Supernaturals.** Nature spirits, *panya'en*, include those who are feared and avoided and those (the *diwata*) who live among large stones in the mountains and are benevolently inclined. **Practitioners.** The *babalyan* functions as both medium and shaman. There are three types: (1) the *bulay*, an old, experienced practitioner who can teach and guide others to become *babalyan* (2) the *mamamulay*, an old *babalyan* who uses root potions as curing agents and who actively transfers his knowledge to others in order to increase the number of *babalyan*, and (3) the *kapunglaw*, an experienced intermediary and religious go-between who dances and sings to attract and summon the benevolent nature spirits. All three act as intermediaries, since the healing action of the medicinal roots is dependent on the power of the benevolent *panya'en*. The principal activities of the *babalyan* are curing ceremonies, *magkabaro*. While dancing, the *babalyan* stops and touches portions of the patient's body, at each touch removing the "pain" from the afflicted parts. The objects removed include stones, leaves, roots, worms, snakes, etc. The latter are believed to be "thrown" into the body of anyone who makes fun of or otherwise offends the *panya'en*, thus making him ill and a candidate for treatment by the *babalyan*. **Soul, death, and afterlife.** A person has five souls, one, the *kiyarowa*, is located in the head; the other four, *pa'yo*, are in the hands and feet. The *kiyarowa* leaves the head during dreams, but the *pa'yo* remain. During sleep, the *kiyarowa* wanders freely and is in danger of being taken captive by a *panya'en* (nature spirit). Soul capture induces illness, which must be diagnosed and treated by a *babalyan*, who attempts to return the soul to the patient's body. If the *babalyan* cannot return the *kiyarowa*, either by enlisting the aid of a benevolent *panya'en* or by propitiating the malevolent *panya'en* by means of songs and dances, death ensues. The body of a deceased person is enclosed in a bamboo coffin and buried in a grave in the ground, together with minimal grave furniture, such as a bowl and a spear. Mourning lasts three days, during which time the surviving spouse remains covered (secluded) under a mat or blanket, and relatives maintain a fire at the foot of the grave.

BIBLIOGRAPHY. Beyer 1917; Estel 1952; Miller 1905; Schebesta 1952-57; Venturello 1907, 1908; Warren 1953, 1959, 1964.

BISAYAS

THE BISAYAN ISLANDS—chiefly Samar, Leyte, Bohol, Cebu, Negros, Panay, and Masbate—encircle the Visayan Sea in the central Philippines at approximately 10°-12° N. Spanish claims to the Philippines were first laid in the Bisayas, and modern Cebu City, founded in 1565, has the distinction of being the first Spanish settlement and the oldest city in the Philippines. There has been much speculation concerning the name Bisayas (Visayas) for these islands and their coastal inhabitants, most particularly with respect to a possible historical connection with the people of the same name in the Brunei Bay area of northern Borneo (see under the entry for *Bisaya* in Volume 1). Others have seen in the name evidence for a relationship with the tenth-century kingdom of Srivijaya, centered on Sumatra. Although it does not appear that Srivijaya or its Javanese successor kingdom, Madjapahit, ever exercized other than nominal hegemony in the Philippines (Rausa-Gomez 1967), the indirect influence of these early Hinduized centers is evident throughout the southern islands in respect to such things as religious nomenclature, mythology, and writing (cf. Kroeber 1918; Benedict 1916). It appears that Brunei was an important entrepôt under both Srivijaya and Madjapahit and that it was most likely Hinduized and (later) Islamized Malayans of Brunei descent who colonized the coastal estuaries of Panay and the neighboring islands, laying the foundations of the pre-Spanish Bisayan culture described in the accounts of the earliest explorers (cf. Santaren 1956; Bewsher 1956; Carroll 1960). The modern population of the Bisayan islands, estimated at around 7 million, is made up of remnant Negrito or Negritolike groups in the foothills of Panay and Negros, generally referred to as Ati (see elsewhere in this volume under *Negritos*); scattered groups of swidden-farming, Proto-Malay hill tribesmen, chiefly on Panay and Negros and generally referred to as *bukidnon* (see below under *Sulod* and *Magahat*); and the numerically superior and politically dominant lowland Christian Filipino population, referred to generically as Bisayans and by speech categories as Sugbuhanon (Cebuano); Hiligaynon (Ilongo, Panayano); Waray-waray (Samar-Leyte, Samareño); Aklan (Aklanon); Hantik (Antiqueño, Hamtikanon, Pantikanon); Hiniraya (Kiniraya, Binukidnon); Banton, etc. [see elsewhere in this volume under

Christian Filipinos]. Specific aspects of contemporary Christian Bisayan culture have been described by, among others, Hart (1954, 1969); Nurge (1965); Arens (1956a, 1956b, 1956c); Quisumbing (1965); Lieban (1967); and Gonzalez (1965). More general discussions are contained in Beyer (1912-23, Section A, Set 1, *vols. 1-5*); Tangco (1951); and Eggan et al. (1956).

BIBLIOGRAPHY. Arens 1956a, 1956b, 1956c; Benedict 1916; Bewsher 1956; Beyer 1912-23; Carroll 1960; Eggan et al. 1956; Gonzalez 1965; Hart 1954, 1969; Kroeber 1918; Lieban 1967; Nurge 1965; Quisumbing 1965; Rausa-Gomez 1967; Santaren 1956; Tangco 1951.

SULOD*

Synonyms. *Buki, Bukidnon, Mundo, Putian*

ORIENTATION. Mountain people, inhabiting the banks of the Panay River between Mt. Siya and Mt. Baloy in central Panay Island. Generally called *bukidnon* or *montesses* by lowlanders, meaning literally "mountain dwellers." To distinguish them from the *ati* (Negritos) who live in the foothills, the Christian lowlanders have given these hill tribesmen distinct names. Those in the mountains of Capiz and Aklan are called *mundo;* those in Iloilo are called, interchangeably, *buki, putian, sulod;* and those from the uplands of Antique are called *buki.* The dialects of these upland peoples are genetically related and very similar to lowland Kiniraya (called Hiniraya by Hiligaynon speakers). The mountain dialects, however, are characterized by many archaic expressions, thus accounting for the difficulty which Kiniraya-speaking lowlanders meet when talking to these upland dwellers. Most of the mountain people are monolingual.

SETTLEMENT PATTERN AND HOUSING. Small, autonomous settlements, *puro*, consisting of from five to seven houses, one or two houses being clustered on each of a number of adjoining hills. Normally, a *puro* is located on top of a high ridge, although a settlement is occasionally found at the foot of a fingerlike slope, beside a river or stream, since such places serve as "watch-towers," where the inhabitants can see and guard their *kaingin* from wild animals. The stream or riverside preference is due to the fact that

streams are an important source of water and riverine foods. The house is a poorly constructed, four-walled, one-room dwelling, raised about three meters on bamboo or timber posts and supported on all sides by props. The roof is of cogon thatch and the walls of flattened bamboo or the bark of trees. Bamboo slats are the preferred material for flooring. In front of the house is a small, low, pyramidlike hut—an improvised structure covered with long cogon grass roofing which touches the ground. This hut is called an *urub* and is used for emergency purposes, such as the sudden occurrence of storms.

ECONOMY. Subsistence is chiefly by shifting cultivation of upland rice (20 varieties), maize, sweet potatoes (9 varieties), and other edible tubers, supplemented by hunting, fishing, and gathering. The Sulod do not stay in one place for more than two years, due primarily to their pattern of land use. The tough grasses and secondary growth that usually follow the harvest render the swidden (*kaingin*) difficult to recultivate, particularly as the Sulod do not have work animals or plowing implements. Hence they move to another place where trees are growing abundantly and where the soil is free of grass. The abandoned site is called *lati* and may be used again after five or more years, when the second growth has become established.

KINSHIP AND MARRIAGE. Kinship is reckoned bilaterally to include all consanguineal and affinal kin of both the father and the mother. In any one settlement, almost all the inhabitants are related either by blood or by marriage. The basic unit of kinship is the nuclear family, consisting of the father, the mother, and their child or children. Children are named after renowned ancestors, after objects bearing significant meaning in Sulod life, and after qualities and deeds indicating superiority. Most Sulod are monogamous. However, the relatively well-to-do practice polygyny (*dapli*), which is permitted provided the man can pay the bride-price. In this system of marriage, it is always the latest wife who negotiates for the succeeding marriage. Normally, marriages are arranged between parents. To initiate a first marriage, the man makes his intentions known to his parents, who in turn approach the parents of the girl. The latter usually ask the boy's parents to return after a few weeks, since they have to talk the matter over with their daughter and many relatives. When the scheduled date arrives, the parents and relatives of the couple come together to discuss the marriage arrangements. This second meeting is called *pamalaye*, an elaborate occasion and a time for merrymaking. While the drinking and eating are going on, the spokesman for the boy stands up and starts the *pamalaye* in poetry called *siday*. He speaks of the lonely, lost bird seeking comfort in the warm nest of another.

---

*The author of this entry is F. Landa Jocano, Associate Professor of Anthropology, University of the Philippines. His data are based on fieldwork among the Sulod in 1957, 1958, and 1959.

The spokesman for the girl stands and rebuts this love offering by saying that the nest is reserved for another bird, etc. This battle of wits usually lasts for one night unless the spokesman for the girl gives up earlier and shakes the hand of his opponent. The girl's parents usually ask for *pangayo*, consisting of a sum of money, jewelry, a number of fighting bolos, several spears, and the wedding attire for the bride. Sometimes a dwelling will be demanded, which may either be occupied by the parents of the girl or given to the couple. The value of the *pangayo* depends on the social and economic position of the girl in the community. Aside from the *pangayo*, the boy is obliged to work for the girl's parents for two harvests. This "bride service" is called *panghagad*. The wedding, *punsyon*, takes place after the *panghagad*. The spokesman of the groom takes a sip of *pangasi* (rice wine) from the *tayuk*, a long piece of reed which serves as a straw, and stands up. He opens the affair by challenging, in poetry, his opponent to bring out the "flower of the house." The spokesman for the girl takes a sip of the wine from the same *tayuk*, coughs a little, stands up, and answers his opponent. This joust lasts for several hours. After this dialogue, the bride and her "court of honor" are covered with blankets and individually presented to the groom, who must select his bride from these girls. In order not to commit mistakes, thus causing embarrassment, the bride is always brought in last. When the man identifies his bride, he removes the cover and kisses her hands. He then feeds her with his right hand, signifying his authority over her. The bride, in turn, feeds the man with her left hand, signifying her acceptance of such authority.

SOCIOPOLITICAL ORGANIZATION. Leadership is assumed by the oldest man in each settlement. The leader, called *parangkuton* or "counselor," directs activities such as hunting, house building, and moving to a new *kaingin* site. He also settles disputes and heads annual social and religious activities. He is assisted by a young man called the *timbang*. When the *parangkuton* dies, the next oldest man in the settlement assumes leadership.

RELIGION. Religion is an intimate part of Sulod life. Every activity is in conformity to the wishes of spirits and deities, and the Sulod does everything within his power to please these divinities, even to the extent of going into debt in order to celebrate a proper ceremony for the chief spirit known as *diwata*. There are 16 annual ceremonies and a number of minor ones, most of which are conducted by the religious leader (medium, medicine man) known as *baylan*.

Death and burial. When a Sulod dies, everyone in the community condoles the bereaved family by contributing material things needed for the *balasan*, "wake of the dead." If the deceased was an important man, a *parangkuton* or a *baylan*, for example, he is not buried in the ground. A coffin is prepared for him by chopping down a large tree, cutting it to a convenient length, shaping it like a boat and hollowing it out. Carvings are made on the cover and on the sides. The corpse is encoffined and the slits glued with a gumlike sap. Then the coffin is placed underneath a special shed made of cogon grass, called the *kantang*, which has been built on top of a solitary hill. Finally, a hole is bored in the bottom of one end of the coffin and a small bamboo tube called *pasuk* inserted to facilitate the flow of the *tagas* or decomposing body fluids. After two or three months, the bones are removed, washed, wrapped in a black cloth (*baghuk*), and suspended under the eaves of the house. If the deceased is an ordinary man, he is simply buried in the ground, to one side of a *kantang*.

BIBLIOGRAPHY. Jocano 1958a, 1958b, 1964, 1968.

MAGAHAT

Synonyms. *Bukidnon, Buquitnon*

ORIENTATION. Shifting cultivators in the mountainous areas of southeastern Negros, in the municipalities of Tanjay, Santa Catalina, Bayawan (Tolong), and Siaton, at elevations of 1,000 to 3,000 feet. Generally called Bukidnon or Buquitnon; those on tributaries of the upper Tayabanan are known as Magahat, referring to a custom whereby the near relatives of a deceased person may go on a raiding party to the coastal regions to kill; if successful they return home and bury their dead relative (Oracion 1954: 12). Predominately "Indonesian" (Proto-Malay) in physical type. The language is a mixture of Sugbuhanon and Hiligaynon, both lowland Christian Filipino languages. There has been considerable penetration of the area in recent decades by Christian Filipinos pioneering hill agriculture and by logging operations. Magahat culture is in general similar to that of the Sulod of Panay.

BIBLIOGRAPHY. Oracion 1954, 1955, 1964, 1965, 1967b.

MINDORO

ALTHOUGH it is the seventh largest island of the Philippines and lies only 160 kilometers southwest of Manila, Mindoro has remained relatively unexplored and unexploited until modern times. It has actually been only since the 1950s, and the eradication of malaria from the coastal lowlands, that Tagalog and Bisayan farmers have begun moving into Mindoro in large numbers. The pagan tribal groups in the rugged mountainous interior, probably numbering between 20,000 and 30,000, are still, with the exception of the Hanunóo, relatively little known. These groups are customarily referred to by the collective term Mangyan (Mangianes, Manghianis, Manguianes), a term formerly applied as well to the interior upland peoples of nearby Tablas and Calamian. *Mangyan* is used by most Mindoro pagans to designate a tribesman in the general sense of "man" or "person," and by some as an ethnonym, e.g., Hanunóo, *hanunu'u mangyan,* "real" or "genuine" *mangyan* (Conklin 1954b: 32; Tweddell 1970). Tweddell divides speakers of Mangyan languages into two groups: (1) a northern group including Iraya (6,000-8,000); Alangan (3,000); and Tadyawan, numbering some 1,500 to 2,000 and including Conklin's Tagaydan (Tagaidan), Nauhan, and Pula; and (2) a southern group including Batangan (4,000); Hanunóo (6,000); and Buhid (Bu'id, Bukid, Buhil, Buquil), numbering around 6,000. The Ratagnon, totaling some 2,000 persons in the extreme southwest part of the island, are apparently recent immigrants from Cuyonon; while the term Bangon, given as a distinct ethnic group designation by Conklin (1949a), is according to Tweddell a generic exonym for people in the center of the island, i.e. Batangan (Tweddell 1970). The Batangan-Alangan groups in the rugged central uplands are by all accounts the most primitive on the island, still making and wearing bark cloth and, in some areas, leading a seminomadic existence, relying principally on hunting, gathering, and the intermittent cultivation of root crops. The

Mindoro pagans speak mutually unintelligible languages, all of which, however, are Malayo-Polynesian and members of Conklin's (1952) Central Philippines group, i.e. Dyen's (1965) Sulic Hesion. Dyen's data seem to point to an affiliation with Tagalic for his Irayic (northern) grouping of Mindoro languages; whereas his Hanunoic (southern) grouping is definitely related to Bisayan. A dual categorization of Mindoro pagans was likewise followed by Beyer, but primarily on physical and cultural grounds, i.e. a northern group of predominantly short Mongol types with some Negrito admixture, culturally less advanced than the southerners, whom Beyer characterized as of predominantly Indonesian physical type (Beyer 1917: 54). Estel (1952), in a review of more recently collected data, has characterized the more primitive northern groups, e.g. Alangan, as primarily Veddoid in contrast to those in the south, e.g. Hanunóo, whom he calls Early Asiatic. He finds no evidence of Negrito admixture on Mindoro. The culturally advanced Hanunóo and Buhid, characterized by semipermanent, dryrice agriculture, weaving, pottery making, metal working, and literacy in an Indic-derived script, have been studied principally by H. C. Conklin. The central and northern groups have received less attention. Maceda, reporting on the Alangan in the vicinity of Mt. Halcon, notes the presence of communal houses raised on piles, with family areas marked off by individual hearths. The occupants comprise a residential kin group, united by ties of consanguinity and affinity, with the hearth of the headman near the entrance and a separate area within the house reserved for bachelors (Maceda 1967a: 103-55). Muratake and Kikuchi (1968), reporting on brief fieldwork among the centrally located Batangan, describe patrilineally-oriented "axial" family lines within local groups consisting of persons related through essentially bilateral (ambilateral) kin ties. The cultural isolation of the Mindoro pagans will probably not continue much longer. Christian

Filipino farmers, now over 300,000 in number, have occupied much of the coastal lowlands, and homesteaders are already encroaching on the upland territories of the tribesmen (Tweddell 1970: 190); while on the plains inland from San Teodoro on the northeast coast, Iraya tribesmen have been settled by the government in towns and on reservations, where many work as wage labor for Christian Filipinos (Maceda 1967a). As of 1950, however, the Hanunóo remained remarkably unaffected by outside influences other than occasional trading trips to the coastal lowlands (Conklin 1954b).

BIBLIOGRAPHY. Beyer 1917; Conklin 1949a, 1952, 1954b; Dyen 1965; Estel 1952; Maceda 1967a; Miller 1912; Muratake and Kikuchi 1968; Tweddell 1970.

HANUNOO

Synonyms. *Bulalakao, Hanono-o, Hampangan, Mangyan*

ORIENTATION. **Location and identification.** The Hanunóo occupy some 800 square kilometers of forest- and grass-covered hinterland, the municipalities of Mansalay and Bulalacao, in extreme southern Mindoro. The principal economic activity of these pagan mountaineers, and the focus of much of their cultural life, is swidden agriculture, in particular the growing of rice. The people refer to themselves as *mangyan* ("man," "tribesman," "pagan") or as *hanunu'u mangyan* ("real," "genuine") *mangyan* (Conklin 1954b: 32; Tweddell 1970). The physical type is Proto-Malay ("Early Asiatic"); both sexes file the teeth and stain them black, chew betel, and wear the hair long. The loin cloth and wrap-around skirt are standard garb (Conklin 1954b, 1957). **Demography.** Estimated 6,000 (Conklin 1954b). **Linguistic affiliation.** Monolingual, speaking dialects of a single language most closely related to languages of the central Philippines (Conklin 1954b, 1953b). The Hanunóo are up to 60 percent literate in an ancient Indic-derived script, once widespread in the Philippines but now found only on southern Mindoro and central Palawan (Conklin 1949b; Postma 1968; Francisco 1966; Gardner and Maliwanag 1939-41). The script, inscribed on bamboo, is associated among the Hanunóo with adolescent courting patterns and the recording and learning of highly metaphorical love songs (*ambahan*), a kind of "literary language" couched in archaic (obsolete) Hanunóo (Conklin 1949b, 1955b). **Cultural relations.** Culturally conservative, preserving much of what may be considered a pre-Spanish Bisayan culture (Conklin 1954b: 58-59). As of the early 1950s, untouched by outside influences such as schools and missions. Main contacts are in form of trading expeditions to coastal (Filipino) towns; in respect to trade in items such as metel, glass beads, and salt, the Hanunóo function as middlemen between the coast and their neighbors immediately to the north, the Buhid (Conklin 1953a).

SETTLEMENT PATTERN AND HOUSING. **Settlement pattern.** Semipermanent, nucleated, autonomous settlements, averaging five to six single-family houses (range two to twelve or more) and containing no more than 50 persons. Settlement sites are often on valley slopes or spurs overlooking a mountain stream, and are named for the nearest prominent geographic feature. The settlement considered as a social group, however, usually goes by the name of one of its eldest residents. Settlements within an hour's easy walking distance of one another may be geographically grouped into unnamed neighborhood communities averaging 100 to 150 persons (Conklin 1954a, 1957). Neighborhoods often coincide with named geographic areas, e.g. Yagaw on the eastern slopes of Mt. Yagaw, drained by the upper tributaries of the Wawan River. Settlement and neighborhood affiliation may be lost through change in residence, but area affiliation is for life. Thus conscious cultural identity and ethnocentric attitudes are most strongly associated with the geographic area (Conklin 1954b: 44-47). **Housing.** Single-family, pile dwellings of sturdy wood and bamboo construction, walled and with thatched hip roofs. Several houses may be arranged in an end-to-end pattern, linked by open verandas. Storehouses (granaries) are smaller replicas of dwellings, but lacking verandas; they are occasionally built in the manner of tree houses. [Conklin 1954b, 1957.]

ECONOMY. The Hanunóo are primarily reliant on integral shifting cultivation for their staple food supply. Fishing, more important nowadays than hunting, provides most of the meat protein. Surplus crops are traded to the lowlands for salt, metal, and ritually important glass beads. **Agriculture.** Primary swiddens are intercropped, first to maize, followed by rice, and maize, beans, and sugarcane may be planted in the main swiddens just before the rice harvest. Secondary dry-field swiddens are usually planted to sweet potatoes and other root crops. Swiddens are fallowed after two years or so—longer if intercropped with bananas and papayas. Rice is of primary concern to the Hanunóo, in terms of both ritual importance and prestige value, but bananas and root crops (sweet potatoes, yams, taro) provide more than one-half of all food consumed (Conklin 1954b: 192).

Conklin's systematic studies of Hanunóo agricultural practices provide an impressive demonstration of the ways in which these people combine a remarkable fund of pragmatic knowledge concerning soil types, erosion, crop rotation, and the like with reliance on such things as stellar lore, augury, and dream interpretation (Conklin 1954b, 1957). **Hunting and fishing.** Wild pig, deer, monkeys, and (formerly) wild water buffalo are hunted with bows and poisoned arrows, spears, traps, and dogs. Fire surrounds, involving 50 or more men, are (or were) used also, although all these techniques are used less often now than formerly. Fishing is, however, still important, and fish, together with crustaceans, provide a good part of all meat eaten. [Conklin 1954b: 71.] **Domestic animals.** The meat of domesticated pigs and chickens is consumed only on festive occasions, as is the meat of humped cattle; these latter animals are never used for agricultural labor. **Industrial arts.** Men forge knives and other implements from imported scrap iron, using the double piston (Malayan) bellows. Basketry is well developed, with the baskets decorated with red dyed rattan, and women plant, pick, gin, and weave cotton for clothing and blankets. Clay cooking pots are traded in from the neighboring Buhid. [Conklin 1954b; 1957, plates 8 & 33.] **Trade.** Locally grown rice, maize, bananas, cacao, and tobacco are traded along the coast for scrap iron, needles, kettles, beads, and red cloth. Some of these items, in turn, are traded to the neighboring Buhid in return for clay cooking pots. Most goods are valued in terms of strings of European glass beads—the common standard of value throughout the pagan interior of southern Mindoro. The beads, important also in curing and religious rites, are obtained from coastal Filipinos—as were the old heirloom bronze gongs and porcelain jars, of Moro and Chinese origin respectively. [Conklin 1954b: 52, 1953a, 1957.] **Property.** Trees, spears, and beads are individually owned, but land may be held by individuals only in usufruct (Conklin 1954b: 48). Bronze gongs and porcelain jars (Conklin 1957: 11) are presumably family-owned heirloom property.

KIN GROUPS. Descent is bilateral. The only corporate kin group is the family, consisting normally of a man, his wife, and their offspring. This is the only group sharing collective responsibility in legal and economic crises, including swidden work (Conklin 1957: 12). The local, named settlement is composed in the majority of cases of a noncorporate, exogamous, residential kin group, termed by Conklin (1949b) the *local family group,* which "respects as advisors its eldest male members and consists usually of a man and his wife or wives, their unmarried children, and the families of their married daughters" (Conklin 1949b: 7). Following Murdock (1949: 64), this may be termed a matrideme (Conklin 1954b, 1957: 13). Nu-

clear families are free to shift residence from one settlement to another, but this is always near the close personal kindred of either the husband or the wife. **Kin terminology.** Conklin (1954b: 79) gives the following kin terms (cf. also Conklin 1964: 36-37):

PaFa	*laki*
PaMo	*idu*
Fa	*ama*
Mo	*ina*
PaBr	*bapa*
PaSi	*bayi*
ElSb	*aka*
YoSb	*ari*
1st Cousin	*insan*
2nd Cousin	*arwa*
3rd Cousin	*atlu*
4th Cousin	*baliw-sanga*
Ch	*anak*

MARRIAGE AND FAMILY. **Courtship.** In connection with major socioreligious feasts termed *panludan,* boys and girls engage in a highly stylized pattern of courtship involving the exchange of love songs (*ambahan* or *urukay*). A verse, chanted first by the boy, must be answered by the girl, with great emphasis being placed on one's cleverness in choosing a suitable verse to fit the particular circumstance. Large repertories of these highly metaphorical verses are maintained, for which purpose they are inscribed on bamboo "manuscripts" in an ancient Indic-derived script. The songs are chanted or sung to the accompaniment of small fiddles, guitars, nose flutes, and jew's harps of local manufacture. [Conklin 1949b, 1955b; Postma 1965.] **Mode.** By bride service and mutual agreement of the two families concerned. There is no exchange of goods, no bride-price, and no formal ceremony. Elopement does occur as an alternative mode. [Conklin 1954b: 47.] **Form.** Monogamy is the norm, but (sororal) polygyny and (fraternal) polyandry are allowed and do occur (Conklin 1954b: 47). **Residence.** Ideally matrilocal, in the settlement of the wife's parents—and statistically so, in 80 percent of Conklin's test cases. Subsequent shifts to bilocality and ultimately back to matrilocality or neolocality do occur. [Conklin 1954b, 1957.] **Extension of incest taboos.** Marriage is traditionally proscribed within bilateral, kindredlike categories maximally extended to include all of Ego's consanguineal relatives and their spouses, but regional endogamy (above the local settlement level) leads to frequent marriages between known kinsmen, requiring ritual cleansing (Conklin 1964: 49). **Domestic unit.** The household is made up normally of a nuclear family consisting of a man, his wife, and their unmarried children. **Divorce and secondary marriage.** The levirate and sororate are favored but are not obligatory. **Inheritance.** Bilateral (Conklin 1954b: 48).

SOCIOPOLITICAL ORGANIZATION. Great emphasis is placed on the autonomy of the local group, i.e. the named settlement consisting in the majority of instances of a residential kin group or matrideme. Such settlements are loosely stratified and predominantly egalitarian: some prestige accompanies the status of eldest within a group of kinsmen or the position of skilled weaver, smith, or medium, but there are no full-time specialists and no headmen, chiefs, or slaves. Differences based on wealth appear to be minimal, and although glass beads are valued in a ritual sense, and old bronze gongs, porcelain jars, and cattle are mentioned, it does not appear that these things enter into a pattern of wealth accumulation to any significant degree. Disputes are settled by the eldest relatives of the disputants. Judgment normally results in payment of a fine in glass beads or other goods, and recourse may be had to ordeal by hot water to settle an argument. Murder is by common agreement avenged by the closest relatives of the victim. Warfare, either actual or traditional, is absent. [Conklin 1954b: 48, 1957.]

RELIGION. **Supernaturals.** Named deities mythologically associated with creation are known, but are relatively unimportant in everyday life. More important are a host of spirits, including ghosts of the recent dead and souls of the living, who are in control of supernatural powers, such as the ability to be invisible or to cause to be invisible. The all-important souls of the recent dead ordinarily function as benign guardian spirits (*kalag*), as do the various nature spirits who guard over mountains, rocks, forests, and the like. But all these can be transformed into evil beings (*labang*), potentially harmful to mortals. Benign spirits, if angered by lapses in propitiatory behavior or infractions of adat, may permit their evil counterparts to harm the living. [Conklin 1954b: 277ff., 255 footnote.] **Practitioners.** Evil spirits, *labang*, may attack a man's soul, thus causing illness or even death. Illness is treated by massage specialists, herbalists, and mediums (*balyanan*), the latter having the ability to send their spirit familiars to combat the evil spirit

causing an illness or to extract harmful objects from the patient's body. Paraphernalia includes carefully guarded stones, the residing places of the spirit familiars. The medium works in a darkened room, chanting and waving leaves and other plant parts over the patient's body, but apparently does not enter a trance state. [Conklin 1954b: 234ff.] **Ceremonies.** Mediums are present at feasts and rituals for deceased kinsmen, local supernaturals, and swidden crops, especially rice. Food offerings, consisting most often of cooked rice, pig blood, or prepared betel quids, are placed in miniature spirit houses, but the most pleasing offering to the spirits, and an important prerequisite to all dealings with them, consists of strings of European glass beads. The most important ceremonial events of the Hanunóo year are the *panludan*, festivals for the ghosts of the recent dead. [Conklin 1954b, 1957.] **Death.** The ghosts of the recent dead are of utmost importance to the welfare of the living. To please these spirits and keep them well disposed, the bones of deceased members of the community are regularly exhumed one year after burial. The bones are bundled, fed, talked to, and danced with at a large, expensive socioreligious festival, *panludan,* for which special dance pavilions, bone houses, and offering structures are erected. The bones are consulted at this time about future events such as crops and harvests, and the *panludan* is an occasion, as well, for merry-making, courting, singing, and dancing (cf. Conklin 1955b). Following the ceremony, the cleaned bones are placed, with certain valuables, in a cave niche with the remains of other close relatives. There is little convincing evidence that the Hanunóo ever practiced jar burial, either in caves or elsewhere. [Conklin 1954b: 54ff., 85.]

BIBLIOGRAPHY. Conklin 1949a, 1949b, 1953a, 1953b, 1954a, 1954b, 1955a, 1955b, 1957, 1958, 1960a, 1960b, 1964; Francisco 1966; Gardner and Maliwanag 1939-41; Murdock 1949; Postma 1965, 1968; Tweddell 1970.

LUZON

LUZON IS THE ranking Philippine island in size and population, and Manila one of the chief cities of Southeast Asia, yet within sight of the capital are mountains whose inhabitants remain largely unchanged by the four centuries of Western contact that have transformed the lowlands. While Christian Filipinos, chiefly Tagalogs and Ilocanos,

occupy the coastal plains and broad river valleys opening into the interior, the northwestern portion of the island is dominated by a spectacular mountain mass centered on the Cordillera Central, with peaks reaching 9,000 feet, the home of settled, rice-terracing pagans known chiefly through the publications of R. F. Barton and A. E. Jenks on two of these peoples, the Ifugao and Bontok. The intermediate foothill areas to the north, east, and south of this mountain mass are occupied by semipermanent, dry-rice cultivators (Apayao, Gaddang, Ilongot) and remnant Negrito or "Negroid" groups. The pagan population of the interior hills and mountains totals altogether less than 350,000, or some 3.7 percent of Luzon's 1948 population of slightly over 9 million (Eggan et al. 1956: *1*, 292). Data accumulated since World War II strongly indicate a development in situ of the majority of mountain languages and cultures from a common base, with linguistic differentiation having taken place largely within the Christian era (Eggan 1954); and the probable contribution of coastal lowland peoples to the ethnic makeup of the mountain provinces, e.g. as refugees from Spanish oppression, has been persuasively argued by Keesing (1962a) and supported by evidence of close linguistic ties between, e.g., Ilocano-Ibanag and the northern group of mountain languages (Fox et al. 1965). These findings largely refute the earlier formulations of culture history that invoked separate migrations from the Asian mainland to account for cultural differences among modern mountain tribes (cf. Beyer 1947; Keesing and Keesing 1934). Most notable among such differences is a general distinction between a northeastern zone of dry-rice cultivators (Apayao, Mountain Tinggian, Northern Kalinga, Pagan Gaddang) and a southwestern zone of terraced, wet-rice agriculture (Ifugao, Bontok, Kankanai, Ibaloi), with, among the terracing groups, considerable more complexity of social and religious institutions. Although the derivation of all Philippine peoples lies ultimately on the Asian mainland, there seems to be no compelling evidence at present to assign the appearance of wet-rice terracing on Luzon to a specific prehistoric or protohistoric migration. Rather, the evidence points to a relatively late development, possibly as a local adaptation to favorable ecological factors (Keesing 1962a: 318ff.). And Eggan (1941, 1954, 1963) has argued convincingly for the local development of village complexity with associated residence and wealth patterns as a response to population increase and stability made possible by permanent field cropping. Certainly the role

of gold should not be overlooked in attempts to reconstruct the early history of insular Southeast Asia, in particular its role in protohistoric trade and resultant mountain-lowland contacts and the diffusion of artifacts and ideas from the mainland. And the historic penetration of Spain into interior Luzon was largely dictated by attempts to gain control of the ancient Benguet gold mines in the mountains inland from the southern Ilocos coast, and midway on the trade routes from the coast to the rice-terracing pagans of the high cordillera. [See Scott 1970; Keesing 1962a.] Early names for the mountain peoples reflect the direction of the Spanish quest for gold; thus the term Igorot, which for a time gained currency in the scientific literature as a generic for all Luzon hill tribes, was originally a Spanish borrowing from Tagal or Iloko *i-golot* ("mountaineer"), used initially to refer to the Ibaloi-Kankanai peoples of Benguet but later extended on Spanish maps (as Igolotes or Ygolotes) to include Bontok and Ifugao (Scott 1966: 154ff.).

The grouping of the Luzon mountain peoples under four regional headings—North, Central, South, and Southeast—in the pages that follow generally conforms to that arrived at by Fox et al. (1965) after a glottochronological examination of the linguistic evidence, with certain modifications based on the linguistic conclusions of Thomas and Healey (1962) and the (largely) historical-cultural classification of these peoples by Keesing and Keesing (1934) and Keesing (1962a). The rationale for these modifications is explained in the introductory statements to each of the regional divisions. Data on the major lowland Christian peoples of Luzon—Tagalog, Ilocano, Pangasinan, Pampangan, and Bikol—are entered elsewhere in this volume under *Christian Filipinos*, as is information on the so-called "minor" Christian groups—the Ibanag (Kagayan, Cagayanes), Itawes (Itavi), Gaddang, and Isinai (Isinay) of the Cagayan Valley, and the Sambal (Sambali) of Zambales Province northwest of Manila. Information on Zambales Negritos and various remnant Negritolike or "Negroid" populations of northern and eastern Luzon (e.g. Dumagats) will be found under the general heading of *Negritos* and in the relevant subsections thereof.

BIBLIOGRAPHY. Beyer 1947; Eggan 1941, 1954, 1963; Eggan et al. 1956; Fox et al. 1965; Keesing 1962a; Keesing and Keesing 1934; Scott 1966, 1970; Thomas and Healey 1962.

CENTRAL GROUPS

THE SLOPES OF Mount Data in western Bontok feed the headwaters of the upper Abra, Chico, and Magat river systems, thus constituting the topographic center of North Luzon's Mountain Province. It is in this centrally located region, especially among the Ifugao, that technical proficiency in the terracing and irrigation of wet rice reaches its highest level, being also marked among the neighboring Bontok, Lepanto, and extreme Southern Kalinga (Tinglayan), but becoming less so as one moves north into Kalinga and Tinggian territory or south among the Kankanai and Ibaloi. [DeRaedt 1964; Scott 1958b.] It is also in this region that one finds the so-called *ato*, or village ward system, with its associated ceremonial and social institutions, developed to its fullest extent among the Lapanto-Bontok but with elements of the complex evident among the neighboring Ifugao and Southern Kalinga—who together with Lepanto (Northern Kankanai) and Bontok constitute a closely related linguistic subgroup within the Northern Philippine family of languages (Thomas and Healey 1962: 30; Eggan 1954). This evident degree of centrality with respect to a variety of cultural and linguistic features would seem to justify the grouping of at least Bontok-Lepanto and Ifugao together for purposes of descriptive presentation. Although Southern Kalinga might on linguistic grounds be included in this classification, the cultural features (other than wet rice) that would link them to Bontok-Lepanto appear most marked in the extreme south (Tinglayan area). The basic cultural affiliation of Kalinga appears to be with Tinggian and Apayao, farther north, and they have been so grouped in the present volume.

BIBLIOGRAPHY. DeRaedt 1964; Eggan 1954; Scott 1958b; Thomas and Healey 1962.

IFUGAO

Synonyms. *Ifugaw, Ipugao, Yfugao*

ORIENTATION. **Location and identification.** Known for their intricate ritual and legal systems and their remarkable development of agricultural terracing, the Ifugao are among the best described of all groups in the Philippines. The traditional Ifugao region, roughly equivalent to modern Ifugao Province, covers slightly less than 750 square miles in the Central Cordillera of northern Luzon. This is a region of rugged uplands, drained by tributaries of the Magat, a major branch of the upper Cagayan. Ifugao [from the Gaddang pronunciation of *ipugao*, "the people who live on the known earth" (Barton 1946: 10)] is the usual generic exonym. The most common "subgroup" designations, actually names taken from population centers or geographic locations, include: Banaue (Banawi, Benauwe), Bunhian (Bungian), Mayoyao (Mayoyo, Mayaoyao, Mayawyaw), Halipan (Salipan, Silipan), Hapao (Sapao, Japao, Hapaw), and Kiangan (Quiangan). The latter term is most often used by neighboring groups to refer to Ifugao in general (Conklin 1968). Terms such as Kallahan (Kalasan, Kalanguyya) and Hanglulu refer to what are apparently southwestern dialect-linked groups or languages in the upper Kayapa River area of northwestern Nueva Vizcaya Province (Conklin 1968: iv; Reid 1971: 22). There are regional differences, most noticeable perhaps with respect to the northerly Mayoyao, and the degree of "Ifugaoness" in fact becomes less as one approaches borders with neighboring groups such as Bontok. Supravillage political institutions are lacking, and the Ifugao have never constituted a "tribe" in this sense. Nevertheless, the various traditional regions of Ifugaoland do share a linguistic and cultural heritage, centered according to myth in Kiangan—the locale of much of Barton's fieldwork. And there is in fact a remarkably high degree of cultural interdependence throughout the Ifugao region (Conklin 1968). **Linguistic affiliation.** Malayo-Polynesian. Classed by Conklin (1952) within his Northern Group of Philippine languages, and by Dyen (1965) within a North Cordilleran Cluster of his Cordilleran Hesion. The closest relationships of Ifugao seem to be with Bontok and Kankanai, with a probable date of separation around 900 A.D. (Fox et al. 1965). **Demography.** Twentieth century estimates have ranged from 60,000 to over 100,000, with a 1960 census figure of 76,800 (Conklin 1968). Densities in some places approach 400 per square mile. **History and cultural relations.** The origins of Ifugao were attributed by Beyer to the migration of an "Indonesian" population from the Asian mainland about 800-500 B.C. (Fox 1956). Eggan (1954) and others have questioned the theory of specific migrations linked to specific culture complexes as a way of explaining differences among contemporary groups, preferring to regard many of these as local developments out of a generalized base common to much of the area. The origins of wet rice, and specifically of the spectacular terracing of the Ifugao, are unknown, although they have been the subject of much speculation (cf. Spencer and Hale 1961; Keesing 1962a: 338ff.). It is reasonably certain that the Ifugao have been in their present area for at least the past three centuries (Conklin 1968) and that their terracing systems are at least that old if not older. Ifugao culture has shown a remarkable degree of persistence, despite the introduction of municipalities, schools, roads, and missions. Although some have adopted Christianity and to a large extent given up the traditional life, for the majority of Ifugao the pagan religion continues as the major integrative force that binds together, through myth and ritual, the whole fabric of society (Lambrecht 1971).

SETTLEMENT PATTERN AND HOUSING. **Settlement pattern.** The general pattern is reportedly one of small, named hamlets of 8 to 12 houses (30 or more persons) located on hillocks or spurs along the sides of a mountain valley. Houses are built on multilevel terraces, invariably in close proximity to rice fields. The well-developed *ato* (ward) system of the Bontok is absent, although according to Lambrecht (1929: 123), the "different parts" of the more extensive villages are individually named. Loofs (1965), on the basis of observations in Banaue, disputes the stereotype of microvillages, calling attention to the actual clustering of hamlets into what might be termed settlement areas of several hundred houses. This pattern would seem to be confirmed by Conklin's mapping of north-central Ifugao, showing clearly defined clusters of hamlets within named agricultural districts (Conklin 1972). Although apparently lacking the composite nature of the large Bontok villages, settlement areas in Banaue were found by Loofs to contain associated "megalithic" elements, such as paved stone houses and communal platforms with upright stone backrests. Among the northerly Mayoyao, settlement clusters are lacking, with houses dispersed on the rice fields, which in turn are laid out on broad valley bottoms. [Barton 1922: 412; Lambrecht 1929; Conklin 1967b.] **Housing.** Well-made timber and thatch granaries and dwellings, raised on four posts, with characteristic pyramidal roofs. Framing is pegged or tenoned and mortised, and wall planks are set in grooves in top and bottom plates. Furnishings and ornamentation are minimal; door panels are occasionally decorated with carved human figures, and there was formerly a shelf for the skulls of enemy heads taken in warfare and of animals slain at feasts of merit. Less permanent structures, e.g. *agamang* (houses for the unmarried, including pubescent girls), may be built directly on the ground. [Lambrecht 1929; Scott 1966.]

ECONOMY. According to Barton (1922: 397) subsistence is derived mainly from agriculture (84 percent). Close to 10 percent is derived from aquatic fauna, such as minnows and snails grown in flooded rice fields. **Agriculture.** Sweet potatoes, grown on hillside swiddens, provide an important staple, though they rank low in prestige value. Rice and taro are grown on multipurpose "pond fields" (Conklin 1967b). Terracing, utilizing walls of earth and stone, is extensive, extending in many cases for a thousand feet or more up a mountainside. Irrigation is controlled by elaborate systems of dykes and sluices, and fields may be intermittently drained and planted to dry crops, such as camotes and legumes. The fields are worked wholly with wooden spades and digging sticks. Labor may be employed for harvesting, payment being in bundles of rice (Lambrecht 1932: 135). All stages of rice cultivation are accompanied by ritual, and harvesting is a gay social time. Rice is the prestige crop, and a man's status is determined by his rice fields (Barton 1922: 400). Secondary crops include corn, grown in sweet potato fields and ground into meal, taro, yams, cowpeas, lima beans, okra, greengrams and other legumes, sugarcane, and tobacco. Cotton, beans, radishes, cabbage, lettuce, peas, and mustard are planted on soggy piles of rice stalks in the rice fields after harvest (Barton 1922: 405-06). Tree crops include coffee (a cash crop), jackfruit, grapefruit, rattan, citrus, areca, coconut, banana, guava, and cacao. The integral nature of agricultural activities, and their cycling through time, are discussed in Conklin (1967b). **Agricultural districts.** Conklin's intensive survey of a 40 square mile portion of north-central Ifugao disclosed a division of the area into some 25 discrete agriculturally defined "districts" (*himpuntona'an*), traditional geographic units with ritual functions. The focal center of an agricultural district is a named, ritual plot, the first to be planted and harvested each year. Matters of irrigation and land use (of prime importance to Ifugao agriculturists) tend to be set in a regional framework involving contiguous and related catchment areas, usually comprising several agricultural districts. [Conklin 1967b.] **Hunting.** Deer, wild buffalo, and pigs are hunted with spears and dogs, and often by teams of up to ten hunters. Civet cat, wild cat, python, iguana, and cobra are hunted and eaten. Monkeys are hunted, but not eaten. Fruit bats are netted, pigs are sometimes caught in a pitfall. Locusts, crickets, and ants are caught and eaten. [Barton 1922: 392-95.] **Fishing.** The *ginga*, or water clam, found in rice fields, is the most important animal food; *dolog* (tilapia fish), minnows, eels, frogs, and snails are caught and eaten (Barton 1922: 396). **Gathering.** A large variety of wild plants are gathered and eaten, but are not a major item of diet (Barton 1922: 397). **Domestic animals.** Water buffalo (purchased in the lowlands), pigs, goats, and chickens. The last are kept at night in baskets beneath the house. Animals are killed only for sacrifice and feasts of merit and are eaten afterward. Sows are leased (Barton 1922: 421). **Industrial arts.** Lambrecht shows an illustration of a sugarcane press (1955: 27). Smithing, basketry, woodworking, and weaving are present, but are artistically uninspired. Carved wooden figures of deities and gods are made locally and used in religious rituals. **Trade.** Formerly barter. Nowadays rice and money are media of exchange. Coffee is the main export crop; livestock, cotton, brass wire, cloth, beads, crude steel, and Chinese jars and gongs are imported. There is some internal trade in knives, pots, spears, and salt. Men often become traders, traveling through the Mountain Province and into the lowlands. [Barton 1922: 426-27.] **Property.** According to Barton, "family" property consists of rice land, forest land, and heirlooms, held in trust for future generations and sold only in emergencies, with the consent of kinsmen and upon performance of an *ibuy* ceremony. Personal property includes houses, valuable trees, and crops of sweet potatoes, which may be sold without ceremony. Property law with respect to sale, mortgaging, indebtedness, and the like is well developed. [Barton 1919.] **Land tenure.** Tenure of rice and nearby forest land is perpetual. Untilled grasslands and forests distant from any settlement are public property with reference to the inhabitants of a common watershed area (Conklin 1967b). Barton adds that unowned land becomes the property of anyone who clears and plants it; with sweet potato fields, which must be fallowed after three years or so, the planter owns the land until it goes fallow (Barton 1919: 43-44). Inheritance of irrigated land is, according to Conklin (1967b), strictly cognatic and primogeniturally weighted. **Water rights.** Rights and duties rigidly prescribed by custom law, e.g. a spring belongs to the owner of the land, who may sell rights to excess water; water that is feeding an area may not be diverted; a man intending to construct an irrigation ditch may sell shares in same; damaging ditches is punishable by fine, beating, or even death. [Barton 1919: 59-60.]

KINSHIP. Each sibling group is the center of a (theoretically) exogamous *bilateral kindred*, reckoned vertically to great-great-grandparents and laterally to third cousins. One's kindred is activated on occasion, e.g. at marriage (marriage is an alliance between kindreds, called "families" by Barton). The kindred is collectively responsible for the actions (and welfare) of its members, and feuding is (or was) common (Eggan 1967). Corporate ownership of land and heirloom property is, according to Goodenough (1955), confined to members of what he terms a *non-unilineal descent group*—which others (e.g. Hoebel 1954: 104-05) have equated with the bilateral kindred (see also Davenport 1959). Eggan (1967) mentions also the *cognatic stock*, a regional bilateral descent group

including those persons in a particular region [probably including a "core" group of aristocrats] claiming descent from a common deified culture hero(s). Beyer's "clan districts" (Beyer and Barton 1911) appear to be the same as Conklin's "agricultural districts" termed by him "the largest territorial units of traditional social and cultural importance." Conklin's districts cannot, however, be defined as localized kin groups (Conklin 1973). **Kin terminology.** Barton (1919: 110) gives the following terms for Kiangan:

GrPa	apo
Fa, FaBr, MoBr	ama, ulitao
Mo, MoSi, FaSi	ina, ulitao
Sibling, cousin ("all kin of Ego's generation")	tulang
Child, nephew/niece	anak, amanaon
GrCh	apo
Pa-in-law	ama, ina
Br/Si-in-law	aidu
Wife	inaya

MARRIAGE AND FAMILY. **Mode.** For children of families lacking property, courtship revolves around *agamang*, girls' dormitories, and several trial marriages may precede a permanent union (Barton 1938). Wealthy families usually arrange the marriages of their children, utilizing go-betweens, with concomitant assignment of the property they will inherit. Families exchange pigs and gifts at the time of betrothal and maintain close liaison thereafter. Marriage proper consists of four ceremonies, each with pig or chicken sacrifice, feasting, and consultation of bile sacs for omens. In the Kiangan area, the final ceremony is marked by gifts of jars, cloth, and knives by the husband's to the wife's family. [Barton 1919: 17-23.] **Form.** Monogamy the norm, but polygyny practiced by wealthy on occasion. First wife has authority of highest status (Barton 1919: 17). **Extension of incest taboos.** First-cousin marriage forbidden in theory and practice; marriage to more distant cousins possible with payment of fines in livestock (Barton 1919: 18). There is strict brother-sister avoidance with respect to sleeping arrangements, sexual joking, and the like. **Inheritance.** Children of both sexes may inherit from either parent, with primogeniture a deciding factor in cases of more than one child. Debts may be inherited, with no distinction according to sex. Illegitimate children are supported by the father's family, but do not inherit from his estate. [Barton 1919: 36-38, 51.] **Residence.** Optional, and at the convenience of the young couple. They may choose to live initially with either his or her parents (Barton 1919: 24, 26), but a couple normally builds a house as near as possible to the largest rice field holding inherited by either partner at marriage (Conklin 1967b). **Domestic unit.** Houses are small and normally contain a nuclear family. Children old enough to care for themselves go to live in boys' or girls' houses (*agamang*), which may be specially built huts or disused houses (Lambrecht 1935: 170). **Divorce.** May occur at any time by mutual consent, but less frequent after first child. If one partner objects, damages may be claimed. Reasons include bad omens, childlessness, cruelty, desertion, adultery, change of affection. If there are no children, each spouse retains property he or she brought into marriage through inheritance, while property acquired jointly during marriage is divided equally. All property, whether individual or joint, is assigned to children if there are any. The spouse who takes the children (the woman has priority in this regard) manages the property for each child until his marriage. [Barton 1919: 18, 30, 33.] **Secondary marriage.** A surviving spouse may remarry only after payment of *gibu* to family of deceased partner. This is less if the survivor marries a kinsman of same (Barton 1919: 27, 29). **Adoption.** Rare, usually only by wealthy, who adopt sibling's children. Adopted child receives almost equal inheritance rights (Barton 1919: 34).

SOCIOPOLITICAL ORGANIZATION. **Political organization.** The Ifugao are often cited as having achieved an elaborate legal system and an impressive level of technological efficiency without a corresponding development of governmental institutions (cf. Hoebel 1949). Chiefs, councils, and politically defined districts or other units are lacking in the traditional culture. Kinship serves to unite to some extent the people in a particular valley or watershed area, but prior to United States occupation, feelings of solidarity rarely extended much beyond the local area. Beyond this "home region" lay zones of increasingly less friendly contact, culminating in an outer "war zone," the locale of headhunting raids (Barton 1930: 113ff.). Conklin's "agricultural districts" appear to be the same as Barton's "home regions" (Conklin 1973). **Social differentiation.** Traditionally based on accumulation of wealth in form of rice lands, water buffalo, and slaves—the latter for sale in the lowlands. *Kadangyan* are wealthy aristocrats who validate their superior status by feast-giving and display of family heirlooms, such as hornbill headdresses, gold beads, swords, gongs, and old Chinese jars. *Kadangyan* families own sufficient rice land to achieve a surplus, whereas *natumok* families, with relatively little land, must borrow rice from *kadangyan* at high rates of interest, thus militating against their ever acquiring the necessary wealth to achieve *kadangyan* status. The very poor, with no land, are *nawatwat*, including servants and tenants on the lands of the wealthy. *Kadangyan* families tend to intermarry, although class lines vary in degree of distinctiveness, being less pronounced in the south (Barton 1922: 418). *Kadangyan* have no political power per se, although their prestige and influence, by virtue of ownership of wealth, may be considerable.

Achievement of full *kadangyan* status, in a ritual sense, is symbolized by a massive hardwood lounging bench, *hagabi,* made with considerable expenditure of labor by villagers. In Kiangan region, the candidate must have sponsored a lengthy and expensive period of feasting and ritual, *uyauwe,* and must provide food and rice wine during the making of the *hagabi* and a feast on the occasion of its installation on a paved platform outside his house. [Barton 1919: 67, 1922: 418, 1946: 126ff.; Baguilat 1940.] Poverty-stricken families formerly sold children into slavery, and children, like rice fields, might also be mortgaged against outstanding debts. Slaves, whether by debt or capture in warfare, were ordinarily sold to lowlanders. If kept by Ifugao, they were often freed, and children of slaves were considered freemen (Barton 1919: 35-36, 1946: 138). **Social control and justice.** The functions of government are (or were) accomplished by the operation of collective kinship obligations, including the threat of blood feud, together with common understanding of the adat or custom law given the people by ancestor heroes, in particular the inviolability of personal and property rights. This system of private law is facilitated by go-betweens (*monbaga*), respected men of wealth skilled in knowledge of genealogy and adat, who negotiate and witness property dealings, marriage transactions, and the like, and who are paid for their services. The effectiveness of a *monbaga* depends in part on his having a large and powerful kin group, who in effect stand behind his decisions. Death and fines are the main punishments, but they vary according to relative rank and kinship considerations. In general, "might makes right," and offenses committed by distant kinsmen or "aliens" are more likely to be avenged by outright killing. Ordeals may be invoked, and include the use of hot water or metal as well as dueling and wrestling. [Barton 1919: 57, 61, 75-77, 96.] **Warfare.** Disputes arising from violations of personal and property rights inevitably involve kinsmen on both sides. Within the local area, these are settled whenever possible by negotiation and the payment of fines. Kinsmen on one side or the other may, however, resort to killing, leading to protracted blood feuds. Feuding, accompanied by headhunting, was common before United States occupation, in particular between regions where ties of kinship were few or nonexistent. Raids into enemy territory were also profitable, since the women and children taken captive could be enslaved and sold to lowlanders. Headhunting expeditions occasionally involved 100 or more men, but tactics were limited to ambush, and unfavorable omens (e.g. bird calls or the positions of stars) frequently led to abandonment or postponement of the project. Enemy heads were displayed on skull shelves at the front of the houses of expedition leaders, enhancing their prestige and that of their kinsmen. It does not appear, however, that heads had any particular religious significance; nor does it appear that either heads or human sacrifice were a necessary part of religious ritual. Barton (1919: 109) comments that peace was never made between villages or districts and that peace between feuding kindreds, if concluded at all, was usually instigated by a case of intermarriage. Peacemaking ceremonies, involving go-betweens, are described by Barton (1946: 160ff.), but the well-developed peace-pact institutions of the Kalinga were by all accounts lacking among the Ifugao. [Barton 1919: 77ff; Lambrecht 1938: 445ff.]

RELIGION. Barton (1946: 19) characterizes Ifugao religion as pantheistic and, outside of India, the most extensive and pervasive such system yet reported. The Ifugao divide the universe into five regions: the known earth (*puga, pugao*); skyworld (*kabunian*); underworld (*dalum*); downstream region (*lagod*); and upstream region (*daiya*). The people traditionally refer to themselves as *i-pugao* (Ifugao), inhabitants of the known earth. **Supernaturals.** All five regions are inhabited by vast numbers of spirits, most with individual names, and listed by Barton in 35 categories, including hero ancestors, celestial bodies, natural phenomena, diseases, agriculture (Barton 1946: 11-12). Deities are invoked by priests in chanting sessions lasting five or more hours; invocations must be in a set order, and a priest may know of up to 1,500 deities. All deities have different natures and powers, but all are immortal, able to change form, become invisible, and move through space (Barton 1946: 14-18). **Practitioners.** Adult males traditionally function as priests within their own kindreds, invoking the spirits of departed ancestors within their own or closely related lines. Since United States occupation, the priestly function has, however, become more generalized. The role of priest, voluntary and learned by apprenticeship, is not a full-time occupation; payment is in meat and drink as well as the prestige of having a "good voice." [Barton 1946: 14, 99; 1938: 113.] **Ceremonies.** Most rites involve a number of priests (up to 15) chanting myths and invoking separate sets of deities simultaneously. The usual ritual pattern: *gonob*—invocation of deities; *duyun*—prayer to deities; *aiyag*—invitation to deity to possess priest; *hikkop*—possession of priest; *torbal*—exhortation to deity. Ancestral spirits are included in *gonob* and *aiyag* (invocation and invitation). Rites always involve an offering—from betel or chicken claw to pig and chicken—and the ritual consumption of rice wine, by spirits through priests, is an integral and continuing part of any rite. Most are performed beneath the house or granary, more rarely in field or forest. Most common are: augury, using bile sacs and livers of chickens and pigs; omenology, mainly bird calls; hunting; hill farm and rice cultivation. Other rites are associated with prestige feasts, head-

hunting, debt collection, sorcery, peace making, divorce. [Barton 1946: 99-126, 138-169; Lambrecht 1932, 1935, 1938, 1939, 1941, 1955, 1957.] Myth-magic is an important aspect of ritual, i.e. the belief that recitation of a myth gives the priest power over the deities and hero ancestors who appear in it. Myths, many of which have names, are likewise invoked as entities or personalities in their own right (Barton 1946: 203, 1955: 4-11). The narrative literature includes a series of epic romances, *hudhud*, recounting exploits of hero ancestors and sung in poetic meter by specialists, e.g. women at harvest time. They do not, however, figure in the ritual life (Daguio 1952; Lambrecht 1965, 1967). **Illness and medicine.** Illness is commonly caused by deities acting with the consent of the ancestors, and must be treated by priests through the medium of divinatory and curing rites (Barton 1946: 169-70). Illness and death can also be the result of sorcery or the "evil eye" (Barton 1946: 140-41, 1919: 70-72). **Soul, death, and afterlife.** If the deities take and return the soul, a man is sick; if they keep it, he dies. The corpse is washed and all orifices plugged, after which it is tied in a sitting position in an honorary death chair and, if of *kadangyan* status, given an insignia (hornbill beak for men, brass figurine for women). The body sits in state, guarded by a fire and corpse tender, for up to thirteen days, depending on the wealth of the deceased. A wake is held each night until the burial in a family sepulcher (a chamber at the end of a tunnel cut into soft rock) along with the remains of others—alternatively in a sealed coffin kept beneath the house or in a granarylike mausoleum. A second burial may be held three to five years after the first, especially if the deceased is unhappy and causing illness among the living. In some areas, males and females are buried separately (brother-sister avoidance), and children are buried in jars. [Barton 1946: 170-72, 179, 193-94, 197-98.]

BIBLIOGRAPHY. Baguilat 1940; Barton 1919, 1922, 1930, 1938, 1946, 1955; Beyer 1912-23: Sect. A, Set 14, *vols. 1-2, 9-16;* Beyer and Barton 1911; Conklin 1952, 1967a, 1967b, 1968, 1972, 1973; Daguio 1952; Davenport 1959; Dyen 1965; Eggan 1954, 1967; Fox 1956; Fox et al. 1965; Goodenough 1955; Hoebel 1949, 1954; Keesing 1962a; Lambrecht 1929, 1932, 1935, 1938, 1939, 1941, 1953, 1954, 1955, 1957, 1965, 1967, 1971; Loofs 1965; Reid 1971; Scott 1966; Spencer and Hale 1961; Villaverde 1909.

BONTOK

Synonyms. *Bontoc, Bontoc Igorot, Guianes, Igorot*

ORIENTATION. **Location and identification.** The Bontok culture type, noted for village wards (*ato*) with ceremonial stone platforms, men's houses, and girls' dormitories, centers on the steep gorge country of the upper Chico River system in the Cordillera Central of northern Luzon—the area of modern Bontok Subprovince, with Ifugao and Kankanai to the south and west, and Kalinga to the north. Although Bontok-speakers share a common origin tradition and ritual cycle, together with mutual rules of war and headhunting, uniformity of house styles, and the like, there is considerable diversity with respect to custom and dialect. Local settlements are autonomous, and the people identify themselves by the names of these settlements, the largest of which, Bontok (from *funtak*, "mountain," cf. Jenks 1905: 33), has since Spanish times been used as a generic exonym for the group as a whole. [Keesing 1949.] **Linguistic affiliation.** Most closely related to Kankanai (Lepanto). Bontok, Kankanai, Kalinga, and Ifugao appear to form a subgroup within the northern Luzon group of Philippine languages (Fox et al. 1965). **Demography.** Keesing (1949: 579) gives a 1930 figure for Bontok Subprovince of between 30,000 and 40,000, living in 32 villages. According to the 1960 Census, some 78,000 persons claimed Bontok as their native language. **History and cultural relations.** Eggan postulates a relatively late shift to wet-rice agriculture, resulting in increased population and the development of large, concentrated settlements. Characteristic features of Bontok, such as the village ward (*ato*) system, have spread to neighboring groups, e.g. Northern Kankanai. [Eggan 1963.] The Spanish in 1859 created the "comandancia" of Bontok, with its seat at the native town of that name, but Spanish control remained minimal and largely punitive. American occupation of the area, beginning in 1902, gradually brought about the cessation of headhunting, the extension of peace pacts and interregional trade, and the introduction of schools and missions. As of the early 1930s, however, the basic features of Bontok culture remained largely unchanged. [Keesing 1949: 579, 1962a: 92ff.]

SETTLEMENT PATTERN AND HOUSING. **Settlement pattern.** Compact villages or "towns" of from 300 to 2,000 persons, located near streams and surrounded by terraced rice fields. Sites may be adjacent to valley bottoms or on steep hillsides, with houses on stone-walled terraces (cf. Birket-Smith 1952). Settlements are divided into residential sections or "wards" (*ato*) ranging in number from as few as 6 to as many as 18, and containing from 14 to 50 houses. Each *ato* has as its ritual center a stone-paved platform, the site of former headhunting ceremonies, containing stone back rests, carved posts for display of enemy heads, and a stone-walled men's "clubhouse." [Jenks 1905: 48; Keesing 1949: 581; Cole 1945: 140.] **Housing.** Public buildings include the *pabafunan,* a low, grounded building with stone walls

and grass roof on a wooden frame, which, together with its stone-paved front court or ritual platform, provides a combination unmarried men's dormitory, council house, and clubhouse for male members of the *ato*. An *ato* usually contains in addition an unmarried girls' dormitory (*olag*), a hutlike structure built directly on the ground of mud and stone with a grass roof. Dwelling houses are ordinarily of one story with an earth floor and with storage and sleeping rooms, but rather small. Finer houses (*fayu*), belonging to wealthy aristocrat families, are likewise built directly on the ground but may be of two (or even three) stories, with pineboard walls, high pyramidal grass roofs, a rear wall of stone, and separate rooms for rice pounding, cooking, storage, and sleeping. These may be built by village work parties. Additional structures include well-made, pine-boarded granaries set on log foundations and stone-walled pig pens. [Jenks 1905: 50ff.; Keesing 1949.]

ECONOMY. **Agriculture.** Dry fields, bounded by stone walls, are used for sweet potatoes, maize, millet, and beans, and may be on hillsides or on valley flats near the houses. Stonewalled rice terraces are constructed on the hillsides and are irrigated by one of three methods: (1) diverting a stream into a high level field and allowing it to flow downhill (2) using weirs and dams, which sometimes entails the construction of raised wooden troughs to carry the water, or (3) carrying water to the fields in pots. All persons with fields bordering a waterway, or using a dam, cooperate in the construction. Water flow to individual fields is controlled by sluices and according to agreement by the owners. Field preparation begins with turning the soil and fertilizing with pig manure and compost when rice seedlings are transplanted. Young plants are protected with scarecrows, some driven by waterpower. Harvesting five months later is done by both sexes, breaking off single ears. Sweet potatoes may be planted in rice fields after the harvest. [Jenks 1905: 88-106.] **Hunting and fishing.** Wild buffalo, much sought after for use in marriage feasts, are hunted by large teams with the aid of dogs. Wild hogs are trapped in pits, and an occasional deer is killed; wild cocks, cats, and birds are snared and eaten. Fishing is done by stream diversion, driving fish into large traps or nets, or catching by hand. Snails and crabs are collected. [Jenks 1905: 81-87.] **Domestic animals.** Water buffalo, pigs, chickens, dogs, and a few cats. Pigs are penned and, like dogs, buffalo, and fowl, are usually eaten only at ceremonies. Hog raising is an important aspect of the culture, especially among the wealthy, and boars' tusks along with buffalo horns are given symbolic value (Birket-Smith 1952). [Jenks 1905: 107-11.] **Industrial arts.** Metal forging and working may be specialized within a community, a double piston bellows being used with charcoal to forge spear blades from imported bar iron. Brass items, such as smoking pipes, are cast by the lost wax process, but the largest proportion of artifacts are made of wood, particularly bamboo —digging sticks, knives, spears, furniture—stone being very little used in this regard. Large stone double mortars are, however, used for pounding rice (Birket-Smith 1952). Clothing is made of sewn bark or else woven from cotton or twisted bast fibers. Pottery, made by women, is a localized industry, as is the production of salt from brackish hot springs. Fermented sugarcane juice (*basi*), fermented rice (*tapey*), and a "soured stew" (*safueng*) are the chief beverages, besides water. Various meats, including locust, are preserved (fermented) by salting down in tightly covered gourds and jars. Rice beer, stored in large Chinese jars and drunk from cups, is an important accompaniment to religious feasts (Birket-Smith 1952). [Jenks 1905: 111-33, 139-48.] **Trade.** Local craft specialization is marked, and there is considerable intervillage trade in such items as spear blades, pipes, baskets, hats, beeswax, pottery, salt, *basi*, and breech cloths. Cotton cloth, brass wire, clothing, blankets, and axes are the main items imported into the Bontok area in exchange for rice. Unthreshed rice (in small bunches or "handfulls") serves as a standard of value in most transactions. [Jenks 1905: 152-59.] **Property.** Fields, houses, granaries, and items of movable property are owned either individually or jointly by spouses if they were acquired jointly. Land may be sold (for rice or other goods), but usually only in case of emergency. Rice fields may be leased in return for one-half the crop. Salt springs and irrigation springs are not owned, but held in common. Usable trees are owned individually, but ownership of nearby forest lands may be held in common. [Jenks 1905: 159-63.]

KIN GROUPS. Bilateral, with some skewing toward patrilineality, e.g. with respect to *ato* affiliations of males. An *ato* is ideally made up of a "set of patrilineal and patrilocal households," although Ego-based kinship circles (kindreds) nowadays cut across *ato* boundaries (Keesing 1949: 588, 592). Eggan (1963: 352) suspects that bilateral descent groups with corporate rights to land, similar to the "main families" of nearby Sagada, may have existed formerly, but information on this point is inconclusive. The wife upon marriage always belongs to the same *ato* as her husband (Wilson 1953b: 117). Little attention is paid to genealogies except among aristocrats, who reckon status according to genealogical nearness to senior descent lines (Keesing 1949: 594). **Kin terminology.** Himes (1964) gives the following terms of reference (additional lists are contained in Keesing 1949: 592 and Kroeber 1919: 76-77):

GrPa	*ikit*
Fa, FaBr, MoBr	*ama*
Mo, MoSi, FaSi	*ina*
Sibling	*aki*
ElSib	*yuna*
YoSib	*anuchi*
Cousin	*kayong*
Ch	*anak*
Nephew/niece	*ka-anakan*
GrCh	*apo*

MARRIAGE AND FAMILY. **Mode.** Courtship and choice of a mate in most instances take place within the institution of the girls' dormitory (*olag*), although aristocratic families tend to arrange the marriages of their children. The period of "trial marriage," during which the boy works for the girl's father but sleeps with her in the *olag*, normally leads to "permanent" marriage with the onset of pregnancy. Marriage is marked by a ceremony, provision of a house by the girl's parents, and property gifts from both sets of parents (Jenks 1905: 68). Marriage customs vary with class (Keesing 1949: 596). **Form.** Generally monogamy, with polygyny permitted (Jenks 1905: 59). **Extension of incest taboos.** Strict brother/sister avoidance results in avoidance of *olag* in boy's own *ato* or in subterfuges (Keesing 1949: 589). Marriage and/or sex is prohibited between a man and his mother, step-mother, mother's sister, daughter, step-daughter, sister, first cousin, and brother's widow (Jenks 1905: 68). **Residence.** Jenks (1905: 69) suggests neolocal, with the girl's father providing the house; whereas Keesing (1949: 568) says that the house is customarily provided by the groom's family and that residence is primarily patrilocal. **Domestic unit.** Comprises parents and young children, since older children live in the boys' or girls' houses, coming home for meals (Keesing 1949: 585). **Inheritance.** Property is owned individually unless acquired jointly by a married couple or inherited jointly by siblings. Children of both sexes inherit from parents at marriage, in return for support, with some preference for the eldest child. The order of inheritance is: lineal descendants, ascendants, siblings and their descendants, surviving spouse, executor in the event of no kinsmen (Jenks 1905: 164-65). According to Birket-Smith (1952), those who contribute most to the death feast of a deceased family head receive the greater part of the inheritance. **Divorce.** Rare when there are children, but absence of children is common cause for divorce. House goes to wife if both spouses agree to divorce, otherwise to plaintiff (Jenks 1905: 69-70). Rich and/or older men may take young girls as wives (Keesing 1949: 590). **Adoption.** Orphans may be taken in by kinsmen, together with their property, which is returned at marriage. Otherwise they are adopted as "servants" and do not receive property, only a house at marriage (Jenks 1905: 70).

SOCIOPOLITICAL ORGANIZATION. **Political organization.** The *ato* (ward or section within a village) is the major political grouping and is governed by the elders (*intugtukan*), who act as a court and in war and peace negotiations (Jenks 1905: 49, 167-68). Each *ato* is bounded and named and has a stone platform ritual center, which is also a men's "clubhouse" and council house. Although there is no *ato* chief or headman, high ranking *kadangyan* (wealthy aristocrats) wield much power in the council of elders (Keesing 1949: 598). [The 18 *ato* making up Bontoc town average 1.5 *kadangyan* each (Wilson 1953b: 115).] A village or town is a federation of *ato*, and although they may act together in certain ritual and economic activities, they remain politically autonomous (Keesing 1949: 584). There is some movement of residence between *ato*, usually when an individual enjoys more favorable property rights elsewhere, or his wife is of a higher status (Keesing 1949: 587). It seems clear from the remarks of Cawed-Oteyza (1965), Reid (1961), and others that a man's full status as an *ato* member is only achieved at marriage. **Social stratification.** The *kadangyan* or *kachangyan* (Iloko, *baknang*) comprise an aristocracy made up of current titleholders or "heads" of senior patrilineal lines, together with their immediate kin. The status is inherited from father to eldest son, is supported by wealth, and is validated by the performance of major ceremonies involving animal sacrifice and public feasting. For barrio Guinang, north of Bontoc town, Reid (1961) describes a wedding ceremony complex (*chono*), whereby household heads undertake a series of progressively more expensive feasts, culminating in those requiring the slaughter of many buffalo. Completion of the required series of feasts, which may continue over many years, validates a man's full marital status and his claim to membership in a higher status family line. The village declares a *chono* period, lasting up to two months, once every five years or so. Differential rank within the *kadangyan* class depends not only on ability to sponsor major feasts but also on the genealogical nearness of households and their heads to senior descent lines (Keesing 1949: 494-95). *Kadangyan* own most rice fields, give feasts from which they gain prestige, and sponsor the *ato*. Wealth is measured in granaries, buffalo, pigs, beads, gold earrings, bronze gongs, and porcelain jars. Others who own land form a majority middle class, often with marital links to *kadangyan* households. The lowest stratum is the *pusi* or *kokitak*, a class of indebted and bonded serfs who own little property and who sharecrop and work for *kadangyan* (Keesing 1949: 595). *Kadangyan* tend to form an endogamous class, even to the extent of condoning first-cousin marriage, with higher status maintained through strategic marriages, which often unite *ato* into alliances. In general, seniority is a principle of respect: senior generations enjoy respect and authority over juniors, older siblings have authority over younger, etc. (Keesing 1949: 593). **Social control and justice.** The *ato*, acting through its council of elders, is the

normal ritual and legal unit, the guardian of myth and adat. Procedures include trial by ordeal and liver divination, and there are set penalties for stealing and fines for assault, which are paid in livestock (Jenks 1905: 169-70). **Warfare.** According to legend, the *ato* with its stone platform was designated by Lumawig as the institution for the performance of headhunting ritual. The taking of a human head was not a prerequisite to marriage, nor were heads an essential part of religious ceremonies; headhunting was, however, an important avenue to prestige and power within the community and was perpetuated by desire for revenge arising out of endemic intervillage warfare. The taking of a head was celebrated by the *ato* in a month-long series of ceremonies and feasts, during which time *ato* members might be tattooed. Special tattoos were, however, reserved only for successful warriors. Heads were buried beneath the stones in front of the men's "clubhouse" (*pabafunan*) or, in the case of Bontoc town, were kept in a special headhouse (*fawi*). In some cases they were subsequently unearthed and stored in baskets within the clubhouse or *fawi*. The jaws were cleaned and boiled and used as handles for old and valued bronze gongs. Battles were fought with shields, spears, and axes, following a challenge between *ato* or whole settlements, but there was no conquest, plundering, or enslavement of the enemy. Peace pacts and formal peace-breaking ceremonies were usually concluded between two *ato* on behalf of their respective villages. [Jenks 1905: 176-88.]

RELIGION. **Supernaturals.** Of most importance are spirits of the dead, *anito*, who inhabit a spirit world in the nearby mountains similar in all respects to the land of the living. No action of any import can be taken without first consulting the *anito*, who give their answers through the calls of certain birds (Reid 1961: 55; Jenks 1905: 198). The spirits of the dead, with the exception of one's closest relatives, are the cause of injury, illness, and death. Lumawig, characterized as a supreme being by Jenks, personifies the forces of nature and is the legendary creator, friend, and teacher of the Bontok, all of whom share in what Cole has called a "Lumawig Cult" (Cole 1945: 142). [Jenks 1905: 196ff.] **Practitioners.** *Patay* are an hereditary class of priests who perform monthly ceremonies to Lumawig; they are divided into three categories: *waku*, who announce rest days and ceremonies; *patay*, who conduct the ceremonies; and the unnamed weather specialists. Old people may become *insupak*, healers who treat injuries and illnesses by exorcising the offending *anito* spirit. Their procedures include touching or stroking the afflicted part, gentle exhalations, and repetitious formulas, but they do not engage in dancing or swinging, nor do they enter a trance state. Any household head, and in fact any person, may at one time or another perform minor rituals and propitiatory acts designed to influence *anito*. [Jenks 1905: 198ff.] **Ceremonies.** Ceremonies generally take the form of religious festivals (*kanyau* or *cañao*) involving the entire membership of an *ato* and including dancing, animal sacrifice, ritual songs and prayers, and the taking of omens from the gall bladders of pigs. The *ato* elders participate in or direct many of these activities (Cawed-Oteyza 1965). Jenks lists ten agricultural ceremonies marking germination and transplanting of rice, protection of seedlings, harvest, and planting of sweet potatoes and beans. He also mentions three rituals controlling climate (to bring rain, to end rain, to dispel cold and fog). Every ten days or so, a sacred day of rest is observed (*tengao*), and upon the return of a successful headhunting party to the *ato* the *kafokab* ceremony is performed (Jenks 1905: 206-14). Birket-Smith (1952) describes what appear to be ritual fishing expeditions by men following a headhunting or harvest ceremony, and Cawed-Oteyza (1965: 343) describes ritual stone fights between the men of Bontoc and Samoki—neighboring communities—designed to increase the size of sweet potato tubers. In addition, aristocratic *kadangyan* families sponsor periodic status-validating feasts and animal sacrifices (see under *Social stratification*). **Soul, death, and afterlife.** When death occurs, the ancestral *anito* are invited to a family meal of chicken and the body is washed, dressed, placed in a death chair, and put on view for five days or so. There may be a feast, with a display of sacrificed buffalo heads on poles. For deceased family heads, burial is in an unused rice field, in a hollowed-out log coffin surmounted by buffalo horns. The unmarried dead are buried near the house in stone-lined graves without coffins. Women and children do not attend burials, which are followed by a buffalo feast, then a fish feast. [Jenks 1905: 74ff.]

BIBLIOGRAPHY. Beyer 1912-23 (Sect. A, Set 15); Birket-Smith 1952; Cawed-Oteyza 1965; Cole 1945; Eggan 1963; Fox et al. 1965; Himes 1964; Jenks 1905; Keesing 1949, 1962a; Kroeber 1919; Reid 1961; Wilson 1953b.

LEPANTO (SAGADA)

Synonyms. *Katangnang, Lepanto Igorot, Northern Kankanai, Sagada Igorot*

ORIENTATION. **Location and identification.** Speakers of Northern Kankanai languages occupy some 30 villages or "towns" in the western portion of Bontok Subprovince and adjacent Ilocos Sur Province, once a portion of the old Spanish "comandancia" of Lepanto (Keesing 1938). According to Moss (1920a: 344), the people call themselves Katangnang, presumably related to Kataugnan, an older name for the Northern Kankanai or Lepanto dialect (Keesing 1962a: 93). It is probable, however, that ethnic identification is more commonly with one's village or local settlement area (cf. Eggan 1960: 25). Vanoverbergh (1952, 1953b, 1954b) and Aquino (1954) have described the ceremonial customs of Bauko and Payeo, respectively, but the bulk of the literature on this region, by Eggan, Scott, and Pacyaya, concerns the inhabitants of the modern municipality of Sagada, only a few miles west, as the crow flies, from Bontoc town. Keesing (1962a: 4, 93) describes the Lepantos as "industrious, group-minded, and ceremonious farmers," practitioners of intensive wet-rice terracing like their immediate neighbors to the west, the Bontok. Similarities to the Bontok culture type are marked, including the division of settlements into "wards," each with a men's "clubhouse" and girls' "dormitory," male "priesthoods," and socially stratified "classes," with validation of status and attainment of prestige gained through sponsorship of expensive quasi-religious feasts. These and other similarities in myth and ritual are attributed by Eggan (1960) to relatively recent borrowing from Bontok. **Geography.** Eastern shoulder of the Central Cordillera at approximately 5,000 feet, an area of partly eroded limestone basins drained by tributaries of the upper Abra and Chico river systems. The region is largely deforested, with a nine-month rainy season and a temperature range of 40° to 90° F. (Eggan 1960: 25; Scott 1966: 220-21). **Linguistic affiliation.** Fox et al. (1965) find a high (80 percent) shared basic vocabulary as between Northern Kankanai (Bauko) and Bontok, with an indicated time separation of less than 600 years, from which they conclude that the two groups shared a common culture as recently as around 1400 A.D. **Demography.** The Lepanto Igorot or Northern Kankanai number approximately 35,000 (Keesing 1962a: 93) of whom some 10,000 reside in Sagada municipality (Eggan 1960: 25). **History and cultural relations.** Sagada early came under the jurisdiction of the Spanish military government, and there has been a long history of acculturation, chiefly as a result of mission schools and churches established since the Spanish-American War. Despite these influences, Sagada has retained much of the indigenous culture, including the annual round of ceremonial activities. Changes in house styles and technology are discussed in Pacyaya (1964) and in other aspects of culture in Pacyaya (1971) and Eggan and Pacyaya (1962).

SETTLEMENT PATTERN AND HOUSING. **Settlement pattern.** Compact settlements or "towns," which in 1932 contained an average of 145 houses totaling 600 to 700 persons (Keesing 1938). Sagada proper, with a population of 3,000, is composed of two named territorial divisions, each further subdivided into wards (*dapay*), corresponding to the Bontok *ato*.

Housing. Dwelling houses are similar to those of Bontok, and may be of two or three stories. Sleeping quarters are within a low boxlike room at ground level, while upper stories are used for storage. These older style houses are, however, rapidly being replaced by modern structures modeled on those of lowland Filipinos (Pacyaya 1964).

ECONOMY. Wet-rice terracing and most other aspects of the basic economy are similar to Bontok (cf. Scott 1966: 220-36).

KIN GROUPS. Sagada has six major bilateral (non-unilineal) descent groups or "families," subdivided into lesser groups, and tracing ancestry back eight to ten generations from founding male ancestors whose names they take. The individual Sagadan is potentially a member of a large number of such groups; in practice, membership is activated according to the actual or potential benefits to be derived. These groups do not control marriage, but they do conduct certain ceremonial activities and hold corporate rights to certain hillsides and trees, exercised through appointed "wardens." Corporate ownership does not, however, extend to rights in rice land, perhaps because the groups stem from an earlier period of shifting agriculture. The personal kindred, reckoned vertically to great-great-grandparents and laterally to third cousins, is responsible for revenge and wergild and defines the ideal exogamic range. [Eggan 1960.] **Kinship terminology.** Eggan (1960: 32-33) gives the following terms:

	Reference	Address
GrPa	alapo	alapo
Fa	ama	ama
FaBr, MoBr	alitao	ama
Mo	ina	ina
MoSi, FaSi	ikit	ina
Sib	etad, besat	besat
Older/Younger Sib	iona/innodi	iona/innodi
Cousin	pingsan	besat
Ch	anak	anak
Nephew/niece	kanakan	anak, kanakan
GrCh	apo	apo

MARRIAGE AND FAMILY. Similar in practically all respects to Bontok (cf. Eggan 1960).

SOCIOPOLITICAL ORGANIZATION. Sagada proper is divided in two, Dagdag and Demang, by irrigation streams. The two groups occasionally take opposite sides in ceremonies and games, including an annual "rock fight" among boys, and may formerly have buried each other's dead. Each has its own sacred grove, guardian spirits, and sacred springs. These two divisions are further subdivided into 12 wards (dapay), each with a ceremonial platform and men's and girls' houses. Households within a ward form a cooperative unit, obon, which is not, however, kinship based. Residence following marriage is variable, and there is no evidence of ward patrilocality as alleged by Keesing (1949) for Bontok wards. Dapay are governed by councils of elders, amama, which also organize rituals. [Eggan 1960.] **Social stratification.** Kadangyan are the wealthier and kodo the poorer people, although according to Eggan the actual range of wealth differences is not great. The wealthy are expected to validate their position by elaborate and expensive marriage celebrations (bayas) at periodic intervals, but of perhaps greater significance is the fact that certain kadangyan customs, e.g. particular burial practices and special ceremonial obligations, are associated with membership in certain descent groups, regardless of whether the individual is rich or poor (Eggan 1960: 31). This is in all probability related to Keesing's (1938) observation that those with fewer resources frequently impoverish themselves, going in debt to the wealthy to obtain the necessary animals for sacrifice and feast giving.

RELIGION. Sagadan religious ideas and ceremonial practices are generally similar to those of Bontok (cf. Eggan 1960; Eggan and Scott 1963, 1965; Scott 1966, 1967; Pacyaya 1971). The spirits of deceased ancestors (anitos) make up the most important category of supernaturals, and relatively great emphasis is placed on death ceremonies ensuring the future welfare of the soul in the "house of the anitos." The full cycle of death rituals, performed only for married persons, includes initial placement of the corpse in a death chair, encoffinment and burial in ancestral caves or stone-lined mausoleums below ground, and a lengthy mourning period, which is gradually terminated by a series of animal sacrifices. The unmarried are buried in jars near the house or in a nearby camote field. [Eggan 1960; Solheim 1959; Pacyaya 1961.]

BIBLIOGRAPHY. Aquino 1954; Bacdayan 1967b; Eggan 1960; Eggan and Pacyaya 1962; Eggan and Scott 1963, 1965; Fox et al. 1965; Keesing 1938, 1949, 1962a; Moss 1920a; Pacyaya 1961, 1964, 1971; Robertson 1914; Scott 1966, 1967; Solheim 1959; Vanoverbergh 1952, 1953b, 1954b.

SOUTHERN GROUPS

THE PAGAN PEOPLES of Benguet Subprovince—Ibaloi and Kankanai—are less well known than those of neighboring Ifugao and Bontok. The bulk of the available ethnographic data pertains to the linguistically distinct Ibaloi, whose traditional homeland appears to have been in the region of Kabayan, an ancient, gold-bearing district on the upper Agno River, in what is now east-central

Benguet (Keesing 1962a: 52). DeRaedt (1964: 262ff.) argues for a relatively late introduction of wet rice into this area, thus accounting for some of the differences in social institutions and religious representations as between the Ibaloi and the Ifugao and Bontok to the northeast. Kankanai speakers are found in northern Benguet (the so-called "southern Kankanai") and in western Bontok (the "northern Kankanai" or Lepanto). Aside from language, however, there appears to be little that is distinctively "Kankanai" in these areas. Those to the north, e.g. Sagada, have been heavily influenced by Bontok and could perhaps in most respects be considered a westward extension of the Bontok culture type (cf. Eggan 1960); those to the south appear to have acculturated to a large extent to the Ibaloi culture type (cf. Moss 1920b). In short, the Kankanai—inhabitants of the old military district of Lepanto—appear at best nowadays as a linguistic category; culturally they are perhaps best considered in relation to Bontok on the one hand and Ibaloi on the other, a procedure followed in the subgrouping of these peoples in the present volume.

BIBLIOGRAPHY. DeRaedt 1964; Eggan 1960; Keesing 1962a; Moss 1920b.

IBALOI

Synonyms. *Benguet Igorots, Benguetanos, Ibaloy, Inibaloi, Inibaloy, Inibiloi, Nabaloi*

ORIENTATION. Ibaloi speakers, totaling close to 60,000, occupy the southernmost heights of the Cordillera Central, in southern Benguet Subprovince and the adjacent mountain areas of Pangasinan, La Union, and Nueva Vizcaya. To the east, high mountain ranges separate the Ibaloi from their traditional enemies, the Ifugao; to the north are the linguistically distinct but culturally similar Kankanai; to the south and west are Pangasinan and Ilocano-speaking lowland Christian Filipinos (Keesing 1962a: 51; Moss 1920b: 211; Barnett 1967). According to Scheerer (1905: 98), the people call themselves Ibaloi and their language Nabaloi (possibly from Ilocano *i* "inhabitant of" and *baliu* "beyond the river," i.e. "stranger"). Local terms and customs vary, however; there has been considerable intermarriage with Kankanai in the northern sectors, while lowland acculturative influences are especially noticeable in the south and particularly around the Baguio-La Trinidad area, a ma-

jor market center and focus of recently introduced commercial crop and livestock production. Ethnographic data on the Ibaloi largely pertain to irrigated-rice growers in the more settled valleys; the more remote mountain settlements, particularly in peripheral areas, are virtually unknown. New commercial ventures, added to the old resource of gold, have increased the traditionally powerful position of wealthy aristocrats, and the accumulation of wealth, with its attendant socioreligious connotations, constitutes a major theme in Ibaloi culture. Christianity, schools, gold mining, cash crops, and wage labor have brought changes in material life, together with questioning of indigenous religious and ceremonial practices, with their heavy demands for expenditure of ritual wealth (Keesing 1962a; Barnett 1967; Moss 1920b).

SETTLEMENT PATTERN AND HOUSING. Houses are for the most part scattered in fields or on hillsides within a settlement area. "River settlements," e.g. along the Agno, stress wet-rice growing, while "mountain settlements" on ridges and slopes grow more root crops (Keesing 1962a: 49). According to Barnett (1967), most settlements are small, consisting of 20 or so households nestled in narrow mountain valleys. Houses, raised about five feet on posts, resemble those of the Ifugao, each with a pyramidal thatched roof surmounting a single, walled room, with space above for storage of rice bundles. Walls of older style houses are of hewn pine boards, fitted to grooves in the sills, and framing timbers are mortised. A removable ladder leads to a single door fitted with a sliding wooden latch, and windows are provided with wooden shutters, which slide in grooves in the framing. [Moss 1920b; Scott 1966: 175ff.] According to Moss (1920b), houses of the rich may have up to five or more rooms, and Scheerer (1905: plate 70) shows what presumably is a house of this type, which appears to be modeled on those of lowland Filipinos.

ECONOMY. Subsistence mainly from agriculture, with hunting and fishing relatively minor sources of food. Commercial crop and livestock production and wage labor have been introduced into some areas. The growing of rice occupies a central position in Ibaloi culture; rice is the ideal ritual food and rice beer a necessary accompaniment to most religious festivals (cf. Barnett 1967). Tubers (sweet potato, taro, cassava) are important sources of food and, together with beans and maize, constitute the bulk of the diet among the less well-to-do. The meat of pigs, dogs, chickens, carabao, horses, and cattle is consumed only on occasions of religious and status-validating feasts. Minnows, frogs, snails, locusts, and fruit (mainly bananas) round out the diet. Sugarcane is processed into wine, less popular than rice beer. Wet-rice fields are terraced, in some cases with stone walls, and water buffalo are used in some areas for plowing and harrowing. [Moss 1920b; Barnett 1967.] **Domestic animals.** Wealthy families may own up to 1,000 head of cattle, many for export to the lowlands, as well as large numbers of horses, water buffalo, and pigs—the latter frequently cared for by the poor on a share basis. Dogs intended for sacrifice are usually purchased in the lowlands and fattened locally. [Moss 1920b.] **Industries.** Metal working does not appear highly developed, although there is some mining and panning of gold. Cloth and pottery are mostly purchased from the lowlands. [Moss 1920b.] **Trade.** The city of Baguio has developed as a major trade center, where Ibaloi exchange coffee, gold dust, and cattle for such things as cloth, salt, tobacco, pottery, dogs, and pigs. Purchases may also be made with money earned as labor in mining, lumbering, and porterage. [Moss 1920b; Barnett 1967.]

KINSHIP AND MARRIAGE. Kinship appears to be reckoned bilaterally, with the personal kindred activated on occasions such as death feasts (cf. Leaño 1965). First-cousin marriage is theoretically prohibited, but occurs in practice, particularly among the well-to-do, who also arrange the marriages of their offspring. Parents on both sides furnish animals for slaughter at betrothal and marriage rites. Residence may be briefly matrilocal until the young couple set up their own residence, at which time they also receive their inheritances of land. The household normally consists of a couple and their unmarried offspring. Divorce is common in the early stages of marriage, but rarely occurs after children are born. Inheritance appears to be bilateral with both sexes inheriting, although eldest sons apparently receive preference with respect to agricultural land. [Moss 1920b; Barnett 1967; Wilson 1953b.] **Kin terminology.** Kroeber (1919) gives the following terms, obtained from C. R. Moss:

Fa	ama
Mo	ina
So, Da	anaka
Sib	agi
GrPa	apo
GrCh	apo
MoBr, FaBr	pang-ama-an
MoSi, FaSi	pang-ina-an
Nephew/niece	pang-anak-ana
Cousin	kasingsing
Spouse	asawa

SOCIOPOLITICAL ORGANIZATION. Ibaloi settlements lack the division into wards with associated men's and girls' houses characteristic of Lepanto and Bontok, although they claim they once had communal sleeping houses (Moss 1920b: 214). Each settlement has its own council (tongtong) of old and wise men (impanama), which always includes any local mem-

bers of the wealthy and powerful class of aristocrats. The council decides offenses against the adat and imposes fines, usually a pig or carabao. Warfare and headhunting, directed at ancient enemies such as Ifugao and related peoples to the east, ceased some time after the coming of the Spanish in 1829 (Moss 1920b). **Social stratification.** There is a reportedly marked differentiation between the rich (baknang) and the poor (abitug), with a considerable concentration of power and influence in the hands of the former. The baknang favor class-endogamous marriages, frequently with near relatives, with the result that most are kinsmen by blood or marriage (Moss 1920b). Baknang are required by custom to sponsor prestige-validating feasts (pashit), at which progressively larger numbers of animals are slaughtered. These begin soon after marriage and may continue over many years, with some individuals repeating the cycle to further enhance prestige. These so-called marriage feasts, seldom held in Benguet nowadays (Barnett 1967), appear to be part of a larger pattern whereby an individual attempts to enhance his prestige, and ultimately his status in the spirit world, by the accumulation and distribution of wealth in the form of feasts and sacrifices—gifts which please the ancestral spirits and predispose them to grant larger harvests and bigger herds, which in turn can be converted to even greater ritual expenditure. The demands of this system on the poor are considerable, forcing them to borrow from the rich, who in turn get richer. [Leaño 1965; Barnett 1967.]

RELIGION. **Supernaturals.** Deified ancestral culture heroes, the greatest of whom is Kabigat, are called collectively kabunian, a term which in some areas, and possibly under Christian influence, has been interpreted in the sense of a supreme being. Natural forces, e.g. thunder, and heavenly bodies, e.g. sun and moon, are invoked in prayers and ritual songs, and there are numerous classes of malevolent spirits who inhabit high mountains or deep forests. [Moss 1920b.] Most important of all are the souls of the dead, the "spirit relatives" (kaamaran), who must be fed and their desires and needs satisfied lest they visit illness and misfortune on the living or fail to intercede on their behalf with higher beings, the kabunian. Earthly status is perpetuated within the spirit world, e.g. those who were wealthy aristocrats on earth join a separate class of spirits in the land of the dead, but maintenance of status in the spirit world depends on the proper performance of ritual sacrifices by one's living kinsmen. The spirit relatives communicate their needs and advice to the living through dreams and omens and by possessing the bodies of kinsmen or mediums. By keeping his spirit relatives happy and satisfied, a man can ensure good fortune for himself, specifically increase in wealth and prestige and thus a favored place in the spirit world when he dies. In truth, the Ibaloi constitute a community of the living and the dead, a system of interdependent relationships, the social and economic consequences of which are discussed above under *Social stratification*. [Leaño 1965; Moss 1920b.] **Practitioners.** The term *mambunung* (lit., "prayer sayer"), usually glossed as "priest," appears to have referred originally to males who, through a religious experience or "call" and a subsequent apprenticeship, learned lengthy prayers and formulas, addressed mainly to *kabunian* deities, together with the complex ritual sequences of the major ceremonies. According to Wilson (1953a), they were formerly important and influential members of village councils, with regard to making war and concluding peace and officiating at trials by ordeal. Nowadays the term appears to have been extended to include diviners, dream interpreters, and mediums, oftentimes women. *Mambunung* in this latter sense may divine the cause of an illness and the proper curative ritual, usually involving animal sacrifice, prayers, and recitation of sacred songs and stories. Dancing, drumming, trance, and the like are apparently not features of these curative rites (Moss 1920b). Spirits of the dead can possess the bodies of living kinsmen or of persons proficient in "seeing" spirits (mediums), through whom they "speak," communicating their desires and advice to mortals. According to Leaño (1965), *mambunung*, male or female, can also be possessed by spirits, although they cannot see them as can true "spirit see-ers." **Ceremonies.** According to Moss (1920b: 289), the Ibaloi know some 40 different classes of ceremonies having to do with illness (the most numerous), war and peace, witchcraft, birth, death, and rice (cf. Claerhoudt 1966). Most involve an initial invocation and invitation to the spirits, ritual drinking of rice beer (*tapey*), the lengthy recitation of prayers and formulas, and the ritual killing of a pig or other animal. Rice and pork are divine foods, i.e. desired by the spirits, a quality not possessed by water buffalo, sweet potato, or taro (Leaño 1965: 165). Certain major ceremonies or ceremonial cycles, e.g. the *pashit* "marriage feast" cycles and the lengthy series of funerary death feasts, are integral parts of the ritual wealth and status-validating complex that motivates so much of traditional Ibaloi behavior. In sponsoring a series of increasingly expensive *pashit* feasts, involving the slaughter of many animals, the consumption of much rice and beer, and the dedication of other valuables, a man shares his wealth with his living kinsmen and spirit relatives and shows his gratitude to the latter for their help in making wealth accumulation possible. Sponsorship of a *pashit* cycle symbolizes as well the gradual separation of a married couple from their families of orientation—an essential step toward achieving independent status of one's spirit in the spirit world (Leaño 1965). Although *pashit* have virtually disappeared from the modern

scene, the lengthiness and cost of obligatory funeral rituals have if anything increased (Barnett 1967: 316). **Soul, death, and afterlife.** Man has at least two "souls," one of which (*adia*) is prone to travel; should it meet with misfortune while absent from the body, a man may sicken or die. A "life line" or guardian spirit or "soul" (*kaajongan*) at death goes to Mt. Pulag in the east (Leaño 1965; Moss 1920b: 273). According to Leaño, the spirit of a deceased person must be made aware of its new status, for which purpose the corpse is placed in a death chair (*aradan*), where it can observe relatives mourning and preparing for the funeral. According to Moss (1920b), the chair is fitted with a hole in the seat and a vessel beneath to catch the fluids of bodily decomposition. Moss, whose data pertain to Kabayan in northern Ibaloi territory, reports the period from death to burial, known as *siling*, as lasting several months in the case of a wealthy aristocrat, during which time the deceased's herds of buffalo, horses, etc. are slaughtered in a lengthy series of ritual feasts, the expenses of which must be partially met by members of the deceased's kindred. Leaño's data, from Trinidad municipality and later in time, indicate earlier burial (probably for hygenic reasons), followed by a month or more of funerary feasts. These latter are occasions for performance of the Song for the Dead (*du-dyang*), all-night affairs in which experienced singers of both sexes engage in a highly stylized form of communication directed at the spirit of the deceased, encouraging it to depart peacefully and well disposed toward the living. During these postburial death feasts the body of the deceased may be represented by a *dagba*, a cylindrical salt basket made of bamboo and placed in the death chair (Leaño 1965: 167ff.). Burial, according to Leaño, is preferably in a grave beneath the house of the deceased (Leaño 1965: 186). According to Moss (1920b: 329ff.), the body is encoffined and buried in the ground or in a natural cave. The rich in Kabayan may be buried within rock mounds or in artificially made rock chambers. The latter, in the form of [family?] mausoleums capable of containing a number of coffins, require months of hard labor involving heating the rock with fire followed by sudden cooling with water.

BIBLIOGRAPHY. Barnett 1967; Claerhoudt 1966; Keesing 1962a; Kroeber 1919; Leaño 1965; Moss 1920b, 1924; Moss and Kroeber 1919; Scheerer 1905; Scott 1966; Wilson 1953a, 1953b.

KANKANAI

Synonyms. *Igorot, Kankanay, Kakanay, Southern Kankanai*

ORIENTATION. According to Moss (1920a: 344), the Igorots of what is now northwestern Benguet Subprovince and the adjacent high country of northern La Union and southern Ilocos Sur "speak the same dialect, have similar customs, and call themselves by the same name, 'Kakanay' or 'Kankanay.'" The Kankanai homeland, on the eastern edge of the Cordillera Central, and drained by the headwaters of the Amburayan, comprises portions of the old Spanish comandancias of Amburayan and Lepanto—a region of ancient gold and copper mines, early targets in a long history of Spanish attempts to gain control of the interior highlands. The indigenous cultures of this "southern Igorot" area, notably Kankanai and Ibaloi, have undoubtedly undergone acculturative changes as a result of Spanish, and later American, exploitation of this mineral rich region. [Keesing 1962a: chap. 4.] Although recognizing the linguistic similarity of the "southern" Kankanai to their neighbors to the north, the Lepanto or "northern" Kankanai, Moss felt that on cultural grounds the two should probably be regarded as separate groups, a procedure later followed by Keesing, who estimated the population of the "Kankanai, or southern Kankanai" at approximately 30,000 persons living in some 150 settled localities (Keesing 1962a: 93 and map facing p. 95). Wet rice is grown on terraced fields, although these are not as extensive or well made as among the Bontok and Ifugao; scattered settlements are the rule, and the compact towns of the Lepanto and Bontok are absent, as are also, apparently, the institutions of village wards, men's "clubhouses," and girls' "dormitories." Differences in wealth are, however, marked, and, as among the Ibaloi, the wealthy tend to have considerable power. Ritual life and customary law are in general similar to Ibaloi, according to Moss. [Moss 1920a; Keesing 1962a: 93; Barton 1930: 300-01.] On the other hand, Bello (1967), reporting on recent fieldwork in Bakun, in northwestern Benguet not far from the Bontok border, was impressed by similarities to culture types farther north and east, and by stories of earlier migration from Lepanto (specifically Besao, near Sagada). Aside from the few observations on ceremonial customs, cited above, relatively little is actually known about the northern Benguet area, making it difficult to determine what, if anything, is distinctively "Kankanai," aside from language; and to what extent the culture type may reflect borrowing or actual migration from Bontok or the effects of the local mining economy on such things as native patterns of wealth accumulation and social stratification. To be considered also in this connection would be directional change subsumed under Eggan's concept of "cultural drift," wherein the Kankanai culture type would be best understood in the light of generalized culture trends in other parts of Mountain Province (Eggan 1963).

BIBLIOGRAPHY. Barton 1930; Bello 1967; Eggan 1963; Keesing 1962a; Moss 1920a.

NORTHERN GROUPS

NORTH OF THE MT. DATA-BONTOK area, the high Cordillera gradually gives way to a jumble of broken mountains and hills under 4,000 feet, with main river valleys at considerably lower altitudes. The languages of this northern one-third of Luzon Island—coastal Iloko and Ibanag, as well as inland Tinggian, Apayao, Kalinga, and Gaddang—are closely enough related to constitute a subgroup within the northern Philippine family of languages (Thomas and Healey 1962). Furthermore, the findings of Fox et al. (1965), that each of the interior languages, with the partial exception of Northern Kalinga, is more closely related to coastal Iloko-Ibanag than it is to any other language, lends support to Keesing's (1962a) view of these mountain peoples as relatively late offshoots from surrounding lowland populations. The heart of this area is an upland watershed drained by tributaries of the Abulug, Tineg, and middle Chico, flowing north, west, and east, respectively. Much of this region is covered with dense tropical forest, supporting integral swiddening systems devoted to the cultivation of mountain rice (Apayao, Mountain Tinggian, Northern Kalinga, Pagan Gaddang). Population is sparse, in marked contrast to the remainder of the Cordillera, where wet-rice terracing predominates. Basic cultural patterns among the Apayao, Northern Kalinga, Pagan Gaddang (and probably Mountain Tinggian) appear markedly similar, e.g. the basically egalitarian, endogamous, kin-based settlement area made up of scattered hamlets, wherein leadership is diffuse and based essentially on a reputation for bravery and a personal charisma signified by accumulated ritual wealth in ancient jars, beads, and gongs. In this respect the Apayao *mengal*, renowned warriors-headhunters, recall the Bagobo *magani*, the "warrior chiefs" of the Davao Gulf hinterland on Mindanao. One is further reminded here of Laura Benedict's demonstration of close parallels in respect to these and other elements of socioreligious culture between the pagan Bagobo and the lowland Filipinos (Tagal, Ilocano, Bisayan) portrayed in the earliest Spanish accounts of three centuries ago (Benedict 1916: 250ff.). In this view, the so-called "valley" Tinggian of the middle Abra, as well as the Southern Kalinga of Lubuagan—settled agriculturists in large villages where kin-based institutions give way to considerations of wealth based on ownership of rice fields—would, like Bontok, Lepanto, and Ifugao, be seen as the product of indigenous culture change operating on an essentially similar base widespread throughout the Philippines, and most likely initiated by the introduction (or local development) of wet-rice terracing into central Mountain Province at some time in the past (cf. Eggan 1963).

BIBLIOGRAPHY. Benedict 1916; Eggan 1963; Fox et al. 1965; Keesing 1962a; Thomas and Healey 1962.

KALINGA

Synonyms. *Calinga, Kalingga*

ORIENTATION. **Location.** The drainage area of the middle Chico and its tributaries, the Mabaca, Saltan, Bananid, and Tanudan, roughly conterminous with modern Kalinga Subprovince, with Apayao to the north and Bontok to the south. **Identification.** The term Kalinga is said to have its origins in the word for "enemy" among lowland Christians (e.g. Ibanag) farther down the Chico, and was widely used in Spanish times for mountain people adjacent to the middle Cagayan valley (Keesing 1962a: 223). Beyer (1917: 49) stressed diversity in physical type, language, and culture and regarded the so-called Kalinga as probably consisting of several distinct peoples. Dozier (1966), although aware of what he calls subcultural differences, stresses the fact of twentieth-century linguistic and cultural integration, regarding the modern Kalinga as having the "most compelling sense of tribal awareness" of any of the Mountain Province peoples (Dozier 1967: vii). This development he attributes to the spread of the peace pact institution throughout Kalinga, together with pacification subsequent to American occupation. Dozier's view of Kalinga culture is, however, disputed in some important respects by Takaki (1969). Settlements along the Saltan and Mabaca rivers in Balbalan district (the "Northern Kalinga") have been studied by Dozier. Barton (1949) and Bacdayan (1967a) describe selected aspects of the "Southern Kalinga" around Lubuagan, while those farther south, in Tinglayan, are dealt with briefly in an unpublished paper by Folkmar (1906). The "Eastern Kalinga" (Madukayan, east of the Tanudan River) are known chiefly through papers by Scott (1958a, 1958b, 1960). **Geography.** High, rugged terrain of the Cordillera Central. Settlements are in lower valleys, at about 2,000 feet, with thick, semitropical vegetation. Steep mountain slopes are covered with cogon grass, and pine trees grow on the higher mountain ridges. **Linguistic affiliation.** Linguists appear to agree that Kalinga belongs with most of the other languages of northern Luzon in a single language family. There is an apparent disagreement, based wholly on lexicostatistical evidence, as to whether Kalinga subgroups with Ilocano, Tinggian, Apayao, Ibanag, and Gaddang (Thomas and Healey 1962) or with Bontok, Ifugao, and Kankanay (Fox et al. 1965); a suggested resolution has been to place Northern Kalinga (Balbalasan) with the former and Southern Kalinga (Lubuagan) with the latter (Thomas and Healey 1962: 31). According to Dozier's informants, all Kalinga dialects are mutually intelligible, but this judgment may have been influenced by the widespread usage nowadays of phonetically simplified Kalinga, heavily influenced by Ilocano (Dozier 1966: xvi). **Demography.** About 40,000, with major concentration around Lubuagan Municipal District (Dozier 1966: 11). **History and cultural relations.** The evidence for anything like a Kalinga culture type in other than relatively recent times is obscure. Early American reports considered the Northern Kalinga as one culturally with their neighbors to the west, the Tinggian, and the Southern Kalinga of Tinglayan as "first cousins" of the Bontoks, leaving "Kalinga" to refer to a "strange nomadic people in the eastern foothills" (Dozier 1966: 32). The modern Kalinga are probably descendants of a number of different peoples, migrants into the area from lowland Abra and Cagayan. The Kalinga region until recent times has apparently been one of much local differentiation with respect to physical type, language, and culture, due in part to isolation of small endogamous populations (cf. Eggan 1963: 350), and, beginning in early Spanish times, the opening up of northern Kalinga to influences from Tinggian and beyond. The rather marked differences between north and south Kalinga can be seen as due in part to these various differentiating factors, including (and perhaps of most importance) the relatively recent introduction into southern Kalinga of wet-rice terracing from neighboring Bontok. [Dozier 1966: 32-35; Eggan 1963.] The Kalinga as a whole, however, are distinguished nowadays from neighboring groups not only by a network of mutually intelligible dialects but also by a characteristic organization into endogamous regions or "territories" and by the widespread development of peace pacts among these regions.

SETTLEMENT PATTERN AND HOUSING. **Settlement pattern.** Northern Kalinga hamlets of 6 to 30 households, clustered in canyon or small hill slope terraces, average 5.5 persons per house. Southern Kalinga settlements or "towns" may contain well over 200 houses, with an average of 4.8 per household (Dozier 1966: 12). **Housing.** House types vary among different groups and even within the same village, but most are on piles, rectangular or square with a single room, of split or plaited bamboo, with a thatched grass roof and a fire pit. Octagonal houses are found in the south. [Dozier 1966: 12-13; Barton 1949: 10; Scott 1966: 174, 195-98, 201.]

ECONOMY. **Agriculture.** Irrigated and terraced wet rice, by all accounts introduced from Bontok, is more important in Southern Kalinga (sometimes called the granary of the Mountain Province), although it is in the process of spreading to Northern Kalinga as well (Keesing 1962a: 223; Scott 1958b). The flooded fields are turned with spade or stick, then trampled, more use being made in the south of plows pulled by water buffalo (Dozier 1966: 143-48). Dry-rice fields are cleared by extended household members, left to dry out for a month, burned in May before the rains, and planted with the use of dibble sticks. Other swidden crops include: beans, sweet potatoes (less important than among neighboring groups, such as Bontok), maize, sugarcane, and taro. Betel, tobacco, and coffee are also grown. [Dozier 1966: 135-48.] **Hunting and fishing.** Wild pig, deer, and game fowl are plentiful and frequently hunted with dogs and spears or, more recently, though illegally, with rifles. Formerly hunting was governed by bird omens. Traps may also be used, especially for birds. Fish and mussels are taken from streams with hooks, and eels are speared. [Dozier 1966: 132-35.] **Domestic animals.** The Northern Kalinga keep few horses or cattle, and water buffalo, where present, are butchered primarily for food, whereas pigs and chickens are preferred for ritual sacrifice and distribution at religious festivals (Dozier 1966: 148). Water buffalo are of greater importance among the Southern Kalinga, where the distribution of their meat at religious feasts confers prestige, and where these animals serve as a standard of value with respect to purchase of land (Barton 1949: 73-75, 107). **Industrial arts.** Iron working (most highly developed in the north), basketry, and pottery making are widespread, but nowhere a specialty. Cotton cloth is still woven in the south, but Northern Kalinga buy their clothes or make them of bark cloth (Dozier 1966: 127-30). **Trade.** The *abuyog* relationship of the Kalinga appears to have been similar to the highly formalized and ritualized pacts between trading partners of distant regions, characteristic of Ifugao and widespread throughout the Philippines. Trading was by all accounts greatly increased by the opening up of Spanish trails into the mountains, and it is most likely that the well-known peace pact institution of the Kalingas was a natural outgrowth of these earlier trading pacts. [Barton 1949: 145; Dozier 1966: 212-13.] **Property.** Barton's discussion of Lubuagan property law holds in general for all Kalinga. Irrigated rice terraces, house sites, and livestock are now the most valued property, along with family heirlooms—

ancient Chinese jars, plates, gongs, and beads. Swidden land is customarily abandoned after use, although if it is potentially irrigable, the original cultivator or his descendants can claim right of ownership. Inherited property (*tawid*) is distinguished from that acquired by a couple after marriage (*ginatang*); the former, e.g. wet-rice fields, is considered as being held in trust for future generations and is not easily alienated. Rights to water go to the first to use a source, but no one is denied the use of water. Disputes are mediated by regional leaders in the north, but in the south there are special supervisors of water rights. [Barton 1949: 84-136; Dozier 1966: 149-58.]

KINSHIP. Kinship is reckoned bilaterally. Each sibling group is the nucleus of a kinship circle or personal kindred, which includes descendants through both pairs of great-grandparents (grandparents in the south), together with their spouses. The members of the overlapping kindreds within an endogamous geographical region (*boboloy*) consider themselves kinsmen, and Dozier (1966: 56) suggests the use of Murdock's "deme" for this kinship group "whose members were, until recently, bound to one another by common residence and consanguinity." Beyond the level of the nuclear family, however, there is little evidence in traditional Kalinga culture for bilateral descent groups with corporate control of property, although something of the sort appears to be developing within wealthy aristocratic family lines in the south (Dozier 1966: 118). Economic activities are commonly shared by members of an extended household—two to four closely related nuclear families living in a contiguous area. Kalinga society is strongly kin oriented, although changes are occurring in the traditional pattern, especially in the south, reportedly associated with the introduction of permanent field wet-rice agriculture and resultant increased population density and community size. [Dozier 1966: 53-84; Barton 1949: 32ff.; Eggan 1963.] **Kinship terminology.** Basically Eskimo (Dozier 1966: 70-74):

	Address	Reference
GrPa	apo	apo
Fa	ama	(si) ama
Mo	ina	(si) ina
FaBr, MoBr, FaSiHu, MoSiHu	ama	olitog
MoSi, FaSi, FaBrWi, MoBrWi	ina	ikit
Sibling	sonodko	sonod
Eldest sib	....	pangngo
Youngest sib	....	odidi
Cousin (1st)	kapinsan	kapinsan
Cousin (2d)	kapinsan	kapidow
Cousin (3d)	....	kapitlo
Child	anakko	anak
Nephew/niece	(name)	amonakon
GrCh	apo (apok)	apo (apok)

MARRIAGE AND FAMILY. **Mode.** Adolescent girls in South Kalinga usually sleep together in the homes of widows, while boys sleep in vacant houses (*obog*). Nighttime visiting of girls by boys is permitted, although only engaged couples are supposed to have intercourse. Northern Kalinga, who strongly disapprove of this custom, expect adolescents to remain in the homes of the (closely related) extended family household at night; sexual contact, if it occurs, is performed secretly and without parental approval. [Dozier 1966: 64, 98; Barton 1949: 40ff.] Free choice is everywhere replacing the older form of contract marriage, which in North Kalinga is handled by go-betweens and begins with a feast and gift exchange, *banat*. This is followed over the years by other feasts, omen taking, and, when the couple have reached marriageable age, a valuable gift of heirloom beads and porcelains from the boy's family to the girl. At this stage (*ingngilin*), the couple are expected—and may be forced if unwilling—to cohabit as husband and wife. The major wedding feast (*pasingan, among*) occurs some months later (in Southern Kalinga not until the birth of the first child) and is the occasion for *banbansak*, the competitive exchange of gifts—heirloom jars and plates, water buffalo, rice lands—between the kindreds of the newly married couple. In the north, the bulk of such gifts is contributed by the boy's relatives, in an ostentatious validation of kindred wealth and prestige. [Dozier 1966: 98-104.] **Form.** Monogamy. Concubines (*dagdaga*) may be taken, although usually only by the wealthy, and children inherit almost equally (Dozier 1966: 105; Barton 1949: 58ff.). **Marriage rules.** Regional endogamy is quite strongly adhered to and was formerly enforced. Marriage is everywhere prohibited with a first cousin; northerners frown upon marriage with a second cousin and, like southerners, freely permit marriage between third cousins (Dozier 1966: 68). **Residence.** According to the ideal pattern, still found in the south, the couple joins the extended family household of the wife's parents, in a house provided by the latter (Dozier 1966: 61-62). **Domestic unit.** Nuclear family with occasional elderly grandparents, and with servants among the wealthy. Cooperation between households in economic tasks is based on an extended family pattern (Dozier 1966: 60-63). **Inheritance.** Children receive inheritance from both sets of parents at marriage, with the best fields going to the first married and house sites going to daughters. Children are expected to support and make offerings for parents (Dozier 1966: 155-57). **Divorce.** Childlessness is the main reason for divorce (up to 50 percent in Northern Kalinga), and a marriage is not regarded as permanent until children are born. Other reasons are poor hospitality and laziness in a wife (Dozier 1966: 106-07).

SOCIOPOLITICAL ORGANIZATION. **Political organization.** The Kalinga as a whole have never been a political unit. Members of overlapping kindreds within endogamous geographic regions (*boboloy*) consider themselves kinsmen, traditionally at enmity with other regions except for formalized trading relations and, more recently, interregional peace pacts. *Boboloy* in North Kalinga average 10 to 12 hamlets, with a total population of around 500 to 700, but are considerably larger in the south, due to the introduction of wet-rice agriculture. Barton (1949) interpreted this Southern Kalinga development as one of incipient statehood based on the importance of territorial ties, a view later corrected by Dozier (1966) and Eggan (1963). Authority within the region was traditionally held by renowned warrior-headhunters (*mangngol*), who, as avengers of wrongs committed against their kinsmen, possessed both prestige and material wealth (cf. Dozier 1966: 202ff.). Nowadays regional leaders, *pangngat* (S. Kal.) or *lakay* (N. Kal.), men possessed of wealth, wisdom, and a dash of charisma, arbitrate disputes and act as pact holders in the peace pacts that have opened up Kalinga society by permitting migration and even marriage outside the traditional regions. [Dozier 1966: 55-60, 119; Barton 1949: 137ff.; Eggan 1963.] **Social stratification.** Wealth in such things as rice fields and livestock has replaced headhunting prowess as a measure of status, giving the wealthy man a respected voice in boasting sessions, still a feature of most regional gatherings. The *baknang*, or well-to-do, have emerged as a class grouping, particularly in the south, where they constitute an incipient aristocracy, the *kadangyan*. This term is not used in the north, where there are simply the rich, *baknang*, and the poor, *kapos*. [Dozier 1966: 116-18.] **Social control and justice.** Renowned headhunters who had also demonstrated their charisma through wealth accumulation, oratorical powers, and knowledge of custom law formerly functioned as arbiters in intraregional disputes. Nowadays regional leaders (*pangngat*) mediate disputes and impose fines after judging public opinion and consulting the kindreds involved. They do not constitute a formal council, but meet informally at regional gatherings. The decisions of *pangngats* are grounded in an extensive body of custom law, well documented by Barton (1949). Interregional peace pact meetings, discussions among representative regional leaders, are occasions for flowery oratory and demonstration of judicial wisdom, avenues to greater prestige. [Dozier 1966: 119-21; Barton 1949: 147ff.] **Warfare.** The personal kindred is everywhere responsible for avenging an injury, death, or wrongdoing inflicted on any one of its members (Dozier 1966: 67). Within the endogamous region, conflicts were, and are, settled whenever possible by mediation through regional leaders. Extraregional disputes and feuds were formerly settled by blood vengeance, most often in the form of headhunting raids. Headhunting was a major avenue to prestige and renown, but does not appear to have been associated with agricultural or fertility rites.

A newly-taken head was displayed in a basketlike receptacle, later boiled, broken up, and its parts distributed among the warriors as trophies. Most prized were lower jaw bones, used as handles for gongs. Pitched battles (*botad*) between regions occur nowadays despite the existence of peace pacts—possibly in response to curtailment of headhunting and private revenge. [Dozier 1966: 197-212; Barton 1949: 154-56.] Peace pacts (*bodong*), dating from the turn of the century, developed out of indigenous institutions such as trading partnerships and intraregional arbitration. A pact is held by two individuals from different regions on behalf of their respective kinship circles, but the pact is binding on the entire region. Pacts are formalized at large gatherings (*lonok*), where their particular provisions are worked out by discussion and arbitration among regional leaders skilled in oratory and custom law. Subsequent gatherings (*dolnat*) mark pact renewals or transfers to new holders. [Dozier 1966: 212-37; Barton 1949: 167-200.]

RELIGION. **Supernaturals.** The world of the supernatural is not clearly conceptualized, and names and attributes of spirits vary from region to region. In Northern Kalinga, offerings are made to the spirits of deceased ancestors (*anitos*) at funeral ceremonies, but the people are more concerned with various classes of malevolent spirits, who, if not propitiated in prayers, chants, and sacrifices, take revenge on the living by causing illness and misfortune. Southern Kalinga pay more attention to the ancestral spirits, and death rites are more elaborate in the south. Kaboniyan, the creator-god, although benevolently inclined, is seldom invoked. Witchcraft and sorcery are known causes of misfortune, but are not overly feared. Fear of poisoning is, however, widespread. [Dozier 1966: 159-63, 181ff.; Barton 1949: 17-27.] **Practitioners.** According to Barton (1949: 24), male "priests" formerly officiated at headhunting rites. Nowadays female mediums or shamans [*mangalisig* (S. Kal.), *mandadawak*, or *manganito* (N. Kal.)] conduct curing rites and perform at various rituals for community welfare. Each has her own repertory of spirit helpers, chants, and paraphernalia, which novices must learn from established practitioners. Illness is caused mainly by malevolently inclined spirits who may capture or destroy the soul, and it is the task of the medium, with the aid of her spirit helpers, to restore the soul to the patient's body. [Dozier 1966: 173-78.] **Ceremonies.** Mainly concern life cycle, agriculture, and formerly headhunting, now community welfare. Mediums make the offerings and prayer chants. Life cycle rituals vary in north and south: common and most important are six *kontad* ceremonies for a child during its first two years, all involving animal sacrifice and feasts (Dozier 1966: 265-66). **Soul, death, and afterlife.** The conception of an afterlife is vague. The spirit of the deceased must be sent on its way with proper ceremonial, but its existence in the hereafter is not particularly dependent on the status of the deceased when alive. The corpse is placed in a death chair for up to ten days, guarded by the surviving spouse while relatives mourn and prepare rice beer for the wake. Pigs and carabao are sacrificed for adults, pigs only for a child, and wakes are generally festive. Wealthy adults are buried in stone and plaster graves (mausoleums, according to Barton) and formerly were reburied in jars. The grave is covered with a thatch arbor, under which offerings may be placed. A year of mourning taboos, during which the surviving spouse may not remarry, is ended by a *kolias* feast. [Dozier 1966: 112-14; Barton 1949: 25-26.]

BIBLIOGRAPHY. Bacdayan 1967a; Barton 1949; Beyer 1917; Dozier 1966, 1967; Eggan 1963; Folkmar 1906; Fox et al. 1965; Keesing 1962a; Scott 1958a, 1958b, 1960, 1966; Takaki 1969; Thomas and Healey 1962.

TINGGIAN

Synonyms. *Tinguian, Tinguianes, Itneg*

ORIENTATION. **Location and identification.** Tinggian or Itneg speakers as a whole show considerable variation. The most homogeneous concentration consists of the so-called "valley" Tinggian studied by Cole in 1907, pagan, wet-rice agriculturists along the valley floors of the Abra and its tributaries in northwestern Abra Province, west of the Cordillera Central, a region of grass-covered, rolling hills and lush, tropical valley vegetation several hundred feet above sea level. The "mountain" Tinggian (relatively few in number) in the high Cordillera country of eastern Abra are primarily growers of rice and root crops in dry fields. The name Tinggian is derived from the Iloko word for "mountain" and is not used by the people themselves, who prefer the term Itneg (possibly from *i-tineg*, "people of the Tineg River"). There has been much intermixture with neighboring groups—Bontok to the south, Kalinga and Apayao to the east and north. Marked influences from the coast, dating back to early Chinese trade, have in recent decades been exacerbated by the penetration of Christian Ilocano settlers into the middle reaches of the Abra. Cole in fact saw the valley Tinggian as descendants of a pre-Spanish coastal population—the modern Ilocano—and as relative newcomers to their present habitat (Cole 1922: 486). [Cole 1922; Keesing 1962a: 121-22.] **Linguistic affiliation.** Grouped by Thomas and Healey (1962) with Iloko, Ibanag, Apayao, Kalinga, and Gaddang in an Iloko-Cagayan branch of the Northern Philippine family of languages. The relation of Iloko and Tinggian is particularly close, with an indicated date of separation around 1200 A.D. (Fox et al. 1965: 109). **Demography.** Beyer's estimate in 1916 was 27,800 (Beyer 1917: 74); whereas Cole (1922: 238) felt that only about 20,000 individuals could be properly classed as Tinggian. **History and cultural relations.** The Spanish established a mission and garrison at Bangued in 1598 and later constructed a major trail or military "road" through Abra from the coast. The Tinggian have for centuries carried on trade with neighboring hill tribesmen and with lowlanders, despite their hostility to the latter as "Christians" and (until relatively recently) the carrying out of frequent headhunting raids against the former. Subsequent to American occupation, the Tinggian became more peaceably inclined, and the influence of Ilocanos increased to the point where Cole in 1922 could predict the not-too-distant assimilation of valley Tinggians into lowland Ilocano society—a trend later confirmed by Eggan. [Cole 1922: 242-46; Eggan 1956.]

SETTLEMENT PATTERN AND HOUSING. **Settlement pattern.** Villages or "towns," formerly stockaded, consist of clusters of barrios around a central nucleus with a central authority, the village headman or *lakay*. Many reach a "considerable size," i.e. larger than Bontok settlements. There are no village wards, men's houses, or girls' dormitories. [Eggan 1941: 13; Keesing 1962a: 121; Cole 1922: 359.] **Housing.** Generally similar to Ilocano, consisting of one or two rooms with a covered or uncovered porch made of wood, bamboo strips and grass thatch for roof, standing on piles about five feet high. The ground area may be enclosed to keep chickens or goods (Cole 1922: 363-65).

ECONOMY. **Agriculture.** Rice is important as food, standard of value, and medium of exchange, and the rice cycle is surrounded by religious sacrifice and omenology. The valley Tinggian grow most of their rice on irrigated terraces; upland swiddens are also planted to rice, as well as sweet potatoes, maize, sugarcane, and cotton. Keesing, citing Cole, points out that terrace walls, although Lepanto-like, are generally low and of earth; Ilocano-like elements include granary styles, the buffalo-drawn plow, and the use of the rice-knife for harvesting (Keesing 1962a: 121). Gardens are planted to vegetables, tobacco, taro, bananas, citrus fruits, and herbs. Both areca and coconut palms are important. Although betel is chewed less frequently now than formerly, it continues to be used in religious offerings. The only native alcoholic drink is fermented sugarcane juice, *basi*. [Cole 1922: 387-409.] **Hunting and fishing.** Hunting is for sport rather than sustenance, whereas fishing provides a somewhat more important source of meat. Dogs are used to drive deer, wild pigs, wild water buffalo, and wild chickens into nets for spearing, and blowguns are used for birds. Fish are taken in traps and nets,

also with line and spear and (occasionally) poison. [Cole 1922: 378-85.] **Domestic animals.** Dogs, pigs (unpenned), chickens, water buffalo (prestige wealth), and, more recently, horses, goats, and cattle (Cole 1922: 411). **Industrial arts.** Smithies using piston bellows, anvil, and hammer were more common formerly than they are now. Spinning and weaving are done on frame looms by women, who also make bark cloth, baskets, mats, dyes, cordage. Women are potters, and pots are plain and slowly burned in dung fires. [Cole 1922: 413-30.] **Trade.** Trade with coastal areas extends far back in time and has been uninterrupted in recent decades (Cole 1922: 489). Peace pacts with Kalinga preceded American occupation and increased trade and travel in an easterly direction (Eggan 1941: 17).

KINSHIP. Reckoned bilaterally (Cole 1922: 359), with personal kindreds probably important in life cycle ceremonies. The kin terminology classes all cousins together, and while the system is widely extended, the effective range of obligations is less than among Bontok and Ifugao—in this respect approximating more to Ilocano (Eggan 1941: 14).

MARRIAGE AND FAMILY. **Mode.** Arranged by parents through intermediaries when children are young. A bride-price (livestock, jars, blankets, rice) is partially paid at an initial betrothal ceremony, the rest is deferred until later or may be withheld until the husband's death and paid from his estate. [Cole 1922: 278-79.] **Form.** Monogamy, with frequent concubinage (Cole 1922: 279). **Extension of incest taboos.** Marriage with up to second cousins forbidden, together with step-sister, wife's sister, wife's mother (Cole 1922: 278, 361). **Residence.** Nowadays neolocal, but there are tales of former initial patrilocality (Cole 1922: 282). **Inheritance.** Property (including land) inherited by parents or acquired jointly during marriage divided equally among children, but boys get livestock and girls get beads. If there are no children, property goes to parents, siblings, and to the wife until she remarries. [Cole 1922: 361.] **Divorce.** Not uncommon, according to Cole (1922: 283), but difficult and expensive, according to Eggan (1941: 15). If the man is to blame, his kin must repay the deferred remainder of the bride-price; if it is the woman, bride-price is refunded.

SOCIOPOLITICAL ORGANIZATION. **Political organization.** The village is the political unit and is headed by a *lakay*, chosen by elders from among the wealthy and influential men of the village. The position is ordinarily held for life and may be passed on to a son, although a *lakay* may, with cause, be removed from office by an informal council of elders, who also assist him in the arbitration and judgment of disputes. Formerly there were temporary alliances of two or three villages for defense. [Cole 1922: 359;

Eggan 1941.] **Social differentiation.** Eggan regards distinctions based on wealth as being more marked among Tinggian than among Bontok and Ifugao, and Cole (1922: 345ff.) describes sponsorship of a progressive series of major religious festivals, requiring large expenditures of wealth, whereby a man gains increased social prestige. Wealth is measured in ancient jars, gongs, and beads as well as in rice fields and livestock. To fulfill ceremonial obligations, the poor are often forced to borrow (e.g. rice) from the rich—loans that must be repaid with interest by debt service. [Cole 1922: 360; Eggan 1941; Keesing 1962a: 121.] **Social control and justice.** The headman (*lakay*) and elders interpret the law according to custom and the ancestors. Murder is punished by blood revenge or by payment of fines; stealing by fines in carabao, jars, or money. Enforcement is solely by weight of public opinion. [Cole 1922: 361-62.] **Warfare.** Headhunting between villages more than 10 or 15 miles apart was formerly endemic. A headhunting raid by all the able-bodied men of a village was a necessary part of the funeral rites for a deceased adult member of the village community. In addition, individuals went out singly to avenge a death or to gain prestige by taking a head. Weapons included knives, head axes, spears, and shields, with ambush the favorite tactic. Captured heads were impaled on sharpened bamboo poles and exhibited beside the village entrance, following which neighboring villagers were invited to a feast, at the conclusion of which the head was broken up and the brains added to the ceremonial sugarcane wine and consumed by qualified participants. Pieces of the skull were distributed to the warriors as souvenirs of the hunt. [Cole 1922: 371-78.]

RELIGION. **Supernaturals.** A pantheon of named deities or spirits, generally termed *anito*, and including Kadaklan ("the greatest"), his wife, Agemem, and their two sons, Adam and Baliyen. Kaboniyan, often identified with Kadaklan, appears as culture hero—teacher and giver of rice, jars, gongs, and beads. Some deities live in the sky, some in the earth, some in village guardian stones. Some are benevolent, some evilly inclined. Most attention is paid these "natural" spirits, whereas spirits of deceased mortals receive no sacrifices nor are they worshipped. [Cole 1922: 295-301.] **Practitioners.** Mediums (*alopogan*) are usually women, although the role is not barred to men, and men usually conduct the communal ceremonies (Eggan 1941: 16). The skills, learned by apprenticeship, include knowledge of healing with plants, charms, and magic and the taking of omens. *Dawak* rituals, during which the spirits enter the body of the medium and "speak" through her, are an important part of most curing rites, but can occur as units in the larger welfare and prestige ceremonies. A medium's specialized skills include recitation of ritual myths, *diam*,

which accompany most ceremonies and explain their supernatural origin as gifts of culture heroes. [Eggan 1956; Cole 1915, 1922: 301-14.] **Ceremonies.** Ritual and festival life among the valley Tinggian is highly elaborated. Performance or sponsorship of minor ceremonies—curing, birth, offerings to guardian stones, house construction, rice culture—is available to anyone, whereas major status-validating ceremonies may only be sponsored by those who have inherited the right or acquired it through dreams or omens, and who have the necessary wealth. A man aspires to give a series of such ceremonies over a period of years, finally earning the right to perform *sayang*, the greatest social and religious event in Tinggian life. *Sayang*, originally a 17-day ceremony, is held in any one community only about once in every seven years, requiring the erection of special ritual structures, large quantities of rice and sugarcane wine, and numerous sacrificial pigs, chickens, and dogs. Mediums and their helpers perform elaborate *dawak* rituals, during which spirit visitors partake of sacrificial food and drink. Sponsorship ensures the health and good fortune not only of the sponsor and his family but of the entire community. [Cole 1922: 315-58.] **Soul, death, and afterlife.** Sickness and death are usually attributed to spirits, but may also be caused by sorcery and/or poisoning (Cole 1922: 305). The corpse is washed, dressed, and placed in a death chair, where it remains during a period of family mourning, formerly lifted by a ritual headhunt by all able-bodied men of the village. [Cole (p. 372) sees this custom as similar to human sacrifice on such occasions in other parts of the Philippines, in both cases to furnish a companion or slave for the departing soul of the deceased.] Burial is in a stone-lined niche grave beneath the house, a kind of mausoleum for the reception of multiple burials. A *layog* death feast, at which a chair is present for the deceased, is held several months to a year after burial. The departed soul goes to a "spirit town," Maglawa, where it joins the ancestors. [Cole 1922: 283-94.]

BIBLIOGRAPHY. Beyer 1917; Cole 1915, 1922; Eggan 1941, 1956; Fox et al. 1965; Keesing 1962a; Thomas and Healey 1962.

APAYAO

Synonyms. *Apayaw, Isneg, Isnag, Isned, Itneg, Mandaya, Kalina', Payao*

ORIENTATION. **Location and identification.** Riverine shifting cultivators along the banks of the Apayao (Abulug) and Matalag in Apayao Subprovince, extreme northern Luzon. Bounded on the south by dry-rice cultivating Mountain Tinggian and Northern Kalinga, whom they resemble physically, and on the north, east, and west by lowland Christian Filipinos, mainly Ilocano and Ibanag. The people nowadays feel a sense of collective identity, symbolized by the use of a common ethnonym, Isneg or Isnag, in the sense of "we the people" as over against neighboring groups such as Kalinga (Keesing 1962b: 3). The term Isneg is probably of Iloko origin, i.e. *i-tineg*, "people of the Tineg River," an old lowlander name for mountain pagans of the Abra-Apayao region (Vanoverbergh 1932: 15ff.). Local groups are, however, most commonly called by the name of a stream or local geographic feature, to which is added the prefix *i* ("people," "inhabitants of," thus *ibolo*, a "native of Bolo"). The commonly accepted exonym, Apayao, derives from the Spanish version of the Isneg name for their major river, i.e. *apayaw* (*abulug* in Ibanag). Local variations in custom and dialect were formerly more marked than at present. Vanoverbergh defines five dialects, the most distinctive of which occurs along the Matalag River in the south, a region which also differs culturally from the northern groups along the Apayao and its tributaries. [Keesing 1962b; Vanoverbergh 1932.] **Geography.** The Isneg live mainly in the southwestern highlands on the Abra-Ilocos border, a region drained by the Apayao River system flowing generally north and east into the China Sea. Highland elevations rarely exceed 4,000 feet, and much of the Isneg territory consists of a maze of humid, malarial valleys and foothills covered with tropical forest and savanna grass. Settlement is sparse, averaging only eight persons per square mile (Keesing 1962b: 3). Travel is chiefly by canoes and bamboo rafts. **Linguistic affiliation.** Classed by Thomas and Healey (1962) with Kalinga, Tinggian, Ilocano, and Ibanag in an Iloko-Cagayan branch of the Northern Philippine family of languages. Wilson (1947a: 8) finds evidence of former use of an ancient script, although indigenous writing of any kind is denied by Vanoverbergh (1936-38: 126). **Demography.** Approximately 11,000 (Keesing 1962b). **History and culture contact.** Keesing (1962b: 2) supposes that the modern Apayao may be descendants of an old coastal population that retreated into the hills, possibly as a result of Spanish pressures. They were among the most dedicated headhunters of the Cordillera until the establishment of military control about 1913, followed by the introduction of civil government some ten years later. Subsequent decades have seen the establishment of government and mission schools, along with sporadic conversions to Christianity. [Keesing 1962b; Vanoverbergh 1932: 57ff., 1936-38: 136ff.; Wilson 1947a: 2.]

SETTLEMENT PATTERN AND HOUSING. **Settlement pattern.** Named settlement areas are made up of hamlets or hamlet clusters, located two to three miles apart, along a section of river or stream. Settlement areas, averaging 240 persons, are occupied over many generations, and the people in an area feel themselves closely related. The typical hamlet contains some 85 persons living in from four to eight houses, surrounded by bamboo fences, granaries, and groves of coconut and betel. Settlement is more or less permanent, with resort to temporary housing when fields become too distant and until fallowed land nearer the home base can be reopened. Inhabitants of neighboring hamlets within a settlement area intermarry, attend one another's religious festivals, and formerly cooperated in headhunting raids into outlying areas. [Keesing 1962b; Vanoverbergh 1932.] **Housing.** The multifamily houses, among the most substantially built of any on the Cordillera, are rectangular in shape and raised on piles six or more feet above the ground. Framing is of complex design, utilizing massive wooden beams joined by mortise and tenon. Walls, with windows, are of hewn boards or woven bamboo, floors of bamboo laid on heavy wooden joists. The central floor space, in rare instances divided into separate family compartments, is surrounded by a low, narrow platform for sitting and storage. Roofs, well made of thatch or bamboo, are high and arched in a characteristic gothic effect, with the ends extended somewhat to create a hooded appearance. A raised annex, sometimes attached to one end of the structure, was reportedly a sleeping area for men in former times. [Keesing 1962b: 4; Scott 1966: 187-94; Vanoverbergh 1953a.]

ECONOMY. **Agriculture.** Slash-and-burn hillside rice, the main crop and prestige food, is ritually important, with elaborate attention given to all phases of rice growing and harvesting. Fields are cut and burned by men, but the planting and harvesting of rice are in the women's hands. Fields are used for one year, followed by four or more years in fallow. Important secondary crops include yams and taro, followed by maize, sweet potatoes (less important than elsewhere in the Philippines), sugarcane (for wine), and bananas —all grown in fenced gardens in former swiddens. Peas, beans, and leafy vegetables are also grown, and tobacco is raised as a trade crop. Arboriculture includes fruit trees, coconuts, areca, and bamboo. Wild fruits, leaves, roots, mushrooms, honey, insects, and larvae provide important additions to the food supply. [Vanoverbergh 1941, 1954a.] **Fishing and hunting.** Fish are taken in fresh water streams and rivers with nets, traps, and hooks and by damming and poisoning. Wild boar and deer are hunted with dogs and spears; bows with poisoned arrows are used occasionally and may be a borrowing from neighboring "Negritos." A great variety of traps, snares, and nets are used chiefly for birds, which are also taken by liming. Hunters observe the flight of omen birds, and the lower jaws of boars are preserved in the houses as trophies of the hunt. [Vanoverbergh 1954a.] **Domestic animals.** Dogs are important for hunting and also as ritual sacrifice, while pigs provide meat for ceremonious feasting and ritual killing. Goats and water buffalo, less numerous, are occasionally killed for food. [Keesing 1962b; Vanoverbergh 1954a.] **Industrial arts.** Metal working, basketry, and mat making are widespread, but weaving and pottery making are unknown. The making of bamboo rafts, dugout canoes, and plank bottom boats of Spanish design is important. [Vanoverbergh 1954a.] **Trade.** Livestock, cloth, ceramics, metal, and salt are acquired from the lowlands in return for tobacco, coconuts, cacao, vegetables, mats, rattan, honey, and wax (Keesing 1962b; Vanoverbergh 1954a.) **Property.** Ancient jars, plates, and beads of Asiatic origin attain a particularly high value among the Apayao, according to Keesing. Jars and beads, classified under numerous subtypes, are exchanged in marriage and are important as heirloom property, as injury payments, and in establishing group alliances. They are also signs of wealth and status. [Keesing 1962b: 7; Vanoverbergh 1954a: 158-63, 174-76.]

KINSHIP. Bilateral, Ego-based kinship circles, rarely reckoned beyond third cousins, overlap within settlement areas (Keesing 1962b: 11). **Kin terminology.** Vanoverbergh (1936-38: 184) gives the following kin terms:

Fa	ama
Mo	ina
Sib	waxi
Eldest sib	manakam
Youngest sib	udiyan
FaBr, MoBr	ulitag
FaSi, MoSi	ikit
1st cousin	kapinsan
2d cousin	kapiduwa
3d cousin	kapilo
So, Da, Ch	babbin, ababbin

MARRIAGE AND FAMILY. Supercision is performed on boys at about age ten, an uncircumcized male being considered unclean and offensive to women (Vanoverbergh 1954a: 185). Boys and girls may blacken the teeth, but tooth filing is apparently unknown. Both sexes tattoo, and tattooing is widespread. **Mode.** Parents' consent is usually sought for marriage, which involves a bride-price (tadug), characterized by haggling and paid in jars, beads, plates, and cloth. Payment is ideally made at a main ceremony (manakit), although it may be spread out over a three- to ten-year period, during which the husband resides in the wife's parents' household in a bride-service relationship. Marriage appears to be hamlet-exogamous, but endogamous within the settlement area. [Vanoverbergh 1936-38: 191-211; Wilson 1947a: 8, 17.] **Form.** Polygyny is allowed and frequent (Vanoverbergh 1936-38: 189). **Extension of incest taboos.** Sibling and first-cousin marriage prohibited, as well as marriage between lineal relations. Second-cousin mar-

riage is frowned upon, but does occur occasionally. [Vanoverbergh 1936-38: 191.] **Residence.** Initially with the bride's parents until the bride-price is paid off (up to ten years), otherwise patrilocal residence (in the groom's parental household) is favored, but appears also to depend on property rights of spouses (Vanoverbergh 1936-38: 206; Keesing 1962b: 13-14). **Household.** Keesing's statistics (1962b: 4) indicate an average of 10-15 persons per household, while Vanoverbergh states that couples reside in the parental household of either the husband or wife for a considerable portion of their married life (1936-38: 82). In addition, wealthy men of mengal status seek to form polygynous households. **Inheritance.** Men and women own separate property, but can acquire joint property after marriage. Daughters inherit from the mother, sons from the father, with shares usually given at marriage. Property does not seem to pass to a spouse, but remains within the personal kindred, unless it was joint property. Debts are inherited. [Vanoverbergh 1936-38: 217-26.] **Divorce.** Adultery and laziness (but not barrenness) are common reasons for divorce by both men and women, and divorce is "not infrequent." Couples simply separate, returning to the natal home. If the wife is at fault, then both sets of parents must haggle over return of the tadug, with apportionment of blame easily leading to feuds. Small children go with the mother, while older children may choose which parent to follow, and may inherit from that parent. [Vanoverbergh 1936-38: 219-23.]

SOCIOPOLITICAL ORGANIZATION. Leadership in Apayao communities is diffuse, with power and influence traditionally coincident with wealth and headhunting prowess. Mengal, famed warriors rich in heirloom wealth such as ancient jars, beads, and porcelain plates, and with large kin followings built up through polygynous marriages, attain leadership status over wide areas. Such positions, symbolized according to Wilson (1947a: 12) by the wearing of a red turban, were entirely dependent on personal ability and charisma, however, and were not inherited. [Keesing 1962b: 9-10.] **Social differentiation.** Highest prestige was traditionally enjoyed by men of mengal status, achieved through success in headhunting, coincident with acquisition of wealth in heirloom jars, beads, and plates. Leading mengal arbitrate disputes and sponsor major ceremonies. [Keesing 1962b: 7-8; Vanoverbergh 1941: 283.] **Social control and justice.** Leading mengal decide most issues by informal discussion and may serve as arbitrators in serious disputes. Raids against an offender's household to gain compensation may be undertaken by victims and their kin. Fear of shaming by public opinion is said to be the most important deterrent to antisocial behavior. [Vanoverbergh 1936-38: 152, 163.] **Warfare.** Dedicated headhunters until government control in the 1920s, with ambush the usual tactic. Taking of a head (the skull cap rather than the entire skull) was the minimum qualification for warrior status, signaled by a special arm tattoo. Raids, led by *mengal* for revenge and/or prestige, were preceded by public boasting, thus placing the entire community under threat of retaliation from the announced victims and effectively involving all able-bodied males in the planned raid. [Keesing 1962b: 8; Vanoverbergh 1936-38: 122, 137; Wilson 1947a: 16.]

RELIGION. **Supernaturals.** Aboriginally a pantheon of over 300 spirits in human, animal, giant, and monster forms and of various humors, with Anglabbang, protector of the Isneg and tutelary spirit of headhunters, of highest rank. Spirits (*anito*) were propitiated formerly by the offering of enemy heads, nowadays by the heads of sacrificed dogs. In addition to *anito*, ghosts (*balanoban*) of "bad" people annoy the living but can be fended off with magic. Relatively little attention is paid to ancestral spirits, although they can and do communicate with the living through the person of the shaman. Some spirits (*anito*) are former mortals, but not all *kaduduwa* (souls) achieve *anito* status. [Vanoverbergh 1936-38: 137, 234-35; 1953-55: 76, 97-80; Keesing 1962b: 14.] **Practitioners.** *Dorarakit* are female shamans who mediate between men and spirits (*anito*) or souls (*kaduduwa*) in cases of illness and in the conduct of public rituals. They are chosen in infancy, learn secret formulas, and are paid in kind. [Vanoverbergh 1936-38: 131, 196-98.] **Ceremonies.** Each stage of rice field preparation and planting is accompanied by bird omenology and religious ritual, and the harvest by a major ceremony with pig or dog sacrifice. The most important of Apayao ceremonies is the *sayam*, performed after taking a head, after completion of a new house, or when coming out of mourning. Rich men demonstrate their status by holding *sayam* more often than others; they garner prestige because the feasting, lasting several days, requires the slaughter of many pigs and the preparation of much rice and sugarcane wine. *Sayam* includes the *tonton* rites of veneration for the spirits, featuring the ritual presentation of an enemy head (nowadays a dog's head) and the boasting recitations of leading *mengal*, who gather around a stone and pound it in unison with long bamboo poles (in the manner of women pounding rice). [Vanoverbergh 1941: 337-40; 1953-55: 233-57.] **Illness and medicine.** Four kidney-eating spirits are responsible for most sickness, which is cured by shamans, who may use herbal medicines or "suck out" the cause of illness. [Vanoverbergh 1936-38: 237-40.] **Soul, death, and afterlife.** After death there is separation into *balanoban* (body) and *kaduduwa*. The former eventually decays, the latter is transported to the realm of the dead (Aglalannawan). The corpse is washed and dressed, placed on a bier to the ac-

companiment of female lamentations, and guarded until burial, some five or six days later. Formerly wooden coffins or jars were interred in graves beneath the house, but now burial takes place in cemeteries. Grave goods include food, clothing, headaxes, knives, and dishes. Mourning lasts from one to two months for all members of the household, who must observe taboos specific to each individual. The *obobat* ceremony, performed by a shaman, ends the mourning period and was formerly preceded by the taking of an enemy head. [Vanoverbergh 1936-38: 244-59.]

BIBLIOGRAPHY. Keesing 1962b; Scott 1966; Thomas and Healey 1962; Vanoverbergh 1932, 1936-38, 1941, 1950, 1953a, 1953-55, 1954a, 1960; Wilson 1947a.

PAGAN GADDANG*

Synonyms. *Gadan, Gaddanes, Iraya, Yrraya*

ORIENTATION. **Location and identification.** The people or peoples living in scattered settlements in and around the middle Cagayan Valley area, and referred to in early Spanish records as Gaddanes or Yrraya, had by 1900 been almost entirely Christianized and are today largely merged within the dominant Ilocano-Ibanag population of the Cagayan lowlands (cf. Lambrecht 1959, 1960). Small pockets of non-Christian Gaddang are still found in southeastern Kalinga, eastern Bontok, and adjacent Isabela Province, where rivers tributary to the Cagayan intersect the eastern slopes and foothills of the Cordillera Central. Scattered pagan settlements extend from the headwaters of these rivers down almost to the valley plain, where they become interspersed with those of Christian Ilocanos and Cagayanos (Ibanags). Pagan Gaddangs are also found east of the Cagayan, in the Katalangan River Valley (Beyer 1917: 43). The more numerous Christian Gaddang are found in the Magat Valley area of northwestern Nueva Vizcaya, and scattered through much of Isabela Province. Beyer (1917: 24) divided all Gaddang into five dialect subgroups: Gaddang proper, Yogad, Maddukayang, Katalangan, and Iraya. Some of these are names of rivers or former military districts, whereas Iraya (Yrraya) is an old Spanish term, derived from the Ibanag word for "upriver" (Keesing 1962a: 238). Although there is considerable variation between groups, due in part to differential acculturation to lowland populations, the Pagan Gaddang constitute a linguistic group sharing a basic culture—symbolized by legendary descent from a common founding ancestor and maintained by widespread trading partnerships and peace pacts between communities. The only ethnographic account of these

---

*This summary of non-Christian Gaddang culture is based. unless otherwise specified, on Wallace (1967).

people are those by Wallace (1967, 1969), based on fieldwork in two communities overlooking the Cagayan Valley near San Mateo in the southern Gaddang area, a region unsuited to integral swidden agriculture and presumably marginal to the traditional Gaddang habitat farther north. This has necessitated cultural adjustments that appear to be forcing these Gaddang increasingly into the orbit of a pervasive and expanding lowland Filipino economy. **Linguistic affiliation.** Despite Keesing's allegation (1962a: 239), based on Pittman (1952), of marked differences between Gaddang and Ibanag, the lexicostatistical subgrouping of Gaddang with Ibanag (plus Ilocano, Tinggian, and Apayao) by Fox et al. (1965) is essentially in agreement with that arrived at by Thomas and Healey (1962). **Demography.** Pagans estimated at around 2,500 by Wallace (1967: 9). Christian Gaddang number 25,000 according to the 1960 Census.

SETTLEMENT PATTERN AND HOUSING. Settlements range in size from two to fifteen or so houses (average four persons per house), located above a stream with swiddens on surrounding steep valley slopes. Spacing of dwellings is irregular, although those of close kin tend to cluster. Houses are rectangular and raised on piles, with walls of bamboo and thatched roofs. They are regarded as temporary affairs, to be abandoned when the group shifts location to open new swiddens. Separate granaries, similar in size and shape to the houses, are more highly valued. Furnishings are scant, but usually include a few old and highly valued beads and gongs. Earlier reports mention tree houses up to 20 or more feet above the ground (Beyer 1917; Keesing 1962a: 239).

ECONOMY. The traditional pattern is one of integral swidden agriculture in well-forested areas, supplemented by hunting, fishing, and sale or barter of forest products. Much of the southern Gaddang area is, however, deforested and covered with cogon grass, resulting in poor yields, overcropping, and frequent moves to new locations. Here the traditional subsistence economy has been supplemented by the raising of cash crops, such as maize and tobacco, and by hiring out as wage labor. **Agriculture.** Swidden rice is most valued, both as food and for ritual use. Legumes and cucurbits are intercropped with rice, and following the harvest the swiddens are planted to sweet potatoes, millet, garlic, gourds, legumes, and (most important nowadays) tobacco. Additional crops include bananas, sugarcane (for wine), peppers, taro, and yams. Sweet potatoes and millet, relatively unimportant in the south, are grown as staples in some other Gaddang areas (cf. Keesing 1962a: 239). **Domestic animals.** Pigs, water buffalo, dogs, cats, and chickens. The southern Gaddang diet is largely vegetarian; pigs and dogs are consumed on the average of once a year at religious festivals, chickens somewhat oftener. Water

buffalo are not sacrificed or eaten, but rather rented out to lowlanders for cash income. **Property.** A household that has cleared a swidden has exclusive right to its use and the products thereof, and the permission of the original clearing household must be obtained before an abandoned swidden can be reopened. Inheritances traditionally consist of carabao, pigs, heirloom beads and gongs, and clothing, although the concept of land as inheritable property is gaining currency in the south.

KIN GROUPS. Bilateral personal kindreds (*inananak*), formerly the effective units in revenge and wergild, are theoretically reckoned vertically to great-great-great-great-grandparents and laterally to fifth cousins. In practice, however, genealogical knowledge is slight, and the effective exogamic range of the kindred extends only to first cousins. There are in addition cognatic descent groups composed of individuals who trace their ancestry ambilineally to the founder of the group, either male or female, who lived many generations ago. The term *inafafu* refers both to the founder and to the group as a whole. These groups have no known corporate features, nor do they regulate marriage, and their social significance appears weakened nowadays by a general lack of genealogical knowledge. They do appear, however, to have been associated in the past with known geographic regions, and are linked in native thinking as branches of a Gaddang "family tree," whereby all Gaddang are descended from a common legendary ancestor, Pangafu. Settlements tend to be nonendogamous with respect to marriage, and are thus linked by extended and affinal kin ties, but the effective social and economic units are the individual households (*tabalayan*), usually a nuclear family but often containing a dependent relative.

MARRIAGE. Although marriage with a second cousin is permissible, marriage partners are usually sought beyond the confines of the local settlement, partly in an attempt to extend the geographic range of kin ties. Courtship is informal, occurring usually on occasions of religious festivals, with choice nowadays relatively free, although child betrothal seems formerly to have been the rule. A go-between conducts the arrangements, which are sealed by the gift of an heirloom bead (valued at as much as one carabao) from the boy's to the girl's family. Marriage is concluded by an elaborate feast when the couple receive their shares of inherited property from both sets of parents. Postmarital residence is initially matrilocal (in the girl's father's settlement) during a one-year period of bride service, after which the couple reside neolocally. Institutionalized spouse exchange (*solyad*) between two couples exists in some Gaddang areas, apparently in an attempt to broaden the range of kin ties (Wallace 1969). **Kin terminology.** Bilateral and generational, of

Eskimo type. Brother-sister avoidance lacking. [Wallace 1967: 143-52.]

SOCIOPOLITICAL ORGANIZATION. Leadership within a Gaddang community appears traditionally to have depended on a combination of bravery, knowledge of custom law, oratorical skills, and (perhaps) ownership of wealth. These qualities were epitomized in the status of *mingal*, the renowned warrior-headhunter. Settlements are politically autonomous, although linked by a peace pact system (*pudon*), probably borrowed from Kalinga. Pact holders were formerly limited to men of *mingal* status. In addition, trading partnerships (*kolak*, "sibling") between Gaddang and with lowlanders facilitate travel and intermarriage throughout the area. **Social differentiation.** Not marked nowadays, and *mingal* no longer achieve renown through headhunting prowess. Social status is, however, achieved through sponsorship of a series of increasingly expensive *anitu* rites, requiring the accumulation and redistribution of household wealth in rice and pigs, and leading to the title of *kamaran*, "wealthy family." **Warfare.** The Gaddang were confirmed headhunters until World War II, and are still greatly feared by lowlanders. Social status, revenge, and good harvests are among the reasons given for taking heads, which were exhibited on bamboo poles and at length buried. Only the jaw bone and teeth were preserved, the former as gong handles and the latter (together with finger bones) as necklaces.

RELIGION. **Supernaturals.** Dufafa, the "earth world," and Kalekay, the "up-after world," are both subsumed within the category Ilosa, in mythology the place where the culture hero, Nanolay, performed his creative deeds. Nanolay, creator and benevolent deity, is identified with Kalekay, as are also the souls of the dead, who dwell there as ancestral spirits. The concept of an afterworld is vague, however, and neither Nanolay nor the ancestral spirits are propitiated; the latter are, however, invited to be present at religious feasts. The main concern of the Gaddang is with the "earth world" and in particular with various classes of malevolent spirits and ghouls, the chief cause of illness and misfortune. Supernatural power, *anitu*, is apparently thought to reside in certain objects, *unting*, which, when hung within a house, serve to consecrate it as a fitting "temple" for household rituals. *Unting* include bundles of clothing and old beads, the former property of parents and grandparents of the housefather, as well as boards crudely carved in the shape of human heads. **Practitioners.** Although laymen frequently sponsor religious rites and ceremonies, the actual performance of ritual acts is left to part-time specialists who function as priest-mediums, i.e. "those who communicate with spirits." Most numerous are female mediums, *mekamong*, who specialize in cur-

ing, purification, and divinatory rites, on occasion entering a trance state while possessed by spirits. Paraphernalia includes beads, baskets, bowls, rice, betel, and tobacco. Male priests, *mebayin*, specialize in long ritual chants sung in an esoteric "spirit" language. **Ceremonies.** Illness, due to malevolent spirits and/or the breaking of cultural taboos, is a major concern, and curing-purificatory rites are numerous. Apparently, however, neither soul loss nor the breaking of the incest taboo is considered a major cause of illness or death. Agricultural, life cycle, and curing rites are on the whole household affairs; only headhunting ceremonies in the past involved the entire community. *Anitu* rites, likewise sponsored by households, are nowadays major festive occasions for pig sacrifice, drinking, dancing, and courting, during which participants pay little nominal attention to the ritual activities of the priest-mediums. These rites, in a series of seven, each more elaborate and expensive, are performed for or by an individual during his lifetime, first as child and later as married householder. A man hopes to accumulate the necessary wealth to perform the entire series, thus ensuring health, good fortune, and social status to himself and his household (in this world, however, rather than the hereafter). It is not clear to what extent these rites are in addition thought to benefit the spiritual well-being of the entire community. **Death.** Death should ideally take place outside the dwelling, in a specially constructed death house, where the corpse remains for several days. A dwelling in which a death has occurred must be abandoned, lest illness or misfortune befall its inhabitants. The spouse of the deceased undergoes a five-month period of mourning and avoidance.

BIBLIOGRAPHY. Beyer 1917; Fox et al. 1965; Keesing 1962a; Lambrecht 1959, 1960; Pittman 1952; Thomas and Healey 1962; Wallace 1967, 1969.

SOUTHEASTERN GROUPS

THE HEADWATERS of the upper Cagayan have their origin south and east of the central Luzon mountain range, in the Sierra Madre and Caraballo Sur ranges in southern Nueva Vizcaya. Between the upper Cagayan and the upper Magat to the north and west—the old Spanish "Ituy"—lies a region of rather dry and barren foothills, relatively unknown and unexploited under the Spanish, whose interests lay farther west, among the gold-rich "Igorots" of Benguet. East of Benguet were the pagan "Ilongots," relatively unknown to the early Spanish chroniclers. [Keesing 1962a: 270, 296ff.] Modern Nueva Vizcaya is populated chiefly by Christian Filipinos—Isinai, Ilocanos, Tagalogs, Gaddangs—growing wet rice in the lowland valleys and plains. Of the remaining pagan hill tribes, the best known are the Ilongots of the Conway and Casiguran rivers, tributaries of the upper Cagayan in southernmost Nueva Vizcaya. This whole area apparently remained marginal to the main thrust of Spanish penetration and to those forces that shaped the cultural evolution of the central Mountain Province peoples. The Ilongot studied by R. and M. Rosaldo lack most or all of the familiar Mountain Province institutions, such as men's houses; their way of life appears anarchic, the code of ethics situational; settlement is dispersed and fluid, as households move, divide, and merge to "follow the swiddens or flee from the law" (Rosaldo 1970c). East of the Cagayan headwaters and northwest of Baler Bay the Egongut (Ilungut) are mixed with so-called Negritos—Dumagat or Baluga groups showing evidence of Negroid or Papuan-like admixture (Beyer 1917: 47, 59; Fox 1953a: 174). Linguistically, at least, both peoples—Ilongot and Baler Dumagat—appear marginal to the rest of northern Luzon (cf. Thomas and Healey 1962, who posit a split-off date from a Philippine superstock at around 1100 B.C.). The implications, if any, of this early date for Ilongot cultural history are not altogether clear. In many respects, the Ilongot culture type resembles that of other dry-rice cultivators of Luzon—Apayao, Northern Kalinga, Pagan Gaddang. The people have been dry-rice cultivators since at least 1700, and root crops are nowadays, at least, clearly secondary to rice. Evidence of earlier affiliations, if any, with the seminomadic, root-cropping, hunting and gathering "Baluga" populations of the Baler coast would appear to have been erased by later contact with Isinai and Gaddang.

BIBLIOGRAPHY. Beyer 1917; Fox 1953a; Keesing 1962a; Rosaldo 1970c; Thomas and Healey 1962.

ILONGOT*

Synonyms. *Ibilao, Ibilaw, Ilungut, Iyongut, Lingotes*

---

*The authors of this entry, Renato and Michelle Rosaldo, conducted fieldwork among the Ilongot in 1967-69 and are at present teaching in the Department of Anthropology at Stanford University. A few linguistic and comparative notes have been added by the editor.

ORIENTATION. **Location and identification.** Scattered settlements of pagan swidden agriculturists in southern Nueva Vizcaya Province (lat. 16° - 16° 15′, long. 121° 15′ - 121° 40′), a region of rolling hills 1,000 to 3,000 feet above sea level, drained by the headwaters of the Cagayan River. Beyer (1917: 47-48) distinguished three dialect subgroups: (1) Egongut (Ipagi Egongot), northwest of coastal Baler and mixed with Negrito-like groups (2) Italon, the "true" Ilongot in the headwaters of the Cagayan, and (3) Abaka (Ibilao) in southwestern Nueva Vizcaya. Christian Gaddang, Isinai, Tagalog, and Ilocano occupy the surrounding valley lowlands, and a few settlements of acculturated "Ilongot" are found along the coast in the region of Baler Bay. The people refer to themselves and their language as *bugkalut* (untranslated) or *qirungut* ("from the forest"), the latter term probably accounting for the Tagalog (and Spanish) variant, "Ilongot." **Linguistic affiliation.** Malayo-Polynesian, seemingly only distantly related to neighboring Philippine languages. Thomas and Healey (1962) indicate a separation date from the Philippine superstock at about 1100 B.C. (cf. Dyen 1965). **Demography.** Approximately 2,500. **History and cultural relations.** The Ilongot continue to this day as an enclave of distinctive, self-conscious conservatism, noted since the sixteenth century for its resistance to pressures from the European world, and, unlike swidden farmers in many parts of the Philippines, they have never entered into symbiotic relations with wet-rice cultivators in the nearby lowlands. Spanish military exploration of the upper Cagayan area—the old "Ituy"—commenced in 1561, followed by the establishment of Dominican missions in 1612, but as late as 1850 the reports continue to mention the "fierceness" of the Ilongots. Even at the time of American occupation, census takers described three-quarters of the Nueva Vizcaya population as unsubjugated and wild (Keesing 1962a: 173, 195, 297). Under American administration, the Ilongot continued untouched and unpacified, as testified by the murder of William Jones, an ethnologist, in 1909. Recent decades have seen the development of airstrips by the New Tribes Mission, the expansion of the lumbering industry, and the encroachment of rural Filipinos into Ilongot territory. Incidents between Ilongots and settlers have been frequent, with open conflict reaching the Manila headlines in 1961.

SETTLEMENT PATTERN AND HOUSING. **Settlement pattern.** The Ilongot, numbering close to 2,500, and occupying an area of some 325 square miles, are divided into 13 named, localized dialect groups (mean population 180; range 64 to 307), each made up of several settlements. A settlement is comprised of 4 to 9 households, 5 to 15 nuclear families, and 40 to 70 persons; households are rarely adjacent to one another, but always within calling distance. Where there is missionary influence, households cluster and form "barrios" near an airstrip. Distinctive structures, such as men's houses, are lacking. **Housing.** The squarish, domestic house (*kamari*) is raised 6 to 15 feet above the ground, with a pyramidal roof, either raising to a central point or with a lengthened central beam at the apex. An outer wall of woven grass or bamboo encloses an unpartitioned central floor space surrounded by a slightly raised six-foot-wide platform, on which are one to three fireplaces—one per nuclear family. Field houses (*qabun*) are temporary affairs, smaller than domestic houses.

ECONOMY. Subsistence based mainly on shifting, dry-rice farming and hunting, with some fishing and gathering. The diet consists of rice, root crops, vegetables, wild pigs, deer, wild birds, and fish. Neither irrigation nor domestic animals are used in cultivation. **Agriculture.** New fields are cut and burned annually. Rice is intercropped with maize and manioc, and following the rice harvest a swidden may be planted to tobacco and vegetables. Fields to be abandoned are planted to sweet potatoes, bananas, or sugarcane. A swidden may be used from one to five years if cut from heavy forest growth, followed by an eight- to ten-year fallow. After a second cultivation, fields are indefinitely abandoned, and households may move as much as 20 miles to a new, thickly forested area. Houses are initially close together, but as new fields are cut at increasingly greater distances, the settlement tends to assume a dispersed pattern until at length the cycle begins again. **Hunting and fishing.** Men hunt communally with dogs at least twice a week, the meat being for immediate consumption and shared equally among all householders. Group hunts without dogs, lasting from three to five days, provide meat which is dried for sale or to be eaten during bride-price meetings. Meat from individual hunts is personal property, dried in strips and sold for cash or trade goods. Fish are taken in nets, traps, and by spearing. Small streams may be dammed and their courses diverted, and fish may also be stunned with poison, with or without damming. These latter techniques are joint ventures, with up to 250 persons dividing the catch. **Gathering.** Forest plant foods include fruits and ferns (seasonally) and hearts of palm and rattan (year around). Betel nuts are gathered throughout the year. **Domestic animals.** Dogs live inside the house and are used for hunting, but are never eaten. Pigs and chickens, kept in special structures near the house, are primarily for sale; the people seldom eat domesticated animals "because they eat excrement." **Industrial arts.** The status of the craftsman is not marked. Adult males forge their knives and agricultural implements (hoes and picks) and weave rattan baskets; women weave and sew. **Trade.** The trade language is Ilocano in the north and Tagalog in the south, with traders either coming to the borders of Ilongot territory or Ilongots hiking to lowland towns. Dried meat, captured fawns, pigs, and chickens are exchanged for bullets, liquor, cloth, salt, and knives. Within the Ilongot area there is minor trade for certain baskets and metalwork, but the bulk of such exchange occurs in the context of bride-price payments and gifts between kinsmen. **Property.** Land traditionally belongs to those who clear it; it is a free and public good. Other property is individually held and rarely inherited.

KIN GROUPS. Ilongot kinship is bilateral. There are no descent groups, but descent is primary in determining affiliation to a *be:rtan*, a putatively geographically-linked and ambilaterally-claimed category of affiliation evoked in contexts of oratory and public discussion. In one sense, a *be:rtan* is not a clan, corporate body, or discrete group of any kind, but rather an affirmation of allegiance given in a particular context or situation. In another sense, the Ilongot are at present divided into 13 mutually exclusive, relatively endogamous, local dialect groups, bearing *be:rtan* names. The *be:rtan* in this sense of the local group comprised of several settlements is the maximal unit for revenge raids in response to past beheadings. *Be:rtan* labels may be used with aggregates of persons to assert radical opposition (a possible translation is "kind, species"), as in bride-price discussions, where "we versus they" is spoken of in the language of raiding and head-taking. Or, it may be used to assert radical closeness, where a stranger is invited to speak at a peace meeting and claims the *be:rtan* of the local group. According to folk etymology, *be:rtan* labels, which may be geographical markers, plant names, place names, or color terms, mean that people once had their houses by, e.g., a *peknar* ("plain"), *biaw* ("Miscanthus"), or *kidmay* ("place name"). In fact *be:rtan* and "place name" are indistinguishable lexically, with the context unambiguously eliciting one or the other. An individual inherits his *be:rtan* from either parent, and could thus in theory have an infinite number, passed down from distant ancestors. In fact, however, no individual claims more than four, in part due to the fact that genealogical memory does not extend beyond the grandparental generation. Generally, a man prefers his father's *be:rtan* and a woman her mother's. Where relevant, if the husband's kin complete the bride-price payments, the children of both sexes take on the father's *be:rtan*. As an individual grows older and enters a wider net of social relations he acquires or "activates" more *be:rtan*. **Kin terminology.** Kin terminology (of reference) is Hawaiian in type: five generations are distinguished, and sex differences are ignored in generations plus two (*qapu*) and minus two (*makaqapu*). In generation minus one (*qanak*), there is an optional distinction for collaterals based on sex of Ego (if male, *makaquitaqu;* if female *makaqikit*); plus one generation distinguishes sex (male, *taqu;* female, *qikit*). Ego's own generation is denoted with a single term (*katanqagi*), with optional distinctions based on relative age (if elder, *qeka;* if younger, *qagi*) and same sex versus opposite sex (male referent, *raki;* female referent, *be:kur*). Affinal terminology is restricted to spouse's generation [spouse (*beqyek*), spouse's *katanqagi* and *katanqagi*'s spouse (*qaum*)] and spouse's first ascending generation (*qapu*). *Qaum* and *qapu* are self-reciprocals, but the reciprocals represent assymetrical kin types, i.e. *qaum* is "spouse's sibling/sibling's spouse," and *qapu* is "spouse's parent/child's spouse." The spouse's consanguine in each case cannot be named and requires otherwise "respectful" behavior.

MARRIAGE AND FAMILY. **Adolescence and courtship.** Girls as babies and boys before their teens have their ears pierced, without ceremony. At about 15, a member of either sex may decide to have his teeth filed and coated with a black sap. Filing may be accompanied by a feast and oaths, but is explained by aesthetic rather than symbolic or social considerations. Participation in a successful headhunt confers a marked change in status and is expected of all youths, preferably before they marry. Youths and maidens exchange betel and occasionally sleep together before they are recognized as couples. Formal discussion and marital exchanges generally follow a period when the young man is informally associated with his wife through casual field labor, gifts, and sex; pregnancy creates a crisis of gift-giving and threatened violence, usually resolved by marriage. **Marriage rules.** Since leadership within a community generally resides with sets of male siblings, close marriages are preferred, and sets of siblings or close cousins often marry into sets of siblings. Marriage within the nuclear family is proscribed; second-cousin marriage is preferred. Sexual relations with spouse's siblings are prohibited, although levirate and sororate are a common form of second marriage on death of spouse. **Mode.** Marriage among the Kakidugen River Ilongot (northwestern region) is by mutual consent of the man and woman concerned; bride-price payments (*laNu*) are made in the case of marriages with distant *be:rtan,* and, in the case of disputes, to quell the anger of the wife's kinsmen. Among groups in the lower Kasiknan area (northeastern region), a protracted series of payments accompanies any marriage, and serves as an occasion to air and settle grievances among kinsmen. The series of payments involves an initial, often hostile, confrontation (*puqrut*) with high stakes—guns and bullets, metal pots, cloth, jewelry, knives—followed by a series of *piqyat*, where meat and goods are given to individual affines, and finally *laNu* ("buying the woman"). From the girl's side, there is an *qarakad*, where, following a *laNu,* pounded rice and liquor are brought to the house of the man's kin and the girl's family renews its claim. **Form.** The family is monogamous and consists of husband and wife along with those offspring and/or adopted children who regularly sleep within the parental household. **Domestic unit and postmarital residence.** A household may include one to three families living under a single roof in an unpartitioned structure, each with its own hearth and sleeping area. Residence upon marriage, and for some time thereafter, is matrilocal: a household is comprised of parents and youngest married daughter(s), own or adopted. Two married sisters with their husbands and children may also comprise a household. The domestic cycle is simple: sons marry out and daughters stay home, leaving the parental household in turn when younger daughters marry. A married couple may return to the man's natal community only on completion of bride-price payments.

SOCIOPOLITICAL ORGANIZATION. Ilongot society is an ordered anarchy; ideologically all men are equal, and no political specialist or leader exists. In practice, community leadership tends to reside in sets of male siblings, especially those skilled in oratory, genealogical knowledge, or custom law. Power of persuasion is held by the most eloquent speaker at public discussions, one who has mastered the art of *puruN*, oratory—predominantly an adult male skill; women claim not to understand *puruN*. The eloquent speaker cannot apply sanctions, however; instead he manipulates oratorical conversation toward a kind of consensus, which he may have discovered through private discussions prior to the public meeting. The orator (or orators) within a settlement becomes particularly important in extrasettlement gatherings, such as peace meetings, where the best of local orators are pitted against their peers. As a "mediator" at such meetings, when the topic may be the number of guns given in payment for heads taken, the orator assumes importance as the representative of his local group, aiding in setting the time and place of the meeting and staking his prestige and often his community's safety on its success. **Social control and justice.** Formal litigation is absent, although bride-price discussions often turn to personal grievances, in which a man may demand metal pots or other commodities in payment for a former threat to his person or in exchange for commodities he has given in prior bride-price meetings. When an immediate "legal" response is required, e.g. for petty theft (cash, a dog), test by ordeal may be demanded by the offended party. Betel exchange, swearing by salt, and occasional sacrifices are also ritual elements of "legal" situations. **Warfare.** Head-taking is practiced by the contemporary Ilongot; and most men have taken a head. An unsettled feud, a death in the household, a young bachelor who "needs" to take a head, are among the conditions that make a man wish to "relieve his heart." Often he will make a *binatan,* a vow of personal sacrifice (eat no rice from a granary, avoid sex, and so on) until he participates in a head-taking. Head-taking is expected of all men, preferably before they marry; it marks a change in status, seen in the ability to wear cowrie shells, head feathers, and red hornbill ornaments. It is not a means of acquiring soul stuff, personal power, or crop increase, nor is it restricted to vendettalike vengeance. Raiding parties range from 1 to 40 in number. Before a party sets out, the members line up before a household and a priest calls the souls of the victims into a bamboo receptacle. As the party sets out, omen birds are listened for in the forest. Music of the violin and reed flute, associated with killing in daily life, may be played in the forest. When killing, a man "scores" for being the first to strike or shoot, the first to reach the body or to actually cut the head, and for being the first or second to throw the head after it is taken. The head is not kept as a trophy, although the hands traditionally were taken home for the children to chop up. A pig is sacrificed amidst singing and dancing after the party returns home. Peace may be established through a series of debates and exchanges, similar to payment for a bride. Visits, marriage, and even joint raiding may in fact follow a peace. The ritual bonds of a pact are rarely binding, however; in the absence of marriage, enmity is renewed within two generations.

RELIGION. Ilongots remained isolated from major religions until the 1950s, when Protestant groups began substantial conversions. The indigenous religion is characterized by the lack of structure and hierarchy apparent in the society generally. Religious specialists, *be:rtan*-based taboos, and beings generally identified as ancestors all figure weakly in the individual-oriented system of beliefs. **Supernaturals.** Divine beings include an overseer-creator associated with the sun; ancestors; other spirits, including personal familiars; and a series of spirits-in-nature. Of the latter, *qagimeN* is probably the most feared and powerful, as man's "companion-in-the-forest," giver of disease, and guardian of the chase and of headhunting; his female counterpart, the "maiden," holds parallel dominion over the gardens. Other spirits, primarily givers of disease, may be attached to persons and give power; these are usually associated with geographical features, typical symptoms, and plants that cure them. Personal experiences, such as dreams, may

yield charms for hunting or health. **Practitioners.** Many persons have unique spiritual associations, arising from illness, visions, and the like. But of these, only a few are shamans, qualified to conduct major diagnostic and curing sacrifices, preside over special chants, and summon the souls of headhunting victims. Anyone cured by a shaman shares in his spirit's power and can conduct minor ceremonies with its help. Other people can suck out disease, divine with a bow, and perform rites inherited from kin. **Ceremonies.** Aside from headhunting and peace-making rituals and occasional sacrifices for severe illness, ceremonies are rarely communal. Only agricultural rituals have anything like cyclical regularity, and these concentrate around the harvest. **Illness and medicine.** Disease and misfortune are caused by contamination, usually from spirits who lick or urinate on a person, from ancestors who long for the company of the living, or from forest or field guardians annoyed by excessive human abuse. A spirit leaving a sick person may be contagious, as may a man's evil thought or curse; tabooed foods cause illness and some plants have power such that cutting one causes stomach ache. Except when specialists perform sacrifices, cures typically involve invoking and then chasing a spirit by manipulating plants (about 700 are used in magic) or objects, and calling, threatening, blowing away, smoking, steaming, bathing, beating, drinking. A medicine may turn on a spirit and make it sick; a contagious plant, burned or beaten, banishes its symptom; a weed or an object—roof thatch, a specially forked stick—is invoked because of its analogy to a disease or to health. **Soul, death, and afterlife.** All men have a spirit that travels during sleep and survives death as a spirit dangerous to the living. Burial practices involve banishment of the deceased's spirit by sweeping, smoking, bathing, and invocation. A corpse is wrapped in bark or boxed, and buried near the home, sitting or curled on its right side, its valuable goods hung on a post at the foot of the grave. Corpses of young children may be placed high in trees in their bark shrouds; their proximity in the earth is regarded as both painful and dangerous.

BIBLIOGRAPHY. Barrows 1910a; Beyer 1917; Dyen 1965; Jones 1908-09; Keesing 1962a; Rideout 1912; M. Rosaldo 1971, 1972; R. Rosaldo 1970a, 1970b; Thomas and Healey 1962; Tugby 1966; Turnbull 1929; Wilson 1947b.

PART III. BATAN-BOTEL TOBAGO

THE BABUYAN AND BATAN archipelagoes stretch north from Luzon to within 70 miles of the island of Lanyu (Botel Tobago), which in turn lies only 45 miles off the southern coast of Formosa (modern Taiwan). These various islands, each of which in clear weather is visible from its nearest neighbor, must have provided a series of natural stepping stones for earlier movements of men and ideas back and forth between Formosa and the Philippines—and ultimately between the Philippines and the Asian mainland. The languages and cultures of this island chain evidence affinities on the one hand to those of the northern Philippines and on the other to those of Formosa's east coast, but do not readily fit known classifications for either region. The 5,400 or so inhabitants of the Babuyan islands are mostly farmers of Iloko and Ibanag extraction, recent settlers from nearby Luzon. These islands, like those of the Batan group farther north, are noted archeologically for protohistoric jar burials in association with stone cairns (Beyer 1947: 213; Solheim 1960; deBeauclair 1969a). The 10,000 inhabitants of the Batanese islands are located principally on Batan (Divatan), Itbayat (Ditbayat), and Sabtang (Sabbang). These people, termed collectively Batanese or Ivatan, speak one or another of two indigenous languages—Ivatanen or Itbayaten—although they have otherwise assimilated almost completely to the dominant lowland Christian Filipino culture pattern. Batan in the early eighteenth century appears to have been relatively densely populated, with the inhabitants concentrated in "towns" on the island's outer circumference, the interior being planted to taro, yams, sweet potatoes, sugarcane, and millet, supplemented in some areas by maize and tobacco. Houses, made of wood and thatched with grass, were built low to the ground and close together, each with a fenced enclosure for pigs. Solheim (1971) calls attention to the extensive use of stone in the form of walls, fences, paving, and the like. Wealthy "chiefs and principals" exercised considerable power within local areas and validated their status by sponsorship of large public feasts, at which family heirloom wealth was displayed in the form of gold and silver ornaments. Gold, highly valued and the principal status symbol, was obtained in trade from Luzon, but was worked locally, as was silver. Seasonal fishing for flying fish involved crews of up to 16 rowers in large, double-prowed boats built up of planks fitted together with wooden pegs and equipped with mat sails. Vengeance and feuding were common, and raiding and warfare endemic, although there is no evidence of headhunting. Buffalo hide and rattan armor included bell-shaped contrivances extending from throat to knee. Combatants crouched in these with only the head exposed, approaching one another with short hops until within spearing range. [Gonzalez Alonso 1966; Scheerer 1906; Kano 1946-52 (2, 57-75, "Ethnological Notes on Batan Islanders Dwelling in Manila"); Yamada 1965; Kikuchi 1966.] With respect to such things as boat and house construction, fishing techniques, gold culture, jar burial, and the like, Ivatan (Batanese) culture appears to have been markedly similar to that of the Yami of Botel Tobago. These and other affinities between the Ivatan and Yami peoples are likewise noted by Mabuchi, who calls attention to Yami traditions of ancestral origins on Batan (I-batan) and of former marriage and trade relations with the Batanese (Mabuchi 1956, citing earlier work by Utsurikawa 1931 and Asai 1936). And, conversely, Yamada (1967) cites Itbayat stories of traveling to Dihami (Yami, i.e. Botel Tobago). Contact evidently ceased some three hundred years ago, just prior to first Spanish contact [Yamada (1967), citing Kano (1946-52) and Ogawa and Asai (1935); independently confirmed by deBeauclair (1959a)]. Thus there seems little doubt about the existence of cultural similarities and past historical contact between Batan and Botel Tobago, although ethnological and archeological knowledge is as yet insufficient to allow anything like a definitive interpretation of the meaning of these facts for the culture history of the area. Linguistically, Batan and Botel Tobago appear to be closely related. Asai (1936) placed Yami with Ivatan in a "Batan group" (cited in Yamada 1967: 146), a placement accepted by Dyen, who therefore excluded Yami from consideration as a Formosan language on the grounds that "Ivatan seems clearly to be a member of the Philippine group of languages" (Dyen 1963: 203). Dyen's later (1965) placement of Ivatan was, however, coordinate with the northern Philippine languages but ungrouped with any one of them, a placement which agrees with that of Thomas and Healey (1962), who propose a splitting-off date for Ivatan of around 1,100 B.C., well before the differentiation of the Philippine language stock into its northern and central components. This uncertainty regarding Ivatan places

Yami and Ivatan in a marginal position with respect to both the Philippines and Formosa, a fact reflected in Ferrell's (nonlexicostatistical) inclusion of Yami among his Paiwanic (Formosan) languages, while at the same time acknowledging Yami's close ties with Ivatan. Much turns on the ultimate relation of the Formosan languages to those of the Philippines, an important key here being the need for greater ethnological and archeological knowledge of the Bashi Strait area and its peoples—the islanders of Batan and Botel Tobago (Ferrell 1969a: 60).

BIBLIOGRAPHY. Asai 1936; deBeauclair 1959a, 1969a; Beyer 1947; Dyen 1963, 1965; Ferrell 1969a; Gonzalez Alonso 1966; Kano 1946-52; Kikuchi 1966; Mabuchi 1956; Ogawa and Asai 1935; Scheerer 1906; Solheim 1960, 1971; Thomas and Healey 1962; Utsurikawa 1931; Yamada 1965, 1967.

YAMI

ORIENTATION. **Location and identification.** Sedentary agriculturists of Indonesian stock, occupying the single small island of Lanyu some 40 miles off the southern tip of Formosa. The European name for this island, Botel Tobago, may be related to the word for gold in some dialects of northern Luzon and the Batan islands, reflecting the former importance of these areas in early trade with China and the West. The name Yami, probably derived from Batanese (Ivatan) *i-ami*, "people from the north," was first recorded as an exonym by Ryuzo Torii in 1897 and rapidly gained general currency in government and academic publications. [Mabuchi 1956: 1-2.] **Geography.** Lanyu is of volcanic origin, 45 square kilometers in area, with mountains averaging 500 meters in height. Short, rapid streams flow from interior catchment areas into narrow, coastal plains. The climate is tropical and monsoonal, with violent storms from May through August. Rainfall is relatively heavy but unpredictable. Land fauna is limited, and hunting is restricted mainly to birds. Marine resources, however, are abundant, and fishing is an important aspect of the economy. **Linguistic affiliation.** Yami is not usually classed as a Formosan language. Its affiliations seem rather to be with the languages of the Batan islands (Ivatan, Itbayaten) farther south. These latter, although ultimately related to the Philippine languages,

appear to have split off at a relatively early date. [Dyen 1963; Thomas and Healey 1962.] **Demography.** Slightly over 1,400 in 1954, representing an increase from the immediate postwar period but slightly less than the first enumeration in 1906 (Mabuchi 1956). This figure had reportedly increased to 1,550 in 1956 (deBeauclair 1957) and to 1,996 in 1964 (Wei and Wang 1966). These figures, if accurate, indicate a rapid increase in population during the past two decades. **History and cultural relations.** Basic cultural and linguistic ties appear to lie to the south, most specifically with the Batan islands; and myths and legends point to regular contact between Batan and Botel Tobago in the period just prior to Spanish conquest of the Philippines. Although contemporary Yami have little knowledge of, or interest in, the island of Formosa, it is likely that their culture history is in some measure tied to that of the larger island—in particular with that of the Ami and other peoples of the east coast littoral (Ferrell 1969a: 58). While Japanese colonial rule by and large protected and secluded the Yami from outside contact, the post-World War II period has witnessed the introduction of schools and missions and some degree of Taiwanese immigration. As of the mid-1950s, however, the Yami were practicing a way of life relatively little changed from that of their ancestors (cf. deBeauclair 1957).

SETTLEMENT PATTERN AND HOUSING. **Settlement pattern.** A total of six compactly settled villages (*ili*), located around the outer circumference of the island, on rocky slopes behind high tide line. According to Wei and Liu (1962: 17), villages average 260 persons (range 183-321), and 69 households (range 46-100). Boathouses are located on the beach below the village, while on both sides and to the rear stretch irrigated and terraced taro fields. Much use is made of stones for retaining walls, foundation walls, steps, paving, and the like. A village consists of extremely closely spaced home lots or compounds, separated by narrow paved walkways, each with a main dwelling (*bagai, wagai*), workshop (*makaran*), pile-raised resting platform (*tagakal*), pig pen, and granary. Public buildings such as men's houses are absent. **Housing.** Architecture to some extent reflects the need for protection against the violent winds and rains of tropical storms. Main houses are semisubterranean, multiroomed affairs on three levels, constructed within excavated areas surrounded by stone retaining walls. Floors and walls are of hewn planks fitted together with wooden pegs or lashings, while roofs are of multilayered bundles of grass thatch securely fastened to wooden rafters. Relief from the dark, cramped quarters within these houses is provided by the light, airy atmosphere of the raised resting platforms. Workshops comprise a planked upper room, used by men for basketry and net making, and an unfloored cellar room, reached by stone steps, which is used by women for weaving. In front of main dwellings are stone uprights used by the inhabitants as backrests. House beams are not carved or decorated except for carved goat horns on the center post of the main dwelling. [Okuda et al. 1941a: 4, 20; Wei and Liu 1962: 8-17; Kano and Segawa 1956: 32-73.]

ECONOMY. **Agriculture.** Subsistence based primarily on settled agriculture. Major crops, with percentage of land planted to each as of 1937, are: swamp taro 41 percent, sweet potatoes 27 percent, dry taro 19 percent, yams 9 percent, millet 4 percent (Okuda et al. 1941a: 8). Other crops include sugarcane (as condiment, not liquor), bananas, breadfruit, betel, abaca, coconuts, ginger, pumpkins, melons, and cucumbers. Okuda et al. (1941a: 22-26) comment on the absence of legumes and leafy vegetables among the cultivated crops, but point out that this seeming lack is made up by the gathering of a great variety (some 22 kinds) of wild food plants. Lower slopes in the immediate vicinity of a village are devoted to the raising of swamp taro on permanent fields, irrigated and (where necessary) terraced, with water for irrigation diverted from mountain streams by systems of ditches and bamboo troughs. Higher slopes and mountain sides are devoted to the slash-and-burn cultivation of Italian millet, dry taro, and sweet potatoes. While women grow the all-important food crop, swamp taro, as well as sweet potatoes, the cultivation of yams is in the hands of males. The ritually important millet is grown by members of agricultural associations, *chichipunan*. The chief agricultural tool is the digging stick; no use is made of animal power, and the fields are not manured. Millet and sweet potatoes can be rotated in dry fields for up to three years, followed by a three- to five-year fallow; wet fields planted to taro produce continuously for up to five years, after which they may be dried and fallowed for two to five years (Okuda et al. 1941a: 40-41). [Kano and Segawa 1956; Okuda et al. 1941a.] **Hunting and fishing.** Hunting is of relatively little importance, but fishing and the collection of shellfish supply an important component of the diet. Fish are taken by spearing, netting, and with hook and line, a considerable portion being dried for future consumption. Among the most important economic activities is the seasonal fishing for flying fish, the largest catches being made at night from boats, using torches and scoop nets. The annual run of the sacred flying fish, lasting for several months, has achieved a considerable importance in Yami life and thought; it is the focus of fishing associations, the members of which cooperatively build and own large fishing boats and carry out important magical and ritual acts to ensure an abundant flying-fish harvest; and it is the basis for calculating the start of a new year and for intercalating the Yami lunar calendar (Lin 1961; Leach 1950). [Kano and Sewaga 1956: 172-229; Kano 1944; Wei and Liu 1962: 118-23; Okuda et al. 1939b: 13-18.] **Domestic animals.** Pigs, the responsibility of women, are kept in pens and fed a cooked mash of taro stalks and leaves. Goats are left to roam in communal pastures, with individual ownership shown by distinctive notches cut in the animals' ears. The meat of domesticated animals, including chicken, is consumed only on festival or ritual occasions. [Okuda et al. 1941a: 42-46; Kano and Segawa 1956: 166-68.] **Industrial arts.** Men are skilled carpenters and boatbuilders, and in addition they do iron smithing, silversmithing (completely tabooed to women), and pottery manufacture. Women spin and weave abaca, ramie, hibiscus, and other fibers, using a horizontal backstrap loom. Botel Tobago is perhaps best known for its large, double-prowed, plank fishing canoes (*chinurikuran*), which are fitted together with wooden pegs and extensively decorated with incised geometric designs. Such boats are capable of carrying a crew of ten oarsmen (cf. Kano 1938b). Equally well known are the conical helmets of silver worn by men on ritual and social occasions. Yami tradition points to Batan (and ultimately Luzon) as the original source of gold and silver, although the latter was in more recent times obtained by melting down Japanese coins. Balancing scales and other tools of the silversmith appear to date from ancient times (Kano 1941c; deBeauclair 1969b). Pottery making is limited to specialists and to a single month during the year. Pots are shaped by hand, using a wooden paddle and a flat, round stone. Small clay figurines are made for amusement or as children's toys. [Kano and Segawa 1956: 281-418.] **Property.** The Yami attach considerable importance to property rights, with fishing grounds, pasture lands, fields, house lots, and the like individually named and bounded by well-known natural features or by stone walls and walks. According to Wei and Liu (1962: 130), unexploited mountain lands and certain natural resources, such as named fishing grounds, are village owned. At the other extreme, such movables as silver helmets, ornaments, and gold foil are individually owned. The prime example of family-owned property would appear to be the plots of wet-taro land, which can be inherited, sold, exchanged, or offered as indemnity. Wet-taro land is normally inherited patrilineally, although a father can if he wishes give a favored daughter some as a dowry (Wei and Liu 1962: 152). Houses, small boats, and domestic animals also appear to fall within the category of family property. It appears, however, from the reports of Wei and Liu, that rights to the use of house lots, dry fields, pastures, and irrigation systems are conditional on membership in what they call patrilineages (*asa satengu*)—probably corporate ambilineal ramages. The owners of large, ritually consecrated, fishing boats are members of fishing associations, ideally made up of family heads related in the male line (although in practice this is seldom wholly the case). What Wei and Liu call lineages also appear to hold title to such things as old Chinese jars, distinctive designs cut in the hulls of boats and notched in goats' ears, and ritual staffs ornamented with carved goats' horns (Wei and Liu 1962: 139; Kano and Segawa 1956: 59). [Wei and Liu 1962: 69, 134-39, 152; Okuda et al. 1939a, 1941b; Kano and Segawa 1956.]

MARRIAGE AND FAMILY. **Mode.** Infant betrothal was formerly common; nowadays the pattern appears to be one of relatively free premarital sex, followed by betrothal negotiated through a go-between and symbolized by a gift of beads and betel to the girl's parents. The wedding is a relatively simple affair, marked by a feast at the home of the bride, after which the girl is formally escorted to the home of the groom's family. Property exchange is minimal, and bride-price absent. [Wei and Liu 1962: 74-75; Mabuchi 1960.] **Form.** Strict monogamy (Wei and Liu 1962: 67). **Marriage rules.** Marriages are, by and large, village endogamous, up to 72 percent according to Okuda et al. (1939a: 6). Wei and Liu's "patrilineages" are agamous, although segments thereof are statistically strongly exogamic (1962: 69). According to Wei and Liu (1962: 61, 73), the limited personal kindred (*ripus*), extended laterally to include first cousins, constitutes the effective incest group, preferred mar-

riages being with second or third cousins. Okuda et al. (1939a: 5), however, report that second cousin marriage is prohibited. **Residence.** Wei and Liu (1962: 30) report the incidence of patrilocal marriages for all six villages on Botel Tobago at around 84 percent. Exceptions occur mainly in families with no sons, where a married daughter may live matrilocally until her eldest son can assume the position of family head. According to Okuda et al. (1939a: 5), a married son lives initially in a small house near that of his father, while cooking together with his parents' family. The birth of a first child brings complete independence from the father's household, marked by construction of a new house, a change of name (i.e. teknonymy), and a change in status of close affinal relatives from *icharua* to *ripus*. The building of a new house and its associated ritual consecration is not undertaken lightly, requiring several years of preliminary planning to accumulate the huge amounts of foodstuffs customarily distributed at such a ceremony. **Domestic unit.** The independent nuclear family, averaging 4.7 persons (Wei and Liu 1962: 17; Mabuchi 1960: 138). **Inheritance.** Lands, boats, and houses are inherited patrilineally. At a man's death, his house, his small fishing boat, and on occasion his silver helmet are broken up and the parts distributed to his sons, with the eldest receiving the ornamental center house post. If there are no direct male heirs, a married daughter living matrilocally may assume temporary administrative duties until her son reaches marriageable age, or (a more likely alternative) ownership of the house lot reverts to the "patrilineage" (Wei and Liu 1962: 35). Wet-taro fields are inherited by a man's sons, with small portions by tradition going to anyone (usually a man's brother, his son, or his wife's brother) who helped carry his corpse to the cemetery. [Wei and Liu 1962; Mabuchi 1960: 138.] **Divorce and secondary marriage.** Divorce, initiated by either spouse, is said to be relatively common nowadays. According to Okuda et al. (1939a: 7), marriages are especially brittle before the birth of a first child. Causes are most often conflict between a bride and her mother-in-law or else adultery on either side. Charges of adultery can often be reconciled by payment of wet-taro land as indemnity, but if separation ensues, male children usually stay with the father, while girls return with their mother to her natal family. Secondary marriages are permissible, although both the levirate and sororate are theoretically forbidden, occurring only after payment of a ritual fine (Wei and Liu 1962: 25, 61).

KIN GROUPS. Discrepancies in the literature on kinship and marriage may be in part the result of inadequate documentation of what is apparently a considerable degree of intervillage variation in these and other respects (deBeauclair 1957). Okuda et al. (1939a) emphasize the collectivity of the village, stressing village endogamy, distinctive origin legends, communal fields and fishing grounds, communal religious festivals, and the common village cemetery (a wife is buried in the cemetery of her husband's village). In effect, they saw the members of a village as essentially a localized kin group united by ties of blood and marriage. Tadao Kano (1941a, 1944), studying legendary genealogies, found evidence that led him to classify the people of Imurud village into two groups—those of "stone descent" and those of "wood descent," i.e. "stone people" vs. "wood people," reminiscent of traditional dichotomies, sometimes with social and/or ritual connotations, common throughout much of Indonesia. Toichi Mabuchi, alluding to Kano's evidence and also to the conceptual importance in Yami culture of patrilocal residence and patrilineal inheritance of valued property, raised the possibility of a unilineal (patrilinear) tendency within an essentially bilateral society (Mabuchi 1956). Murdock (1960: 2-3), after weighing the evidence, classified the Yami as a bilateral society of Eskimo type, denying any trace of unilineal organization.

In 1957, a team of researchers from Taiwan's Academia Sinica (Institute of Ethnology), headed by H. L. Wei, spent four months among the Yami surveying patterns of social organization in all six villages. Their report (Wei and Liu 1962) introduced what they called the Yami's "patrilineage system," existing side by side with characteristic bilateral features such as the personal kindred. The evidence presented by Wei and Liu for "patrilineal descent" and the division of villages into localized, corporate "patrilineages" is unclear as it stands, part of the confusion evidently being due to overreliance on informants' statements of an idealized model (Nakane and Wang 1963). There is said to be a tendency "in principle" toward patrilocal residence and the localization of patrilineally related households within the village, but this is nowhere documented by actual mapping, leading one to suspect that it is more a matter of claiming a kind of putative descent from ancestors who are said to have once been so localized. Wei and Liu state that patrilineages "own" water rights and certain lineage lands, with families enjoying what appear to be usufruct rights, but here again the evidence is unconvincing—certainly wet-taro land is individually (family) owned, with full rights of alienation. In summary, it would appear that Yami kin relationships are basically organized around the bilateral principle, with the limited personal kindred (ripus) of greatest importance. There appears, however, to be an incipient development (perhaps an outcome of earlier contacts with Batan and ultimately northern Luzon) of what Davenport (1959) calls localized, nonunilinear, descent groups, membership in which may be determined by some optative or ambilineal principle. In the Yami's case, it is residence at marriage; where the couple settles in or near the house lot of the man's parents and the girl automatically gives up membership in her natal group; children born to this marriage affiliate with their parents' group. Access to land and water rights is dependent on membership in such a group, including common residence within the confines of a single village. **The bilateral kindred.** Ego's bilateral kindred are called upon for economic and social support on occasions such as weddings, funerals, and the ritual consecration of new houses and boats —all significant social and ceremonial events along the individual lifeline. Incest taboos apply most stringently to members of the *ripus*, the minimal personal kindred reckoned laterally to include first cousins. In practice, the *ripus* usually includes a wife's father or brother, these affinal relatives (*icharua*) being commonly shifted to *ripus* status following the birth of a first child. This enlarged *ripus* circle ordinarily constitutes the blood vengeance group and the active burial party at a man's death. [Wei and Liu 1962: 55-60; Okuda et al. 1939a: 14-16.] **The "patrilineage."** According to Wei and Liu (1962), Yami villages contain anywhere from two to eight named groups, which the authors term "patrilineages." The house lots of the members of a patrilineage are ideally contiguous, i.e. the members "in principle" form localized, patrilocal units or divisions within the village community (Wei and Liu 1962: 9). Household heads are males, and the inheritance and administration of property is predominantly in the hands of males. Lineage names indicate former location within an ancestral home (e.g. *sira du avak*, "those of the center") or else vegetational characteristics of ancestral fields. The recurrence of the same lineage name in more than one village is not, however, an indication of blood relationship; persons are considered lineage mates only if they reside in the same village, and those who leave forfeit their lineage memberships as well as their land and water rights (Wei and Liu 1962: 18, 41). Lineages "own" what might be termed genealogical stories (deBeauclair 1959a) dealing with the adventures of ancestral heroes and their wanderings over various parts of Botel Tobago and offlying islands. Going back as many as 19 generations, in some cases to "stone" or "wood" origins, in others to intermarriage between a Botel Tobago woman and an Ivatan (Batan) man, these stories appear to incorporate what might be termed lineage pedigrees traceable through the male line, although information on this latter point is obscure (Wei and Liu 1962: 45ff.; deBeauclair 1959a). Lineages (*asa satengu*, "one branch") are agamous with respect to marriage, whereas sublineages (*asa itetenguan*, "many branches," no more than five generations in depth), are strongly exogamic (Wei and Liu 1962: 33, 69). The eldest male in the highest generation within a lineage succeeds to the office of *ipapuipungut*, charged with responsibility for upkeep of wet-taro irrigation systems and allotment of water therefrom, as well as direction of millet cultivation groups (Wei and Liu 1962: 33, 51). Lineages appear to "own" such things as irrigation systems, markings on canoes, and notches in goats' ears. It likewise appears from the account by Wei and Liu (1962: 36, 134-38) that millet fields and possibly other dry fields, as well as certain pasture and forest lands, are lineage property, with individuals or families enjoying usufruct rights by virtue of membership in the lineage. The millet cultivation group (*chichipunan*), in principle composed of the adult men of a sublineage, is directed by the *ipapuipungut* in the sowing of millet and associated ritual, as well as in the harvest and its distribution among the families of association members (Wei and Liu 1962: 123-25). It appears from the account by Wei and Liu that membership in the important fishing associations (*kakavang*) is likewise lineage-based and that the large, ritually consecrated canoes bear distinctive lineage markings (1962: 52, 118ff.). According to Okuda et al. (1939a: 19-22), the members of a fishing association, who construct their boat in common and share in the seasonal catch of flying fish, are in Imurud village usually "closely related," although in other villages this appears to be less so, and members of the same household may in fact belong to different associations. Nor do the member households of any one of the Imurud associations, said by Wei and Liu (1962) to be lineage-based and thus presumably residentially segregated, group themselves within contiguous residential areas within the village, a fact confirmed by Kano's (1944) mapping of Imurud associations by household membership. **Kin terminology.** Lineal terms for uncles and aunts, cousin terms of "Eskimo" type (Murdock 1960: 140). Wei and Liu (1962: 83-84) give the following terms of reference:

PaFa	akai
PaMo	akes
Fa	ama
Mo	ina
PaBr	marang
PaSi	kaminang
ElBr, ElSi	kaka
YoBr, YoSi	wali
Sb	kakte
1st cousin	kateisa
2d cousin	kapusing
3d cousin	kapurogan
Ch	anak
SbCh	anak no kakte
GrCh	apu

Teknonymy. With the birth of a first son, a man changes his name to "father of so-and-so." When his son in turn has a son, he again changes his name to "grandfather of so-and-so," and should he have a great grandchild, the event will be reflected in still another name change (Wei and Liu 1962: 106-10).

SOCIOPOLITICAL ORGANIZATION. Traditionally, there has been no village chief or headman, the lead-

ership being in the hands of village elders (*rarake*), who attain their status by virtue of age, character, and wealth. Some are also "lineage" heads (*ipapuipungut*), although there appears to be no necessary connection between the two statuses (Wei and Liu 1962: 153ff.). **Social differentiation.** Although the Yami lack age-grades, men's houses, and formal social classes, wealth differentiation is a major avenue to individual (and family) prestige and status—and wealthy men have considerable influence in village affairs. It appears that the dynamics of Yami life are largely associated with the accumulation, display, and distribution of wealth—particularly in the form of foodstuffs such as pigs and taro—at major religious festivals, such as the consecration of a new house or a large fishing boat. Families proudly display collections of goats' horns and pigs' jaws as mementos of past achievements in what amount to periodic feasts of merit—at which family members wear elaborate silver and wood ritual helmets, gold and silver breast ornaments, and strings of old and valued beads, while displaying carved and ornamented ritual staffs and ancient Chinese jars. Such events may take on a competitive tone, in which challenges are given between villages, each represented by a wealthy family who displays, with suitable boasting, its wealth, e.g. a particularly large and fine wet-taro tuber or a large silver helmet. These are carefully judged by assembled elders as to quality as well as quantity, the defeated side eventually retreating amid the boastful jibes of the winners. [Wei and Liu 1962: 145-55; deBeauclair 1959b; Kano and Segawa 1956: 76-137.] It is probable, although not specifically so stated in the literature, that sponsorship of festivals marking the ritual consecration of new houses and large fishing boats is analogous to so-called feasts of merit elsewhere in Southeast Asia, whereby a family, under the leadership of an ambitious housefather, sponsors an (often progressive) series of major undertakings requiring the recruitment of considerable labor and the expenditure of considerable wealth. The sponsorship of feasts of merit confers enhanced spiritual status on the sponsors, reflected in increased social prestige—which is in turn a reflection of the fact that enactment of these ceremonies also benefits the spiritual well-being of the entire community. **Social control and justice.** Disputes, arising chiefly over charges of adultery and violation of property rights, are normally settled by negotiation and payment of compensation—traditionally in pieces of gold foil, glass beads, or wet-taro land. Close bilateral relatives on both sides take leading roles in negotiations, although, according to deBeauclair (1957), the rich men of a village also intervened in disputes prior to the introduction of modern government. Should negotiations fail, the relatives of the injured party may issue a verbal challenge, which, if accepted by the other side, may lead to physical conflict, i.e. stone, stick, and sword fights between relatives on both sides or a duel between two champions. Such conflicts consist largely of noise and bravado; should a participant be accidentally killed, the perpetrator would flee to the mountains, thus precipitating the recruitment of a formal blood vengeance group from among the male *ripus* of the murdered man; according to Wei and Liu (1962), the leader of such a group should be an elder of the deceased's patrilineage, usually a brave and experienced warrior (*makakangasia,* from *makakangam* meaning warrior). [Wei and Liu 1962: 62-63, 153-68.] **Warfare.** According to deBeauclair (1958), intervillage fighting and feuding were common formerly and still occur occasionally, and there are traditions of pitched "battles" involving up to 80 persons on a side, the result of disputes over such things as fishing rights and charges of adultery. Weapons included spears, clubs, and stones (but apparently no slings), together with shields, headgear and body armor of rattan or fish skin (cf. Kano and Segawa 1956: 132-37). Yami warfare appears, however, to have been largely a matter of boasting and bravado, with hostilities ceasing at the first sign of serious bloodshed. Unlike the majority of tribes on the Formosan mainland, the Yami of Botel Tobago have by all accounts never participated in headhunting practices. [deBeauclair 1958.]

RELIGION. **Supernaturals.** The Yami conceive of a layered upperworld inhabited by named deities called collectively *tau roto* ("people above"). These deities may punish mortals with fire, rain, or thunderstorms if offerings to them are neglected. They are especially fond of millet, which, along with taro and pig, is offered them at a yearly ceremony termed *miparos* (Mabuchi 1956: 16). There is also, apparently, an underworld, likewise inhabited by spirits, who are not, however, those of the dead. Of more immediate concern than the *tau roto* are various classes of terrestrial spirits, known collectively as *anito.* Although the spirits or ghosts of the recent dead are potentially harmful and thus classed among the *anito,* a family's more remote ancestral spirits can give protection and help on occasion. The *anito* are greatly feared and are the objects of innumerable food offerings as well as rather spectacular exorcistic rites, e.g. at the dedication of a new fishing boat (cf. Kano and Segawa 1956: 350-51). Canoe figureheads are sometimes carved in the form of an anthropomorphic figure of Magamaog, a mythical being in Yami legend; otherwise there is little interest in artistic portrayal of the supernatural (Kano and Segawa 1956: 290). [deBeauclair 1957; Mabuchi 1956.] **Practitioners.** Certain individuals (*romiak*), male or female, are thought to be endowed with magic power and the ability to enter trance states, during which they predict the outcome of disease or recover lost objects (deBeauclair 1957, 1959b: 194); and Kano and Segawa (1956: 442) describe a "medicine woman" treating a patient by

chanting, massage, and brandishing a sword to exorcise evil spirits. It appears, however, that most ceremonies are carried out by household or association heads, and that the position of priest was never developed to any great extent among the Yami. There is little information on witchcraft and sorcery, although soil from a cemetery is greatly feared and appears to be used in something like sorcery (deBeauclair 1957). **Ceremonies.** Okuda et al. (1939a) list numerous household ceremonies, e.g. thanking the spirits for the millet harvest, although major occasions along the life cycle, e.g. marriage and death, are not particularly elaborated in a ceremonial sense. Recurrent ceremonies include those at the beginning of the sacred flying-fish season, when crew members assemble in their boats in full ceremonial attire, including silver helmets, to participate in the ritual of "calling" the flying fish and of smearing nearby rocks with the blood of a sacrificed cock (Wei and Liu 1962: 118-23). The male members of agricultural associations annually enact the ritual sowing of the sacred millet while wearing their silver helmets and other ceremonial attire; following the harvest they gather in a circle around a wooden mortar to enact the ritual pounding (*mirachi*) of the millet (Wei and Liu 1962: 123-25; Kano and Segawa 1956: 164-65). The Yami's greatest efforts are reserved, however, for quasi-religious events such as the consecration of a new fishing boat or the completion of a new house—festival occasions that take on the character of feasts of merit, whereby families enhance their social standing within the village community (cf. deBeauclair 1959b; Kano and Segawa 1956: 282-359). Major ceremonies, such as the consecration and launching of a new fishing boat, require the accumulation of large quantities of food, especially pork and wet taro, and on such occasions the meat is carefully divided for distribution into ranked portions. Millet, the sacred food beloved by the gods, is in boiled form served as food and offered as sacrifice on practically all ceremonial occasions (Wei and Liu 1962: 145ff.). **Soul, death, and afterlife.** The main soul (*pa'ad, pagad*), located in the head, leaves the body only at death, when it travels to a land of the dead said by some to be on two small islands within the Batan Archipelago. Minor souls reside in the joints, e.g. the knees and shoulders, and may leave the body temporarily. Capture of the *pa'ad* by evil spirits, *anito,* is a major cause of illness, and gold foil or heirloom beads are applied to the patient's body to strengthen his soul in its struggle with the *anito.* [Liu 1959; Wei and Liu 1962: 63-64.] Should these or various exorcistic measures fail, the person dies. Burial in a village cemetery occurs within a day or so after death. The corpse, in a sitting position with elbows and knees drawn up and sharply flexed against the chest, is bundled in cloth and tied securely with cord. The bundled body is placed for a time on a stone seat outside the house while relations bid it goodbye, after which it is carried by a burial party to the cemetery outside the village. [Wei and Liu 1962: 63-64.] The actual burial party, close male relatives of the deceased, is kept small, partly because of an overwhelming fear of cemeteries and any contact with the dead, and partly because its members must be compensated in gold, beads, or wet-taro land. Burial is in a grave lined (in somewhat the manner of a cist) with hewn boards. Members of the burial party wear full armor and brandish spears to ward off evil *anito*. Mourning, which continues for three days, during which stringent taboos are placed on family members, is ended by a feast. [Liu 1959; Kano and Segawa 1956: 444-45.] A man who has lived a good life and who dies in his own home is buried in the vil-

lage cemetery according to the procedures outlined above. The corpses of those who die "bad" deaths, e.g. away from home, may be exposed on a ledge near the sea (Liu 1959), and there is evidence of jar burial at some time in the past (Kano 1941a).

BIBLIOGRAPHY. Asai 1936; deBeauclair 1957, 1958, 1959a, 1959b, 1969b; Davenport 1959; Dyen 1963; Ferrell 1969a; Kano 1936, 1938a, 1938b, 1941a, 1941b, 1941c, 1944; Kano and Segawa 1956; Leach 1950; Lin 1961; Liu 1959; Mabuchi 1956, 1960; Murdock 1960; Nakane and Wang 1963; Okuda et al. 1939a, 1939b, 1941a, 1941b; Thomas and Healey 1962; Torii 1902; Utsurikawa 1931; Wei and Liu 1962; Wei and Wang 1966.

PART IV. FORMOSA

As POINTED OUT by Ferrell, Taiwan's geographical location is critical for any understanding of the prehistoric movement of people and ideas along the coast of mainland Asia or out into the island world of the Philippines and Indonesia:

In Taiwan, aboriginal cultures of mainland origin, though showing also influences from the Philippines or other regions to the south, were still flourishing when Han-Chinese and Europeans began the modern development of the island in the 17th century A.D. The long continuity of these ancient mainland-derived cultures among Formosan populations speaking Austronesian languages, and the lack of evidence so far for any non-Austronesian indigenous languages in Taiwan, along with internal linguistic indications of considerable antiquity in Taiwan for the Formosan languages in general, appear to add support to the venerable theories that the Austronesian languages probably originally spread into the Pacific from mainland East Asia, and that the non-Han languages spoken by the ancient Yüeh peoples of the China coast may have been Austronesian [1969a: 3].

The Austronesian languages of Formosa have been classed by Dyen (1963, 1971) and others into at least two distinctive and presumably ancient groupings, viz. *Atayalic*, including Atayal and Sedeq, and *Tsouic*, including Tsou, Kanakanabu, and Sa'aroa. *Paiwanic*, provisionally including all remaining aboriginal languages, whether living or extinct, is less well defined. The Atayalics and Tsouics, swidden-farming headhunters of the rugged mountainous interior, have been identified with the early prehistoric cultures that moved out from the mainland about 2,500 B.C. (Chang and Stuiver 1966; Chang 1970). The Paiwanics, on the other hand, have been generally plains and foothill peoples, seemingly subject to cultural influences from island Indonesia and the Pacific (Chang 1957). [For additional discussion of early culture history see Mabuchi (1964, 1970a); Kano (1946-52); C. L. Chen (1968, chapter 10); Ling

(1955, 1958, 1962).] Taiwan's aboriginal population, generally estimated at somewhat over 200,000, has been subject to some three hundred years of increasingly intensive Sinicization concomitant with settlement of the lowlands by immigrants from China's southeast coastal provinces. Early Hindu and Muslim trade contacts are summarized by Ferrell (1966), while the short-lived Dutch period is covered in Davidson (1905) and Campbell (1903). Formosa (1911) summarizes much of the early Japanese effort at control and pacification of the native population, while Utsurikawa et al. (1935) and Mabuchi (1954c) reconstruct early tribal migrations based on intensive study of local genealogies and legends. More recent culture change, including Christian missionization since 1949, is discussed in Kokubu and Kaneko (1962), Ferrell (1969b), Tang (1970), and Nettleship (1970). General ethnological studies include C. L. Chen (1968) and Chijiiwa (1960) on material culture; Furuno (1945), Agawa and Asai (1935), Ho (1967), and Kaneko (1957) on ritual, myth, and legend; Okada (1942), Masuda (1942), Wei (1956, 1958c, 1965), and Mabuchi (1960, 1970a) on social organization; and general surveys by Kojima (1915-22), Sayama (1913-21), Suzuki (1932), and Teikoku-gakushiin (Académie Impériale) 1941. The many attempts at classification of the aboriginal peoples, including use of such terms as *Kaoshantsu* ("mountain tribes") and *P'ingp'ufan* ("plains tribes"), are summarized in Mabuchi (1954a, 1954b) and C. L. Chen (1968), and discussed in K. C. Chen (1967), C. L. Chen (1958a), Ferrell (1969a), Wang (1966, 1967), and Wei and Wang (1966). The ordering of groups in the present volume follows Ferrell (1969a) in the use of a primarily geographic-historical basis for classification, since, in terms of present knowledge, there appears to be remarkably little consistency in either the cultural or the linguistic data as one moves from area to area or group to group.

BIBLIOGRAPHY. Agawa and Asai 1935; Chang 1957, 1970; Chang and Stuiver 1966; Campbell 1903; C. L. Chen 1958a, 1968; K. C. Chen 1967; Chijiiwa 1960; Davidson 1905; Dyen 1963, 1971; Ferrell 1966, 1969a, 1969b; Formosa 1911; Furuno 1945; Ho 1967; Kaneko 1957; Kano 1946-52; Kojima 1915-22; Kokubu and Kaneko 1962; Ling 1955, 1958, 1962; Mabuchi 1954a, 1954b, 1954c, 1960, 1964, 1970a; Masuda 1942; Nettleship 1970; Okada 1942; Sayama 1913-21; Suzuki 1932; Tang 1970; Teikoku-gakushiin 1941; Utsurikawa et al. 1935; Wang 1966, 1967; Wei 1956, 1958c, 1965; Wei and Wang 1966.

CHINESE

THE MODERN peopling of Taiwan from coastal China, only 115 miles distant, began in the sixteenth century with scattered enclaves of pirates and privateers engaged on one side or the other of dynastic wars on the mainland. By the early 1800s, this beginning trickle had grown to two million and had absorbed or driven into the hills most of the plains-dwelling aborigines. As of the mid-1960s, Taiwan's ethnic Chinese numbered over 13 million, one-third of whom were living in cities of 100,000 or more, a consequence of the massive urbanization and industrialization that has taken place since 1949 and the establishment on Taiwan of the Nationalist government-in-exile. The Taiwanese are still, however, predominantly a rural agricultural peasantry, settled throughout the fertile coastal plains and everywhere pushing inland, up the valley floors and terraced hillsides on lands formerly claimed by the aborigines. These coastal plains, which account for only about one-third of Taiwan's total land area, support over 98 percent of the total population, with an overall average density of 2,700 per square mile, among the highest in the world (American University 1969: 15). Taiwan's Chinese are comprised chiefly of immigrants from the southeast coastal provinces of Fukien and Kwangtung. Hokkien speakers from Fukien arrived first and pre-empted the best lands, particularly those on the fertile western plains. Hakka speakers from Kwangtung came later and had to be content with marginal lands in the foothills and along the east coast. These two strains continue to comprise the overwhelming majority of the rural peasantry. They share generally similar physical characteristics and a broadly common cultural heritage, the main difference being linguistic (American University 1969: 35). Government schools are, however, encouraging the official use of Mandarin and the study of the Han cultural heritage. The Hokkien, with 80 percent of the Chinese-speaking population, are clearly the major ethnic group on the island, and the term Formosan Chinese or Taiwanese is often used to refer to this dominant group (Wolf 1972: 8). It is principally on this group that a series of modern studies of Chinese life and culture have appeared (cf. Gallin 1966; Wolf 1968, 1972; Barnett 1970; Ahern 1973; Diamond 1969; Pasternak 1972).

BIBLIOGRAPHY. Ahern 1973; American University 1969; Barnett 1970; Diamond 1969; Gallin 1966; Long 1960; Pasternak 1972; Wolf 1968, 1972.

EASTERN LOWLAND GROUPS

THE PEOPLES of Ferrell's "Littoral Culture Complex" (1969a: 51-58) are (or were) scattered over the low plains inland from Taiwan's north, east, and southwest coasts. The Ami, with a population approaching 90,000, and the Puyuma (pop. 6,000) have in each case retained at least some degree of ethnolinguistic identity. Peoples such as the Ketagalan (Ketangalan or Basai, and including Turubiawan, Qauqaut, and Linau) and Kuvalan (Kulavan, Kavalan, Kuwarawan, Kiwarawa) of the Taipei-Ilan area, and the Siraya [also known as Sideia or Sinkan and including the subgroups Tevorang (Taivuan), Tamsui, Takaraian (Makatau), Pangsoia, Dolatok, and Longkiau (Loncjou)], inland from Tainan, are mentioned in early Chinese and Dutch accounts [summarized in Ferrell (1969a, 1971) and deBeauclair (1970b)], but have long since been absorbed into the coastal Chinese population and (except for a few speakers of Kuvalan) are linguistically extinct. [See Kokubu and Kaneko (1962) for bibliographical references to Chinese and Japanese sources.] Traditions of overseas origin tend to set these littoral cultures off, as a group, from the rest of aboriginal Formosa, as do a series of other traits—pile dwellings, dugout canoes, elaborate cosmogonic/theogonic myths, division of villages into wards, with men's houses and age grades—which Ferrell (1969a: 58) believes may reflect the movement of people and/or ideas into eastern Formosa, in probably relatively recent times, from somewhere to the south, possibly the Philippines. [On the other hand, the ancient platform houses of the Siraya are thought by some to be evidence of Polynesian/Micronesian connections (cf. Li 1957a).]

BIBLIOGRAPHY. deBeauclair 1970b; Campbell 1903; Candidius 1628; Dapper 1670; Ferrell 1969a, 1971; Kokubu and Kaneko 1962; Li 1957a; Ogilby 1671; Struys 1684; Valentyn 1724-26.

AMI*

Synonyms. *Amia, Mo-amiami, Mo-qami, Pangtsah*

ORIENTATION. **Identification.** Ryuzo Torii, in the late nineteenth century, appears to have been the first to apply the term Ami to the indigenous inhabitants of Taiwan's east coast between Hualien and Taitung. Partly on the basis of differences in dialect and custom, Y. Ino in 1899 classified the Ami into five geographically named subgroups, later combined by T. Kano into a more or less standard three-fold classification: (1) a northern group, including the Nanshih (Nansei) Ami (2) a central group, including the Siukuluan (Shukoran, Shukuoluan, Hsiukulan, Hsiukuluan) and Haian (Coastal) Ami, and (3) a southern group, including the Peinan (Hinan, Pinam) and

Hengchun (Koshun) Ami. The people themselves appear to identify most strongly with localized villages or village complexes, the most thoroughly studied of which, Vataan and Tavarong of the Siukuluan Ami, are mentioned in seventeenth-century Dutch sources. [Liu et al. 1965: 6-7; Mabuchi 1954a; Ferrell 1969a.] **Location.** The coastal plain and interior rift valley paralleling Taiwan's east coast for some 150 kilometers, roughly from Taitung in the south to Hualien in the north (22° 45'-24° N. Lat., 121° 10'-121° 40' E. Long.). The majority of villages (33 among the central Ami) are on the middle and upper reaches of the Hualien, Siukuluan, and Peinan river systems. [Liu et al. 1965: 13-26.] **Geography.** Monsoonal tropical to subtropical climate. High temperatures and heavy rainfall are interrupted by a short "dry" season from December through January. Winds of typhoon force periodically strike the east coast between May and November, causing much damage (Liu et al. 1965: 2-3). **Linguistic affiliation.** Malayopolynesian. Ferrell's (1969a) classification of Ami as a member of the Paiwanic group of Formosan native languages is tentatively accepted by Dyen (1971), who also lists the following reported dialect names: Baran (Falanao, Maran), Kibi (Kiwit), Taparon (Tavalon), Tauran (Nataoran, Amis), and Sabari. **Demography.** The 1960 census lists 87,345 speakers of Ami (K. C. Chen 1967: 39), making them the largest of Taiwan's aboriginal groups, with the highest rate of increase—from 52,000 in 1939 (Wei and Wang 1966: 119-21). **History and culture contact.** It is T. Mabuchi's view that the Ami may be composed of several more or less unrelated ethnic elements (Mabuchi 1956: 9). According to Liu et al. (1965: 10-12), the origin legends of central Ami villages all contain the motif of a universal flood and brother-sister incest, widespread throughout East Asia; and some investigators have identified the "Sanasai" of these legends with Lutao (Green Island) off the Taitung coast, along with the possibility of a later element having arrived by migration from some unidentified region farther to the south (Ferrell 1969a: 53). The ethnic history of these people is further complicated by widespread internal migration throughout the latter half of the nineteenth century, the result of headhunting raids and military pressures from neighboring Atayal and Puyuma (Mabuchi 1960: 134; Utsurikawa et al. 1935). The aboriginal culture was seriously disrupted by Japanese colonial policies subsequent to 1900, and in recent decades the Ami have been increasingly exposed to the acculturative pressures of an expanding Taiwanese peasantry. In addition, Christian missions have succeeded in nominally converting most Ami (Li et al. 1962: 12-13). The matrilineal clan system, often cited as characteristic of all Ami, is most developed among the central groups; the more heavily Sinicized northern Ami lack most of these matrilineal features (Mabuchi 1960: 133-34).

---

*This summary focuses on the central Ami and in particular on the large village complex, Vataan; it does not attempt to cover the considerable cultural variation among other Ami villages and subgroups.

SETTLEMENT PATTERN AND HOUSING. **Settlement pattern.** Compact, permanent villages, averaging 600-700 inhabitants (Mabuchi 1960: 133), and located for the most part on coastal plains or on the broad alluvial plains of the interior rift valley. The central Ami village of Vataan, with a 1958 population of 2,362 persons living in six named hamlets, has reportedly been at its present site along a tributary of the Hualien river for upward of a hundred years, with a population in 1894 of over 2,000 (Li et al. 1962: 6, 448). Public buildings formerly included one or more men's (age-grade) houses and a village temple or "ancestor house." Villages were enclosed within dense bamboo thickets, with bachelors' dormitories, located at strategic entrance points, serving as guard houses. The "ancestor house" (*kakitaan*), the home of the chief priest, served as a village ceremonial structure on occasions such as the completion of a successful headhunt; main posts were elaborately carved and decorated, and there was a skull shelf in the yard in front of the structure. The construction of public buildings resembled that of private dwellings, except that the roofs of men's houses sloped close to the ground, eliminating the use of side walls. [Li et al. 1962: 191-95; C. L. Chen 1968: 261ff.] **Housing.** Dwelling houses are rectangular in shape, with walls and floors of bamboo or planks, and with thatched roofs. The interior flooring is raised a foot or so above the ground on short piles. Posts and rafters may be incised and painted with geometric designs (Heine-Geldern's "ornamental style," according to Ferrell 1969a: 52). Ami houses still tend to be large, kin-group dwellings (Ferrell 1969a: 52), with an average of 9.5 persons per house in central and southern villages, according to Mabuchi (1960). Southern Ami houses were formerly partitioned into five or more rooms with multiple functions (Sayama 1913-21: *1*, 20-21), and Vataan houses nowadays may be divided by plank partitions into separate compartments, although this is not traditional. Millet granaries are separate from dwellings and are raised slightly above the ground on piles. [Li et al. 1962: 169-80.]

ECONOMY. Agriculture, supplemented in former times by hunting and to a somewhat lesser extent by fresh-water fishing, remains the chief source of food. Vataan informants state that they learned wet-rice cultivation from neighboring Sinicized tribes about 70 years ago. Although they open an occasional swidden on nearby hillsides, Vataan villagers rely increasingly nowadays on wet rice, along with sugarcane as a commercial crop, utilizing modern techniques of irrigation, animal power, and chemical fertilizers. [For additional localized descriptions of economic practices in central Ami villages, see Sayama 1913-21: *1*, 37-43, 47-51; Kojima 1915-22: *2*, *pt. 1*, 31-48, 126-32.] **Agriculture.** Traditionally slash and burn, with millet (*havai*) the most highly valued and ritually impor-

tant crop and sweet potatoes (*vunga*) the staple. Other crops included sorghum and dry rice (for liquor), maize, taro, beans, sugarcane, and bananas. Swiddens were used for four to six years, with a fallow of up to twenty years, with intercropping a common practice. Cutting and burning of new fields was done by members of the younger age-classes under the direction of elders, after which the fields were distributed among the extended family working units. [Li et al. 1962: 15-42, 447-48.] **Hunting and fishing.** Game animals such as wild boar, deer, and monkeys formerly supplied an important supplement to the diet. Hunting parties, consisting of co-members of an age-class, engaged in extended game drives, using dogs and fire, together with bows and arrows and spears. Communal hunting on village-owned hunting grounds occurred in association with religious ceremonies and seems to have had ritual significance. The meat of large game animals was carefully divided and distributed according to rank and age-class membership, with women strictly excluded from all phases of hunting activities. [Li et al. 1962: 45-58, 449-50.] Fishing in nearby rivers is nowadays much more important than hunting as a source of protein, and is accomplished with nets, spears, traps, poison, dams, and weirs. Communal fishing following important religious ceremonies was an essential ritual activity in former times (Li et al. 1962: 450). **Domestic animals.** Dogs, important for hunting, were not eaten, whereas pigs and chickens served mainly as ritual sacrifice. Water buffalo are a recent introduction, along with wet rice; they are used solely for plowing and transportation and have no ritual significance. [Li et al. 1962: 85-90, 450.] **Industrial arts.** Clothing, originally of bark cloth, was more recently made from animal skins or woven from native-grown hemp or cotton. Caps and helmets of rattan, bamboo, and skin were decorated with shell beads and feathers according to rank and class. Among the central Ami, pottery is manufactured in Tavarong village by the paddle-and-anvil method and traded to other villages, such as Vataan. Carpentry and wood carving are not as highly developed as among some neighboring groups. The Vataan Ami do some forging and other iron work; although they use the Indonesian double piston bellows, they say they learned the technique in recent times from the Chinese. While some crafts are sex linked, e.g. women make pottery, craft specialization appears weakly developed. [Li et al. 1962: 451-61.] **Property.** Although the concept of private (family) ownership of agricultural land has become widespread since its introduction by the Japanese and the wholesale adoption of wet-rice agriculture, land appears formerly to have belonged in principle to the village. Agricultural land was divided into sections worked by members of junior men's age-grades. Hunting and fishing territories were likewise divided into sections under the control of administrators or wardens appointed by the various age-grades. Family property, administered by the eldest female within the household, includes the house and kitchen garden as well as heirloom wealth in antique bronze bells and glass beads. Private ownership of weapons, looms, and the like is sex linked, as is inheritance of same. [Liu et al. 1965: 211-27, 267; Li et al. 1962: 133.]

MARRIAGE AND FAMILY. **Mode.** Young people in theory have considerable freedom in the choice of a mate, but approval by the girl's parents is virtually mandatory before a marriage can take place. The ceremony is minimal, consisting mostly of welcoming the groom into the bride's home. "*Ambil-anak*" marriage, with payment of bride-price and patrilocal residence—the traditional resort of families lacking female heirs—is increasingly popular nowadays, even among families with marriageable daughters. Liu et al. (1965: 45) see this as one aspect of a change among the Vataan Ami in the direction of patrilineality. **Form.** Strict monogamy (Liu et al. 1965: 34, 126). **Marriage rules.** Among the Vataan Ami, the effective range of incest prohibitions extends to fourth cousins on the maternal side and to second cousins on the paternal side. The Tavarong Ami also extend incest rules bilaterally, but only so far as third cousins on the maternal side. [Liu et al. 1965: 132-35.] **Residence.** A couple traditionally took up residence in the home of the bride's parents, although families lacking daughters could resort to "*ambil-anak*" marriages with payment of bride-price and patrilocal residence. Increasing Sinicization is resulting in a trend toward patrilineality and patrilocal marriage, according to Liu et al. (1965: 32, 45). **Domestic unit.** In principle, the matrilocal extended family. In actuality, some 50 percent of Vataan households consist of nuclear families—attributable presumably to recent outmigration to new settlements. The position of household head usually descends to the eldest daughter, who traditionally stays on and, with her husband, inherits the homestead. [Liu et al. 1965: 33-34, 45-46.] **Divorce and secondary marriage.** Among the Vataan Ami, divorce is "frequent" and both sororate and levirate preferred and common (Liu et al. 1965: 126, 139, 147). **Adoption.** Occurs in about 3 percent of households in Vataan, most often the child of a relative (Liu et al. 1965: 36).

KIN GROUPS. **Descent.** Matrilineal. **Kin groups.** The bilateral personal kindred (*ngangasawan*), defined to include fourth cousins on the mother's side and second cousins on the father's side, constitutes the effective exogamic category. Including affinal relatives, it provides the membership of raiding (vengeance) parties, as well as support in the form of labor and gifts on occasions such as marriage and death (Liu et al. 1965: 70, 262). The basic kin group and nowa-

days the basic landowning unit is the matrilocal extended family, residing in a single household. The eldest woman within this group, usually the mother or grandmother, acts as household head, succession to this position being by primogeniture within the matrilineal line (Liu et al. 1965: 260). According to Mabuchi (1960: 133), the central and southern Ami are organized into some 50 matrilineal clans, subdivided into more or less local lineages. Vataan village, with over 2,000 inhabitants, is, according to Liu et al., organized into seven named matrilineal kin groups, the largest of which, *pakadodangai*, is named for the wooden mortar in which, according to myth, an ancestral sibling pair escaped the universal deluge. This kin group numbers 1,300—over half the total population. Because of its size, exact genealogical relationships are no longer traceable, and membership is subdivided into numerous lineage groups, the senior of which provides the hereditary priestly line, *kakitaan*, whose house, fronted by a skull shelf, was formerly the ritual center for village headhunting rites. The second largest kin group, subdivided into eight lineages, numbers 600 within Vataan but is widely dispersed in other central Ami villages as well (Liu et al. 1965: 260-61). These are noncorporate kin groups, serving to define the limits of certain rights and duties of members—who are distinguished by the observance of distinctive food taboos and ritual customs, such as funerary rites. Although marriage within Vataan is reported to be some 94 percent village endogamous (Liu et al. 1965: 132), the clans themselves are nonexogamous (Li et al. 1962: 8). Mabuchi (1960: 133) reports both lineage and clan exogamy among southern Ami and sporadically among the central groups, but considers this an incipient local development, the result of extensive internal migration, brought on by the military pressures of neighboring groups. Although exact genealogical relationships among members of a clan cannot always be stated, the members of the senior or most direct line of descent from an original or founding ancestor can always trace their genealogy (Liu et al. 1965: 45-46). In Vataan, the *pakadodangai* claim descent from mythical ancestors who first settled the area; other matriclans or lineages within the village appear to represent groups that migrated in from elsewhere and were given land by the *pakadodangai* (Liu et al. 1965: 62). The senior line of the largest *pakadodangai* lineage apparently constitutes an hereditary priestly line (*kakitaan*), and as such furnishes a kind of chief priest for Vataan village, in charge of important harvest and headhunting rituals. Certain other family lines possess hereditary rights to other ritual activities, e.g. those having to do with blacksmithing and stone fishing weirs. Larger lineages possess in addition a kind of talking chief (*utsingapaai*, "one who speaks well") and a genealogical expert (*mamikitots*). [Liu et al. 1965.] **Kin terminology.** Liu et al. (1965:

79ff.) give the following Vataan terms of reference (cf. also Mabuchi 1960: 134):

PaFa	*kudar*
PaMo	*kadau*
Fa	*mama*
Mo	*ina*
PaBr	*vake*
PaSi	*vai*
OSb	*kaka*
YSb	*sava*
Sb	*putong*
Ch	*wawa*
PaBrCh	*wawa no vake*
PaSiCh	*wawa no vai*
SbCh	*wawa no putong*

The Ami practice a system of naming similar to that of the Atayal and Saisiat, whereby the parent's name is linked to that of the child, patronymic for a boy, matronymic for a girl. [Liu et al. 1965: 121-22; Kojima 1915-22: 2, *pt. 2*, 95-98, 205-08.]

SOCIOPOLITICAL ORGANIZATION. Sociopolitical organization appears complex, although generalization is made difficult by differences, including those in terminology, among northern, central, and southern groups. The most fully described village, Vataan, may in fact be atypical, due in part to its large size, composite structure, and considerable degree of acculturation. Chen and Coe, basing their statements on a study of Tavarong, characterize Ami society as definitely hierarchical, with the gods at the top, including the ancestral gods whose way of life is to be followed. Next are the *kakitaan* (priestly) families, who carry out the will of the gods, assisted by the *saparangau*, leaders chosen from the older age-grades. The majority of the population is arranged in age-grades, each dependent on the one above for precepts and instructions in proper behavior. This whole structure is annually reaffirmed in the all-important *irisin* ceremony. [Chen and Coe 1954.] Ami society appears to be characterized by what might be termed a dualistic power structure. Secular authority seems clearly based in the male age-grade system, with women expressly excluded from age-grades and men's houses (the educational and administrative centers of the village) and thus from political life. At the same time, it seems evident that ritual authority has its basis in the female-oriented matrilineage system, although here again it is the brothers of lineage women who actually function as priests. In retrospect, the age-grade system has the appearance of having been superimposed on an original kin-based society, with positions of leadership grounded in (largely) ritual status derived from genealogical nearness to an original "founding" line. The result has been a kind of split between secular and ritual leadership. [For localized descriptions of sociopolitical structures in central Ami villages see Sayama 1913-21: 2, 25-30; Kojima 1915-22: 2, *pt. 1*: 145-57.]

Political organization. According to C. L. Chen (1965), political power in northern (Nanshih) Ami villages is vested in a "chiefs' assembly," composed of men chosen from among the *papuro'ai* (lit.: "one who speaks"), leaders or monitors of the mature age-grades. A man who seeks this office must be an eloquent speaker, skilled in ritual and hunting, and wealthy enough to sponsor a feast and display his wealth before all other *papuro'ai*. A speaker, elected by the chiefs' assembly from among its members, is the "high chief" in the village, although hunting, warfare, and headhunting are the responsibility of another high chief, who is elected from among the warrior chiefs of the various age-grades. Other assemblies or councils (of elders, of all males, of all age-grade monitors) mitigate to some extent the power of the chiefs' assembly. A somewhat similar system of secular "chiefs" (*saparangau*), leaders of proven ability chosen from the ranks of the more mature age-grades, is described by Chen and Coe (1954) for the central Ami village of Tavarong. Political power here is in the hands of these older men, who are seated at important ceremonies in order of their rank (Furuno 1945: 285ff.). Chen and Coe see these "chiefs" as intermediaries between the laity and the hereditary priestly families (*kakitaan*), ritual specialists and interpreters of the will of the gods. The situation in the central Ami village of Vataan, most fully described of all Ami villages, is apparently somewhat atypical. Here the village (*niaroh*) is divided into hamlets or sections (*kuan*), each with a headman or representative (*kakisowal*, "eloquent speaker"). From among the *kakisowal* are elected the members (*komod*) of a village council, administrators of fishing and hunting rights and other village-owned property. From among the council membership, in turn, there is chosen a "high chief" (*sapalungau*), a genealogical/ritual specialist who sets the dates for major festivals and presides over meetings and ceremonies. He is entitled to special headgear and is surrounded by taboos that set him off from the rest of the population. The term means literally "one who promotes germination," and as priest he specializes, according to Li et al. (1962: 8-9), in agricultural ritual; and according to Wang (1961: 176), his personal deities all have to do with agriculture. As summarized by Liu et al. (1965: 169-88, 265-67), leadership in Vataan is in the hands of a high chief, assisted by hamlet headmen and age-class leaders, with the high chief acting additionally in the capacity of a chief priest. This kind of political hierarchy, with its by-passing of the traditional rights of the *kakitaan* priestly families, has progressed farthest in Vataan—probably as a consequence of Taiwanese acculturative pressures. **Social differentiation.** Secular power in Ami villages appears everywhere to have been traditionally in the hands of men's age-grades. Among the Vataan Ami, the young men (*kapah*), comprising seven named grades (age-sets or classes), sleep in bachelors' houses, where they are at the beck and call of older men, performing a variety of services and in former times functioning as warriors. The middle-aged males (*matoasai*), comprising four named grades, provide the active leadership within the village, while the *kalas*, with two grades, comprise the older men, retired from active life but highly respected. [Liu et al. 1965: 266-67.] A large village such as Vataan may have up to three men's houses, one each for the young, middle-aged, and elderly, with in addition bachelors' dormitories which serve as watch stations near entrances to the village. Initiation of a new grade or class of boys of 15 or so years of age occurs on the average of every five years in Vataan. At this important event, held in the main men's house (*sajuratan*), each existing class moves up a step in the hierarchy, although keeping its own name. In Vataan and most northern Ami villages, these names are traditional, according to a set series which recurs cyclically over time (Liu et al. 1965: 190-209). When a new class is formed, a leader or monitor ("speaker") is chosen, who ordinarily keeps this position for life. Each class in addition has a ritual specialist for hunting activities (formerly including headhunting) and a distributor of meat. [Liu et al. 1965; Chen and Coe 1954.] In addition to the age-grade systems, descriptions of Tavarong village society mention what amount to class differences based on traditional, kin-based, ritual prerogatives. According to S. M. Jen (1958), the Tavarong *kakitaan* lineages constitute a kind of hereditary nobility; as direct descendants of the legendary ancestor-founders, they "own" the village lands and the ancestor house (*kakitaan*) where they perform rituals for the village welfare. The remainder of the population—laity or "civilians"—is largely landless and in a sense tenants of the *kakitaan* lineages. Certain of the higher civilian grades may, however, administer certain lands and ritually serve the *kakitaan*. These "higher civilians" appear to correspond to Chen and Coe's (1954) "chiefs" (*saparangau*), intermediaries between the laity and the *kakitaan* priests. According to Liu et al. (1965: 183-86), these class differences are marked by differences in house style and decoration, e.g. only the *kakitaan* ancestor houses may carry carved human and animal figures on the main posts. **Social control and justice.** Blood vengeance (the responsibility of members of the personal kindred, *ngangasawan*) appears formerly to have been the rule in serious cases such as the killing, whether accidental or not, of a fellow villager. Nowadays the offender, with his near maternal kin, flees to a neighboring village while go-betweens usually manage to arrange payment of compensation in lieu of blood vengeance. Less serious cases are usually settled (in Vataan) by the high chief, with bilateral kindred on both sides consulted and liable for payment of whatever fine is imposed—most often a pig. [Liu et al. 1965: 70-71, 229-39.] **Warfare.** Headhunting, which ceased some 40 to 50 years ago, was carried out by Vataan villagers against other Ami—e.g. the village of Tsikasowan to the north—but also as part of a prolonged and disruptive state of hostilities with neighboring Atayal, Bunun, and Puyuma peoples. According to Liu et al., the taking of an enemy head was an integral part of the annual *irisin* renewal ceremony, celebrated at Vataan soon after the end of the millet harvest—a statement seemingly in agreement with the observation by Furuno (1945: 82) that a prime motivation for headhunting was to ensure an abundant millet crop. A headhunting party consisted usually of members of a particular age-grade. The head was brought back to the village men's house for a four-day celebration, after which the skull was cleaned and placed on the skull shelf before the village "ancestor house," *kakitaan*. Weapons included bows and arrows and spears. Although warriors carried shields, no use was made of body armor. Villages were formerly fortified with sharpened bamboos and earthen trenches. [Liu et al. 1965: 239-50, 268-69; Sayama 1913-21: *1*, 25-29; *2*, 140-41.]

RELIGION. **Supernaturals.** The Ami are noted for their well-developed theogony and associated body of cosmogonic myths, traits that distinguish them from most other aboriginal groups on Formosa. Named deities include a female sun goddess, a male moon god, and tutelary deities of war, headhunting, harvest, etc., as well as of specialist groups such as shamans and priests. Ancestral gods, *tatakusan*, are numerous and important. The ghosts or spirits, *karia*, of people who have died unnatural deaths are especially dangerous and can cause illness in the living. [Chen and Coe 1954.] **Practitioners.** Priests specialize in memorizing lengthy origin myths, including long genealogies of named ancestral and other deities (the Ami reckon some 59 generations since an act of brother-sister incest produced the first ancestors). These are invoked as part of the ritual accompanying any religious ceremony. The status of priest, largely defunct as of 1954, is inherited by primogeniture within certain matrilineages, specifically within those family lines (*kakitaan*) claiming direct descent from the ancestors who first settled the village or local area. Brothers of women of the lineage are most often the actual performers of ritual, although the status is inherited through their sisters. *Kakitaan* families formerly owned and maintained ceremonial houses ("ancestor" or "head" houses), the senior of which functioned as a ceremonial center for the entire village. The last of these *kakitaan* houses, famed for its carved wooden posts depicting human and animal figures, was moved in 1958 from Tavarong to Taipei (Jen 1958). According to Chen and Coe (1954), the *kakitaan* priests functioned chiefly at ceremonies, e.g. the *mihavai* harvest ritual, having to do with the staple crops, millet and rice. Wang (1961: 177) and Li et al. (1962: 10-12), on the other hand, indicate that their main concern was with headhunting and skull rituals. [Chen and Coe 1954: 251-55.] Shamans (*sikawasai*, lit.: "spirit owners"), of either sex but usually women, were still functioning in Tavarong village in 1954. Those in Vataan formed a hierarchy: (1) senior grade, *aisudan* (2) ordinary grade, *tsikawasai*, and (3) apprentices and assistants (Liu et al. 1965: 265; Li et al. 1962: 10-12). Individuals who become *sikawasai* are frequently abnormal or unstable personality types, a prime consideration being the ability to go into a trance state, during which the person is possessed by his or her spirit familiar. Individuals are "chosen" (a frequent sign being chronic illness) and apprenticed at an early age. *Sikawasai* specialize in getting back strayed or lost souls, a common cause of illness or death. Techniques include dancing, chanting, rubbing the patient's body with leaves, and sacrificial offerings of wine, pork, and ricecakes. Choice of treatment is determined by *milao* divination, whereby the practitioner "reads" the severed ends of a split bamboo, a method similar to one found in Borneo and Assam, according to N. Utsurikawa (cited in Chen and Coe 1954: 252). [Chen and Coe 1954; Furuno 1945: 213-20.] **Ceremonies.** The most important of all Ami ceremonies is *irisin* (*irising*, *ilisin*), held annually in the fall after the millet harvest. As described by Chen and Coe (1954) for Tavarong village, this is an eight-day religious festival, held at the start of the new year and emphasizing village renewal and fertility. The ceremonial aspects are managed by the leading *kakitaan* family, represented by its female head and her brother, who together perform such rituals as the serving of consecrated betel, washing and cleansing rites, and the sacrificial offering of wine, pork, and betel to the gods. Special events include group dancing by the village shamans and the imparting of instructions for proper behavior by *saparangau* chiefs to age-grade leaders, the latter in turn repeating these to their age-mates. The festival ends with ritual fishing by the entire village and an offering of fish to the gods. [According to Wang (1961: 178), the period of ritual consecration, with accompanying taboos on food and sex, that is associated with any major ceremony is always broken by a ritual fishing expedition.] Liu et al. (1965: 239-50) state that *irisin* in Vataan village was formerly an occasion for headhunting and rededication of the village skull shelf. [See Furuno (1945: 43-73, 220-60) for detailed descriptions of agricultural rites, the majority of which have to do with millet.] **Soul, death, and afterlife.** Furuno (1945: 16-17) reports belief in two souls, one good and one bad, residing on the right and left shoulder, respectively. According to Liu et al., the Vataan Ami hold to a theory of three souls, one in the head and one on each shoulder. The spirits of persons who have died unnatural deaths are greatly feared; they can cause ill-

ness, probably including illness due to soul loss—a frequent complaint treated by shamans. The souls of those who die a "good" (i.e. natural) death go to an upperworld, where they inhabit a level corresponding to their rank prior to death. The souls of headhunt victims, suicides, and those without relatives go to an underworld. The corpse, washed and dressed, lies in state for a day, after which it is wrapped in a mat and buried in a board-lined grave in the yard outside the house. Mourning is ended by a sacrificial feast, at which a shaman symbolically washes the new ancestral spirit. The corpse of a chief or priest is displayed in a sitting position for some days before burial, and the death feast is marked by the consumption of much rice wine and the slaughter of many pigs. [Liu et al. 1965: 152-67, 264-65; Chen and Coe 1954; Furuno 1945: 22-25; Sayama 1913-21: *1*, 49-50.]

BIBLIOGRAPHY. C. L. Chen 1965, 1968; Chen and Coe 1954; K. C. Chen 1967; Dyen 1971; Ferrell 1969a; Furuno 1945; Jen 1958; Kojima 1915-22; Li et al. 1962; Liu et al. 1965; Mabuchi 1954a, 1956, 1960; Sayama 1913-21; Utsurikawa et al. 1935; Wang 1961; Wei 1961; Wei and Wang 1966.

PUYUMA

Synonyms. *Panapanayan, Piuma, Pilam, Pelam, Pyuma*

ORIENTATION. **Identification.** The Puyuma speak one language and consider themselves to be of one stock, although they have never formed a tribe in a political sense (Schröder 1967: 12). There is no indigenous name for the people as a whole, ethnoidentification being with the village, the largest of which, Puyuma (in modern Taiwanese, Nanwang), has achieved currency as a generic exonym. Older Japanese publications favored the term Panapanayan—a place name prominent in legendary accounts of ancestral wanderings—but this usage has not gained general currency (Mabuchi 1954a: 7). Terms such as Hasshaban and Pa-she-fan are, according to Schröder (1967: 11), derived from Japanese and Chinese expressions for "eight-settlement aborigines," referring to the traditional number of villages—now expanded to ten—sharing legendary accounts and ritual enactments pertaining to a common ancestral heritage (cf. Utsurikawa et al. 1935: 336ff.). Legend divides these villages into two categories, one claiming "stone origin," the other "bamboo origin," in association with tales of ancestral survivors from a universal deluge and their landing near the coast at a place called Panapanayan or Ruvua'an (Ruvoahan, Revoaqan). According to L. S. Sung (1964: 78ff.), the stone ancestry—Ruvua'an category has as its leading village Katipol (Taiwanese: Chihpen), in association with the villages of Kasavakan (Chienho), Rikavon (Lichia), Alipai (Pinglang), Vankiu (Panchiu), Tamalakao (Taiping), and Mulivulivuk (Ch'ulu)—all together totaling some 4,400 people in 1964 (Wei and Wang 1966: 55). The bamboo ancestry—Panapanayan category has as its leading village Puyuma (Nanwang, Pinan, Hinan), in association with the villages of Pinaski (Pinglang) and Apapolo (Paoshang)—all together totaling about 1,700 people. Although the two categories differ with respect to dialect and cultural usages, these are slight and due mainly to differing degree of contact with neighboring peoples, according to Schröder (1967: 12-13). H. L. Wei (1962), who equates Ruvua'an with Panapanayan as one and the same place, regards the two categories, Katipol and Pinan, as essentially two branches of a single stem. **Location.** Peinan District of Taitung County, on Taiwan's southeast coast. Some ten villages located within a 20-km. radius of the port city of Taitung—an alluvial plain watered by the Peinan, Tanan, and Chihpan rivers. Bounded on the north by the Ami and on the west and south by the Paiwan-Rukai peoples. **Linguistic affiliation.** Malayopolynesian. Classed within the Paiwanic division of Formosan aboriginal languages by Ferrell (1969a). Dyen (1971) gives the following reported dialect names: Chipon (Kata-tipol, Pyuma), Pinan (Hinan, Pilam), Sanwhai, Tsarisen (Tsalisen), Saprek, Katsausan, and Kale-whan. **Demography.** Slightly over 6,000 in 1964 (Wei and Wang 1966). **History and cultural relations.** There has been a considerable degree of contact and intermarriage with neighboring groups. This is particularly true of the more united and stronger Katipol village group in its relations with Paiwan and Rukai; whereas the Puyuma (Pinan) group has always felt closer ties with the Ami (Mabuchi 1954a; Schröder 1967). Ferrell (1969a: 54) cites Ogawa and Asai (1935) to the effect that some myths mention overseas origins (cf. stories of obtaining millet from Votul, identified by some as Botel Tobago), while according to other versions the Puyuma and Ami both emerged from stone and bamboo on Taiwan's east coast. The myths likewise include deluge and sibling incest motifs, the latter associated with survival in a wooden mortar (Schröder 1967: 17, 35). Utsurikawa et al. (1935: 333ff.) trace historic migrations from the coast inland, spreading north and south, those to the south becoming Paiwanized through intermarriage at the upper-class levels. Kokubu and Kaneko (1962) stress the former military prowess of the Puyuma—rulers over a considerable portion of southeastern Taiwan (cf. Mabuchi 1966: 132). The age-grade system, famed for the quality of its spiritual and military training, was discontinued in the late 1950s, and the Puyuma are today strongly Sinicized. Young people converse nowadays in Chinese, the only language taught in the local schools, and resist completely the indigenous religion, turning either to Christianity or to Chinese folk religions (Schröder 1967).

SETTLEMENT PATTERN AND HOUSING. **Settlement pattern.** Permanent villages, with an average population of around 600 (Mabuchi 1960), although the leading villages of Puyuma (Nanwang) and Katipol in 1963 contained some 1,100 and 1,300 ethnic Puyuma, respectively. Villages were formerly fortified with hedges and fences, and village gates were guarded by warriors (Schröder 1967). L. S. Sung (1964) describes men's houses (*parakuan*), ancestral spirit houses (*karumaan*), and boys' dormitories (*takoban*), the latter, in Nanwang village, being circular in shape and elevated on piles some 15-20 feet above the ground. The spirit houses contain sacred spears and other paraphernalia and may be decorated with carved ancestor sculptures similar to those of the eastern Paiwan (Ferrell 1969a; Chen 1968: 272-75; Wei et al. 1954: 18ff.). **Housing.** The aboriginal house was a one-room, rectangular structure built directly on the ground, with walls of bamboo or planks and a thatched and gabled roof. Nowadays housing is largely of Chinese style, and the larger Puyuma villages have a sizable Chinese population. [Chen 1968: 262-64; Wei and Wang 1966: 55.]

ECONOMY. **Agriculture.** Material life and economic pursuits are nowadays little different from those of the surrounding Chinese. Subsistence is derived mainly from agriculture, in particular the growing of irrigated rice, although some rice, together with sweet potatoes, maize, millet, taro, and beans is grown on dry fields. Millet, along with various tubers and cucurbits, was more important formerly and, in the form of cakes and wine, continues as the principal ritual food. Sugarcane, pineapples, and peanuts are raised as commercial crops. [Schröder 1967; Chen 1968.] **Hunting and fishing.** Nowadays of relatively little importance, although hunting, once an important source of food, continues as a ritual activity in association with major religious festivals. Hunting for deer is done principally with dogs and guns. Techniques utilizing fire and traps were formerly important as well. [Schröder 1967; Chen 1968.] **Domestic animals.** Originally pigs, dogs, and chickens. Dogs are especially valued for hunting, while pigs appear to be raised principally for sale to Chinese. The water buffalo was introduced, along with the growing of irrigated rice, some 70 years ago, and has no ritual significance. [Schröder 1967.] **Property.** Hunting grounds, rivers, and arable land are owned by aristocrat members of chiefly family lines. Commoners hold usufruct rights to the land they cultivate and pay tribute in products of hunting, fishing, and agriculture to the aristocrats. [Teikoku-gakushiin 1941.]

MARRIAGE AND FAMILY. **Mode.** Wei (1962: 66) stresses the inevitability of a bride-price, approved by the girl's maternal uncle, as a necessary accompaniment to any marriage; and Schröder (1967: 20) writes that the "price for the bride is very high." Mabuchi,

123

on the other hand, denies the existence of any significant bride-price (1960: 135). There is some evidence for what amounts to gift exchange prior to the birth of the first child, followed by a series of increasingly expensive exchanges, likened to potlatching by Wei et al. (1954: 23), in which the groom's family incurs significantly greater expense in the form of land, labor, and valuables given to the bride's family. **Form.** Strict monogamy (Sung 1964: 79; Mabuchi 1960: 135). **Marriage rules.** Most marriages are village-endogamous, but there is no strict rule about clan (ritual group) exogamy. Incest prohibitions are defined bilaterally, to include third cousins (Sung 1964: 71). **Residence.** Matrilocal in principle, although according to Wei, the custom of *"ambil-anak"* marriage and contact with the ambilineal Paiwan has introduced an increasingly strong element of patrilocality. The actual incidence of matrilocal marriages in all Puyuma villages stood at around 60 percent in the early 1950s (Wei 1962: 78). According to Mabuchi (1960), patrilocality is a "moderately frequent" alternative, now as in the past. **Household.** Although Mabuchi (1960) denies the existence of extended family households, the reports of Wei (1962: 66-79), Sung (1964: 79), and Schröder (1967: 14) all indicate the existence in both Puyuma and Katipol villages of something like a matrilocal stem family household, averaging between six and seven members. Wei makes the added comment that households of twenty or more members were common formerly. The status of family head is inherited by primogeniture within the female line, although the eldest brother of the female household head acts as guardian (Wei 1962: 79). **Inheritance.** Arable land, dwelling houses, and pigs—as well as the position of family head—are inherited from mothers to daughters, usually the eldest daughters. Betel nut trees, bamboo thickets, cattle and weapons —as well as the position of village chief—are passed on from fathers to sons, usually eldest sons (Utsurikawa et al. 1935: 335). **Divorce.** Persons with histories of from five to ten divorces and remarriages are "no rarity" (Schröder 1967: 20).

KINSHIP. **Descent.** Matrilineal, according to Wei (1962). Bilateral, with ambilineal or multilineal affiliation with ritual groups, according to Mabuchi (1960). **Kin groups.** For Nanwang (Puyuma) village, Wei (1962) and Wei et al. (1954) describe a "matrilineal clan-lineage system" within a localized dual division or "moiety" structure. Chiefly family lines, tracing their ancestry back to original or founding ancestors, maintain spirit houses and function as the genealogical cores of larger groups (six in Puyuma village), which Wei terms "matriclans," but which are regarded by Mabuchi (1960) as nonunilineal descent groups ("ritual groups") with optional (ambilateral) modes of affiliation. According to Wei, his clans are "in principle" matrilineal and exogamic. Mabuchi's ritual groups are nonexogamous, although

"the people regard them as composed of actual or presumptive kinsmen." Descent, in the sense of ritual-group affiliation, is conceptually ambilateral. If the parents belong to different ritual groups, their children may enjoy dual affiliation, although in practice the child's ritual group membership is most often determined by the parents' choice of postmarital residence. Since this is most often matrilocal, it follows that the preponderant mode of affiliation is matrilineal. Adults may, in addition, change their ritual group affiliation voluntarily or at the command of ancestral spirits speaking through a shamaness as oracle, with some adults postponing any group affiliation until they have received this supernatural sanction. Membership in a group of this kind involves common participation in agrarian, hunting, headhunting, and curing rituals. Wei (1962: 81) mentions in addition the category of *inajamunan*, an Ego-oriented bilateral kindred, which functions in defining the incest taboo and in channeling mutual aid. **Kin terminology.** Mabuchi (1960: 136) gives the following terms, with the remark that the system follows a generational pattern, with cousin terms of Hawaiian type:

GrPa	*imo*
Fa,FaBr,MoBr	*ama*
Mo,MoSi,FaSi	*ina*
ElSb	*iva*
YoSb	*wadi*
Cousin*	*wa-wadi-an*
Child,nephew/niece	*alak*

* Cousins are in addition terminologically distinguished according to collateral distance from Ego.

SOCIOPOLITICAL ORGANIZATION. **Political organization.** According to Mabuchi (1960), villages tend strongly toward local endogamy and political autonomy. Political control within the village is exercized by heads of chiefly families, one of whom fills the office of local headman or village chief. Succession to this office, although not automatic, tends to take place by selection from among the sons or close bilateral relatives of the former headman. According to Chen (1965: 98-100), the village of Pinan (Puyuma) was composed, until about 1959, of a northern division (*i-ami*) and a southern division (*i-timor*), each with its own named cult house or spirit house maintained by the leading descent group (ritual group) within the division. The two divisions ("moieties") had no exogamous functions with respect to marriage, but functioned rather as religious, economic, and administrative units. Reciprocal relations included enactment of sham battles connected with the military training of age-grades. Each division had a council of six to administer public affairs, together with a priest to supervise ritual activities. These functionaries were mostly heads of powerful descent groups, and the positions tended to be hereditary within chiefly family lines. The positions of paramount village chief and war captain were in recent decades associated with the leading descent group within the northern division, and the men's house of this group was regarded as the administrative center of the entire village. This group likewise retained, through the person of its priest, the right to initiate communal religious rites affecting village welfare. The open ground for the performance of rituals and the training of village youth, together with the place for observing omen birds prior to headhunting expeditions and the place for depositing hunted heads, were all located outside the northern division village gate. [For detailed political histories of the various Puyuma villages, see Utsurikawa et al. 1935: 336ff.]

Social differentiation. According to Mabuchi (1960), two social classes—nobles (i.e. aristocrats) and commoners—with marriage between the two possible under certain conditions. Aristocrats comprise the members of certain chiefly family lines, owners of land, and recipients of tribute from commoners (Teikoku-gakushiin 1941: 23-24). These lines in turn, according to Utsurikawa et al. (1935: 342ff.), form the cores of the larger descent-ritual groups. Members invoke actual or putative genealogical connection with the core group, commoners being defined as those with the more remote connections. Mabuchi (1966) discusses the role of aristocratic intermarriages across ethnic boundaries, a process which has extended the range of genealogical connections and the sphere of political influence into neighboring Paiwan-Rukai villages.

Age-grades. According to C. L. Chen, the Puyuma have the most elaborate system of age-grades and men's houses of any of the aboriginal peoples of Formosa. Although the associated structures, such as the men's houses, have fallen into disuse, the system itself, together with its training features, continued to function in most villages into the late 1950s (Chen 1965: 98; Furuno 1945). Unlike the Ami, the Puyuma lack cyclical sets of age-grade names. A boy is initiated into the system at about age 13, at which time he enters one of the boys' dormitories, where he lives for a period of five years, serving the upper grades and learning tribal lore. At about age 18 he graduates to a new status, that of *maibutan*, during which he was formerly expected to participate in a successful headhunt—since the 1920s replaced by the hunting of wild animals. As a symbol of his changed status, the young man is given a new loincloth by an older man (most often a maternal uncle, according to Sung 1964: 73), who thereafter becomes his guide and mentor. The youth resides in the men's house of his (maternal) ritual group for an approximately four-year period, undergoing military training and subject to the most rigid discipline, e.g. a strict prohibition against contact with the opposite sex. At about age 22, the young man graduates to the status of *bangsalan*, whereupon he is eligible for marriage. Once married, men go to live in their wives' houses and cease to sleep in the men's house (Sayama 1913-21: 8, 40). To enter this system initially, a boy

was expected to participate in a ceremonial prelude to the later *magayau* or headhunting ceremony. This initiatory ceremony, termed *magayagayau*, featured the ritual spearing to death of a captive monkey by the initiates, the driving away of evil spirits by age-grade monitors clothed in banana leaf wrappings and with soot-smeared faces, the running of competitive foot races, and the ritual use of deerskins, miscanthus leaves, and shaved bamboo poles (Chen 1965: 100-03). [Furuno (1945) denies the existence of any ceremony of initiation.]

RELIGION. Sacred songs and prayers are recited by shamanesses and priest-chiefs in an archaic "sacred" language. These, together with myths, sagas, and genealogical recitations—some sacred, some profane—portray theogony and cosmogony in vivid terms. Primeval times, inseparably connected with the ancestors, climax in a universal deluge, the survival of siblings in a wooden mortar, brother-sister incest, and subsequent populating of the world. Ancestral heroes teach man to hunt game and to plant rice, events carefully preserved and re-enacted in contemporary rites and referred to repeatedly in myths and prayers. In the Puyuma conception, the contemporary world of mortals and the world of the ancestors are one. One's goal, and the purpose of most ritual, is attainment of the good and happy life, both in this world and beyond. The truly happy person possesses physical and spiritual vigor, wealth, rank, and prestige—and only the good man achieves all four. Nowadays, according to Schröder's 1964-65 survey of Katipol village, only a handful of families adhere to the old religion; most profess Catholicism or a mixture of Catholic and tribal beliefs. [Schröder 1967.]

Supernaturals. Prehuman deities include a creator, lord over life and death, known under various names (e.g. *dhemawai*) and mentioned in most prayers, although conceptualized in rather vague terms. Also deified are four "owners of the land" (*miaqalop*), administrators of the four parts of the world, messengers and executive organs of the *dhemawai* and superordinate to the lesser deities. These latter, named and of both sexes, are mostly primeval humans endowed with divine attributes—overseers of rivers, forests, and animals, including a brother-sister pair identified with a sacred sun and a profane moon. Likewise in the category of lesser deities are culture heroes, patron deities of crafts and specialities, guardians of village, house, and village gates. Spirits of more recently departed ancestors are regarded as a collectivity, lacking the rank of deities, but much closer to the affairs of men. These ancestral spirits are the immediate source of all good and evil, and religious ritual is directed primarily at them. The spirits of those who have died a "good," i.e. natural, death, are beneficently inclined and in constant communication with their descendants. Those who have died unnatural deaths—e.g. suicides, victims of headhunting, or those who died away from home—make constant demands on the living and are the cause of misfortune; they must be kept at a distance, e.g. they are fed and then banned prior to any ceremony. [Schröder 1967: 33-34.] **Practitioners.** The heads of chiefly families function at times as combined priest-chiefs with respect to larger ritual groups or entire villages (cf. Schröder 1967: 22). The position of chief (*ajawan, ayawan*) is in some instances, however, separate from that of priest (*rahan, ragan*) (Teikoku-gakushiin 1941). According to Schröder, the Puyuma have a well-developed shamanism, with more than 20 shamanesses resident in Katipol alone in 1964. The shaman (*temararamau, tamaramau*), usually a female, undergoes an apprenticeship under an established practitioner, works with the aid of guardian spirits, and may enter a trance state. Shamans specialize in divining the causes of illness and in the treatment of illness by recovering lost souls, exorcising demons, and the like. In Katipol village they are called *puligau* or *purigao*. [Schröder 1967; Furuno 1945: 130ff.] **Ceremonies.** Individualized ritual is minimal, most rites being communal and performed by chiefs, shamanesses, or family heads. Ritual forms include sacrifice, prayer, dance, and song, with betelnuts, beads, and iron fragments indispensable to most rites. Sayama (1913-21: 8) mentions in addition swinging and purificatory hunting. The ritual sequence begins with the banning of demons, followed by the invocation and offering to ancestors and good spirits, together with the ceremony itself, and ends with the blessing of participants (Schröder 1967: 35ff.). Each of the various ritual groups within a village is responsible for different categories of ceremonies, with the most powerful usually in charge of agricultural ritual, in particular rites having to do with the sowing and harvesting of millet. Millet is

sown first in a ritual field or plot (*inufuran*), according to Furuno (1945: 131). [For descriptions of ceremonies having to do with hunting, agriculture, age-grade initiations, headhunting, marriage, and death see Schröder (1967). For additional data on agricultural ritual, see Furuno (1945: 124-32) and Sayama (1913-21: 8).] **Soul, death, and afterlife.** Some Puyuma reportedly believe in the existence of three souls, one on each shoulder and one in the head. Those on the shoulders can leave the body temporarily, causing illness, which is treated by female shamans who recover the lost or straying soul. Should the head soul, or life spirit, leave the body, the person dies. The spirits of those who die "natural" deaths travel to an underworld abode where they dwell peacefully; but the souls of those who die from unnatural or abnormal causes, or far from home, remain dissatisfied and constantly harass the living. "Privileged" souls, i.e. those of chiefs and shamans, are reported to go to a paradise above the firmament (Schröder 1967: 31-32). The corpse is buried the day after death, wrapped in cloth wound round with rope, and interred in a grave beneath the dirt floor of the house (Kojima 1915-22: 2, *pt. 3*, 382-86). Schröder (1967: 29) mentions jar burial, and Sayama (1913-21: 8, 192-93) describes burial beneath the floor of the ancestral spirit house (possibly for chiefly aristocrats and shamans).

BIBLIOGRAPHY. Chen 1965, 1968; Dyen 1971; Ferrell 1969a; Furuno 1945; Kojima 1915-22; Kokubu and Kaneko 1962; Mabuchi 1954a, 1960, 1966; Ogawa and Asai 1935; Sayama 1913-21; Schröder 1967; Sung 1964, 1965; Teikoku-gakushiin 1941; Utsurikawa et al. 1935; Wei 1962; Wei and Wang 1966; Wei et al. 1954.

WESTERN LOWLAND GROUPS

IN HIS ETHNOLINGUISTIC CLASSIFICATION of Formosan aborigines, Ferrell (1969a: 48ff.) defines a "vague grouping" of Paiwanic speakers on Taiwan's western coastal plains and interior foothills, including Hoanya (Hanya, Arikun, and Lloa subgroups), Favorlang (Babuza, Poavosa), Papora (Paposa, Vupuran), Pazeh, Taokas, Luilang, and Saisiat, all except Pazeh and Saisiat nowadays linguistically extinct. All, including the linguistically related Thao (Sao, Shao) of the highland Sun-Moon Lake region, have been heavily Sini-

cized—to the extent that groups such as Favorlang are no longer recognizable, culturally or linguistically, within the predominantly Formosan Chinese population. Only two of these western groups are known in the modern ethnographic literature, the Saisiat (see below under that heading) and the Thao (Chen et al. 1958; H. Li 1955; Tang 1957; Y. Y. Li 1957b). For the rest, there is only the fragmentary information to be culled from early Chinese reports (e.g. Huang 1736), Dutch mission records (summarized in Campbell 1903) and dictionaries (e.g. Happart 1650). Mention in these sources of large earth-platform houses with thatched, oval roofs, boys' dormitories, leather garments, and slab-lined pit burials indicate cultural ties with the inland, mountain-dwelling Rukai, Bunun, and Tsou. Origin legends repeat well-known deluge and sibling incest motifs, but, unlike those of Paiwanic speakers on Taiwan's east coast (e.g. Ami, Puyuma), contain no mention of overseas origin. Ferrell feels that the noticeable degree of diversity among these west-coast languages (his Paiwanic I grouping) argues for their considerable antiquity on the island of Taiwan, and in fact he proposes them as the probable direct descendants of peoples represented by the archeological assemblages of the area, i.e. Lungshanoid farmers appearing sometime in the second millennium B.C. (Ferrell 1969b: 189, citing Chang 1969). [Ferrell 1969a, 1969b.]

BIBLIOGRAPHY. Campbell 1903; Chang 1969; Chen et al. 1958; Ferrell 1969a, 1969b; Happart 1650; Huang 1736; H. Li 1955; Y. Y. Li 1957b; Tang 1957.

SAISIAT

Synonyms. *Saisiyat, Saiset, Saisirat*

ORIENTATION. A remnant population of Paiwanic speakers in the foothills some 20 kilometers inland from the coastal cities of Miaoli and Hsinchu, in northwestern Taiwan. The indigenous culture type, once more widespread on the Hsinchu plains, has been greatly modified by centuries of contact with the mountain-dwelling Atayal to the east and the plains-dwelling Chinese to the west. A population of some 1,300 shifting agriculturists was in the early twentieth century distributed in scattered hamlets along the upper tributaries of the Chung Chiang. Nowadays an estimated 2,800 Saisiat (Wei and Wang 1966: 7) are concentrated in a few large villages, dependent for the most part on wet-rice agriculture and intimately tied to the peasant economy of Taiwan's western coastal plains. A division in the literature into so-called Northern and Southern Saisiat appears to reflect the existence of intermittent ceremonial groupings, rather than any basic dialectal, cultural, or political differentiation. Dyen (1971) lists Taiai, Buiok, and Arikun as modern dialects of Saisiat. [Ferrell 1969a, 1969b: 185-86; Mabuchi 1960, 1966; Wei 1958b.]

SETTLEMENT PATTERN AND ECONOMY. Kojima (1915-22: 3, 64-73) describes a traditional subsistence economy based on swidden farming, with hunting important both socially and emotionally. Millet (*tata*) and glutinous rice are the sacred foods. Taro, yams, and sweet potatoes are important as foodstuffs but are of no ceremonial significance. Domesticated bees are kept for honey, and bees figure symbolically in folklore and religious ritual. Early sources (e.g. Kojima 1915-22: 3, 46) mention settlement in scattered mountainside hamlets of from 20 to 100 inhabitants. More recently, Wei (1958b) has described the loose grouping of hamlets (*rito*) into "villages" (*kinasangan*), although the modern pattern of concentrated village settlement and village headmen would appear to be an adaptation to governmental and other acculturative pressures. Houses within historic times have been large, rectangular, multiroom structures built directly on the ground, with walls of bamboo and thatched, gabled roofs. [Kojima 1915-22; Wei 1958b; Ferrell 1969a.]

KINSHIP AND MARRIAGE. With respect to their social structure, the Saisiat appear generally similar to the Bunun and Tsou, with descent, succession, and inheritance uniformly patrilineal (Mabuchi 1960: 129; C. C. Chen 1967). Some 17 exogamous, nonlocalized patriclans (nowadays with Chinese surnames) regulate marriage and were formerly the "owners" of arable land and hunting territories, usufruct rights to which were exercized by localized clan segments. Government-induced changes in settlement pattern and the widespread adoption of wet rice have, however, altered these traditional concepts in the direction of private ownership of land. According to Wei (1958b), clans (*singrahjo*, given by Furuno (1945: 321-62) as *shinrahjo*, "kin group") are further grouped into six exogamous, named phratries, a pattern again reminiscent of the Bunun and Tsou. Customs surrounding courtship and marriage likewise appear generally similar to those of the Tsou and Bunun. The incisors of both sexes are extracted during late adolescence, probably a precondition to marriage (Kojima 1915-22: 3, 55). Daughter (sister) exchange appears to have been the preferred mode of marriage, and a period of bride service, followed by patrilocal residence, was common in at least some villages. Households (*ahataowan*, from *aha*, "people" and *taowan*, "dwelling") tended to be relatively large (average 7.7, according to C. C. Chen 1967); married sons remained in their father's household until his death, with the eldest as custodian of the family estate. As among the Tsou, marriage prohibitions were extended beyond the paternal clan to all members of the mother's clan and to children of mother's own sisters. [Kojima 1915-22: 3, 108, 116.] **Kin terminology.** Mabuchi (1960: 130) gives the following terms:

GrFa	*bake*
GrMo	*kuku*
Fa	*yama*
Mo	*ina*
PaBr	*pina-yama*
PaSi	*pina-ina*
Sibling, cousin	*ahal*
Child, nephew, niece	*kurkuring*

SOCIOPOLITICAL ORGANIZATION. The hamlets along a stretch of river appear traditionally to have formed a loosely organized entity (*asang*), glossed variously as "village," "district," "tribe," or "cooperative group." The effective units in these districts appear to have been localized segments of clans, exercising usufruct rights to land and cooperating in economic and ritual tasks. Kojima denies the existence of any government institutions at the *asang* level, although he does report their banding together for defense and for performance of the biennial *pasta'ai* ceremony. According to Wei, the Saisiat are comprised of six "tribes" (*asang*), three in the north and three in the south. The *asang*, with a "tribal" chief, is the traditionally basic political, economic, and ceremonial unit, according to Wei (1958b). *Asang* "in principle" claimed ownership rights to land and were in addition the basic units of warfare. The head household of an *asang* chiefly lineage constituted a kind of administrative-ceremonial center, and it was here that headhunting rites were performed in former days. Headhunting was motivated by desire for revenge and honor (successful warriors were entitled to wear special headgear and tattoo their faces according to Atayal-adopted designs) and also, apparently, functioned as a kind of trial by ordeal (Kojima 1915-22: 3, 179-85). For defense, possibly in the antigovernment uprisings of the 1920s, and for performance of *pasta'ai* nowadays, *asang* organize themselves into "confederacies," i.e. northern and southern Saisiat. It is not clear how these traditional structures have adapted to the modern system of concentrated village settlement and government-appointed headmen. [Furuno 1945: 321-62; Wei 1958b; Kojima 1915-22: 3, 167-75, 184.]

RELIGION. The Saisiat have a well-developed pantheon, according to Ferrell (1969a). Spirits (*havun, hapun*) include ancestral spirits, for whom there is an annual ceremony, *pasuvake* (*pas*, "celebrate," and *vake*, "grandfather"). The priest for this ceremony is the head of the "leading" household within a group of related, neighboring households, all of whom participate in the communal eating of consecrated glutinous rice and the sharing of same with the ancestral spirits. The ceremony ends with ritual hunting by the men, i.e. mock hunting with bow and arrow (Furuno 1945: 321-62; Kojima 1915-22: 3, 29ff.). Furuno also describes a millet-sowing ritual utilizing a small sacred plot marked off within a larger field, and said to be a "village" rather than "clan" affair. The best known of Saisiat ceremonies is *pasta'ai*, which is held biennially and which was originally, according to Ferrell, a village renewal—ancestor spirit ceremony similar to the "Five-Year Festival" of the Paiwan. Nowadays it is supposed to represent placation of a mythical tribe of dwarfs, *ta'ai*, that were annihilated by the ancestors of the Saisiat (Ferrell 1968. See also Ferrell 1969b; Kojima 1915-22: 3, 32-37; C. H. Chen 1952; Tang 1955). According to Furuno, the role of priest in *pasta'ai* is hereditary in certain clans; and these priests rank higher than those who figure in certain other communal ceremonies, also hereditary within specified clans. Shamanesses are said to cure illness and to be specialists in divination. Burial appears to take place somewhat randomly in wood lot or field, with the body flexed and interred in a niche grave (Kojima 1915-22: 3, 83ff.).

BIBLIOGRAPHY. C. C. Chen 1967; C. H. Chen 1952; Dyen 1971; Ferrell 1968, 1969a, 1969b; Furuno 1940, 1945; Kojima 1915-22; Lin 1956; Mabuchi 1960, 1966; Tang 1955; Wei 1958b; Wei and Wang 1966; Yang 1956.

CENTRAL MOUNTAIN GROUPS

FOR PURPOSES of descriptive presentation, the present volume follows Ferrell (1969a) and Mabuchi (1966) in grouping together the upland peoples of Formosa's central mountain chain, viz., the Atayal, Bunun, Tsou, Rukai, and Paiwan. This is, however, principally on geographic-ecological-historical grounds and implies little if anything concerning homogeneity of language or culture. The true mountain habitat of these peoples and their relatively long isolation from coastal influences produce a rather sharp contrast with lowland groups such as the Ami and Puyuma, discussed in the preceding sections—groups that have been subject to over a hundred years of Chinese acculturation and, in the case of the Ketangalan, Siraya, and others, complete Sinicization. The mountain cultures maintained their indigenous traditions into the second decade of the twentieth century, and as of the early 1930s there were still informants who had lived through the turn-of-the-century beginning of Japanese pacification and the opening up of the mountains to schools and missions (Mabuchi 1966: 104). Linguistically, the mountain peoples represent all three of the major divisions of the Austronesian languages on Formosa, and although some material traits, such as the importance of millet, seem common to all, they appear to differ considerably with respect to details of sociopolitical organization and religious expression. Differences of this order may stem from basically different historical traditions of some depth, as the linguistic evidence might indicate, or they may represent local, and relatively recent, differentiation out of a common culture base. In considering this latter possibility, the following would seem relevant: the acculturative impact of the strongly patrilineal, ancestor-oriented Chinese; the effects of trade in such things as deer hides and the consequent introduction of wealth differentials; the effect on indigenous sociopolitical patterns of government-forced resettlement at lower altitudes, and the adoption of wet-rice agriculture, negating the traditional importance of hunting and hunting territories.

BIBLIOGRAPHY. Ferrell 1969a; Mabuchi 1966.

PAIWAN-RUKAI

Synonym. *Tsarisen*

ORIENTATION. **Identification.** Although the Rukai are on linguistic and other grounds occasionally classed as a distinct ethnic category (cf. Utsurikawa et al. 1935: 230), numerous cultural similarities with Paiwan—due in large part to recent acculturation of Rukai by adjacent northern Paiwan—have led both Ferrell (1969a) and Mabuchi (1960, 1966) to classify the two together, e.g. Ferrell includes both Paiwan and Rukai in his Paiwan culture complex as a "loose grouping showing much local diversity" (1969a: 40). The Rukai (also known as *tsarisen*, "mountain people") in the early decades of the present century occupied some 22 villages on the upper Sukou, Ihliau, and Tanan rivers—according to Utsurikawa et al. (1935: 231) their legendary homeland, termed Kaliala, bounded on the north by Bunun peoples, on the east by Bunun and Puyuma, and on the south and west by Paiwan. Among the better known Rukai

villages are Budai (Chen 1956b, 1958b) and Taromak (Hsieh 1967, 1968). The Paiwan region, bounded on the north by Rukai and on the west, south, and east by members of the Littoral Culture Complex—Siraya, Puyuma, Ami—is centered historically on the western and southern slopes of Mt. Tawu, where the upper tributaries of the Linpien and Chiatsoushan have their source (Mabuchi 1966: 134). Among the better-known Paiwan villages, numbering some 166 in 1935, are Chala'abus (Rai), Kabiyangan, Bongarid, and Kulalao—all west-central Paiwan (Butsul) villages on the upper Linpien river system. Paiwan speakers are usually divided into "subtribes," e.g. Raval (Ravar, Rabaru), Butsul (Buchoru), Chaobobol (Chakobokoboji, Ooobojan), Parijarijao (Paridarijao, Palilalilao), Pakarokaro (cf. Utsurikawa et al. 1935: 256; Sayama 1913-21: 1-3; Kojima 1915-22: 5, *pt. 1*, 5; Wei 1960). Mabuchi, however, avoids the implications of "tribal" designations by combining Paiwan and Rukai within a framework of 13 "regions," defined most frequently as aggregates of villages within the drainage areas of particular streams (Mabuchi 1954a, 1966). **Location.** Uplands of the Central Mountain range, south of about 23° N. Lat., extending for some 140 kilometers into extreme southerly Taiwan—primarily within modern Pingtung County, but with a recent extension to the east coast, along the Tamali River in Taitung County. Villages are located for the most part on the upper drainage areas of rivers, e.g. the Chiatsoushan, Pulci, Chala'abus, Tamali, and Tachukao. **Linguistic affiliation.** Although not particularly closely related, Rukai and Paiwan are together regarded by Ferrell (1969a: 30) as probable offshoots of the Paiwanic languages (many now extinct) of Taiwan's central west coast region. Dyen (1971) gives the following reported dialect names for Paiwan: Tokubun (Tokovul, Tokuvul), Shimopaiwan (Ka-paiwan-an), Kapiyan (Kaviangan, Kipiyan), Raisha (Tsala'avus), Kunanau (Kulalau), Naibun (Tsa'ovo'ovol), Kachirai (Tsoa-qatsilai), Rikiriki (Raokrik, Laliklik, Lilisha), Tachaban (Patsavan, Patsaval), Tamari (Tsaovali); and for Rukai, Dainan (Taromak), Taramakau (Talamakau, Takamakau), Maga (Tordukana), Tona (Kongadavanu), and Mantauran (Upunuhu, Opunoho). **Demography.** Paiwan, 44,682; Rukai, 6,302 (Wei and Wang 1966: 118). **History and cultural relations.** Highly stylized "monumental" carving on wood and stone, most highly developed within the northwestern Rukai-Paiwan region, has been compared with so-called megalithic art of Assam and Indonesia (cf. Chen 1961), and bronze dagger handles, preserved as ancestral heirlooms, were associated by Kano (1946-52: *1*, 189ff.) with a possible migration of proto-Dongsonian peoples from mainland Southeast Asia. Theories of ancient migrations from the mainland are, however, questioned by Ferrell (1969a: 46-47), who feels that most of the characteristic features of Paiwan-Rukai culture represent local developments on a base carried by Paiwanic speakers, who probably moved into their present territory in prehistoric times from the central western plains of Taiwan. Bronze casting may have persisted among upland groups into relatively recent times, and so-called ancestral heirlooms such as glass beads and ceramic jars may have been acquired as a result of seventeenth century trade with the Dutch. Commercial surpluses such as deerskins, traded to the Dutch and others, may in addition have been responsible for the socially stratified, ramage-type systems, unique in aboriginal Formosa, and frequently compared with similar systems in Polynesia (K. C. Chang 1957). [Ferrell 1969a: 47; deBeauclair 1970a, 1970b. For a view contrasting with that of Ferrell, see Pearson 1970.] The present summary focuses principally on the west-central Paiwan (Butsul). The ethnographic record for this area, and in particular for Chala'abus village, is relatively full, and in addition this is the traditional homeland, from which the Paiwan began moving to the south and east—probably shortly before the arrival of the Dutch in the seventeenth century (Mabuchi 1954b). Principal villages have traditionally been located in the mountains of this northwest homeland, although in recent decades the government has encouraged the relocation of villages at lower altitudes, thus bringing the people in closer contact with lowland Chinese villages and trade centers. Acculturation appears to have been most marked with respect to economic institutions, e.g. cash crops such as cassava have been introduced, along with wet-rice agriculture. While the powers and prerogatives of the old chiefly aristocracies have been curtailed, distinctions based on wealth persist, along with the bilateral kindred and bisexual primogenitural inheritance. Religious rituals, e.g. the millet festivals, have largely disappeared, coincident with the introduction of Christianity and its accelerated acceptance among the less well-to-do. [Kokubu and Kaneko 1962; Chen 1956b; Tang 1970.]

SETTLEMENT PATTERN AND HOUSING. **Settlement pattern.** Indigenous patterns have been altered in recent decades by government resettlement schemes, which have encouraged the movement of hill villages to more accessible locations nearer the plains. Traditionally, concentrated villages averaging 300 inhabitants, although the range extended from less than 100 to close to 1,000 (Mabuchi 1960; Ferrell 1969a). Chala'abus village in 1953 was sited on a hillside, with cultivated fields on the surrounding slopes; houses were arranged in terraced rows, one above the other, with narrow stairways affording communication between rows (Wei 1955). Relations between local groups were in the past frequently hostile, and regional alliances rare; villages were protected by bamboo stockades and stone walls, and young men guarded village gates against surprise raids (Ferrell 1969a; Okada 1950; Kojima 1915-22: 5, pt. 3, 330-34). Until recent decades, most villages

contained at least one ritual house (ancestral spirit house) maintained by the senior chiefly lineage(s) within the village (Wei 1955; Kojima 1915-22: 5, pt. 3, 5). Men's houses are lacking among the upland northwestern Paiwan and adjacent Rukai, although they are (or were) found occasionally among local populations in close contact with the age-graded Puyuma to the north and east (Ferrell 1969a: 44). **Housing.** Among the high altitude northern Paiwan and western Rukai, house sites are constructed by digging into a slope and extending an earth and stone terrace outward. Floors and roofs of these rectangular, semisubterranean houses are of slate or flat stone slabs. Walls may be of slate or hewn wooden boards. The houses of the chiefly aristocracy may carry elaborately carved human and snake designs on wooden walls, posts, and lintels, although this privilege is denied commoners. Houses of senior chiefly lineages tend to be large, fronted with extensive stone paved platforms, which serve as meeting places for villagers. An upright stone pillar represents the founding ancestor(s) of the lineage. [Ferrell 1969a: 43-44; Chen 1968: 261ff.; Wei 1955.] South and east of this highland area, houses tend to be constructed at ground level, with wood plank walls and thatched roofs. Among the extreme southerly Paiwan, Chinese house types, with walls of adobe construction, prevail (Ferrell 1969a; Chen 1968).

ECONOMY. **Agriculture.** Traditionally, slash-and-burn agriculture, with sweet potatoes and taro (preserved by baking in stone ovens) the staple crops. Millet, with at least nine varieties, including glutinous and nonglutinous, is the ceremonial food par excellence. In the form of cakes and wine, it is the favored food of the ancestral spirits, and its growing and harvesting are accompanied by ritual, including ceremonial planting in a ritual field and a prohibition against harvesting with a knife (Kojima 1915-22: 5, pt. 3, 131; Okada 1950). Other crops include beans, peanuts, goosefoot, maize, sorghum, cucurbits, ramie, and tobacco. Wet rice is nowadays grown to a limited extent in some areas, although rice in any form appears to have been formerly tabooed among the western Paiwan (Kojima 1915-22: 5, pt. 2, 390; 5, pt. 3, 302). Intercropping appears to be common; fields may be fenced and animal pests discouraged by the use of clappers worked by lines strung from a temporary field house. Crop rotation is reported by Okada, who indicates a fallow period following four to five years of cropping. According to Chen, millet can be grown for two years on the same swidden, after which it must be fallowed for five to six years; taro requires a longer fallow, but can be grown up to five years on the same field (Okada 1950; Chen 1956b; Kojima 1915-22: 5, pt. 3, 394-95). **Hunting.** Hunting, for food as well as for purposes of trade and ritual, was formerly a prestigeful male occupation.

Deer, wild pigs, goats, leopards, monkeys, and birds were hunted with bows and arrows, spears, and guns. Larger game was pursued by communal hunting parties, aided by dogs and/or fire. Smaller game was taken in a variety of traps, snares, and nets. Deer horns, boars' tusks, leopard and deerskins, and hawk and pheasant feathers were used for personal ornamentation and clothing; and deer and leopard skins, especially, were traded and sold to lowlanders. The head of a chiefly lineage on whose hunting grounds an animal was slain was entitled to a portion of the meat. [Okada 1950; Kojima 1915-22: 5, *pt*. 3, 396-406.] **Fishing.** Fish are taken in rivers, using poison, weirs, nets, bows, and spears (Kojima 1915-22: 5, *pt*. 3, 410-13). **Domestic animals.** Chiefly pigs, dogs, and chickens, the former primarily for consumption at religious festivals. Domesticated bees are also reported. [Okada 1950.] **Industrial arts.** Basketry, weaving, smithing, and especially wood carving. Women are tabooed from hunting and men from weaving. Neither the Paiwan nor the Rukai have any recollection of pottery making, although they do possess heirloom pots. [Okada 1950.] **Property.** Land, including hunting and fishing territories, fields, and house lots, belongs to chiefly lineages. Commoners have rights of usufruct and can transfer these to an eldest child (Okada 1950). Ferrell (1969a: 44) mentions heirloom wealth consisting of old pottery jars, glass beads and bracelets, and bronze dagger handles. [For glass beads, see also Chen 1966; for pottery see Jen 1960.]

MARRIAGE AND FAMILY. **Mode.** Infant betrothal appears to be relatively rare. Young people of both sexes formerly had their teeth blackened and their earlobes pierced. Tattooing, of both sexes, functioned chiefly as a status marker among the aristocracy, or, among young men, as the mark of a successful headhunter. Its connection, if any, with marriage or marriageability, remains unclear (Kojima 1915-22: 5, *pt*. 3, 368-75). According to Mabuchi (1960), a brideprice is required, size depending on relative social class of the bride and groom, i.e. a lower-class man marrying into an aristocratic family must expect to pay a large bride-price. Okada (1950) mentions ironware, pigs, wine, beads, betel, and silver bracelets. Among chiefly families, the bride-price may in addition include cultivable land, together with rights to the labor and tribute of those commoner families working the land (Wei 1955). **Form.** Monogamy (Mabuchi 1960). **Marriage rules.** According to Mabuchi (1960), incest taboos are extended bilaterally to include all second cousins (third cousins among Chala'abus Paiwan, according to Wei 1960), although such rules are apparently applied more strictly among the chiefly aristocracy than among commoners. Marriages among commoners are primarily village endogamous, whereas the higher ranking aristocracy tend to contract village-exogamous marriages for political purposes. **Residence.** Ambilocal (Mabuchi

1960). **Household.** Average household size is slightly less than five persons (Okada 1950; Mabuchi 1960). Since an eldest child (of either sex among the Paiwan) remains with the parents and ultimately inherits the house, whereas younger siblings move out to form new (independent) households, a village normally contains a minority of extended [stem] family households (Wei 1960: 98). **Divorce.** According to Okada's 1933 figures, approximately one-half of all household heads in Rai (Chala'abus) village had experienced divorce from one to ten times, with adultery a major cause of divorce (Okada 1950). **Inheritance.** By primogeniture (either sex among the Paiwan, males among Rukai) with respect to house, house name, and position as household head. Thus in Rai (Chala'abus) village in 1933, household heads were about equally divided between male and female (Okada 1950).

KIN GROUPS. **Descent.** Okada (1950) found no evidence of kin groups based on a unilineal rule of descent. According to Ferrell (1969a: 45-46), kinship is ambilineal and residence ambilocal. Children affiliate with the lineage or "house," i.e. assume the house name (*ngatang a(n) uma*), of the household into which they are born (Wei 1955). Thus affiliation depends on parents' choice of residence—which for eldest siblings, at least, is ambilocal. For the Chala'abus Paiwan, Wei (1960) describes a bilateral personal kindred, on occasion including affines and, for the purpose of defining incest, extended outward to include third cousins. **Kin groups.** Both Ferrell (1969a) and Chang (1957) have called attention to the marked similarity of the Paiwan-Rukai lineage systems to the cognatic ramage-type societies of Polynesia. All households in a village claim varying degrees of genealogical relatedness to a named "chiefly" household(s). The senior (eldest) person in this household (either sex among Paiwan, male among Rukai) functions as religious and temporal leader of all related households; he or she "owns" the land and collects tribute, primarily for redistribution at religious festivals (Ferrell 1969a). Thus for Chala'abus village as of 1953, with a population close to 1,000, Wei (1955, 1960) found 12 chiefly households, the highest ranking of which (house name *ruvaniau*) maintained its ancestral spirit house, with associated skull shelves, as a kind of village temple and provided, in the person of its senior male, the "big chief," the putative owner of one-third of the cultivable land of the village. Wei describes in addition a system of what appear to be named social categories based on relative genealogical closeness to the chiefly lineage(s). [Rukai lineage systems, and associated patterns of class differentiation and political integration—generally similar to those of the Chala'abus Paiwan—are described in Wei 1955, 1960.] Some west-central Paiwan villages, e.g. Chala'abus, report a division into two moietylike categories, neither endogamous nor exogamous. Children inherit membership in one or another of these categories from their parents; should the parents be of opposite divisions, the children's affiliation depends on their parents' choice of post-marital residence (Mabuchi 1960; see also Y. Y. Li 1956).

SOCIOPOLITICAL ORGANIZATION. **Political organization.** Political integration does not normally exceed the level of the local community. Most villages are, however, located within what Mabuchi terms "regions," i.e. the drainage area of a stream or tributary of a major river, wherein chiefly families contract village-exogamous marriages, and villagers attend one another's major religious festivals. Although the aggregate of villages within a region may well be interrelated by kin and affinal ties and by participation in a common ritual language, they fail, characteristically, to form political confederations (Mabuchi 1966). A village may be under the religious and secular authority of a single chief, although the large village of Chala'abus, as reported by Wei, had in 1953 multiple chiefs serving political, religious, and military functions. A "big chief" (*avusamang*), head of the genealogically senior lineage, was assisted by numerous functionaries, mostly near kinsmen. Heads of the 12 or so chiefly families within the village made up an "administrative council," subordinate to the *avusamang* (Wei 1955). Ferrell (1969a: 15ff.) questions whether the assumption of political and administrative powers by "village chiefs," going back at least to the eighteenth century, is indeed an indigenous institution. The secular powers and social distinctiveness of the chiefly aristocracy may in fact date only from the lucrative seventeenth-century trade in deerskins and other forest products and the appointment by Dutch traders of secular chiefs in hill villages. It might be assumed, furthermore, that these changes operated on an older base, similar to surrounding Puyuma and Siraya, whereby chiefs of ritual groups derived their influence from primarily genealogical and ritual considerations. **Social stratification.** According to Wei (1960), the term *mamatsangiran* refers specifically to the senior lineage and household within a local community, i.e. those who claim direct descent from the original founders. The term (variously, *mamatsangilan*, *mazazagilan*) has been used more generally by Okada and others to distinguish a class or category of chiefly aristocracy versus so-called commoners (variously, *atedang*, *koapen*), reflecting a system wherein households are ranked along what amounts to a continuum, based on genealogical closeness to a senior (founding) line. [See above under *Kin groups*.] Heads of high ranking households have chiefly status, with their relative power depending in part on the amount of land "owned." Claims of eminent domain formerly entitled chiefs to tribute in kind and in labor from "commoners" who worked the land under usufructory title.

Chiefs' "domains," wherein according to Okada they maintained order, handled foreign relations, and opened new land, included in some cases whole villages and even (through intermarriage or conquest) tributary rights over portions of other villages. [See Mabuchi (1966) for an analysis of the political and territorial implications of intermarriages among Paiwan chiefly families.] In theory, the chiefly aristocracy is strictly endogamous with respect to marriage; in practice, these rules apply only to the highest rank households, for whom marriages of eldest sons and daughters, at least, are usually class-endogamous and village-exogamous. Otherwise, marriage into a chiefly family is an accepted and favored way for a lower-class male to achieve higher status (probably as the founder of a new line, since, judging by Wei [1955: 107], the class status of the children in such a marriage would follow that of the mother). Title as household head within a chiefly lineage descends, among the Paiwan, to the eldest child, regardless of sex. His or her siblings likewise enjoy chiefly rights and privileges, although their descendants, after a few generations, normally revert to commoner status (Okada 1950; Wei 1955). The sumptuary privileges of the chiefly aristocracy include the right to distinctive house names and to carved crests and other devices on house beams; the right to wear leopard skin cloaks and necklaces of boars' tusks and leopard teeth; the right to tattooing, with chest and arm designs restricted to high ranking chiefs and renowned headhunters (Okada 1950; Ho 1955). The possession of ancient ceramic jars, in some respects resembling the prehistoric pottery of South China, is an additional prerogative of chiefly families, wherein such jars, many of which are named and widely known and valued, are passed down as family heirlooms. According to S. M. Jen (1960), the supernatural origin of the jars, recounted in myths, gives them a magic aura: seed grain stored in them produces abundant crops; beer brewed in them possesses spiritual qualities. Jars, glass beads, and other heirloom objects represent material wealth and as such figure in bride-price negotiations. More importantly, perhaps, they enhance the spiritual charisma of a family and its head—and in this sense they relate to the ritual significance of chiefly lineages and, within a village, of the chiefly household and its head as the nucleus of what was probably originally a cult group comprising the remaining village households, all related (through cognatic, ambilineal ties as a "conical clan") to the core or "founding" line. As pointed out by Ferrell (1969a), the social distinctiveness of the chiefly aristocracy, in particular as this appears related to purely secular considerations, may be an outgrowth of seventeeth-century trade with the Dutch. In sum, it would seem inappropriate to apply the terms and concepts of European feudalism to the Paiwan-Rukai, as is done by Wei (1955, 1960). Thus the "tribute" or "taxes" that "nobles" collect from their commoner "serfs" is (or was) intended primarily for redistribution at religious festivals—a probable indication of the original genealogical/ritual nature of this aristocracy and its associated powers and prerogatives. [Wei 1955, 1960; Okada 1950; Mabuchi 1960, 1966; Ferrell 1969a.] **Age-grades.** Age-grades, and boys' dormitories, absent among the western Paiwan and adjacent Rukai, are found in a few villages farther east, e.g. the east coast Rukai village of Taromak (Hsieh 1968), a reflection, according to Ferrell (1969a), of Puyuma influence. **Social control.** Disputes are judged by chiefs and settled by the imposition of fines—bracelets, glass beads, ironware, pigs. In general the size of the fine varies inversely with the social class of the accused, with aristocrats exempt entirely from prosecution with respect to some crimes, such as stealing (Okada 1950; Wei 1955). **Headhunting.** According to information collected by T. J. Ho from aged informants in Chala'abus village, headhunting was undertaken to avenge a prior death and to gain renown and/or advance one's social status (a commoner could earn the right to the chest tattoo and other prerogatives of aristocrats through headhunting exploits). Raiding parties, consisting of from 2 to 50 men, were guided by dream and bird omenology. Within Chala'abus village, headhunting ritual was the hereditary prerogative of a single chiefly lineage, represented by its priest. After cleaning and removal of the mandible, a newly taken skull was placed on a stone pillar in the paved courtyard fronting the house of the highest ranking (village) chief. Spirits were offered sacrificial pig meat and millet wine, while men who had taken heads in the past danced in full regalia and boasted of their exploits. The skull was eventually removed to the village skull shelf in front of the ancestral spirit house. [Ho 1955; Sayama 1913-21: 8, 143-50; Kojima 1915-22: 5, pt. 3: 208-20; Furuno 1945: 451-63.]

RELIGION. In contrast with the plains-dwelling Ami, Puyuma, and Siraya, the upland Paiwan-Rukai show little concern with cosmogony. Their myths rather emphasize the origins and genealogies of their chiefly families. Typical of such accounts is one which has an ancestral pair emerging from two eggs enclosed within an earthenware jar, the eggs in turn having been produced by the sun following impregnation by a giant snake. [Ferrell 1969a: 44-45. See also T. J. Ho (1967: 1, 81-82) for mention of deluge/incest origin myths among some eastern Paiwan.] Ancestral spirits are important and are placated collectively through the chiefly house(s) to which all members of a village are in varying degrees related. **Supernaturals.** A well-developed pantheon, including Takalaus, god of thunder and lightning and patron of millet culture, and Namati, goddess of life and creation, associated with Qadau ("Sun"). Spirits of all kinds, including the souls of the dead, are *cemas* or

tsumas (Ferrell 1969a). According to Kojima (1915-22: 5, pt. 3, 5) the ancestral spirits include a class of culture heroes, those who in primeval times came down from Mt. Tawu to teach farming and hunting to the Paiwan. Important also are ancestral founders of villages, venerated in ancestral spirit houses maintained by chiefly lineages. **Practitioners.** Male priests (*para'are, paraqalai*) may on occasion be chosen by divination. Most, however, are hereditary within chiefly family lines charged with the conduct of communal ceremonies, e.g. *para'are a maleva*, "priest of the Five-Year Festival" (Wei 1955). Priestesses (*pulingao*) function chiefly as shamans in divinatory and curing rites, during which they enter a trance state while possessed by a tutelary spirit. Ritual paraphernalia include iron knives, pebbles, and pig bones. *Pulingao* specialize in massage, recovery of lost souls, and bottle gourd divination (Kojima 1915-22: 5, pt. 3, 47-49) and may in addition conduct rites along the life cycle such as at birth and death. This profession, restricted to women, is not hereditary. Rather, one receives a supernatural "calling," manifested by fainting or other psychic abnormalities, on occasion induced by swinging (Wu 1965). [Kojima 1915-22: 5, pt. 3, 47-53, 273-79; Okada 1950; Y. Y. Li 1956; Wu 1965; H. Li 1958.] **Ceremonies.** The Chala'abus festival calendar formerly included religious rites at the annual clearing and burning of land for agricultural purposes and, in particular, in conjunction with the sowing and harvesting of millet (for millet and taro rituals, see especially Kojima 1915-22: 5, pt. 3, 131-37). Certain of these communal ceremonies appear to have been the hereditary responsibility of individual chiefly families, e.g. the maintenance of a ritual millet field and the performance of planting ritual in this field by an agricultural priest on behalf of the entire village (Okada 1950; Ferrell 1969a). A ceremony normally includes an invocation and invitation to the spirits by a priest, including "leading" them with smoke from burning millet straws; feeding the spirits with pig meat, millet cakes, and millet wine; and prayer and propitiation of spirits, often in an archaic language. Purification during and after a ceremony may include use of Miscanthus leaves and communal hunting (headhunting in former times). Ritual places include household ancestral shrines, as well as a village "temple" or spirit house maintained by a senior chiefly lineage. Slate skull shelves are (or were) maintained—outside the village for the skulls and bones of slain animals, inside the village for the skulls of slain human enemies (Kojima 1915-22: 5, pt. 3, 62-80). Most characteristic of the Paiwan (but absent among Rukai) is the so-called Five-Year Festival (*maleva*), held formerly by each village on an average of once every five years following the harvest. This was a village-renewal festival, during which the collective ancestral and other spirits were summoned from Mt. Tawu to participate in five days of ceremonial games, ritual, and feasting, and then sent back to their spiritual dwelling place. Festivities included a ritual ball game, in which bark balls, representing various spirits, were tossed in the air by priests while the men of the village competed in catching them on the ends of long bamboo poles (Ferrell 1969a: 45). According to Kojima (1915-22: 5, *pt. 3*, 82-87), the spirits traveled through the entire Paiwan territory, from north to south, receiving a welcome in each village along the way. They then reversed their route, traveling from south to north back toward Mt. Tawu, and getting a send-off in each village on their route. The interval between welcome and send-off was, in the far south, less than one month, but might be as much as a year in northern Butsul villages. **Soul, death, and afterlife.** According to Okada (1950), there is (or was) belief in five *tsumas* (spirits) located on either side of the body; at death the right-hand spirits return to Mt. Tawu, while those identified with the left remain on earth, a cause of illness and misfortune to the living. Burial, with the corpse in a squatting position, bound with long strips of cloth, was formerly in a slate-lined grave beneath the house, with all the members of a single family interred in the same grave (Y. C. Chang 1955). This seems to correlate with archeological reports for southeastern Taiwan of stone-lined cist graves containing multiple burials, some secondary (Pearson 1970).

BIBLIOGRAPHY. deBeauclair 1970a, 1970b; K. C. Chang 1957; Y. C. Chang 1955; Chen 1955, 1956b, 1958b, 1961, 1966, 1968; Dyen 1971; Ferrell 1969a; Furuno 1945; Ho 1955, 1967; Hsieh 1967, 1968; Jen 1960; Kano 1946-52; Kojima 1915-22 (*vol. 5, pts. 1-5*); Kokubu and Kaneko 1962; H. Li 1958; Y. Y. Li 1956; Mabuchi 1954a, 1954b, 1960, 1966; Miyauchi 1937; Okada 1950; Pearson 1970; Sayama 1913-21 (*vol. 8*); Tang 1970; Utsurikawa et al. 1935; Wei 1955, 1960; Wei and Wang 1966; Wu 1964, 1965, 1968.

BUNUN

Synonyms. *Bunum, Vonum, Vunun*

ORIENTATION. **Location and identification.** The Bunun are swidden-farming hilltribesmen, inhabiting a major portion of central Formosa (chiefly Nantou County) on both sides of the Central Mountain range, at about 3,000 feet. They occupy an area of dense forest and open grassland, approximately 120 by 60 kilometers, containing in 1930 some 120 settlements, and drained by the upper tributaries of the Choshui, the Laonung, the Nantzuhsien, and the Hsiukuluan rivers. The area is bounded on all sides by other aboriginal groups—Atayal, Ami, Rukai, Tsou—a fact which has made for considerable ethnic intermixture

and consequent variation among subgroups. [Mabuchi 1952, 1966: 121; Chiu 1966: 5.] Mabuchi divides the Bunun (from the word for "human being") into five "tribes" or subgroups, each characterized by distinctive dialect and cultural features and each maintaining a kind of tribal consciousness through widespread networks of kin and affinal ties. These groups, with their 1932 populations in parentheses, are: Takebaka (1,200), Taketodo (2,250), Takevatan (1,750), Tak'banuath (5,200), and Isbukun (7,700). The same author distinguishes further between what he terms the "homeland" Bunun (the two northernmost groups, Takebaka and Taketodo, on the upper tributaries of the Choshui, south of Sun-Moon Lake) and the "colonial" Bunun, the remaining three groups who have migrated south and east across the Central Mountain range, where they have assimilated in varying degrees with neighboring peoples. Recent descriptions of Bunun culture are for the most part on the Takebaka (cf. Chiu 1962, 1964, 1966) in the extreme northwestern section of the homeland area. [Mabuchi 1952, 1954a: 6-7.] **Linguistic affiliation.** Classed by Ferrell (1969a) within the Paiwanic division of Formosan aboriginal languages, a position tentatively accepted by Dyen (1971), who lists the following reported dialect names: Tamaroan (Tamado'wan, Tamaroau, Northern Bunun), Katoguran (Katongulan, Ketanganau, Central Bunun), Ibaho (Ivaxo, Southern Bunun). **Demography.** Mabuchi's 1932 estimate was 18,000 (1952: 183); whereas Wei's 1964 count stands at 24,000, with 51 administrative villages averaging 475 persons each (Wei and Wang 1966: 7). **History and culture contact.** Some Bunun are said to trace legendary origins to the western coastal plains of Formosa, possibly reflecting an earlier movement into the hills of plains refugees from Chinese pressures and their subsequent intermixture with Atayalic and Tsouic hilltribesmen. Bunun history since the mid-eighteenth century has been one of expansion out of a historic mountain homeland on the upper reaches of the Choshui River south of Sun-Moon Lake, moving south and east across the Central Mountain chain and driving out or absorbing other groups (chiefly Tsou) in the process. [Mabuchi 1952, 1954c: 140.] Transition to the modern period began in the late 1930s, with government-sponsored movement of the people from their scattered mountain hamlets to more concentrated village-type settlements in foothill valleys nearer the plains—and along with this the gradual adoption of wet-rice agriculture. Villages nowadays are in many of their outward aspects indistinguishable from those of Formosan Chinese. Most, however, continue to plant a few crops such as millet and sweet potatoes on nearby hillside swiddens. Although the all-important agrarian and headhunting festivals have disappeared, traditional food taboos continue to be observed, and shamans continue their curing rituals despite the inroads of Christianity on most of the indigenous belief system. [Mabuchi 1970b; de-Beauclair 1956; Coe 1955.] Ferrell emphasizes the cultural eclecticism of the Bunun, partly a result of widespread migration and accompanying absorption and assimilation of other peoples. Thus, although they are linguistically classed with their neighbors on the east, the Ami, they show relatively little resemblance to these people, either physically or culturally; with respect to social organization they are most like the neighboring, but linguistically unrelated, Tsou; and with respect to religious orientation, they resemble superficially the Atayal, their linguistically unrelated neighbors to the north (Ferrell 1969a: 35).

SETTLEMENT PATTERN AND HOUSING. **Settlement pattern.** The aboriginal pattern was one of dispersed homesteads forming loosely defined, agamous hamlets or neighborhoods averaging probably less than 50 persons (Mabuchi 1966), and composed of what appear to have been localized segments of patrilineal clans. Statistics such as those of the 1930 census, listing 120 "villages" with an average population of 150, reflect the beginnings of government resettlement programs and the appointment of "village chiefs," a trend reflected even more strongly in a recent estimate of 475 persons per village (Wei and Wang 1966). [Mabuchi 1952, 1960, 1966.] **Housing.** Traditional dwelling houses resemble those among the Rukai-Paiwan peoples to the south. The rectangular-shaped house is constructed on a level site partially excavated from a hillside and extended outward by means of an earth or stone-walled terrace. House floor and outer front courtyard are slate paved. Side and back walls are of rough slate or stone laid up without mortar, while front walls may be of upright planks or large stone slabs. Gable roofs are covered with slate, thatch, or plank shingles. [Ferrell 1969a.] Men's houses (and age-grading) appear to have been absent among the Bunun. C. C. Chiu mentions for the Takebaka a "tribal house" (a kind of spirit or ancestor house) used for religious ceremonies and village council meetings: walls and roof are of slate, with skull shelves on the outer side of the rear wall (Chiu 1966: 159-60).

ECONOMY. The traditional source of livelihood is slash-and-burn agriculture, with the extended family household the basic economic unit. Traditional crops include millet and sweet potatoes (the staples), along with dry rice (of more importance among the Tsou), maize, taro, beans, and various cucurbits. Wet rice has been grown only since the 1930s, and some hemp is produced nowadays, primarily for sale to Formosan Chinese. The Bunun attach an especially high value to millet, with an annual cycle of millet rituals reportedly more elaborate than that of any other aboriginal group on Formosa. As among the Tsou, the hunting of wild game and the rearing of pigs are of particular social and emotional importance in the traditional culture. [Mabuchi (1952) describes the traditional economy. See Chiu (1966) for an account of economic activities in a modern village strongly acculturated to Formosan Chinese.] **Hunting.** Large catches of game are (or were) taken by surrounds, using fire and/or dogs. The latter serve chiefly for hunting and are never eaten. Hunting, like millet culture, is surrounded by religious taboos and rituals; killed game, weapons (traditionally the bow and arrow), and all other accoutrements of the hunt are strictly taboo to women. Distribution of meat is socially and ritually elaborated, while the skulls and jaws of slain animals are preserved for ritual use. [Mabuchi 1940, 1970a; Sayama 1913-21: 7, 122-23; Chiu 1966.] **Industrial arts.** The Bunun, like the Atayal and Tsou, lack the elaborate carving and painting on wood so characteristic of the surrounding Paiwanic peoples (Ferrell 1969a). They made pottery, of geometric impressed design, into the present century, but are best known for finely woven, multicolored cloth, which, made into jackets and skirts and decorated with glass beads and shells, was worn at religious festivals. Weaving, formerly taboo to men, is now restricted to plain hemp cloth and is done by only a few women (deBeauclair 1956). The Bunun, like the Atayal and Tsou, extracted the lateral incisors of both sexes during late adolescence (Ferrell 1969a), and, according to Chiu (1966: 55) the custom was associated in the minds of the people with later success as a hunter (male) or weaver (female). Both sexes formerly tattooed, said by deBeauclair (1956) to have been associated, for males, with headhunting prowess. **Property.** Members of patrilineal clans are "owners of land," in a magico-religious sense, with respect to the scattered hunting territories of the clan (see under *Religion*). Nonclansmen pay tribute (a portion of any game taken) when hunting on clan territory, thereby assuring the good will of the "owners." In practice, these "ownership" rights appear to be exercised by localized segments of clans—Mabuchi's subclans or lineages. The subclan or patrilineage, in addition, becomes "owner," in both a jural and ritual sense, of any agricultural land cleared and returned to fallow by a member household. [Mabuchi 1952: 194-95, 1970a: 353, 369.]

MARRIAGE AND FAMILY. **Mode.** Nowadays a modest bride-price, consisting of such things as money, clothing, pigs, and metal tools. Sister exchange was formerly more common, with "repayment" often delayed for a generation or so. [Mabuchi 1960; Chiu 1962; Sayama 1913-21: *1*, 154-55.] **Form.** Exclusively monogamous (Mabuchi 1960). **Marriage rules.** Marriage prohibitions are extended to include members of the father's patrilineal clan or phratry; members of the mother's patriclan; individuals whose mothers belonged to the same clan; and first cousin marriage of any kind. Marriage choices under these conditions become considerably restricted, and young men frequently find their brides in quite distant villages. In addition, the ban on marriage with maternal relatives is in practice frequently circumvented. [Mabuchi 1952: 198; 1960, 1970b.] **Residence.** Exclusively patrilocal—no exceptions among 313 cases examined by Mabuchi (1952: 192). **Household.** Mabuchi (1960) reports a traditional pattern of patrilocal extended families averaging slightly under 10 persons per household, a figure higher than that for any other aboriginal group on Formosa. Chiu (1962) reports 50 percent extended family households, 42 percent nuclear, in a Takebaka village studied in 1960. Mabuchi elsewhere (1952: 193) indicates that in fact the composition of the Bunun household may be quite flexible, averaging 10 persons but "often" containing as many as 20 or 30, including a variety of clan or phratry relatives living temporarily under one roof. **Divorce and secondary marriage.** Both common. Either sex may initiate divorce, with return of the bride-price mandatory in cases where the wife is the initiator. Older children stay with the father; small children go initially with the mother but return eventually to the father's kin group. [Chiu 1962.]

KIN GROUPS. **Descent.** Descent, succession, and inheritance consistently patrilineal (Mabuchi 1952: 192). **Kin groups.** The Bunun "tribes" are each characterized by a segmentary organization into patrilineal phratries (dual phratries or "moieties" among the "homeland" Takebaka and Taketodo), clans, subclans, and lineages, with exogamy prevailing at all levels (Mabuchi 1952, 1960). The general term for a nonlocalized, unilineally reckoned category is *sidoq* (*siloq*), used most often for what Mabuchi calls a clan. Localized segments of clans (Mabuchi's subclans) are systematically named and are the effective corporate units with respect to control of hereditary hunting territories. Unnamed patrilineages ("those of the same oven ashes"), consisting of patrilineally related households living in adjacent hamlets, are "owners of arable land" (*taima-qoma*). *Sidoq* membership is inherited through the paternal line, and is symbolized by the observance of distinctive behaviors, e.g. the right to eat a specified category of millet tabooed to nonmembers. At marriage, a woman affiliates with her husband's *sidoq*, losing for life any rights to membership in her natal group. However, the members of her natal clan have a considerable spiritual influence over the lives of her children, symbolized by feasts, gifts, and respectful behavior rendered them by members of the father's clan following the birth of a first child. [Mabuchi 1952, 1960, 1970a.] According to Wei (1957), clan names are associated with events and places that occur in ancestor legends; but according to Mabuchi, the concept of descent from ancestral "founders," and the ties (other than magico-religious) of descent groups to

land, are weakly developed (Mabuchi 1970a: 356). While Ferrell (1969a) writes of "the ranking household of the senior subclan," Wei (1957) comments that although primogeniture is recognized "in principle," all clans and subclans are equal. **Kin terminology.** The system, basically a generational one, is rarely extended beyond the subclans of both parents. In terms of address, however, honorific vocatives for father and mother are applied to all adult members of the mother's patriclan, regardless of generation (Mabuchi 1960). This overriding of the generation principle results in an approximation of Omaha terminology for cross cousins (Mabuchi 1970b). Chiu (1962) lists Takebaka kin terms, while Mabuchi (1960: 132) gives the following reference terms for Bunun (subgroup unspecified):

GrFa	*tama-qo'das*
GrMo	*tina-qo'das*
Fa	*tama*
Mo	*tina*
PaBr	*man-tama*
PaSi	*man-tina*
Sib	*tas'an*
Cousin	*man-tas'an*
Ch	*uvath*
Nephew/niece	*man-uvath*
GrCh	*uvath, man-uvath*

SOCIOPOLITICAL ORGANIZATION. A traditional pattern of politically autonomous hamlets, with those in a given valley or drainage area (i.e. locality) linked by kin and other ties to form what Mabuchi calls ritual groups (see under *Religion*). "Men of influence" exercised an indefinite and fluid authority within a locality (eminent magicians and warriors were called *mamangan*, "possessed of spiritual worthiness"), but formal political organization at the local level was lacking, and "village chiefs" a later creation by government. [Mabuchi 1952: 187ff., 1960, 1970a: 357.] Localities are aggregated into "tribes" through common magico-spiritual and genealogical traditions as well as networks of consanguineal and affinal kin ties. Common traditions and ties maintain a degree of law and order over considerable areas with an average population of 3,600 people. Formal political organization is, however, lacking at this level, and there are no "tribal chiefs." The Bunun "tribes" (Takebaka, Taketodo, Takevatan, Tak'banuath, Isbukun) appear to have evolved from single genealogical-ritual groups through a process of segmentation in response to population increase and subsequent migration. Thus the Taketodo maintain their memory of an original settlement (*atsang todo*) inhabited by the first ancestors (*todo*). [Mabuchi 1952, 1960; Chiu 1966: 9-11.] **Warfare.** Headhunting was important formerly, with distinctive body tattoos the prerogative of the successful warrior. Northern Bunun (Takebaka) raided southern Bunun (Isbukun) as well as surrounding Atayal, Ami, and Tsou. A prospective headhunting party observed a period of sexual abstinence by sleeping in the ritual house, and consultations regarding the results of dream and bird omenology were frequent, both before and during an expedition. Newly-taken heads were boiled and the skin and brains removed, after which the skulls were feted in a week-long religious festival and finally placed on skull shelves along the outside wall of the ritual ("tribal") house. For the Takebaka, Chiu (1966: 156, 212) describes a kind of local "warrior-chief" (*laviong*), a strong, skillful, brave [and probably spiritually potent, *mamangan*] individual selected from among eligible males within a designated unilineal descent group to lead on occasions of warfare and/or headhunting. Chiu likewise reports the occasional occurrence of ritual cannibalism, particularly in those cases where a group has been so fortunate as to take the head of an enemy's *laviong*. The bow and arrow, in some cases poisoned, seems to have been the chief weapon. [Chiu 1966: 206-14.]

RELIGION. Mabuchi (1970a) contrasts the "atheistic" Bunun and Tsou of the central highlands with the "theistic" Ami-Puyuma-Paiwan peoples of southern and eastern Formosa. The latter, with well-developed pantheons, rely to a considerable degree on the intercession of deities and ancestral spirits in human affairs. The Bunun, and to a lesser extent the Tsou, place their reliance instead on the magical manipulation of spiritual power resident in the soul-spirits of living men, animals, and millet. **Supernaturals.** Weakly developed theogony, and little if any development of an ancestor cult. Much attention paid, however, to the soul-spirits (*qanito*) of the living, which, if angered or mistreated, can, independently of their owner-bodies, cause harm to other humans, damage a millet crop, or interfere with the success of a hunting party. An important concept in this regard would seem to be that of *tis'ia*, a kind of miasmic infection capable of emanating on its own volition from the body of a person and potentially harmful to others or to crops such as millet (Mabuchi 1936). These beliefs appear to underlie what Mabuchi calls magico-spiritual "ownership" of hunting territories and arable land by members of descent groups—and the necessity for payment of "tribute" (meat of slain animals, millet beer feasts) before one can successfully hunt or grow crops on land "owned" by a descent group of which one is not a member. [Mabuchi 1970a.] **Practitioners.** According to Coe, millet priests (*lisikidan lus'an*), hereditary in male descent lines, had mostly disappeared, together with traditional millet rituals, by the early 1950s. Male and female shamans (*isingolasan*) were, however, still active in the diagnosis and treatment of illness. The causes of illness are said to be black magic (intrusion of objects in a victim's body) or the activities of *qanito*, evilly disposed spirits or ghosts of the dead. One becomes shaman by apprenticeship and instruction, or, alternatively, by dream visitation and acquisi-

tion of a supernatural helper spirit. Equipment includes bamboo sticks, stones, and Miscanthus leaves, the latter used as a kind of magic straw through which the practitioner sucks the intrusive object (pebble, hair, etc.) from the afflicted portion of the patient's body. According to Coe, the Bunun shamans do not experience true possession, the guardian spirit speaking *to* the shaman, not *through* him. [Coe 1955. See also Chiu 1964; Sayama 1913-21: 7, 90-91.] **Ritual groups and ceremonies.** Mabuchi comments on the unusual development of millet ritual among the Bunun, as compared with other Formosan aborigines. It appears that localized segments of patriclans form what Mabuchi terms ritual groups, defined as "unions of households" that follow the same cycle of millet rituals and observe the same taboos, most specifically the communal eating of sacred millet tabooed to outsiders. [Ritual groups among the Takavatan are called *tastolusan*, according to Ho (1958).] Leaders of ritual groups, hereditary in certain patrilineages, function as priests, specialists in keeping and reading "picture calendars"—long, narrow boards on which carved pictures and signs serve as mnemonic reminders of the sequence and details of ritual performances (including swinging and ball games) peculiar to each ritual group. These ceremonial calendars are generally divided into 12 lunar months, with allowance for a periodic leap year, and are geared to the stages of millet culture, e.g. the year "begins" with the clearing of fields and sowing of millet. Ritual groups maintain ritual fields (Ho 1958), together with what Mabuchi terms "headhouses," or *lumaq* (apparently the ritual or "tribal" house of Chiu 1966: 159-60). Here are stored the priest's paraphernalia, including the shoulder blades of pigs, chicken feet, and deer hooves (Ho 1958). Attached to the outside wall are shelves for the skulls of enemies and the jawbones of animals slain in the hunt, together with a consecrated granary for storage of the group's sacred (i.e. "tabooed") millet. Second in importance only to millet festivals are the annual ceremonies honoring newly-taken heads of enemies and the annual hunting festivals staged by the men of a localized subclan, the "owners" of the headhouse and its skull shelves. These festivals include ritual hunting by the men and the ceremonial sprinkling of skulls with millet beer. [Mabuchi 1936, 1952, 1970a.] **Soul, death, and afterlife.** Belief in good and bad soul-spirits (*qanito*) of the right and left shoulder, respectively (Sayama 1913-21: 7, 62; Mabuchi 1970a). For a mature and respected male dying a "natural" death at home, burial is most often beneath the paved floor of the house or front courtyard, in a stone, slab-lined pit designed for multiple burials. The corpse is arranged in a squatting position with the arms bent upward against the chest, and is wrapped tightly with cloth before being lowered into the pit. These practices, quite early interdicted by government on sanitary grounds, have virtually disappeared from modern Bunun villages. [Sayama 1913-21: 7, 163-65; Chiu 1966: 72; deBeauclair 1956.]

BIBLIOGRAPHY. deBeauclair 1956; Chiu 1962, 1964, 1966; Coe 1955; Dyen 1971; Ferrell 1969a; Ho 1958; Mabuchi 1936, 1940, 1952, 1954a, 1954c, 1960, 1966, 1970a, 1970b; Sayama 1913-21; Wei 1957; Wei and Wang 1966.

TSOU

Synonyms. *Alishan, Arisan, Northern Tsou, Tsu'u, Tsuou, Tzo*

ORIENTATION. **Location.** Swidden-farming hill tribesmen in the vicinity of Mt. Ali in the west central mountains of Taiwan, some 50 kilometers east of Chiai city (120° 40′ S. Long., 23° 25′ N. Lat.). Bounded on the west and south by plains-dwelling Chinese and Sinicized aborigines, and on the north and east by settlements of Bunun hill tribesmen. An area roughly 80 by 20 kilometers, containing in 1931 some 20 settlements at an average of 3,500 feet. Drained in the south by the upper reaches of the Nantzuhsien and Tsengwen rivers and in the north by the Chingshui and Ch'enyulan, upper tributaries of the Choshui. Nearby Yü Shan (Mt. Morrison), the highest peak on Taiwan, figures prominently in Northern Tsou origin myths. [Ferrell 1969a; Mabuchi 1952, 1966; Okada 1942.] **Identification.** Mabuchi divides the Tsouic-speaking peoples into (1) *Northern Tsou* (*tsou,* "people") with four "tribes" or subgroups: Tufuya, Tapangu, Dufutu (Lufutu), and Imutsu (2) *Southern Tsou* with two subgroups: Kanakanabu (Kanabu) and Sa'aroa (La'aroa). The four northern groups are linked by common customs and genealogical traditions, and dialectal and cultural differences among them seem to be of a far lesser magnitude than among the neighboring Bunun, whom they closely resemble with respect to their patriclan organization. They evidence, furthermore, a degree of cohesiveness lacking among the two southern groups, the Kanabu and Sa'aroa. These latter have been considerably reduced in population and relatively more exposed to acculturative influences from the plains, and they diverge rather markedly from the northern culture type with respect to certain features of social organization and religion. The Tsouics as a whole, however, share a number of similarities that set them apart from the rest of Formosa, according to Ferrell (1969a). The Northern Tsou have remained relatively unacculturated until recent decades, and the bulk of the ethnographic literature is specific to these northern groups, particularly the Tapangu–Tufuya, i.e. Wei's Arisan Tsou. [Mabuchi 1952, 1966; Ferrell 1969a; Kojima 1915-22: 4, 262ff.; Wei et al. 1952.] **Linguistic affiliation.** According to Ferrell (1969a) and Dyen (1971), Tsou (i.e. Northern Tsou) and kindred Kanakanabu and Sa'aroa comprise Tsouic, the smallest and by far the most atypical of the three major groups into which the Malayopolynesian languages of Formosa have been classified. Although Ogawa and Asai (1935: 36) classed Kanabu and Sa'aroa as merely dialects of Tsou proper, the differences seem to be greater than this order of classification would imply. Sa'aroa is nowadays lexically as near Paiwanic (Siraya) as to Tsou, due probably to borrowing (Ferrell 1969a: 39). Dyen (1971: 170-71) lists the following reported dialect names: Arisan (Alisan), Haisen (Paitsiana, La'aluwa), Iimutsu, Luhtu (Dufutu, Namakaban, Namahabana, Namakabau, Ruftu), Nagisaru (Nagisaran), Tapangu, Tfuea (Tufuja, Tufuya, Chibora, Tsuihwan). **Demography.** Mabuchi's census figures for 1931 indicate a total at that time of around 2,200, with an average subgroup population of less than 400: Tufuya (664), Tapangu (922), Dufutu (108), Imutsu (24), Kanakanabu (188), and Sa'aroa (291). Wei and Wang report an increase in population since the early 1940s, with the Tsou proper (Northern Tsou) at 3,100 and the total for all Tsouic speakers close to 4,000. [Mabuchi 1966: 126; Wei and Wang 1966.] **History and cultural relations.** Northern Tsou maintain legendary genealogical connections with former dwellers on the western plains, near modern Chiai city, probably reflecting the assimilation, at some time in the past, of plains refugees fleeing from Chinese pressures. Tsou territories in the mountains appear to have formerly been more extensive than at present, and there is good evidence that Tsou raided north into Atayal, and east into what is now Ami territory. Incursions of Formosan Chinese and Sinicized aborigines, beginning in the early eighteenth century, brought epidemics and depopulation, weakening the Tsou and contributing to progressive loss of territory to the expanding Bunun. [Mabuchi 1952, 1966; Wei et al. 1952: 1-17.] Like the Bunun, the Tsou were in the late 1930s moved by government edict into compact villages at lower altitudes, where they were encouraged to grow irrigated rice. These and other pressures, e.g. the tourist industry at nearby Sun-Moon Lake, have brought about many changes in traditional Tsou culture. There is nowadays more frequent intermarriage among the various Tsouic groups, and some Tsou in peripheral villages have even intermarried extensively with neighboring Bunun. [Mabuchi 1966; Kokubu and Kaneko 1962: 37.] Ferrell (1969a: 39) calls attention to the uniqueness on Formosa of certain aspects of Tsouic language and culture, and to the probability that Tsouic cultural origins lie in directions quite different from those of surrounding Paiwanic-speaking peoples. While this may appear superficially to be the case, closer inspection reveals many similarities with Paiwanics and the Indonesian world to the east and south—and any final cultural and linguistic assessment of the Tsou remains at this point an unsettled question.

SETTLEMENT PATTERN AND HOUSING. **Settlement pattern.** Kojima's data of about 1916 indicate a hamletlike pattern, with settlements of three to ten households (ca. 30 to 100 people), located near the banks of rivers or mountain streams (Kojima 1915-22: 4, 96-102). For the territory of the "tribe" or subgroup, e.g. Tapangu, Mabuchi (1960) describes a pattern consisting of a stem or core village (generic *hosa*; specific Tapangu, Tufuya, Dufutu, etc.), genealogically and ritually senior to a varying number of branch or satellite settlements. Each settlement has its men's house, with that of the core village serving as the meeting place for a "tribal" council and as a ritual center for the entire complex. According to Wei et al. (1952: 18-37, 114-31), the men's house (*kuva, kuba*) of the core village is a large structure, fronted by an open plaza for dancing and ceremonies, beyond which, near the entrance to the village, is the ritually important "village tree" (*pa'mumutu*). Behind the men's house, sometimes clustered in a fan-shaped arrangement, are the dwelling houses, some, at least, with the status of clan ancestral houses, according to Wei et al. Fields are scattered on nearby hillsides or river terraces, and paths connect the core village with its satellite settlements, all of which are within walking distance. **Housing.** The oval-shaped dwelling houses (*emo*), with domelike thatched roofs extending nearly to the ground, are unlike those of any other Formosan group (Ferrell 1969a). The floor, of packed mud and sand, is at ground level, and the house lot is enclosed by a low stone wall (Wei et al. 1952: 18-37). Kojima describes the existence formerly of large, extended family households with separate (nuclear family) sleeping platforms and central hearths. A house is considered ritually complete only if it has associated with it a shelf for the bones of animals slain in the hunt, a sacred millet field, and a storage basket or chest for sacred (tabooed) millet (Kojima 1915-22: 4, 99). The wall-less men's houses (*kuva*) are rectangular, raised on piles, with domed, thatched roofs. In former times, they contained skull shelves for the honored trophies of past headhunting raids. Associated orchid plants and banyan trees are considered sacred, the temporary residing places of deities summoned to attend village-wide ceremonies (Ferrell 1969a; Chen 1968: 278).

ECONOMY. As among the Bunun, subsistence relies mainly on dry farming, with hunting of wild game and raising of pigs important both socially and emotionally. Ritually, millet is most important, followed by dry rice. Fishing is important as a source of food, but compared to hunting it is subject to relatively little ritual elaboration. [Mabuchi 1952.] **Agriculture.** Millet (much of it in the form of beer) and sweet potatoes are the staples, supplemented by taro, dry rice, maize, beans, pumpkins, garlic, bananas, and peanuts. Wet rice is a relatively recent introduction. Hemp, tobacco, *croix,* and bamboo are also grown.

Swiddens are used for up to three seasons and then fallowed for four to five years. Millet is sown broadcast, mixed with pumpkin seeds, and in the same manner dry rice is on occasion mixed with maize. No use is made of manure. [Okada 1942; Kojima 1915-22: 4, 106-08.] **Hunting.** Hunting techniques, used on deer, wild boar, leopards, bears, monkeys, and birds, are virtually the same as among the neighboring Bunun. The meat of game animals, along with such items as bears' gall bladders and deerhides, accounts for much of the trade with lowlanders (Kojima 1915-22: 4, 223). The emotional importance of hunting in the traditional culture is reflected in the degree of ritual elaboration, including associated bird divination, second only to that surrounding headhunting in former times. **Domestic animals.** Limited to chickens (mainly for eggs), dogs (for hunting), and pigs (meat sacrificed and eaten at religious festivals). [Okada 1942.] **Industrial arts.** The Tsouic are not especially noted for their material or artistic productions. Like the Bunun and Atayal, they lack the elaborate and decorative carving on wood and stone so characteristic of the Paiwanic peoples. Embroidery, basketry, bamboo craft, and net making are well developed, and weaving and pottery making were done formerly. Highly distinctive of the Tsou are certain traits that seem to relate to northern Asia, such as extensive use of leather clothing (caps, detached sleeves, tight leggings, puckered moccasins) and cylindrical containers of bark. [Ferrell 1969a; Wei et al. 1952: 75-98; Chen 1968.] **Division of labor.** Okada (1942) reports a rather marked sexual division of labor, strictly enforced: men engage in the clearing and burning of fields, hunting, basketry, net making, leathercraft, and weapon making. Women care for pigs, weave, make pottery, embroider, cook, draw water, build pig sheds, weed and care for dry fields. Both sexes engage in the cultivation of spring-sown rice and millet, make millet granaries, and build houses. Strict taboos formerly surrounded certain of these activities, i.e. it was forbidden for a man to touch a garden hoe or a loom or for a woman to enter the men's house, touch weapons, or go near a bone shelf. Sanctions included threat of illness, scarcity of game, and the like. [Okada 1942; Wei et al. 1952: 114-31.] **Property.** As among the Bunun, patrilineal clans are "owners" of hunting territories (*hupa*) in a magico-religious sense, and nonclansmen pay tribute when hunting on clan territory. Ownership rights are in practice exercised by localized patrilineages, and apply regardless of whether the land is used for hunting or farming. Thus at a millet-sowing ritual a representative of the "owning" clan must be present to offer millet beer to the patron deity of the land as a hunting tract (Mabuchi 1952, 1970a: 357). Individual ownership of property is in theory restricted to movables, such as clothing, weapons, and implements, with household heads functioning as trustees with respect to the corporate estates of extended kin groups. The introduction of wet-rice fields and the increased ritual independence of nuclear families is, however, altering this traditional pattern in the direction of private ownership of land and other wealth (Okada 1942; Kojima 1915-22: *4*, 190; Wei et al. 1952: 99-113).

MARRIAGE AND FAMILY. The association, if any, of bodily mutilation and headhunting with initiation and marriageability status is unclear. The ears of both sexes were pierced at around eight years of age. In late puberty, the lateral incisors of both sexes were extracted, and young men when hunting or traveling girdled themselves tightly with two-inch wide belts of rattan. Teeth blackening and tattooing, present to a limited extent among the Sa'aroa and Kanabu, were apparently not practiced by the Northern Tsou (Kojima 1915-22: *4*, 102; Okada 1942). **Mode.** Among the Northern Tsou, early betrothals and arranged marriages are not uncommon, with sister exchange a frequent occurrence in former times. In all cases, bride service for a period of one to three years is obligatory (Mabuchi 1960; Okada 1942). Marriage ceremonies are usually timed to coincide with annual millet festivals. There is an exchange of goods, e.g. rolls of cotton cloth—black for female and red for male, and the bride and groom are fed token grains of sacred millet by their new fathers-in-law, symbolizing the union of the two extended kin groups (Okada 1942; Kojima 1915-22: *4*, 194-97). A married woman becomes a member of her husband's clan. During her early child-bearing years, the men of her natal clan present her with pigs, which she raises and slaughters in a series of feasts for members of her husband's clan, who return these favors with frequent visits and gifts of millet beer. This reciprocal gift-giving has to do with beliefs about the spiritual relationship between the men of a woman's natal clan and the well-being of her children, in particular the uncle-nephew relationship (Mabuchi 1952; Okada 1942). **Form.** Strictly monogamous (Mabuchi 1960). **Residence.** Among Northern Tsou, strictly patrilocal, following an initial period of bride service (Mabuchi 1952, 1960). The Kanakanabu young couple move back and forth until the parents of one or the other die (Kojima 1915-22: *4*, 191). **Marriage rules.** Marriage prohibitions among the Northern Tsou are similar to those among the Bunun, with the exception that the Tsou prohibit marriage between those whose mothers are real sisters, rather than simply clan-mates, as among the Bunun. Like the Bunun, the Tsou prohibit all first cousin marriages, and there are no prescribed or preferred unions. According to Kojima (1915-22: *4*, 192), it is permitted to marry the brother or sister of a dead spouse, but it is not obligatory. [Mabuchi 1952: 191-92; 1960.] **Household.** Nowadays the small, patrilocal extended family, averaging slightly less than six members, is common among the Northern Tsou; whereas the nuclear family household is usual among the Sa'aroa and Kanabu (Mabuchi 1952: 193;

1960; Ferrell 1969a). Okada (1942) reports that named patrilineages were formerly the normal units of common residence, and Kojima describes the earlier existence of large, multifamily structures, containing separate family compartments and separate quarters for unmarried girls; adolescent boys slept in the village men's house (Kojima 1915-22: *4*, 183, 248-50). It is evident that the Tsou nowadays conceive of a "household" as made up of a head house and satellite field houses, with members living in the latter a good part of the time (Mabuchi 1952; Okada 1942). **Inheritance.** Strictly patrilineal, according to Mabuchi (1960). Individual ownership of property is traditionally restricted to movables, such as clothing and weapons (see under *Property*).

DESCENT GROUPS. **Descent.** Descent, succession, and inheritance consistently patrilineal (Mabuchi 1952, 1960). **Descent groups.** According to Mabuchi (1960) and Wei et al. (1952), the Northern Tsou "tribes" or subgroups are each characterized by a segmentary organization into lineages, clans, and phratries, with exogamy theoretically prevailing at all levels. The generic term for a nonlocalized unilineally reckoned category of kinsmen, meaning "of the same dirt floor," is taken by Okada (1942) as evidence that the Tsou "tribes" have evolved through a process of segmentation within what were originally localized residential kin groups. Clans function as "owners," in a magico-religious sense, of hunting territories (Mabuchi 1970a). They are exogamous with respect to marriage, and they avenge the injury or death of a member (Kojima 1915-22: *4*, 156). Clan origins are recounted in legends which invoke male founding ancestors and provide a genealogical basis for activation of interclan ties (Okada 1942). Clan membership is inherited through the paternal line and is symbolized by the right to eat the sacred millet (*faiva*) tabooed to nonmembers. At marriage, a woman affiliates with her husband's clan; her natal clan continues, however, as an important magico-religious influence in her life and particularly in the lives of her children (see under *Marriage and Family*). Within each village, the households of the same patrilineage constitute a distinct ritual, economic, and landholding unit (*ateufutsu-no-emoo*, "those of the same stem house") (Mabuchi 1960, 1970a). It is these localized patrilineages that in practice exercise use rights to farm land and streams. Within this group, only one dwelling merits the term *emoo* (leading, stem, or head house), a ritually complete house with associated animal bone shelf, ritual field, and chest for the storage of the group's sacred millet. [Mabuchi 1952, 1960, 1970a; Wei 1950; Wei et al. 1952: 99-113; Okada 1942.] **Kin terminology.** Okada (1942) lists Dufutu terms, and Wei (1950: 9-10) gives terms for Kanabu and Sa'aroa, as well as Northern Tsou. The following list of reference terms is from Mabuchi (1960: 132-33):

GrFa	*akei*
GrMo	*bai*
Fa	*amo*
Mo	*tno*
PaBr	*amo-tsoni*
PaSi	*ino-tsoni*
Sib	*ohaesa*
Cousin	*popue-nanatoto-ohaesa*
Ch	*oko*
Nephew/niece	*popue-o-okoa*
GrCh	*popue-o-okoa*

SOCIOPOLITICAL ORGANIZATION. **Political organization.** Mabuchi describes the Northern Tsou as made up of four "tribal" territories, each with a chief living in a head village (*hosa*) that is genealogically and ritually senior to a varying number of branch settlements. The "tribe" comprises a single ritual group, wherein branch villages observe the same rituals and taboos as the head village, and wherein the "tribal" chieftain is both secular and religious leader. The senior village men's house serves as a combined administrative, military, and ritual center for the entire complex. Chieftainship is in principle hereditary within chiefly patrilineages, and heads of satellite settlements are likely to be the paternal relatives of the "tribal" chief. These chiefly lines do not, however, constitute a privileged aristocracy as among the Paiwan-Rukai farther south. [Mabuchi 1952, 1960, 1966.] The above account is given added historical depth by Kojima, who describes what appear to have been river drainage districts or domains, each controlled by a hereditary priest-chief (*peonshi*), who might at the same time function as war leader (*ijomu*). Interdomain feuding and headhunting appear to have been endemic. *Peonshi* were entitled to wear distinctive head gear, but they received no tribute and worked their own fields (Kojima 1915-22: 4, 238-58). Okada (1942), drawing on fieldwork of the 1930s and the earlier survey data of Kojima, supposes the Tsou community to have been originally a residential kin group housed in a large, multifamily dwelling, exploiting a section of stream or watershed, and named for an ancestral founder or some vegetative or topographical peculiarity of an original house site. The local community, so defined, was at the same time a ritual group, with its associated skull shelves, ritual field, and store of sacred millet. The house head was ritual leader and, if strong and resourceful, war leader as well. Nuclear families lived part of the year in field houses (*hunou*), which, with increased population, became further removed from the head house (*emo*) and gradually coalesced into branch settlements, economically independent but genealogically and ritually tied to their respective *emo*. With time and increased segmentation, these satellite communities acquired their own ritual accoutrements, including in some cases men's houses. The old ties continue, however, and are ceremonially renewed each year in what have become the head villages (*hosa*) of "tribes" or "tribal complexes."

[Mabuchi 1952, 1960, 1966; Okada 1942; Kojima 1915-22: 4; Wei et al. 1952: 114-31.] **Social differentiation.** According to Mabuchi (1960, 1966), the Tsou have no privileged or chiefly aristocracy, and there are no formal age-grades. They do have the institution of the men's house (*kuva, kuba*), which Ferrell (1969a) believes may have been borrowed from Paiwanic speakers (the Siraya term was *kouva*). Among the Northern Tsou, the central or "tribal" men's house served as a focal point of tribal life, taboo to women. Important matters were discussed here by "men of influence" sitting in council. Unmarried young men slept here, particularly during their initiation—a period of instruction in tribal lore and the arts of war and headhunting. Solemn initiation rites were held annually for both sexes, according to Kojima, following which boys could don leather headgear and girls black headcloths. [Okada 1942; Wei et al. 1952: 133-63; Kojima 1915-22: 4, 142.] **Warfare.** Feuding and headhunting appear to have been endemic in former times, with the history of the Northern Tsou "tribes" largely one of shifting alliances, broken by periods of enmity, both among themselves and with the two southern groups, the Kanabu and Sa'aroa. Tsou headhunters in addition ranged into Atayal territory and east as far as the Ami. And beginning in the early decades of the twentieth century, the Tsou offered notably stiff resistance to government efforts at forced pacification. [Mabuchi 1952, 1960, 1966.] Hostilities under aboriginal conditions appear to have been chiefly concerned with revenge or with individual quests for honor. The warrior with an enemy head to his credit was honored in his home village and was entitled to special headgear and the title of *maotana*, "brave man." Especially brave and successful warriors gained the status of war leader (*ijomu*), second in importance only to that of tribal chief, *peonshi*. Individuals with outstanding abilities or charisma might combine these roles, in the process becoming famous in tribal lore and legend. [Kojima 1915-22: 4, 277-300.] Both Mabuchi and Okada refer to what were apparently tribal-wide military organizations centered in men's houses of head villages, but it would appear that hostilities were most often in the form of small raids organized by individuals in quest of personal honor, or the result of chronic interclan feuding to avenge past killings. Weapons were swords, spears, bows and arrows, and guns. Bird and dream divinations were important, and a leader's reputation in part depended on his skills in these arts (Kojima 1915-22: 4, 88-92). Peace between clans or "tribes" was negotiated in a formal ceremony, during which, according to an old custom, a stone was buried to commemorate the event (Kojima 1915-22: 4, 302). Ceremonies in honor of newly-taken heads, as described by Wei et al. (1952: 133-63) and Tu (1968), lasted for up to five days and were held on the plaza fronting the men's house. Each newly-taken head was displayed on a shield and fed millet beer, while a sacrificial pig, tied to the base of the "village tree," was killed by members of the headhunt party (clothed in red), who stabbed the animal with spears. Following display in a kind of basket made by splitting one end of an unright bamboo pole, the head was retired to a skull shelf within the men's house. Included in the ceremony was the ritual feeding of the divine birds, i.e. those whose voices, through divination, had foretold the success of the expedition (Tu 1968).

RELIGION. Ferrell has noted the enigmatic position of the Tsouic culture type with respect to religious beliefs and institutions. Thus Tsou myths ascribe man's origin to a deliberate act of creation rather than to spontaneous emergence from stone or bamboo or to the union of mythical ancestral deities, and although the myths contain the motif of a universal deluge, they lack the associated brother-sister incest theme so widespread in East Asia. Furthermore, although the lack of ritual concern with ancestral spirits, characteristic of both Bunun and Tsou, distinguishes both groups from surrounding Paiwanic speakers, the Tsouic pantheon of named deities, lacking among the Bunun, is highly characteristic of Paiwanic cultures. [Tu 1959; Ferrell 1966, 1969a.] **Supernaturals.** The Tsou conceive of a class of higher deities (*hicu, hitsu,* "spirit") living in a remote "heaven" and generally well disposed to man. These include a female creator god, Ninevu (Nivenu) and the great male deity, Hamo. More directly concerned with the affairs of men are numerous lower deities, including patrons of such activities as millet culture and the hunt, who are subordinate to Akemameoi (lit. "grandfather old person"), protector of land and villages, punisher of evil and lover of good, spiritual mentor of headhunting and the chase. Akemameoi's "seat" is a large stone at the foot of the village (banyan) tree, fronting the men's house and ceremonial plaza. [Tu 1959; Kojima 1915-22: *4,* 64ff.; Wei et al. 1952: 133-63; Ferrell 1966, 1969a.] **Practitioners.** Among the Northern Tsou, the "tribal" chief (*peonshi*) in his capacity as ritual leader, and sometimes war leader as well, functions as priest with respect to major agricultural and headhunting ceremonies. [The southern Tsouics, i.e. Sa'aroa, are reported to have a hereditary priesthood.] Shamans (*yoiho, ruiho*) of both sexes treat the sick and predict the future. Techniques include prayer, sprinkling of water, and waving of Miscanthus leaves. Although there is little mention in the literature of trance or spirit possession, the shaman does communicate with spirits, according to Wei et al. (1952: 133-63). Among the Northern Tsou, anyone can become shaman by apprenticeship to an established practitioner. Among the Sa'aroa, however, the candidate must be "chosen" or "called" in a dream. [Kojima 1915-22: *4,* 74ff.] **Ceremonies.** The Northern Tsou ceremonial calendar included major annual festivals associated with agriculture, hunting, fishing, headhunting, and initiation. The Sa'aroa also held a major

ceremony once every two or three years, commemorating the bringing of agriculture by a mythical ancestress-hero and featuring the veneration of ancestor relics. Otherwise the Tsou pay little ritual attention to the ancestral spirits. [Kojima 1915-22: *4,* 73; Ferrell 1969a.] Offerings to deities always include millet beer, millet cakes, and pork; while those to the highest gods included in the past a human head, according to Wei et al. (1952: 133-63). Millet festivals feature the sowing of seed in a three-foot square sacred field (*pokaya*), storing the harvest therefrom (the sacred millet) in a holy millet chest or granary, and communal eating of the sacred (tabooed) millet by members of extended kin groups. Associated activities include ritual hunting by males and millet pounding by females, as well as ritual contests between groups of young people. Miscanthus leaves figure prominently in purificatory and exorcistic rites. [Kojima 1915-22: *4,* 76-79; Okada 1942.] **Soul, death, and afterlife.** Man has two souls: *hejo* (*hemo*) resides within the body, and when it departs, the person dies; *pepea* (*piepiya*) travels abreast of the living body, performing the same functions as the two shoulder soul-spirits of the Bunun and Sa'aroa. At death, *hejo* becomes a spirit (*hitsu*) in an afterworld (Hefuehebu), where it lives much as it did on earth. Spirits of noted chiefs and warriors, however, go to a higher heaven, close to the great god Hamo. One's *pepea* becomes a ghost, potentially harmful to the living. [Kojima 1915-22: *4,* 69ff.; Mabuchi 1970a; Wei et al. 1952: 133-63.] According to Okada, the corpse is arranged in a sitting position, with knees drawn up to chin, wrapped in cloth, and buried in a pit beneath the dirt floor of the dwelling. According to Wei et al. (1952: 164-68), slab-covered pits each accommodate one body; when the available floor space is exhausted, the house is moved to a new site. Miscanthus leaves, tied to the ends of long, upright poles, surround the dwelling during five days of mourning, at the end of which relatives purify themselves in the waters of a river and offer millet beer to the spirit of the deceased. [Okada 1942.]

BIBLIOGRAPHY. Chen 1968; Dyen 1971; Ferrell 1966, 1969a; Kojima 1915-22; Kokubu and Kaneko 1962; Mabuchi 1952, 1954a, 1954c, 1960, 1966, 1970a; Ogawa and Asai 1935; Okada 1942; Sayama 1913-21; Tu 1959, 1968; Wei 1950; Wei and Wang 1966; Wei et al. 1952.

ATAYAL

Synonyms. *Atazan, Etall, Itall, Taiyal, Tayal*

ORIENTATION. **Location and identification.** The Atayal occupy some 70 villages on the headwaters of the Choshui, Tatu, Tachia, Ta'an, and Tananao in interior, north-central Taiwan, north of a line from P'uli to Hualien. They are the most widely distributed of Taiwan's aboriginal peoples, occupying nearly one-third of the total mountainous area, and they were formerly the most notorious headhunters on the island. They are commonly divided into three major dialect groups: Seqoleq and Tse'ole' (Se'ole'), together comprising Atayal proper, and Sedeq (Sazek, Sejeq), linguistically and culturally somewhat divergent. The name in each case is derived from the respective dialect word for "human being." Seqoleq speakers, with over 40 percent of an estimated 50,000 population, are the most numerous and widespread of the three, occupying a major central portion of the total Atayal area of some 160 by 120 kilometers (Mabuchi 1966). Tse'ole' (20 percent) occurs primarily in the west and southwest, while Sedeq (38 percent) is spoken principally in the southeast. Dialectal differences coincide with minor differences in social organization, origin legends, and the like. Seqoleq speakers, for example, say that their ancestors emerged from a large rock in the upper Peichiang—Sebayan plateau area, northeast of Sun-Moon Lake. From this southwest "homeland" area, according to Mabuchi, the Seqoleq have migrated, within a span of some five generations, north and east, settling in specific, named drainage areas and forming loosely organized federations of villages for defense. These in turn have become the Seqoleq "tribes" of the literature, e.g. Melqoan, Melipa, Xaqul, Gaogan, etc. Although widely separated nowadays, the Seqoleq federations continue to claim a common origin and to invoke a vague ideology of common descent. Approximately 40 of these so-called tribes were identified by Japanese ethnologists for the Atayal as a whole; some one-half, identified as either Seqoleq or Tse'ole', comprised the "Atayal proper," the focus of the major portion of the Japanese ethnographic effort. Chinese ethnographers have concentrated on the largest of these "tribes," the Kalaisan (Nanao) in the extreme east of the Atayal area, and specifically on the ethnically mixed village of Nanao, nowadays numbering some 1,200 people and located on the coastal plain in close proximity to lowland Chinese (cf. Li et al. 1963). [Mabuchi 1960, 1966; Wei 1963; Ho 1956.] **Linguistic affiliation.** Ferrell (1969a) lists Squliq (Sqolyeq, Seqoleq), and Ci'uli (Tse'ole') as dialects of Atayal. Atayal, together with closely related Sediq (Sedeq), comprise the Atayalic language group, one of the three major groupings of the aboriginal Austronesian languages on Taiwan. **Demography.** According to the 1930 census, there were 32,925 Atayal in 241 villages, totaling 7,040 houses (Norbeck 1950, citing Suzuki 1932). According to a more recent figure, Atayal is spoken by nearly 50,000 persons (Ferrell 1967). **History and cultural relations.** Ferrell (1969a: 32) calls attention to the lack of close similarities between the Atayalics and other peoples

on Formosa as possibly supporting the hypothesis that they represent an ancient stratum pushed back into the mountains by more recent (Paiwanic) arrivals. Although origin legends differ somewhat among subgroups, they generally account for the first appearance of the ancestors and their subsequent migrations within the Atayal area. Some describe emergence from stone; others tell of a universal deluge and survival on Mt. Taihasen, inland from Hualien. Generally, however, there is a conspicuous lack of any orientation to the lowlands or the sea. According to Mabuchi, an early trade route led from the Sebayan plateau "homeland," deep in the mountainous interior, in a generally northeast direction to what is now Ilan County, directly south of Taipei. Here the Atayal came to trade their mountain products with Sinicized Kavalan and Formosan Chinese for salt and iron. This seems also to have been the general direction of historic migrations of Atayal peoples, and it is generally the route of the recently completed east-west highway that has opened up much of the Atayal area to tourism and economic exploitation from the lowlands. [Mabuchi 1954c, 1966; Utsurikawa et al. 1935; Norbeck 1950; Kokubu and Kaneko 1962; Ferrell 1969a, 1969b; S. H. Chen et al. 1950.] The earliest historic mention of the deep mountain Atayal is dated 1722, but isolation in a rugged terrain protected the Atayal from major acculturative change until the advent of Japanese military administration in 1897. From 1903 to 1914, the Japanese conducted over 20 expeditions into Atayal territory in a program of forced pacification and abolition of headhunting. Beginning in the early 1920s, Japan's policy shifted to an emphasis on education, trade, and economic development. Under Japanese and later Formosan Chinese township administration, Atayal settlements have in most instances been moved to lower altitudes, where wet rice is grown alongside the traditional swidden crops. Intensive proselytizing by Christian missionaries began in 1949, with the result that the Atayal are now reported to be nominally 100 percent Christian (Nettleship 1970). As described by Li et al., the Nanao Atayal on the eastern Ilan plains are well on the way to total integration within the Chinese cash crop market economy. Traditional religious festivals are no longer held, and Nanao villagers nowadays attend five Christian churches, four Protestant and one Catholic, while the old *gaga* ritual groups have become cooperative work groups, organized according to church affiliation. [Li et al. 1963: 161ff.; Ho 1956; deBeauclair 1956; S. H. Chen et al. 1950.]

SETTLEMENT PATTERN AND HOUSING. **Settlement pattern.** The aboriginal pattern seems to have been one of scattered settlement in small hamlets or field huts on the high mountain slopes above 1,500 meters (Li et al. 1963: 308; Nettleship 1970; deBeauclair 1956; Sayama 1913-21: 4; Kojima 1915-22: 1, 88-

89; Mabuchi 1966). Beginning about 1900, successive Japanese and later Formosan Chinese governments forced the resettlement of most Atayal in compact villages on the lower slopes of mountain valleys or in foothill areas adjacent to the coastal plain. Villages (*galang*) nowadays average 600 or so inhabitants (Wei and Wang 1966: 6-7), and there is usually a police station, a school, and one or more churches. Public buildings, such as men's houses, were lacking in the traditional culture, although village watch towers, raised 10-30 feet on scaffoldings of long bamboo poles, were among some subgroups occupied by young men as defensive devices (Kojima 1915-22: *1*, 101; C. L. Chen 1968: 284, 282, fig. 98c). According to Sayama (1913-21: *4*), these towers among the Sedeq served as gathering places for unmarried young men and occasionally for young people of both sexes. **Housing.** Among the deep mountain Atayal, houses were constructed in a highly characteristic semisubterranean style that is rarely met with since removal to lower altitudes and exposure to Japanese and Chinese architectural models. In these old-style houses, the floors, rectangular in outline, are excavated three to five feet below the surface and are reached by ladders leading downward from a door at ground level. Walls are of loosely stacked cordwood, placed between uprights, which in turn support a gable roof of thatch, bark, split bamboo, or slate. Houses, along with adjacent granaries on short pilings, are well made, with considerable use of hewn beams and mortise and tenon construction. Pigs are housed in fenced yards with grass-covered huts. Skull shelves were reserved exclusively for heads of slain enemies; trophies of the hunt, such as wild boars' jaws, were hung from house rafters. [Kojima 1915-22: *1*, 92-93; Sayama 1913-21: *4*; Ferrell 1969a; C. L. Chen 1968; deBeauclair 1956.]

ECONOMY. Subsistence traditionally based on dry-field farming, supplemented by hunting and some fishing. Commercial crops such as sugarcane and peanuts, handicrafts, and tourism nowadays provide a cash income whereby the Atayal are increasingly being drawn into the lowland Chinese market economy. **Agriculture.** According to Kojima, millet (*telakis*), sweet potatoes (*ngaxe*), and maize are the staples in the high mountains, where cold precludes the growing of swidden rice. Supplementary crops include taro (*shexe*), manioc, beans, gourds, bananas, tobacco (*tobako*), ginger, and ramie. Millet, in the form of beer and glutinous cakes, is, with the meat of the domestic pig, the food most pleasing to the spirits and thus of prime ceremonial importance. Although the growing of millet is surrounded with ritual prescriptions and prohibitions, many of them performed by men, the activities associated with pig raising, principally in the hands of women, do not appear to have taken on any particular ritual significance. The ritually unimportant sweet potato, formerly the staple food, has been replaced in that capacity by wet rice,

and relegated to the status of pig food, wherever the Atayal have resettled at lower altitudes. Swiddens are used for three to four years and then fallowed for up to ten years. Trees are planted along with crops a year or so before fallowing in an attempt to encourage the quick regeneration of forest at the expense of unwanted Miscanthus grass. Broadcast sowing of millet, intercropping, and crop rotation are all within the traditional cultural inventory. [Yuan 1964; Kojima 1915-22: *1*, 127-31; Okada 1959.] **Hunting and fishing.** Wild boar, deer, goats, and an occasional bear are hunted communally with dogs and guns (formerly bows and arrows), or taken in hemp rope snares and pitfalls. Bats, squirrels, monkeys, bee honey, and larvae also contribute to the diet, while deer horns and bear's gall are traded for salt and iron from the lowlands. Fish are taken principally in communal drives by poisoning streams and pools. [C. L. Chen 1956a "daily life"; Kojima 1915-22: *1*, 132-33.] **Domestic animals.** Traditionally pigs and chickens, the former chiefly for religious sacrifice. Nanao village adjacent to the plains nowadays utilizes water buffalo in connection with wet-rice agriculture. [C. L. Chen 1956a; Yuan 1964; Kojima 1915-22: *1*, 137.] **Industrial arts.** The Atayalics are known for work in rattan, bamboo, and wood, together with weaving and shell bead embroidery; they lack pottery making and decorative carving in stone and wood, traits strongly characteristic of surrounding Paiwanic peoples (Ferrell 1969a). Skill in weaving multicolored cloth from native grown hemp was formerly important to women's status, with the entire process from raw material to finished product taboo to men (Shih 1964). Distinctive items of clothing formerly included ceremonial rattan hats covered with bearskin and deerskin raincoats (Ruey et al. 1955). **Property.** As reported in the literature, the size and composition of land owning groups, i.e. categories whereby native usage defines access to land and the products thereof, appear to vary considerably, although the core is almost always comprised of patrilineally related kinsmen. These categories are not, however, closed, and other kin, including affinals, as well as nonkinsmen, may participate from time to time. In general, hunting and fishing territories tend to be owned by villages or village alliances; whereas ownership of agricultural land, particularly in the more populous and wealthier northern federations, tends to be within families or a group of close kin (brothers; a father and his sons-in-law; cousins; a man and his sisters' husbands). [Okada 1959; Kojima 1915-22: *1*, 260-80; Mabuchi 1966; Wei 1958a.] **Shell bead money.** Strings of shell beads (*aha, kaha, ahita*), either singly or sewn on native hemp cloth, were formerly highly regarded status symbols, as well as serving as a kind of currency in bridewealth and compensation payments. According to Kojima, strings of beads were combined, by tens, into bundles, 50 of which equaled one shell bead skirt. Two of the latter, in turn, equaled one shell bead robe, etc. These various units in addition had standard conversion values in terms of goods such as pigs. Thus compensation in cases of ritual defilement or infringement was commonly paid to a communion group (*qotox neqan*) in shell beads, which were in turn converted to one or more pigs; the latter were then sacrificed and eaten communally by the group. [Chang 1953, 1958; Kojima 1915-22: *1*, 276.]

MARRIAGE AND FAMILY. Premarital sex is considered an affront to the spirits (*rutux*) and is prohibited even among nonrelatives. Facial tattooing, achieved by boys through participation in headhunting expeditions, was formerly a necessary precondition to marriage. The knocking out of upper incisors, at about 13 years of age, appears to have been motivated chiefly by cosmetic considerations. [Kojima 1915-22: *1*, 103ff.; Ferrell 1969a.] **Mode.** A prospective groom relies on a close male relative to make the proposal and carry through negotiations with the girl's family. There may be prolonged haggling (up to four years among some of the northern federations) over the bride-price, traditionally made up of strings of shell money, pigs, and bead-embroidered clothing. Among the Nanao, the girl's family provides a dowry of household utensils, tools, and weapons (Li et al. 1963: 90ff.). According to Kojima (1915-22: *1*, 210-30), and Okada (1959), the bride-price tends to be higher among the wealthier northern federations, e.g. Gaogan. Families with both boys and girls sometimes resort to exchange marriage in lieu of bride-price, although any omission of bride-price, since it is a violation of divinely ordained custom (*gaga*), is an offense to the ancestral spirits and must be compensated by pig sacrifice and ritual feasting (*manyeq gaga*) by members of the feast or communion group (*qotox neqan*). **Form.** Strict monogamy (Wei 1963; Mabuchi 1960). **Extension of incest taboo.** Wei's (1963) "incest group" consists in effect of a skewed bilateral kindred, reckoned laterally to fourth paternal and third maternal cousins. One can, however, marry a third paternal cousin by payment of a compensatory fine (Li et al. 1963: 197; Mabuchi 1966: 114). **Residence.** The normal pattern is a bride-price marriage, followed by patrilocal residence, in which case children belong to the descent group of their father. Should a family lack a direct male heir, an "*ambilanak*" marriage may be resorted to, in which case the couple reside matrilocally and the children belong to the descent group of the mother (Wei 1963; Kojima 1915-22: *1*, 188). Matrilocal marriages also occur as alternatives to payment of a high bride-price, as in the wealthy northern federations. In such cases, children belong to the mother's descent group. Should the couple separate, however, the father may return with his children to his natal group, where the children will affiliate patrilineally. According to Kojima (1915-22: *1*, 243-46), the mother's side seeks to prevent this by providing a large dowry, which the groom must

repay before effecting a separation. Matrilocal marriage under any circumstance is, however, a rare occurrence, according to both Kojima (1915-22: *1*, 243-46) and Okada (1959). **Domestic unit.** According to Wei (1963), nuclear family households occur in roughly one-half of all cases, the remaining one-half being patrilocal stem families in which one married son, ideally the eldest, remains at home and inherits the position of household head. Okada gives an average per household of 4.8 for all Atayal, with a Tse'ole' sample somewhat higher at 6.6 (Okada 1959). **Inheritance.** According to Wei (1963), inheritance rules are strictly patrilineal and, in the case of family headship, by primogeniture. Yuan (1964) and Li et al. (1963: 216) agree with the ideal of patriliny, but point out that among the heavily Christianized Nanao, tilled land is nowadays inherited bilineally within families. **Divorce and secondary marriage.** According to most accounts, divorce is frowned on as displeasing to the ancestral spirits. Among the modern Nanao it does, however, occur with some frequency, accompanied by pig sacrifice and ritual feasting (*manyeq gaga*). Also among the Nanao, it is permissible although not obligatory, for a widower to marry his deceased wife's sister. A bride-price is normally not required in such marriages. [Li et al. 1963: 95, 201; Okada 1959; Kojima 1915-22: *1*, 239.]

KINSHIP. Descent rules appear to vary somewhat among the different Atayal groups, depending on extent of migration and segmentation as well as degree of resettlement and subsequent adoption of wet-rice agriculture. Although the ideological basis of most social relationships stresses the idea of patrilineal descent, strict unilineal exogamy is lacking among the Atayal proper (Mabuchi 1960: 129), with the incest category among the Seqoleq corresponding to a skewed bilateral kindred reckoned five and four ascending generations on the father's and mother's side respectively (Wei 1963). Among the Nanao, those within this relationship are termed *qutux gelu* ("same nine"). Same-generation siblings and cousins of opposite sex who fall within this category call one another *neqan* and observe strict behavioral taboos in one another's presence. A new mother sends gifts to her *neqan* lest their feelings unconsciously affect the well-being of her child (Li et al. 1963: 115-20). The idea of unilineal descent is expressed minimally in a group of neighboring households, the heads of which are brothers; an eldest son normally inherits the parental household and serves as spokesman for his brothers. A more extended idea of unilineal descent is expressed in the Tse'ole' term *gamil* ("root," thus *qotox gamil*, "of one root"), referring to a line or pedigree whereby people invoke descent from a common male ancestor. Each *gamil* maintains its version of a common Tse'ole' legend tracing ancestral origins to Mt. Taihasen. Villages of the "colonial" Atayal in the north and west tend nowadays to be dominated by a single, named "founding" *gamil*, with the village chieftainship hereditary within that *gamil* (Ruey et al. 1955; Okada 1959). Among the eastern Sedeq, according to Mabuchi, a hamlet often consists of a localized patrilineage descended from a founding ancestor (Mabuchi 1960: 129). And the Seqoleq term, *qutux melaxu* ("one head"), refers to a localized group of patrilineal kinsmen glossed as "clan" by Kojima, who says that children take the "clan" of the father if parental postmarital residence is patrilocal, while with matrilocal residence filiation is with the "clan" of the mother (1915-22: *1*, 178-95; cf. *Residence* under *Marriage and Family*). Thus patrilineal descent lines, under various names, tend everywhere to form the basis of social groups, including villages (*qotox ngasal*), ritual groups (*qotox gaga*), hunting groups (*qotox litang*), and feast or communion groups (*qotox neqan*). The ideology of patrilineal descent is, however, tempered among most Atayal by locality considerations, with ritual and other groups tending to include matrilineal, affinal, and even non-kin members. Y. F. Ruey classified villages of the Xaqul federation in the ancient Sebayan plateau "homeland" as bilateral (in S. H. Chen et al. 1950: 57), and it would likewise appear to be these less acculturated, deep mountain federations that Murdock classifies as ambilineal and ambilocal, with descent affiliation according to parents' choice of residence, in turn said to depend frequently on relative availability of arable land (Murdock 1960: 9-10). Matrilocality does occur as an alternative mode where bride-price is high, as in the more northern federations (cf. Okada 1959), and in conjunction with "*ambil-anak*" marriages, but is said to be a relatively rare occurrence under any circumstance (Kojima 1915-22: *1*, 243-46; Okada 1959). **Kin terminology.** Kin terms reflect the generation principle in both Ego's and the first descending generation, with lineal terms for uncles and aunts in the first ascending generation. Generation level is important with respect to behavior among kinsmen, e.g. strict taboos on sexual references and sexual joking between same-generation siblings and cousins of opposite sex (*neqan*) and between a man and his same-generation brothers-in-law (*yanai*). The following Atayal terms of reference are drawn from Mabuchi (1960: 130-31) and Kojima (1915-22: *1*, 180-81). Additional Nanao terms are contained in Li et al. (1963: 180-95):

GrFa	*yutas*
GrMo	*yake*
Fa	*yaba*
Mo	*yaya*
PaBr	*mama*
PaSi	*yata*
ElSib, same sex	*qebusuyan*
YoSib, same sex	*sesuwai*
Sib and cousin, either sex	*metse-sesuwai*
Sib and cousin, opposite sex	*neqan*
Child, either sex	*laqe*

SOCIOPOLITICAL ORGANIZATION. According to Mabuchi (1966), ethno-identification among the Atayal is strongly based on territorial considerations and less so on kinship, although descent may be invoked to justify claims of common ethnicity within a region. **Ritual groups.** The basic unit in Atayal society is the so-called ritual group (*qotox gaga*), an organization of patrilineally related persons observing a common set of taboos and ritual procedures (*gaga*) inherited from a common set of ancestors in order to maintain the spiritual protection of those ancestors. A *gaga* "owns" its ancestral spirits (*rutux*) and shares in the communal eating of its sacred millet (*gaxak*), the latter under the protection of the *gaga* chief/priest, a person skilled in memorizing prayers and ritual sequences, reciting tribal history, and conducting public affairs (Li et al. 1963: 204). Ritual groups tend over time to lose their exclusive kinship basis through the operation of *mbaji gaga* ("buying *gaga*"), whereby, following the necessary bird augury (the "divine bird," *sileq*), nonrelatives may obtain the protection of a group's ancestral spirits by purchasing (formerly with shell money) a portion of its sacred millet, along with knowledge of the obligatory taboos and rituals. Thus the basis for membership becomes more a matter of common residence than of kinship (Wei 1963). In some areas, ritual group equals village, whereas in others a village may be composed of several ritual groups. In like manner the village-cum-ritual group may in some cases correspond to a hunting group or a feast group, in others not. In the southwest "homeland," an entire village federation or "tribe" may comprise a single ritual group (Mabuchi 1966: 112; Kojima 1915-22: *1*, 57). [Li et al. 1963: 90-91, 121-65, 204; Yuan 1964: 153; Wei 1958a: 34, 1963; Kojima 1915-22: *1*, 57-58.] **Political organization.** By all accounts the local settlement was originally a cluster of neighboring hamlets whose inhabitants constituted a localized kin group functioning as a single ritual group. Modern administrative villages (*galang, karan*, "cluster"), with village headmen and other functionaries, were created by successive Japanese and Chinese governments in an effort to gain political control in the tribal areas (Okada 1959). For the village of Nanao, Li et al. (1963: 121-65) describe a village chief (*meraho galang*), elected from among village *gaga* heads. The latter, as "keepers of the holy millet," hold real power, exercised in a village council. The position of village chief tends to be hereditary within a prominent or "founding" patrilineage, and by primogeniture (Wei 1958a; Li et al. 1963: 142ff.). For defense against headhunting, the villages in a drainage area have tended to form loosely organized, named federations or "tribes," termed by Atayal *qotox leliyung* (*leliong*), "those of one river." These so-called "tribes" were rarely political entities, and member villages usually retained political autonomy, with "tribal" chiefs emerging only in wartime and then only temporarily (Mabuchi 1966). For the Nanao Atayal, however, Li et al. (1963: 147ff.) describe a rather elaborate structure of villages organized into regional federations and these in turn into a single superconfederacy, with chiefs and subchiefs at all levels. **Social control.** Headmen and councils judge serious cases and impose fines, the amount of which is usually arbitrated by influential persons representing the two sides. The chief mechanism of social control is, however, the informal working of collective responsibility within the ritual group. He who violates the custom law (*gaga*) of the group sins against the group's ancestral spirits and thus endangers not only his own welfare but that of the entire group. Confession and atonement (pig sacrifice) are necessary lest crops fail or sickness descend. He who sins and fails to confess can be expelled from the group, a kind of ultimate sanction, since he thereby loses not only the group's cooperative labor but, more importantly, the protection of the ancestral spirits (Li et al. 1963: 121-65; Kojima 1915-22: *1*, 346ff.). Those to whom atonement is made, i.e. those whose taboo has been broken and whose ancestors have been thus offended, partake of sacrificed pig meat in a communal ritual known as *manyeq gaga* ("to eat according to the custom"). When thus engaged, they constitute a communion or feast group (*qotox neqan*) which may or may not be the equivalent of a village ritual group; in the southwest "homeland" a feast group may extend throughout the area of an entire village federation (Mabuchi 1960: 130). [Kojima 1915-22: *1*, 313-18, 367-83; Okada 1959; Li et al. 1963: 121-65.] **Social differentiation.** Although Mabuchi's (1966) denial of social or class stratification may hold generally, and perhaps particularly for the southwest "homeland" area, the traditional culture was not without gradations in social status, and it appears to have contained incipient patterns that relate to what are apparently later developments among certain "colonial" subgroups. The traditional culture recognized various degrees of individual achievement, symbolized by a rather elaborate system of graded insignia. Respected *gaga* heads, successful hunters, famed headhunters, and skilled weavers were entitled to such things as copper bracelets, red cloth, and shell-embroidered headbands, with the number and quality depending on degree of fame or expertise achieved. Demonstrated skill in weaving appears to have been intimately associated with the status of women, not only with respect to marriageability but also, apparently, with something like ritual maturity, e.g. a victorious headhunting party was welcomed by all the village women except those who were menstruating and those who did not weave well (Ho 1956: 192). Skilled weavers, like successful headhunters, were entitled to the distinctive Atayal facial tattoo. [Ho 1953, 1956: 170ff.; Chang 1953; Li et al. 1963: 85-87; Kojima 1915-22: *1*, 103; Okada 1959.] Among the

wealthier northern village federations, e.g. Gaogan, the children of the poor were sometimes sold to wealthy families, for whom they became household servants. Although such individuals had no political rights, they could be bought back again by their natal families and they could marry with the consent of their "owning" family. In such cases, the bride-price was considered just compensation and they were thereafter free. [Kojima 1915-22: *1*, 202-03; Okada 1959.] Among the contemporary Nanao in the extreme east and the Miaoli County groups bordering the western plains, as described by Li et al. and Ruey et al., respectively, there is evidence of some degree of social stratification based on wealth. It is unclear, however, whether such differentiation has evolved out of indigenous institutions or as a borrowing from lowland cultures. Nanao villages are loosely stratified by wealth in land and cattle, the latter presumably for sale in lowland markets. Although the landless, who may represent an earlier class of war captives or debt slaves, have no voice in *gaga* or village affairs, the system is open-ended, and vertical mobility is possible (Li et al. 1963: 142-43, 223-24). Among the Wenshui River Atayal in Miaoli County, so-called aristocrats own land and enjoy exclusive rights to ornaments and carved house posts. Aristocrat families demand high bride-prices for their daughters, and aristocrats are exempt from prosecution for certain crimes (Ruey et al. 1955). **Warfare.** Headhunting (*megaga*, "to follow the ancestral custom"), for which the Atayal were notorious, was endemic as late as 1910, but had been virtually eliminated by the 1920s under Japanese pacification. Although the villages in a drainage area (the village federation or "tribe") formed temporary alliances for offense or defense, the typical headhunting raid was carried out by a single individual accompanied by a few village mates. Formal military organizations and initiatory rites were lacking, although most young men participated in raids at one time or another. Disputes arose typically over boundaries of hunting territories, with raids organized chiefly for revenge and for acquisition of individual honor and prestige. The successful headhunter was entitled to special insignia, including the distinctive Atayal facial tattoo. According to T. J. Ho, an enemy head was a necessary accompaniment to ancestor sacrifice ceremonies, while the skull, teeth, and hair, in the form of amulets, provided spiritual protection. In addition, according to Ho, one's status in the afterworld depended in part on one's headhunting prowess while alive. A newly-taken head, with the brain removed, was placed in a net bag and carried to the home village, where it was feted with dancing, pig meat, and millet beer. Warriors drank a token potion of millet beer and blood poured from the head, after which it was added to those already on the village skull shelf in front of the chief's house. The spirits of all these heads became part of the collective *rutux* (spirits, including those of the ancestors) that guarded and protected the village from disaster (Li et al. 1963: 278). Cessation of hostilities was marked by a peace ceremony, which included the burying of a memorial stone. [Ho 1956; Kojima 1915-22: *1*, 357-84.]

RELIGION. **Supernaturals.** The well-developed pantheons of named deities characteristic of the Paiwanic peoples are lacking among the Atayalics. Instead, there are the rather vaguely defined *rutux* (*utux, liutux*), a kind of supernatural collectivity, the most important of which by far are the ancestral spirits, the source of all good and bad fortune among the living and the object of an annual round of ceremonial prayers and pig sacrifices. The rules and demands of the ancestral spirits are called *gaga*. He who faithfully observes or follows the ancestral *gaga* will prosper; he who fails to do so will suffer calamity. Those persons who follow a particular *gaga* heritage constitute a *qotox gaga* or ritual group (see above, under *Sociopolitical Organization*). A ritual group performs its own agricultural ceremonies, under the direction of a chief/priest, and its members cooperate in activities such as hunting, housebuilding, and swiddening. [Ferrell 1969a; Li et al. 1963: 310; Norbeck 1950.] **Practitioners.** *Gaga* chiefs, who also serve as priests in carrying out agricultural ceremonies on behalf of their *gagas,* must be skilled in the memorization of long prayers, the details of ritual procedures, and the knowledge of bird and celestial augury. Among the Nanao Atayal, curers (*mahgok*), who are mostly women, deal with illnesses attributed to ancestral spirits offended by a violation of *gaga*. Diagnosis is by divination, using a glass ball balanced on a horizontally-held bamboo tube. The practitioner prays to the spirits while rubbing the afflicted part with calamus root. Anyone can become *mahgok* by paying an established practitioner and acquiring, along with prayers and medicines, a special strain of millet handed down from teacher to pupil. [Li et al. 1963:

271, 286-87; Kojima 1915-22: *1*, 70-75, 83.] **Ceremonies.** Chiefly agricultural, having to do with sowing and harvesting of millet, wherein *gaga* priests perpetuate their respective strains of sacred millet by sowing and reaping from small ritual fields or plots maintained by each *gaga* group. There is mention of former headhunting ceremonies, and the association of headhunting with annual ancestor sacrifice ceremonies (cf. Okada 1959), but details are unclear, as is the association, if any, of these with the annual cycle of agricultural rituals. [Kojima 1915-22: *1*, 50ff.; Okada 1959; Yuan 1964; Li et al. 1963.] **Soul, death, and afterlife.** The Atayal of Nanao village believe the soul exists in the blood, signified by the beating of the pulse. At death the soul joins a vaguely defined collectivity, the *rutux*, assuming a benevolent guise if the death was a natural one. Burial in Nanao village is nowadays in a wooden coffin in a village cemetery. Formerly the corpse was arranged in a sitting position, with knees drawn up against the chest, wrapped in cloth bindings and interred in a slab-covered pit in the floor beneath the bed. Successive generations of household members continued to be buried in this manner until all available floor space was taken, whereupon the house was moved to a new site. Mourning for near relatives lasted up to one month, with apparently no elaboration of postfunerary or secondary burial rites. [Li et al. 1963: 99-110; Kojima 1915-22: *1*, 155-62.]

BIBLIOGRAPHY. deBeauclair 1956; Chang 1953, 1958; C. L. Chen 1956a, 1968; S. H. Chen et al. 1950; Ferrell 1967, 1969a, 1969b; Ho 1953, 1956; Kojima 1915-22; Kokubu and Kaneko 1962; Li et al. 1963; Mabuchi 1954c, 1960, 1966; Murdock 1960; Nettleship 1970; Norbeck 1950; Okada 1959; Ruey et al. 1955; Sayama 1913-21; Shih 1964; Suzuki 1932; Utsurikawa et al. 1935; Wei 1958a, 1963; Wei and Wang 1966; Yuan 1964.

BIBLIOGRAPHY

ABBREVIATIONS

AA   *American Anthropologist,* various places
BDAA   *Bulletin of the Department of Archaeology and Anthropology,* National Taiwan University, Taipei
BIE   *Bulletin of the Institute of Ethnology,* Academia Sinica, Taipei
Bijd.   *Bijdragen tot de Taal-, Land- en Volkenkunde van Nederlandsch-Indië,* Den Haag
IAE   *International Archives of Ethnography,* Leiden
JEAS   *Journal of East Asiatic Studies (University of Manila, Journal of East Asiatic Studies),* Manila
JRASMB   *Journal of the Royal Asiatic Society, Malayan Branch,* Singapore
JZ   *Jinruigaku Zasshi,* Tokyo
KT   *Koloniaal Tijdschrift,* Den Haag
MGK   *Minzokugaku-kenkyu,* Tokyo
MIE   *Monographs of the Institute of Ethnology,* Academia Sinica, Taipei
MNZ   *Mededeelingen van wege het Nederlandsch Zendelinggenootschap,* Rotterdam
ND   *Nampo Dozoku,* Taihoku, Formosa
OPDAA   *Occasional Papers of the Department of Archaeology and Anthropology,* National Taiwan University, Taipei
PJS   *Philippine Journal of Science,* Manila
PS   *Philippine Studies,* Manila
PSHR   *Philippine Social Sciences and Humanities Review,* Quezon City
PSR   *Philippine Sociological Review,* Quezon City
SMJ   *Sarawak Museum Journal,* Kuching
SWJA   *Southwestern Journal of Anthropology,* Albuquerque
Tijd.   *Tijdschrift voor Indische Taal-, Land- en Volkenkunde,* Batavia
TNAG   *Tijdschrift van het Koninklijk Nederlandsch Aardrijkskundig Genootschap,* Amsterdam, Utrecht, Leiden
TWC   *T'ai-wan wen-hsien chuan-k'an,* Taipei

Abueva, José V., and Raul P. de Guzman, eds.
   1969   *Foundations and dynamics of Filipino government and politics,* Manila, Bookmark.
Achutegui, Pedro S. de, and Miguel A. Bernad
   1961-69   *Religious revolution in the Philippines, Vol. 4,* 2d ed., rev. 1961; *Vol. 2,* 2d ed., rev. 1968; *Vol. 3,* 1969, Manila, Ateneo de Manila Press.
Agoncillo, Teodoro A.
   1965   *The fateful years: Japan's adventure in the Philippines, 1941-45,* 2 vols., Quezon City, R. P. Garcia.
Agoncillo, Teodoro A., and Oscar M. Alfonso
   1960   [1961] *A short history of the Filipino people,* Quezon City, University of the Philippines Press.
Ahern, Emily
   1973   *The cult of the dead in a Chinese village,* Stanford, Stanford University Press.
Alzona, Encarnacion
   1934 [?]   *The Filipino woman: her social, economic, and political status, 1565-1937* (rev.ed.), Manila, Benipayo Press.
American University, Foreign Area Studies
   1969   *Area handbook for the Republic of China,* Washington, D.C., U.S. Government Printing Office.
Amyot, Jacques
   1960   "The Chinese community in Manila," *University of Chicago, Philippine Studies Program, Research Series 2* (University of Chicago Ph.D. dissertation).

Anderson, Gerald, ed.
   1969   *Studies in Philippine church history,* Ithaca, Cornell University Press.
Appell, George N.
   n.d.   "Ethnographic notes on the Iranon Maranao (Illanun) of the Kudat District, Sabah," *Sabah Society Journal* (in press).
Aquino, Simon
   1954   "Life in Payee," *JEAS 3:* 561-611.
Arce, Wilfredo
   1963   "Social organization of the Muslim peoples of Sulu," *PS 11:* 242-66
Arens, Richard
   1956a   "Notes on camote rituals in Leyte and Samar Islands, Philippines," *PJS 85:* 343-47.
   1956b   "Witches and witchcraft in Leyte and Samar Islands, Philippines," *PJS 85:* 451-65.
   1956c   "Animism in the rice ritual of Leyte and Samar," *PSR 4:* 2-6.
Arong, José R.
   1962   "The Badjaw of Sulu," *PSR 10:* 134-46.
Asai, Erin
   1936   *A study of the Yami language, an Indonesian language spoken on Botel Tobago Island,* Leiden, J. Ginsberg (Ph.D. dissertation).

Bacdayan, Albert S.
   1967a   *The peace pact system of the Kalingas in the modern world,* Ithaca, Cornell University, Ph.D. dissertation (UM 67-12, 328).
   1967b   "Religious conversion and social reintegration in a western Bontoc village complex," *Saint Louis Quarterly 5:* 27-40.
Baguilat, Raymundo
   1940   "The Ifugao *hagabi,*" *Philippine Magazine 37:* 65.
Bailen, Jerome B.
   1967   "Studies in physical anthropology on the Philippines" in Mario D. Zamora, ed., *Studies in Philippine Anthropology,* Quezon City, Alemar-Phoenix: 527-58.
Barnard, Myra Lou, et al.
   1955   "Cotabato Manobo survey," *PSHR 20, no. 2:* 121-36.
Barnett, Milton L.
   1967   "Subsistence and transition of agricultural development among the Ibaloi," in Mario D. Zamora, ed., *Studies in Philippine Anthropology,* Quezon City, Alemar-Phoenix: 299-323.
Barnett, William K.
   1970   *An ethnographic description of Sanlei Ts'un, Taiwan, with emphasis on women's roles,* East Lansing, Michigan State University, Ph.D. dissertation (UM 71-2026).
Barrows, David P.
   1910a   "The Ilongot or Ibilao of Luzon," *Popular Science Monthly 77:* 521-37.
   1910b   "The Negrito and allied types in the Philippines," *AA 12:* 358-76.
Barton, Roy Franklin
   1919   "Ifugao law," *University of California Publications in American Archaeology and Ethnology 15:* 1-186.
   1922   "Ifugao economics," *University of California Publications in American Archaeology and Ethnology 15:* 385-446.

1930 *The half-way sun: life among the headhunters of the Philippines*, New York, Brewer and Warren.

1938 *Philippine pagans; the autobiographies of three Ifugaos*, London, Routledge.

1946 "The religion of the Ifugaos," *American Anthropological Association Memoir 65*: 1-219.

1949 *The Kalingas: their institutions and custom law*, Chicago, University of Chicago Press.

1955 "The mythology of the Ifugaos," *American Folklore Society Memoirs 46*: 1-244.

Bean, R. B.
1910 *Racial anatomy of the Philippine Islanders*, Philadelphia, J. B. Lippincott.

Beauclair, Inez de
1956 "Present-day conditions of the aborigines of Formosa (Atayal and Bunun)," *Sociologus 6*: 153-69.

1957 "Field notes on Lan Yü (Botel Tobago)," *BIE 3*: 101-16.

1958 "Fighting and weapons of the Yami of Botel Tobago," *BIE 5*: 87-114.

1959a "Three genealogical stories from Botel Tobago," *BIE 7*: 105-40.

1959b "Display of wealth, gift exchange and food distribution on Botel Tobago," *BIE 8*: 185-210.

1969a "Ethnological research on the Babuyan Islands," *International Committee on Urgent Anthropological and Ethnological Research, Bulletin 11*: 9-12.

1969b "Gold and silver on Botel Tobago: the silver helmet of the Yami," *BIE 27*: 121-27.

1970a "Dutch beads on Formosa? An ethnohistorical note," *BIE 29*: 385-93.

1970b "A note on the Dutch period of Formosa 1622-1662," *BIE 29*: 395-97.

Bello, Moises C.
1967 "Some observations on beliefs and rituals of the Bakun-Kankanay," in Mario D. Zamora, ed., *Studies in Philippine Anthropology*, Quezon City, Alemar-Phoenix: 324-42.

Benedict, Laura Watson
1913 "Bagobo myths," *Journal of American Folklore 26*: 13-63.

1916 "A study of Bagobo ceremonial, magic and myth," *New York Academy of Science, Annals 25*: 1-308.

Bewsher, R. A.
1956 "Bisayan accounts of early Bornean settlements in the Philippines recorded by Father Santaren," *SMJ 7*: 48-53.

Beyer, H. Otley
1912-23 *Beyer Collection of Filipiniana, Section A: History and Ethnology of the Philippine Peoples*, 33 vols., Yale University Library-Yale Anthropology Department (from microfilm of volumes in Harvard University, Peabody Museum of Archaeology and Ethnology, 1966).

1917 *Population of the Philippine Islands in 1916*, Manila, Philippine Education Company.

1947 "Outline review of Philippine archaeology by islands and provinces," *PJS 77*: 205-374.

1948 "Philippine and East Asian archaeology, and its relation to the origin of the Pacific Islands population," *National Research Council of the Philippines, Bulletin 29*: 1-130.

Beyer, H. O., and Roy F. Barton
1911 "An Ifugao burial ceremony," *PJS 6*: 227-52.

Birket-Smith, Kaj
1952 "The rice cultivation and rice harvest feast of the Bontoc Igorot," *Det Kongelige Danske Videnskabernes Selskab, Historisk-filologiske Meddelelser 32*: 1-22.

Blair, Emma H., and James A. Robertson
1903-09 *The Philippine Islands 1493-1898*, 55 vols., Cleveland, Arthur Clark.

Blumentritt, Ferdinand
1896 "Die Nachrichten der Jesuiter missionaere P. Francisco Sanches, P. Llobera und P. Peruga über die Negritos von Mindanao oder die Mamanuas," *IAE 9*: 251-52.

Bornemann, Fritz
1955 "J. M. Garvan's Materialien über die Negritos der Philipinen und P. W. Schmidt's Notizen dazu," *Anthropos 50*: 899-930.

Brilman, D.
1937 *De zending op de Sangi-en Talaud eilanden [The Mission on the Sangihe- and Talaud archipelago]*, Oestgeest, Uitgegeven van den Zendings-studieraad.

Bulatao, Jaime
1962 "Philippine values I: the Manileño's mainsprings," *PS 10*: 45-81.

Cameron, C. R.
1917 *Sulu writing*, Zamboanga.

Campbell, William
1903 *Formosa under the Dutch, described from contemporary records*, London, Kegan Paul.

Candidius, Georgius
1628 "Discours ende cort Verhael van't eylant Formosa [Short account of the inhabitants of Formosa]," reported in S. Van Rechteren, *Journal Gehouden op de reyse ende wederkomste van Oost-Indien*, Zwolle, 1639. [Translated into English in Campbell 1903: 9-25.]

Carroll, John J.
1960 "The word Bisaya in the Philippines and Borneo," *SMJ 9*: 499-541.

Carson, Arthur
1961 *Higher education in the Philippines*, Washington, D.C., U.S. Department of Health, Education, and Welfare, *Bulletin No. 29*.

Casiño, Eric S.
1966 "Lunsay: song-dance of the Jama Mapun of Sulu," *Asian Studies 4*: 316-23.

1967a "Jama Mapun ethnoecology: economic and symbolic," *Asian Studies 5*: 1-32.

1967b "Folk-Islam in the life cycle of the Jama Mapun," *PSR 15*: 34-43.

Cawed-Oteyza, Carmencita
1965 "The culture of the Bontoc Igorots," *Unitas 38*: 317-77.

Cense, A. A., and E. M. Uhlenbeck
1958 *Critical survey of studies on the languages of Borneo*, 's-Gravenhage; Martinus Nijhoff.

Chabot, H. Th.
1969 "Processes of change in Siau," *Bijd. 125*: 94-102.

Chang, Kwang-chih
1953 "Pen-hsi so ts'ang T'ai-wan Atayal-tsu pei-chu piao-pen [Shell beads of the Atayal tribe in the Department collections]," *BDAA 2*: 29-34.

1957 "On the 'Polynesian' complexes in Formosa," *BIE 3*: 89-97.

1958 "T'ai-wan t'u-chu peo-chu wen-hua ts'ung chi ch'i ch'i-yüan yü ch'uan-po [On the shell-bead money complex in Formosa, the Pacific, and the New World]," *Ethnological Society of China, Bulletin 2*: 53-133.

1969 "Fengpitou, Tapenkeng, and the prehistory of Taiwan," *Yale University Publications in Anthropology 73*.

1970 "Prehistoric archaeology of Taiwan," *Asian Perspectives 13*: 59-77.

Chang, Kwang-chih, and Minze Stuiver
1966 "Recent advances in the prehistoric archaeology of Formosa," *National Academy of Sciences, Proceedings 55:* 539-43.

Chang, Yao-ch'i
1955 "Paiwan-tsu chih sheng-ming li-su [Rites of passage among the Paiwan]," *Tai-wan Wen-hsien 6:* 59-67.

Chen, Cheng-hsi
1952 "Taiwan ai-jen ti ku-shih [Story of Negritoes in Taiwan]," *Taiwan Fengwu 2:* 25-28, 39-40.

Chen, Chi-lu
1955 "Tai-wan P'ing-tung Wu-t'ai Rukai-tsu ti chia-tsu ho hun-yin [Family and marriage among the Budai Rukai of Pingtung, Taiwan]," *Ethnological Society of China, Bulletin 1:* 103-23.
1956a "Atayal-tsu ti jih-ch'ang sheng-ho [Daily life of the Atayal]," *BDAA 7:* 56-59.
1956b "Tai-wan P'ing-tung Wu-t'ai Rukai-tsu ti nung-keng fang-fa ho nung-keng i-li [Agricultural methods and rituals of the Budai Rukai of Pingtung, Taiwan]," *Studia Taiwanica 1:* 53-77.
1958a "A cultural configuration of the island of Formosa," *Ethnological Society of China, Bulletin 2:* 1-10.
1958b "Houses and woodcarving of the Budai Rukai," *Ethnological Society of China, Bulletin 2:* 33-52.
1961 "Tai-wan Paiwan-ch'ün chu-tsu mu-tiao piao-pen t'u-lu [Woodcarving of the Paiwan of Taiwan]," *OPDAA 2:* 1-198.
1965 "Age organization and men's house of the Formosan aborigines," *BDAA 25-26:* 93-111.
1966 "Tai-wan Paiwan-ch'ün ti ku liu-li chu chi ch'i ch'uan-ju nien-tai ti t'ui-ts'e [Old glass beads possessed by the Paiwan group of Taiwan and their date of introduction]," *BDAA 28:* 1-6 (English version appears in author's *Material culture of the Formosan aborigines,* chapter 9).
1968 *Material culture of the Formosan aborigines,* Taipei, Taiwan Museum.

Chen, Chi-lu, and Michael D. Coe
1954 "An investigation of Ami religion," *Quarterly Journal of the Taiwan Museum 7:* 249-62.

Chen, Chi-lu, et al.
1958 "Jih-Yüeh-t'an Thao-tsu tiao-ch'a pao'kao [Ethnological researches among the Thao of Sun-Moon Lake, Formosa]," *OPDAA 1:* 1-166.

Chen, Chun-chin
1967 "Tung-ho ts'un sai-hia tsu chih jen-k'ou yü chia-tsu [Population and family system of the Tungho Saisiat]," *BIE 23:* 141-65.

Chen, Kang-chai
1967 *Taiwan aborigines: a genetic study of tribal variation,* Cambridge, Harvard University Press.

Chen, Shao-hsin, et al.
1950 "Shan-ti wen-hua t'e-chi: Rui-yen min-tsu-hsüeh ch'u-pu tiao-ch'a [Special issue on aboriginal culture: report of preliminary ethnological investigations among the Masitobaon Atayal]," *TWC 2:* 1-79.

Chijiiwa, Suketaro
1960 *Taiwan takasagozoku no juka [Houses of the Formosan aborigines],* Tokyo, Maruzen.

Chiu, Chi-chien
1962 "Ch'ia (K'a)-she ch'ün Bunun-tsu ti ch'in-tsu tsu-chih [The kinship organization of the Takebaka Bunun]," *BIE 13:* 133-93.
1964 "Bunun-tsu Ch'ia (K'a)-she ch'ün ti wu-shu [The magic of the Takebaka Bunun]," *BIE 17:* 73-94.
1966 "Bunun-tsu Ch'ia (K'a)-she ch'ün ti she-hui tsu-chih [Social organization of the Takebaka Bunun]," *MIE 7:* 1-266.

Chrétien, Douglas
1963 "A classification of twenty-one Philippine languages," *PJS 91:* 485-506.

Christie, Emerson B.
1909 "The Subanuns of Sindangan Bay," *Bureau of Science, Division of Ethnology Publications 6:* pt. 1, Manila, Bureau of Printing.

Claerhoudt, Alfonso
1966 "The song of a people: Igorot customs in eastern Benguet," *Saint Louis Quarterly 4:* 159-278.

Clifford, Sister Mary Dorita, B.V.N.
1969 "*Iglesia Filipina Independendiente:* The Revolutionary Church," in Gerald Anderson, ed., *Studies in Philippine Church History,* Ithaca, Cornell University Press: 223-55.

Clotet, Fr. José
1889 "Letter from Father José Maria Clotet, Talisayan, May 11, 1889," [Translated by Frank Lynch, S.J., for University of Chicago, Philippine Studies Program, Conference on Mindanao, May 1955 (mimeographed) from *Cartas de los PP. de la Compañia de Jesus de la Mision de Filipinas 9:* 170-84, Manila, 1891].

Coe, Michael D.
1955 "Shamanism in the Bunun tribe, central Formosa," *Ethnos 20:* 181-98.

Cole, Fay-Cooper
1913 "The wild tribes of Davao District, Mindanao," *Field Museum of Natural History, Anthropological Series 12:* 49-203.
1915 "Traditions of the Tinguian," *Field Museum of Natural History, Anthropological Series 14:* 1-226.
1922 "The Tinguian: social, religious, and economic life of a Philippine tribe," *Field Museum of Natural History, Anthropological Series 14:* 231-493.
1945 *The peoples of Malaysia,* New York, van Nostrand.
1956 "The Bukidnon of Mindanao," *Chicago Natural History Museum, Fieldiana: Anthropology 46.*

Combés, Francisco, S. J.
1906 "Historia de las islas de Mindanao, Iolo, y sus adyacentes" (translated in E. H. Blair and J. A. Robertson, eds., *The Philippine Islands 1492-1898,* Cleveland, Arthur H. Clark, 1906: vol. 40, chap. 9).

Concepcion, Mercedes B.
1966 "Analysis and projections of the population of the Philippines," in *First Conference on Population, 1965,* Quezon City, University of the Philippines Press.

Conklin, Harold C.
1949a "Preliminary report on field work on the islands of Mindoro and Palawan, Philippines," *AA 51:* 268-73.
1949b "Bamboo literacy on Mindoro," *Pacific Discovery 2:* 4-11.
1952 "Outline gazetteer of native Philippine ethnic and linguistic groups," New Haven (mimeographed).
1953a "Buhid pottery," *JEAS 3:* 1-12.
1953b "Hanunóo-English vocabulary," *University of California Publications in Linguistics 9:* 1-290.
1954a "An ethnoecological approach to shifting agriculture," *New York Academy of Sciences, Transactions 17:* 133-42.
1954b *The relation of Hanunóo culture to the plant world,* New Haven, Yale University, unpublished Ph.D. thesis (film).
1955a "Hanunóo color categories," *SWJA 11:* 339-44.
1955b "Hanunóo music from the Philippines," *Ethnic Folkways Library Album P 466,* New York, Folkways Records and Service Corporation.
1955c *Preliminary linguistic survey of Mindanao,* Univer-

sity of Chicago, Philippine Studies Program, Mindanao Conference Paper (mimeographed).

1957 *Hanunóo agriculture: a report on an integral system of shifting cultivation in the Philippines*, United Nations, FAO Forestry Development Paper No. 12.

1958 *Betel chewing among the Hanunóo*, Quezon City, National Research Council of the Philippines.

1960a "The cultural significance of land resources among the Hanunóo," *Philadelphia Anthropological Society, Bulletin 13:* 38-42.

1960b "Maling, a Hanunóo girl from the Philippines," in Joseph B. Casagrande, ed., *In the Company of Man*, New York, Harper and Row: 101-18.

1964 "Ethnogenealogical method," in Ward H. Goodenough, ed., *Explorations in Cultural Anthropology: Essays in Honor of George Peter Murdock*, New York, McGraw-Hill: 25-55.

1967a "Ifugao ethnobotany 1905-1965: the 1911 Beyer-Merrill Report in perspective," *Economic Botany 21:* 243-72.

1967b "Some aspects of ethnographic research in Ifugao," *New York Academy of Sciences, Transactions 30:* 99-121.

1968 "Ifugao bibliography," *Yale University, Southeast Asia Studies, Bibliography Series 11.*

1972 "Land use in north central Ifugao," New York, American Geographical Society (a set of 8 maps).

1973 Personal communication (February 1973).

Cooper, John M.
1940 "Andamanese-Semang-Eta cultural relations," *Primitive Man 13:* 29-47.

Corpuz, O. D.
1966 *The Philippines*, Englewood Cliffs, New Jersey, Prentice-Hall.

Daguio, Amador Taguinod
1952 *Hudhud hi Aliguyon: a translation of an Ifugao harvest song with introduction and notes*, Stanford University, unpublished M.A. thesis.

Dapper, O.
1670 *Gedenkwaerdig Bedryf der Nederlandsche Oost-Indische Maetschappye, op de Kuste en in het Keizerrijk van Taising of Sina . . .*, Amsterdam, 1670. [Contains David Wright's "Account of the natives of Formosa," written about 1650.]

Davenport, William
1959 "Nonunilinear descent and descent groups," *AA 61:* 557-72.

Davidson, James W.
1905 *The island of Formosa, past and present*, London, Kelly and Walsh.

Davis, William G., and Mary Hollnsteiner
1969 "Some recent trends in Philippine social anthropology," *Anthropologica, n.s. 11:* 59-84.

Demetrio, Francisco, S. J.
1966 "Death: its origin and related beliefs among the early Filipinos," *PS 14:* 355-95.

DeRaedt, Jules
1964 "Religious representations in northern Luzon," *University of Chicago, Philippine Studies Program, Research Series no. 4* (reprinted from *Saint Louis Quarterly 2:* 245-348).

Diamond, Norma
1969 *K'un Shen: a Taiwan village*, New York, Holt, Rinehart and Winston.

Dinter, B. C. A. J. van
1899 "Eenige geographische en ethnographische aanteekeningen betreffende het eiland Siaoe [Some geographical and ethnological annotations on the island Siau]," *Tijd. 41:* 324-90.

Dozier, Edward P.
1966 *Mountain arbiters: the changing life of a Philippine hill people*, Tucson, University of Arizona Press.

1967 *The Kalinga of northern Luzon, Philippines*, New York, Holt, Rinehart and Winston.

Ducommun, Dolores
1962 "Sisangat: a fishing community of Sulu," *PSR 10:* 91-106.

Dutch East Indies
1933-36 Department van Economische Zaken, Tijdelijk Kantoor voor de Volkstelling [Department of Economic Affairs. Interim Office of the Census], *Volkstelling 1930*, 8 vols., Batavia, Landsdrukkerij.

Dyen, Isidore
1963 "The position of the Malayopolynesian languages of Formosa," *Asian Perspectives 7:* 261-71.

1965 "A lexicostatistical classification of the Austronesian languages," *Indiana University Publications in Anthropology and Linguistics, Memoir 19, International Journal of American Linguistics.*

1971 "The Austronesian languages of Formosa," *Current Trends in Linguistics 8:* 169-99.

Eggan, Fred
1941 "Some aspects of culture change in the northern Philippines," *AA 43:* 11-18.

1954 "Some social institutions in the Mountain Province and their significance for historical and comparative studies," *JEAS 3:* 329-35.

1956 "Ritual myths among the Tinguian," *Journal of American Folklore 69:* 331-39.

1960 "The Sagada Igorots of northern Luzon," in George Peter Murdock, ed., *Social Structure in Southeast Asia*, Chicago, Quadrangle Books: 24-50.

1963 "Cultural drift and social change," *Current Anthropology 4:* 329-35.

1967 "Some aspects of bilateral social systems in the northern Philippines," in Mario D. Zamora, ed., *Studies in Philippine Anthropology, in Honor of H. Otley Beyer*, Quezon City, Alemar-Phoenix: 186-202.

1968 "Philippine social structure," in George M. Guthrie, ed., *Six Perspectives on the Philippines*, Manila, Bookmark: 1-48.

Eggan, Fred, et al.
1956 *Area Handbook on the Philippines*, 4 vols., New Haven, Human Relations Area Files.

Eggan, Fred, and Alfredo Pacyaya
1962 "The Sapilada religion: reformation and accommodation among the Igorots of northern Luzon," *SWJA 18:* 95-113.

Eggan, Fred, and William H. Scott
1963 "Ritual life of the Igorots of Sagada: from birth to adolescence," *Ethnology 2:* 40-45.

1965 "Ritual life of the Igorots of Sagada: courtship and marriage," *Ethnology 4:* 77-111.

Elkins, Richard E.
1964 "The Anit taboo: a Manobo cultural unit," *Practical Anthropology 11:* 185-88.

1968a *Manobo-English dictionary*, Honolulu, University of Hawaii Press.

1968b "Three models of Western Bukidnon Manobo kinship," *Ethnology 7:* 171-90.

Elkins, Richard E., et al.
1969-70 Personal communication from Richard Elkins and members of the Summer Institute of Linguistics, Malaybalay, Bukidnon, consisting of linguistic maps and other data relative to the preliminary definition of a Manobo family of languages on Mindanao, December 1969 and June 1970.

Elwood, Douglas J.
1968   *Churches and sects in the Philippines: a descriptive study of contemporary religious group movements,* Dumaguete City, Philippines, Silliman University.

Eslao, Nina
1966   "The development cycle of the Philippine household in an urban setting," *PSR* 14: 199-208.

Esser, S. J.
1938   "Talan [Languages]," in *Atlas van Tropisch Nederland. Het Koninklijk Aardrijkskundig Genootschap in Samenwerking met den Topografischen Dienst in Nederlandsch-Indies,* 's-Gravenhage, M. Nijhoff.

Estel, Leo
1952   "Racial types on Mindoro," *JEAS* 1: 21-31.
1953   "Racial origin in northern Indonesia," *JEAS* 2: 1-20.

Ferrell, Raleigh
1966   "Myths of the Tsou," *BIE* 22: 169-81.
1967   *Atayal vocabulary (Sqolyeq dialect), selected and translated from Naoyoshi Ogawa's "Atayaru Goshu" (Japanese-Atayal word book, Taihoku 1932),* Taipei.
1968   "Negrito ritual and tradition of small people on Taiwan," in N. Matsumoto and T. Mabuchi, eds., *Folk Religion and the Worldview in the Southwestern Pacific,* Tokyo, Keio Institute of Cultural and Linguistic Studies: 63-72.
1969a   "Taiwan aboriginal groups: problems in cultural and linguistic classification," *MIE* 17: 1-445.
1969b   "Paiwanic ethno-linguistic groups of the west-central Taiwan 'black pottery' culture area," *BIE* 28: 159-96.
1971   "Aboriginal peoples of the southwestern Taiwan plain," *BIE* 32: 217-35.

Flores-Meiser, Enya P.
1969   "Division and integration in a Sibutu barrio (Sulu, Philippines)," in Mario D. Zamora and Zeus A. Salazar, eds., *Anthropology: Range and Relevance,* Quezon City, Kayumanggi Publishers.

Folkmar, Daniel K.
1906   *Social institutions of the Tinglayan Igorot,* original manuscript, H. O. Beyer Collection, Manila (typescript copies in the University of Chicago, Philippine Studies Program).

Formosa, Bureau of Aboriginal Affairs
1911   *Report on the control of the aborigines,* Taihoku, Formosa.

Forrest, Thomas (Capt.)
1779   *A voyage to New Guinea, and the Moluccas, from Balambangan: including an account of Magindanao, Sooloo, and other islands,* London, G. Scott.

Fox, Robert B.
1953a   "The Pinatubo Negritos: their useful plants and material culture," *PJS* 81: 173-414.
1953b   "Social aspects of the rice-wine complex among the Tagbanuwa of Palawan Island, Philippines," *Eighth Pacific Science Congress, Abstracts of Papers,* Quezon City, Philippines.
1954   *Religion and society among the Tagbanuwa of Palawan Island, Philippines,* Ph.D. dissertation, Department of Anthropology, University of Chicago.
1956   "Culture history," in Fred Eggan et al., *Area Handbook on the Philippines,* 4 vols., New Haven, Human Relations Area Files: 250-62.
1957   "A consideration of theories concerning possible affiliations of Mindanao cultures with Borneo, the Celebes, and other regions of the Philippines," *PSR* 5: 2-21.
1967   "Excavations in the Tabon Caves and some problems in Philippine chronology," in Mario D. Zamora, ed., *Studies in Philippine Anthropology in*

Honor of H. Otley Beyer, Quezon City, Alemar-Phoenix: 88-116.

Fox, Robert B., et al.
1965   "A preliminary glottochronology for northern Luzon," *Asian Studies* 3: 103-13.

Frake, Charles O.
1957   "The Subanun of Zamboanga: a linguistic survey," *Ninth Pacific Science Association Congress, Proceedings* 3: 93.
1960   "The Eastern Subanun of Mindanao," in George Peter Murdock, ed., *Social Structure in Southeast Asia,* Chicago, Quadrangle Books: 51-64.
1964   "A structural description of Subanun 'religious behavior'," in Ward H. Goodenough, ed., *Explorations in Cultural Anthropology: Essays in Honor of George Peter Murdock,* New York, McGraw-Hill: 111-29.
1967   *Social organization and shifting cultivation among the Sindangan Subanun,* New Haven, Yale University, Department of Anthropology, Ph.D. dissertation (University Microfilms 67-4151).
1969   "Struck by speech: the Yakan concept of litigation," in Laura Nader, ed., *Law in Culture and Society,* New York, Aldine: 147-67.

Francisco, Juan R.
1963   "Indian influence in the Philippines: with special reference to language and literature," *PSHR* 27: 1-310.
1966   "Palaeographic studies in the Philippines," *SMJ* 13: 417-26.

Frei, Ernest J.
1959   *The historical development of the Philippines national language,* Manila, Bureau of Printing.

Fresnoza, Florencio
1957   *Essentials of the Philippine education system,* Manila, Abiva Publishing House.

Friend, Theodore
1965   *Between two empires: the ordeal of the Philippines, 1929-1946,* New Haven, Yale University Press.

Frieswijk, E.
1902   "Aanteekeningen betreffende de geographische en ethnographischen toestand van het eiland Tahoelandang [Annotations on the geographical and ethnological situation of the island Tahulandang]," *Tijd. BB* 22: 426-39, 469-89.

Furuno, Kiyoto
1940   "Saisiat-zoku no suii girei [Rites of passage of the Saisiat tribe]," *MGK* 6: 19-53.
1945   *Takasagozoku no saigi seikatsu [Religious life of the Formosan aborigines],* Tokyo, Sanseido.

Gallin, Bernard
1966   *Hsin Hsing, Taiwan: a Chinese village in change,* Berkeley, University of California Press.

Gardner, Fletcher, and I. Maliwanag
1939-41 *Indic writings of the Mindoro-Palawan axis,* 3 vols., San Antonio, Witte Memorial Museum.

Garvan, John M.
1931   *The Manobos of Mindanao,* Washington, D.C., U.S. Government Printing Office.
1963   "The Negritos of the Philippines," edited by Hermann Hochegger, *Wiener Beiträge zur Kulturgeschichte und Linguistik* 14 (printed in 1964). [Original manuscripts reproduced in microfilm and published as *Vol. 19* of the Micro-Bibliotheca Anthropos.]

Geoghegan, William H.
1969   "Decision-making and residence on Tagtabon Island," *Working Paper No. 17, Language-Behavior Research Laboratory,* Berkeley, University of California.

Gisbert, Fr. Mateo
1892 *Diccionario Bagobo-Español*, Manila, Establ. Tipo-Lito. de Ramirez.
1902 "The Conquest of Davao," in H. Otley Beyer, comp., *Philippine Ethnographic Series, Moro Set 4, Paper 40.*

Gloria, Manuel
1939 "A visit to the Negritos of Central Panay, Philippine Islands," *Primitive Man 12:* 94-102.

Golay, Frank
1961 *The Philippines: public policy and national economic development*, Ithaca, Cornell University Press.

Gonzalez, Mary
1965 "The Ilongo kinship system and terminology," *PSR 13:* 23-30.

Gonzalez Alonso, Fr. Julio
1966 "The Batanes Islands," *Acta Manilana 2:* 1-136.

Goodenough, Ward H.
1955 "A problem in Malayo-Polynesian social organization," *AA 57:* 71-83.

Gowing, Peter G.
1964 *Mosque and Moro, a study of Muslims in the Philippines*, Manila, Philippine Federation of Christian Churches.
1967 *Islands under the Cross*, Manila, National Council of Churches in the Philippines.

Grossholtz, Jean
1964 *Politics in the Philippines*, Boston, Little, Brown.

Guthrie, George M., ed.
1968 *Six perspectives on the Philippines*, Manila, Bookmark.

Guthrie, George M., and Pepita Jimenez Jacobs
1966 *Child rearing and personality development in the Philippines*, University Park, Pennsylvania State University Press.

Hall, D. G. E.
1968 *A history of South-East Asia*, New York, St. Martin's Press (reprint of 1955 edition).

Happart, Rev. Gilbertus
1650 *Woord-Boek der Favorlangsche Taal* [translated by W. H. Medhurst, *Dictionary of the Favorlang Dialect of the Formosan language, by Gilbertus Happart, written in 1650*, Batavia 1840, and reprinted in W. Campbell, *The Articles of Christian Instruction in Favorlang-Formosan, Dutch and English, from Vertrecht's ms. of 1650*], London, Kegan Paul, Trench, Trübner, 1896, pp. 122-99.

Hart, Donn V.
1954 *Barrio Caticugan: a Visayan Filipino community*, unpublished Ph.D. dissertation, Syracuse University (Source No. 20 in HRAF OA1 Philippines File).
1959 *The Cebuan Filipino dwelling in Caticugan: its construction and cultural aspects*, New Haven, Yale University, Southeast Asia Studies.
1961 *The Philippine plaza complex: a focal point in culture change*, New Haven, Yale University, Southeast Asia Studies.
1965 "From pregnancy through birth in a Bisayan Filipino village," in Donn V. Hart, Phya Anuman Rajadhon and Richard J. Coughlin, *Southeast Asian Birth Customs: Three Studies in Human Reproduction*, New Haven, HRAF Press: 1-113.
1966 "The Filipino farmer and his spirits," *Solidarity 1:* 65-71.
1969 "Bisayan Filipino and Malayan humoral pathologies: folk medicine and ethnohistory in Southeast Asia," Ithaca, Cornell University, *Southeast Asia Studies, Data Paper No. 76.*

Hayden, Joseph R.
1942 *The Philippines: a study in National development*, New York, Macmillan.

Heine-Geldern, Robert
1923 "Südost Asien," in Georg Buschan, ed., *Illustriete Völkerkunde*, Stuttgart, Schrecker und Schröder: Bd. 2: 689-968.

Hickson, S. J.
1889 *A naturalist in North Celebes*, London, J. Murray.

Himes, Ronald S.
1964 "The Bontok kinship system," *PSR 12:* 159-72.

Ho, Ting-jui
1953 "Pen-hsi so ts'ang Atayal-tsu lieh-t'ou i'shih piaopen [Clothing and ornaments related to Atayal headhunting in the Department collections]," *BDAA 2:* 22-29.
1955 "P'ing-tung hsien Lai-i hsiang Paiwan-tsu chih wen-shen yü lieh-t'ou [Tattooing and headhunting of the Chala'abus Paiwan, Pingtung]," *BDAA 6:* 47-49.
1956 "Atayal-tsu lieh-t'ou hsi-su chih yen-chiu [A study of the Atayal headhunters of Taiwan]," *College of Arts, Bulletin 7:* 151-208.
1958 "Bunun-tsu ti su-tso chi-i [Millet rituals of the Bunun]," *BDAA 11:* 92-100.
1967 *A comparative study of myths and legends of Formosan aborigines*, 2 vols., unpublished Ph.D. dissertation, Indiana University (UM 68-7250).

Hoebel, E. Adamson
1949 "Introduction," in Roy F. Barton, *The Kalingas, Their Institutions and Custom Law*, Chicago, University of Chicago Press.
1954 *The law of primitive man*, Cambridge, Harvard University Press.

Hollnsteiner, Mary
1963 *The dynamics of power in a Philippine municipality*, Quezon City, Community Development Research Council.
1967 "Inner Tondo as a way of life," *Saint Louis Quarterly 5:* 13-26.

Hsieh, Jih-chang
1967 "Ta-nan lu-kai tsu hun-yin [Marriage among the Taromak Rukai]," *BIE 23:* 195-227.
1968 "Ta-nan lu-kai tsu chia-hsi chih ch'ih-hsü [Continuation of the family line among the Taromak Rukai]," *BIE 26:* 67-81.

Huang, Shu-ching
1736 "Fan Su Liu K'ao [Six studies of savage customs]," vols. 5-7 in his *T'ai Hai Shih Ch'a Lu [Record of Inquiries in the Taiwan Seas]*, reprinted by the Bank of Taiwan, 1957.

Huke, Robert E., et al.
1963 *Shadows on the land: an economic geography of the Philippines*, Manila, Bookmark.

Hunt, Chester L.
1954 *Cotabato: melting pot of the Philippines: a study on population distribution in and integration of a non-homogenous community*, Manila, UNESCO National Commission of the Philippines.

Isidro, Antonio
1968a *Muslim Christian integration at the Mindanao State University*, University Research Center, Mindanao State University, Marawi City, Philippines.
1968b *Muslim Philippines*, University Research Center, Mindanao State University, Marawi City, Philippines.

Jen, Shien-min
1958 "Hua-lien hsien Ta-pa-lang Ami-tsu ti tsu tz'u [Ancestor house of the Ami tribe at Tavarong]," *BIE 6:* 79-106.

1960 "Tai-wan Paiwan-tsu ti ku t'ao hu [Ancient precious pottery of the Paiwan]," *BIE 9:* 163-224.

Jenks, Albert Ernest
1905 "The Bontoc Igorot," *Department of the Interior Ethnological Survey Publications 1:* 1-266.

Jocano, F. Landa
1958a "The Sulod: a mountain people in central Panay, Philippines," *PS 6:* 401-36.
1958b "Corn and rice rituals among the Sulod of central Panay, Philippines," *PJS 87:* 455-72.
1964 "Notes on the Sulod concept of death, the soul, and the region of the dead," *PS 12:* 51-62.
1966 "Rethinking 'smooth interpersonal relations'," *PSR 14:* 282-91.
1968 *Sulod society: a study of the kinship system and social organization of a mountain people of central Panay,* Quezon City, University of the Philippines Press (*Institute of Asian Studies, Monograph Series 2*).
1969 *Growing up in a Philippine barrio,* New York, Holt, Rinehart and Winston.

Jones, William
1908-09 *The diary of William Jones,* Natural History Museum (typescript).

Kaneko, Erika
1957 "Totenausrichtung und Besiedlungsgeschichte bei den Bergstämmen von Formosa," *Wiener Völkerkundliche Mitteilungen 5:* 102-26.

Kano, Tadao
1936 "Kotosho Yamizoku no shussan ni kansuru fushu [Customs concerning birth among the Yami]," *ND 5:* 6-17.
1938a "Kotosho Yamizoku no awa ni kansuru nokogirei [Millet ritual among the Yami of Botel Tobago]," *MGK 4:* 35-48 (reprinted in *Studies in the Ethnology and Prehistory of Southeast Asia 1* (1946): 380-97.
1938b "Kotosho Yamizoku no oobune kenzo to funamatsuri [Boat-building and associated ritual among the Yami of Botel Tobago]," *JZ 53:* 125-46.
1941a "Kotosho nakken no okan [Burial jar found on Botel Tobago]," *JZ 56:* 117-32.
1941b "Doshokubutsumei yori mitaru Kotosho to Batan shoto to no ruien kankei [Cultural affinities of the Batan Islands and Botel Tobago as viewed from plant and animal names]," *JZ 56:* 434-45.
1941c "Fuirippin shoto, Kotosho narabi ni Taiwan no genju minzoku ni okeru kinbunka [Gold culture among the aborigines of the Philippines, Botel Tobago and Formosa]," *JZ 56:* 465-75.
1944 "Kotosho Yamizoku to tobiuo [The Yami of Botel Tobago and flying fish]," in Yoshitaro Hirano, ed., *Taiheiyoken: Minzoku to bunka [The Pacific Area: Peoples and Cultures],* vol. 1, Tokyo, Kawade Shobo: 503-73.
1946-52 *Tonan Ajiya minzokugaku senshigaku kenkyu [Studies in the ethnology and prehistory of Southeast Asia],* Tokyo, Yashima-shobo (2 vols., both posthumous: *Vol. 1,* 1946; *Vol. 2,* 1952, edited by K. Segawa and T. Mabuchi).

Kano, Tadao, and Kokichi Segawa
1956 *An illustrated ethnography of Formosan aborigines, Vol. 1, The Yami,* Tokyo, Maruzen.

Kaut, Charles
1961 "'Utang na Loob': a system of contractual obligation among Tagalogs," *SWJA 18:* 256-72.

Kavanagh, Joseph J.
1955 "The Iglesia ni Cristo," *PS 3:* 19-42.

Keesing, Felix M.
1938 "Population and land utilization among the Lepanto, northern Philippines," *Congrés International de Geographie, Comptes rendus 2 (3-C):* 458-64.
1949 "Some notes on Bontok social organization, northern Philippines," *AA 51:* 578-601.
1962a *The ethnohistory of northern Luzon,* Stanford, Stanford University Press.
1962b "The Isneg: shifting cultivators of the northern Philippines," *SWJA 18:* 1-19.

Keesing, Felix M., and Marie Keesing
1934 *Taming Philippine headhunters: a study of government and of cultural change in northern Luzon,* London, George Allen and Unwin.

Kennedy, Raymond
1935 *The ethnology of the Greater Sunda Islands,* unpublished Ph.D. dissertation, New Haven, Yale University (UM 67-4797).

Kiefer, Thomas M.
1967 "Power, politics and guns in Jolo: the influence of modern weapons on Tausug legal and economic institutions," *PSR 15:* 21-29.
1968 "Institutionalized friendship and warfare among the Tausug of Jolo," *Ethnology 7:* 225-44.
1969 *Tausug armed conflict: the social organization of military activity in a Philippine Moslem society,* Ph.D. dissertation, Indiana University, Department of Anthropology (also issued as *Research Series No. 7, Philippine Studies Program,* University of Chicago, June 1969).

Kiefer, Thomas M., and Clifford Sather
1970 "Gravemarkers and the repression of sexual symbolism: the case of two Southeast Asian Moslem societies," *Bijd. 126:* 75-90.

Kikuchi, Yasushi
1966 "Philippines-Batan-to no shakai-shoso-kinnen ni okeru henyo [Some aspects of society in the Batan Islands, Philippines]," *MGK 31:* 56-60.

Kojima, Yudo, ed.
1915-22 *Banzoku kanshu chosa hokokusho [Report of investigations on the customs of the Formosan aborigines],* 5 vols., Taihoku, Formosa, Rinji Taiwan Kyukan Chosakai [Government General of Formosa, Special Research Committee on Old Formosan Customs].

Kokubu, Naoichi, and Erika Kaneko
1962 "The tribal peoples of Formosa," *International Committee on Urgent Anthropological and Ethnological Research, Bulletin 5:* 32-38.

Kroeber, Alfred L.
1918 "The history of Philippine civilization as reflected in religious nomenclature," *American Museum of Natural History, Anthropological Papers 19, pt. 2:* 39-67.
1919 "Kinship in the Philippines," *American Museum of Natural History, Anthropological Papers 19:* 73-84.
1943 "Peoples of the Philippines," *American Museum of Natural History, Handbook Series 8, rev. ed.:* 1-244.

Kuder, Edward M.
1945 "The Moros in the Philippines," *Far Eastern Quarterly 4:* 119-26.

Lambrecht, Francis
1929 "Ifugaw villages and houses," *Publications of the Catholic Anthropological Conference 1:* 117-41.
1932 "The Mayawyaw ritual, 1. Rice culture and rice ritual," *Publications of the Catholic Anthropological Conference 4:* 1-167.
1935 "The Mayawyaw ritual, 2. Marriage and marriage ritual," *Publications of the Catholic Anthropological Conference 4:* 169-325.
1938 "The Mayawyaw ritual, 3. Death and death ritual," *Publications of the Catholic Anthropological Conference 4:* 327-493.

1939 "The Mayawyaw ritual, 4. Property and property ritual," *Publications of the Catholic Anthropological Conference* 4: 495-711.

1941 "The Mayawyaw ritual, 5. Go-betweens and priests," *Publications of the Catholic Anthropological Conference* 4: 713-54.

1953 "Genealogical trees of Mayawyaw," *JEAS* 2: 21-28.

1954 "Genealogical tree of Kiangan, Ifugao," *JEAS* 3: 366-69.

1955 "The Mayawyaw ritual, 6. Illness and its ritual," *JEAS* 4: 1-155.

1957 "The Mayawyaw ritual, 7. Hunting and its ritual," *JEAS* 6: 1-28.

1965 "Ifugaw *hudhud* literature," *Saint Louis Quarterly* 3: 191-214.

1967 "The *hudhud* of Dinulawan and Bugan at Gonhadan," *Saint Louis Quarterly* 5: 267-713.

1971 "The main factors of resistance to culture change in Ifugaoland," in Peter G. Gowing and William H. Scott, eds., *Acculturation in the Philippines*, Quezon City, New Day: 83-89.

Lambrecht, G.
1959 "The Gaddang of Isabela and Nueva Vizcaya: survivals of a primitive animistic religion," *PS* 7: 194-218.

1960 "Anitu rites among the Gaddang," *PS* 8: 584-602.

Landé, Carl
1965 *Leaders, factions, and parties: the structure of Philippine politics*, New Haven, Yale University, Southeast Asia Studies.

Laquian, Aprodicio A.
1966 "The city in nation building," Manila, School of Public Administration, University of the Philippines, *Studies in Public Administration No. 8*.

1968 *Slums are for people: The Barrio Magsaysay Pilot Project in Urban Community Development*, Manila, University of the Philippines.

Laufer, Berthold
1907 "The relation of the Chinese to the Philippine Islands," *Smithsonian Miscellaneous Collections* 50: 248-84.

Lawless, Robert
1969 "An evaluation of Philippine culture-personality research," Quezon City, Asian Center, University of the Philippines, *Monograph Series No. 3*.

Leach, E. R.
1950 "Primitive calendars," *Oceania* 20: 245-60.

Leaño, Isabel W.
1965 "The Ibaloy sing for the dead," *PSR* 13: 154-89.

LeBar, Frank M.
1968 "Ritual wealth and culture change in Southeast Asia," *Proceedings, VIIIth International Congress Anthropological and Ethnological Sciences*, Tokyo and Kyoto, 2: 225-27.

Lewis, Henry T.
1971 *Ilocano rice farmers: a comparative study of two Philippine barrios*, Honolulu, University of Hawaii Press.

Li, Hwei
1955 "Jih Yüeh T'an Thao-tsu ti ch'u-sheng ho yü-erh fa [Birth customs and child care among the Thao of Jih Yüeh T'an, Taiwan]," *BDAA* 6: 49-51.

1958 "P'ing-tung hsien Lai-i ts'un wu-shu tzu-liao [Data on magic collected in Chala'abus village, Pingtung County]," *BIE* 6: 107-29.

Li, Yih-yüan
1956 "Lai-i hsiang Paiwan-tsu chung chi-mo jen ti yen-chiu [A study of the 'Chimo' people among the western Paiwan]," *BIE* 1: 55-83.

1957a "T'ai-wan nan-pu Pingpu-tsu p'ing-t'ai-wu ti pi-chiao yen-chiu [On the platform house found among some Pingpu tribes in Formosa]," *BIE* 3: 117-44.

1957b "Thao-tsu ti ching-chi sheng-huo [Economic life of the Thao]," *BDAA* 9-10: 52-99.

Li, Yih-yüan, et al.
1962 "Ma-t'ai-an Ami-tsu ti wu-chih wen-hua [Material culture of the Vataan Ami]," *MIE* 2: 1-461.

1963 "Nan-ao ti Atayal-jen: min-tsu-hsüeh t'ien-yeh tiao-ch'a yü yen-chiu [The Atayal of Nanao: an ethnological investigation]," *MIE* 5: 1-312.

Lieban, Richard W.
1967 *Cebuano sorcery; malign magic in the Philippines*, Berkeley, University of California Press.

Lin, Heng-li
1956 "Saisiat-tsu ai-ling-chi ko ts'u [The songs of the 'Pas-taai']," *BIE* 2: 31-107.

1961 "Yami-li chih-jun fa [Intercalation of the Yami calendar]," *BIE* 12: 41-74.

Ling, Shun-sheng
1955 "Tung-nan Ya ti hsi-ku tsang chi ch'i huan T'ai-p'ing-yang ti fen-pu [The bone-washing burial custom in Southeast Asia and its circum-Pacific distribution]," *Ethnological Society of China, Bulletin 1*: 25-44.

1958 "T'ai-wan t'u-chu-tsu ti tsung-miao yü she-chi [Ancestor temple and earth altar among the Formosan aborigines]," *BIE* 6: 1-57.

1962 "Hua-nan Tung-nan Ya chi Chung Mei-chou ti shu-p'i pu shih ta-pang [Stone bark cloth beaters of South China, Southeast Asia and Central America]," *BIE* 13: 195-219.

Liu, Pin-hsiung
1959 "Lan-yü Yami-tsu sang-tsang ti i-lieh [Burial rites on Botel Tobago Island]," *BIE* 8: 143-83.

Liu, Pin-hsiung, et al.
1965 "Hsiu-ku-luan Ami-tsu ti she-hui tsu-chih [Social structure of the Siukuluan Ami]," *MIE* 8: 1-268.

Llamzon, Teodoro A.
1971 "The Tasaday language so far," *Philippine Journal of Linguistics* 2: 1-30.

Long, Howard R.
1960 *The people of Mushan: life in a Taiwanese village*, Columbia, University of Missouri Press.

Loofs, H. H. E.
1965 "Some remarks on 'Philippine megaliths'," *Asian Studies* 3: 393-402.

Lopez, Rogelio M.
1964 "Some facts about women in Manoboland," *Carolinian* 28: 14ff.

1965 "Manobo belief: there's a soul in every grain of rice," *Sunday Times Magazine* 20: 42.

1968 *Agricultural practices of the Manobo in the interior of Southwestern Cotabato (Mindanao)*, Cebu City, University of San Carlos.

Lynch, Frank
1949 "Ang Mga Asuwang: a Bicol belief," *PSHR* 14: 401-27.

1964 "Social acceptance," in his *Four Readings on Philippine Values*, Quezon City, Institute of Philippine Culture, Ateneo de Manila University Press: 1-21.

1965 "Trends report of studies in social stratification and social mobility in the Philippines," *East Asian Cultural Studies* 4: 163-91.

Lynch, Ralph E.
1955 "The Bukidnons of northern Mindanao, 1945-1955," *University of Chicago, Philippine Studies Program*, Conference on Mindanao, May 1955 (mimeographed).

156

BIBLIOGRAPHY

Mabuchi, Toichi
1936 "Bunun-zoku no matsuri to koyomi [Rituals and picture calendar of the Bunun]," *MGK 2*: 58-80.
1940 "Bunun-zoku ni okeru juniku no bunpai to zoyo [Distribution and presentation of meat among the Bunun]," *Minzokugaku Nempo 2*: 365-452.
1952 "Social organization of the central tribes of Formosa," *IAE 46*: 182-211.
1954a "Takasagozoku no bunrui gakushiteki kaiko [Retrospect on the classification of the Formosan aborigines]," *MGK 18*: 1-11.
1954b "Takasagozoku ni kansuru shakaijinruigaku [Social anthropology of the Formosan aborigines]," *MGK 18*: 86-104.
1954c "Takasagozoku no ido oyobi bunpu [Migration and distribution of the Formosan Aborigines]," *MGK 18*: 123-54.
1956 "On the Yami people," in Tadao Kano and Kokichi Segawa, eds., *An Illustrated Ethnography of Formosan Aborigines, Vol. 1, The Yami*, Tokyo, Maruzen: 1-18.
1960 "The aboriginal peoples of Formosa," in George Peter Murdock, ed., *Social Structure of Southeast Asia*, Chicago, Quadrangle Books: 127-40.
1964 "Tales concerning the origin of grains in the insular area of eastern and southeastern Asia," *Asian Folklore Studies 23*: 1-92.
1966 "Sphere of geographical knowledge and socio-political organization among the mountain peoples of Formosa," *Monumenta Nipponica Monograph 25*: 101-46. [Translation of an article in *Minzokugaku Nempo 3*: 267-311, 1940-41.]
1970a "Magico-religious land ownership in central Formosa and Southeast Asia," *BIE 29*: 349-83.
1970b "A trend toward the Omaha type in the Bunun kinship terminology," in J. Pouillon and P. Maranda, eds., *Echanges et communications. Mélanges offerts à Claude Lévi-Strauss à l'occasion de son 60ème anniversaire*, 2 vols., The Hague, Mouton: 321-46.

Maceda, Marcelino N.
1954 *A survey of the socio-economic, religious and education conditions of the Mamanuas of Northeast Mindanao*, Master's thesis, University of San Carlos.
1956 "Utilization of poisonous roots by the Mamanuas," *Carolinian 19*: 15, 35.
1957 "The full-moon prayer ceremony of the Mamanuas of Northeastern Mindanao," *Anthropos 52*: 277-84.
1963 "Some medicinal plants known to the Mamanua of Northeastern Mindanao, Philippines," *Studia Instituti Anthropos 18*: 133-36.
1964a *The culture of the Mamanua (Northeast Mindanao) as compared with that of the other Negritos of Southeast Asia*, Manila, Catholic Trade School.
1964b "Preliminary report on ethnographic and archaeological fieldwork in the Kulaman Plateau, Island of Mindanao, Philippines," *Anthropos 59*: 75-81.
1966 "Archaeological and socio-anthropological field work in Kulaman Plateau, Southwestern Cotabato," *Science Review 7*: 7.
1967a "A brief report on some Mangyans in northern Oriental Mindoro," *Unitas 40*: 102-55.
1967b "Preliminary studies of the figures and ornamentation of some selected jar covers from Kulaman Plateau (Southwestern Cotabato), Island of Mindanao, Philippines," *Anthropos 62*: 509-32.
1968 "Manobo society: selected patterns and possible change," in Rudolf Rahmann and G. R. Ang, eds., *Dr. H. Otley Beyer: Dean of Philippine Anthropol-*

ogy (*A Commemorative Issue*), Cebu City, University of San Carlos.

MacLeish, Kenneth
1972 "Stone age men of the Philippines," *National Geographic 142*: 219-50.

Madigan, Francis C.
1968 "Problems of growth—the future population of the Philippines," *PS 16*: 3-31.

Majul, Cesar A.
1964 *Political and historical notes on the Old Sulu Sultanate*, International Conference on Asian History, University of Hong Kong (mimeographed).
1966a "Succession in the old Sulu sultanate," *Philippine Historical Review 1*: 24-43.
1966b "Political and historical notes on the old Sulu sultanate," *Philippine Historical Review 1*: 1-23.
1966c "Chinese relationships with the sultanate of Sulu," in Alfonso Felix, ed., *The Chinese in the Philippines*, Manila, Solidaridad Publishing House: 143-60.

Manuel, E. Arsenio
1958 *The Maiden of the Buhong sky, a complete song from the Bagobo folk epic Tuwaang*, Quezon City, University of the Philippines Press.
1961 "Upland Bagobo narratives," *PSHR 26*: 429-552.
1963 "A survey of Philippine folk epics," *Asian Folklore Studies 22*: 1-76.
1969a *Manuvu social organization*, unpublished Ph.D. dissertation, Chicago, University of Chicago.
1969b "Agyu: the Ilianon epic of Mindanao," *Unitas 42, no. 2*: 1-104.

Marche, A.
1884 *Etudes ethnographiques sur les Tagbanuas de L'Ile de Palawan (Philippines)*, Paris, Hachette.

Masuda, Fukutaro
1942 *Nampominzoku no konin: Takasagozoku no konin kenkyu [Marriage among the peoples of Southeast Asia: a study of marriage among the Formosan Aborigines]*, Tokyo, Daiamond-sha.

Matildo, Miguel D.
1953 *A study of the socio-economic, religious, and educational conditions of the Manobos of Agusan*, unpublished M.A. thesis, Cebu City, University of San Carlos. [Ateneo de Manila, University Archives Microfilm, 1968.]

McAmis, Robert D.
1966 "An introduction to the folk tales of the Maranao Muslims of Mindanao in the Southern Philippines," *Translation Series 9, University of Chicago, Philippine Studies Program*.

McGee, T. G.
1967 *The Southeast Asian city: a social geography of the primate cities of Southeast Asia*, London, G. Bell and Sons.

McKaughan, Howard P.
1954 "Notes on Chabacano grammar," *JEAS 3*: 205-43.

McKaughan, Howard P., and Batua Macaraya
1967 *A Maranao dictionary*, Honolulu, University of Hawaii Press.

McPhelin, Michael
1969 "Manila: the primate city," *PS 17*: 781-89.

Mednick, Melvin
1956 "The Moros," in Fred Eggan et al., *Area Handbook on the Philippines*, 4 vols., New Haven, Human Relations Area Files: 4, 1729-74.
1957 "Some problems of Moro history and political organization," *PSR 5*: 39-52.
1961 "Sultans and mayors: the relation of a national to an indigenous political system," *Il Politico 266, no. 1*.

BIBLIOGRAPHY

1965 "Encampment of the lake: the social organization of a Philippine Moslem (Moro) Society," *Research Series 5, University of Chicago, Philippine Studies Program.*

1969 Personal communication.

Miete, A.
1938 "Het adatrecht der Sangihe en Talaudeilanden [Customary law on the Sangihe and Talaud islands]," *KT 27:* 356-71.

Miller, E. Y.
1905 "The Bataks of Palawan," *Philippines Department of the Interior, Ethnological Survey Publications 2:* 179-89.

Miller, Merton
1912 "The Mangyans of Mindoro," *PJS 7 (section D):* 135-57.

Mills, Lennox A.
1925 "British Malaya, 1824-67," *JRASMB 3, pt. 2:* 1-340.

Miyauchi, Etsuzo
1937 "Yuwairu Paiwan-zoku no tsukon-kuiki ni tsuite [On the local exogamous zone among the Paiwan]," *MGK 3:* 78-95.

Montano, J.
1886 *Voyage aux Philippines et en Malaisie,* Paris, Hachette.

Montanus, Arnoldus. *See* Ogilby, John

Montero y Vidal, D. José
1888 *Historia de la piratería Malayo-Mahometana en Mindanao, Joló y Borneo,* Madrid, Manuel Tello.

Moss, Claude R.
1920a "Kankanay ceremonies," *University of California Publications in American Archaeology and Ethnology 15:* 343-84.
1920b "Nabaloi law and ritual," *University of California Publications in American Archaeology and Ethnology 15:* 207-342.
1924 "Nabaloi tales," *University of California Publications in American Archaeology and Ethnology 17:* 227-353.

Moss, Claude R., and Alfred L. Kroeber
1919 "Nabaloi songs," *University of California Publications in American Archaeology and Ethnology 15:* 187-206.

Muratake, Seiichi, and Yasushi Kikuchi
1968 "Social structure of the Batangan in Mindoro, Philippines," *Sha: A Quarterly Record of Social Anthropology 2:* 30-61 (Department of Social Anthropology, Tokyo Metropolitan University).

Murdock, George Peter
1949 *Social structure,* New York, Macmillan.

Murdock, George Peter, ed.
1960 *Social structure in Southeast Asia,* Chicago, Quadrangle Books (*Viking Fund Publications in Anthropology No. 29*).

Nakane, Chie, and Sung-hsing Wang
1963 "Taiwan Yamizoku no shakaisoshiki ni tsuite [On the social organization of the Yami of Formosa]," *MGK 27:* 665-68.

Nettleship, Martin
1970 "Externally caused change in aboriginal culture," *BIE 30:* 83-98.

Newton, Ph.
1920 "Observations on the Negritos of the Philippine Islands," *American Journal of Physical Anthropology 3:* 1-24.

Nimmo, Harry Arlo
1965 "Social organization of the Tawi-Tawi Badjaw," *Ethnology 4:* 421-39.
1967 "The sea nomads: description and analysis," *PS 15:* 209-12.
1968 "Reflections on Bajau history," *PS 16:* 32-59.

Norbeck, Edward
1950 "Folklore of the Atayal of Formosa and the mountain tribes of Luzon," *Anthropological Papers, Museum of Anthropology, University of Michigan 5:* 1-44.

Nurge, Ethel
1965 *Life in a Leyte village,* Seattle, University of Washington Press.

Nydegger, William T., and Corinne Nydegger
1963 *Tarong: an Ilocos barrio in the Philippines,* New York, Wiley.

Ogawa, Naoyoshi, and Erin Asai
1935 *Taiwan takasagozoku densetsushu [Myths and traditions of the Formosan native tribes],* Tokyo, Tokoshoin (Institute of Ethnology, Taihoku Imperial University).

Ogilby, John
1671 *Atlas Chinensis . . . with a relation of the Netherlanders assisting the Tartar against Koxinga and the Chinese fleet . . . collected out of their several writings by Arnoldus Montanus, English'd and adorn'd with above a hundred several sculptures, by John Ogilby, Esq.,* London.

Okada, Yuzuru
1942 "Kita-Tsou-zoku ni okeru kazoku [Family life of the Northern Tsou]," *Mikai shakai ni okeru kazoku [The family in primitive society],* Tokyo, Kobundo Shobo: 87-169.
1950 "Paiwan zokuno kazoku seikatsu [Family life of the Paiwan tribe]," *Mikai shakai no kenkyu [The study of primitive society],* 2d ed., Tokyo, Kobundo Shobo: 46-99 [reprinted from an earlier paper by Okada in *MGK 7:* 1-9 (1941)].
1959 "Atayal-zoku no shakaikosei [Social organization of the Atayal]," *Shakaijinruigaku no kihonmondai [Basic problems in social anthropology],* Tokyo, Yuhikaku: 107-62.

Okuda, Iku, Yuzuru Okada, and Yoichiro Nomura
1939a "Kotosho Yamizoku no shakaisoshiki [Social organization of the Yami of Botel Tobago]," *Shakai Keizai Shigaku [Journal of the Social and Economic History Society]* 8: 1-36.
1939b "Kotosho Yamizoku no rodo to gyoro [Labor and fishing among the Yami of Botel Tobago]," *Shakai Keizai Shigaku [Journal of the Social and Economic History Society]* 9: 1-18.
1941a "Kotosho Yamizoku no nogyo [Agriculture of the Yami of Botel Tobago]," in Taiheiyo-kyokai [Institute of the Pacific. Science Section], ed., *Dainanyo: bunka to nogyo [Greater south seas: its culture and its soil],* Tokyo. Kawade-shobo: 325-72 (1-48).
1941b "Kotosho Yamizoku no zaisansei [Property rights among the Yami of Botel Tobago]," *Shakai Keizai Shigaku [Journal of the Social and Economic History Society]* 11: 57-72.

Oracion, Timoteo S.
1954 "An introduction to the culture of the Magahats of the Upper Tayabanan River Valley, Tolong, Negros Oriental, Philippines," *Silliman Journal 1:* 1-24.
1955 "Ceremonial customs and beliefs connected with Magahat kaingin agriculture," *Silliman Journal 2:* 222-36.
1960 "Notes on the culture of Negritos on Negros Island," *Silliman Journal 7:* 201-18.
1963 "Notes on social structure and social change of Negritos of Negros Island," *PSR 11:* 58-67.
1964 "Kaingin agriculture among the Bukidnons of Southeast Negros, Central Philippines," in Socorro Espiritu and Chester Hunt, eds., *Social Founda-*

BIBLIOGRAPHY

tions of Community Development–Readings in the Philippines, Manila, R. M. Garcia Publishing House: 233-49.

1965 "Magahat pregnancy and birth practices," *PSR 13:* 268-74.

1967a "The Bais Forest Preserve Negritos: some notes on their rituals and ceremonies," in Mario D. Zamora, ed., *Studies in Philippine Anthropology in honor of H. Otley Beyer*, Quezon City, Alemar-Phoenix: 419-42.

1967b "A preliminary report on some culture aspects of the Bukidnons on southeastern Negros Island, Philippines," *Unitas 40:* 156-81.

Pacyaya, Alfredo G.
1961 "Changing customs of marriage, death and burial among the Sagada," *Practical Anthropology 8:* 125-33.
1964 "Acculturation and culture change in Sagada," *Silliman Journal 11:* 14-25.
1971 "Religious acculturation in Sagada," in P. G. Gowing and W. H. Scott, eds., *Acculturation in the Philippines*, Quezon City, New Day: 128-39.

Pal, Agaton P.
1956 "A Philippine barrio: a study of social organizations in relation to planned cultural change," *JEAS 5:* 331-486.
1964 "Dumaguete City: Central Philippines," in Alexander Spoehr, ed., *Pacific Port Towns and Cities: A Symposium*, Honolulu, Bishop Museum: 13-16.

Panganiban, Jose Villa
1961 *Spanish loan-words in the Tagalog language*, Manila, Bureau of Printing.

Pasternak, Burton
1972 *Kinship and community in two Chinese villages*, Stanford, Stanford University Press.

Pearson, Richard
1970 "Archaeological survey in southeastern Taiwan," *BIE 30:* 317-30.

Pelzer, Karl J.
1945 *Pioneer settlement in the Asiatic tropics: studies in land utilization and agricultural colonization in Southeast Asia*, New York, American Geographical Society.

Phelan, John L.
1959 *The Hispanization of the Philippines: Spanish aims and Filipino responses: 1565-1700*, Madison, University of Wisconsin Press.

Philippine Islands (Republic). Bureau of the Census and Statistics
1962-63 *Census of the Philippines, 1960*, Manila.

Pittman, Richard S.
1952 *Notes on the dialect geography of the Philippines*, Summer Institute of Linguistics, Grand Forks, N.D.

Postma, Anton
1965 "The *ambahan* of the Hanunóo-Mangyans of southern Mindoro," *Anthropos 60:* 359-68.
1968 "Contemporary Philippine syllabaries in Mindoro," in Rudolf Rahmann and Gertrude Ang, eds., *Dr. H. Otley Beyer: Dean of Philippine Anthropology, San Carlos Publications, Series E: Miscellaneous Contributions in the Humanities*, No. 1: 71-77.

Quisumbing, Lourdes
1965 "Marriage customs in rural Cebu," *San Carlos Publications, Series A: Humanities No. 3.*

Raats, Pieter J.
1969 "A structural study of Bagobo myths and rites," *San Carlos Publications, Series A: Humanities No. 8.*

Rahmann, Rudolf
1955 "A thunderstorm blood-offering of Mamanua Negritos of northeastern Mindanao," in J. Haekel, ed., *Die Wiener Schule der Völkerkunde: Festschrift der 52 jährigen Bestandes des Instituts der Völkerkunde*, Wien, Horn: 369-71.
1956 "Burial in a standing or sitting position among Philippine Negritos," *Anthropos 51:* 541-42.
1963 "The Negritos of the Philippines and the early Spanish missionaries," in *Festschrift Paul J. Schebesta, Studia Instituti Anthropos 18:* 137-57.

Rahmann, Rudolf, and Marcelino N. Maceda
1955 "Notes on the Negritos of Northern Negros," *Anthropos 50:* 810-36.
1958 "Some notes on the Negritos of Iloilo, Island of Panay," *Anthropos 53:* 864-76.
1962 "Notes on the Negritos of Antique, Island of Panay, Philippines," *Anthropos 57:* 626-43.

Rausa-Gomez, Lourdes
1967 "Sri Vijaya and Madjapahit," *PS 15:* 63-107.

Reber, Anna L.
1966 *The Sulu world in the eighteenth and early nineteenth centuries: a historiographical problem in British writings on Malay piracy*, Master's thesis, Ithaca, Cornell University, Department of History.

Reed, William A.
1904 "Negritos of Zambales," *Department of the Interior, Ethnological Survey Publications 2, part 1*, Manila, Bureau of Printing: 1-90.

Reid, Lawrence
1961 "Ritual and ceremony in Mountain Province," *PSR 9:* 1-82.
1971 "Philippine minor languages: word lists and phonologies," *Oceanic Linguistics Special Publication 8:* 1-239.

Reyes, Wilfredo, L.
1966 "Philippine population growth and health development," in University of the Philippines Population Institute, ed., *First Conference on Population, 1965*, Quezon City, University of the Philippines Press: 112-115.

Reynolds, Harriet R.
1964 "Continuity and change in the Chinese family in the Ilocos provinces, Philippines," Ph.D. dissertation, Hartford Seminary Foundation (UM 65-2677).

Reynolds, Hubert
1966 "The multi-level house of the Manobo in Salangsang and its inter-relations with other aspects of culture," *Silliman Journal 13:* 581-93.

Rideout, Henry Milner
1912 *William Jones: Indian, cowboy, American scholar and anthropologist in the field*, New York, Frederick A. Stokes.

Robertson, James A.
1914 "The Igorots of Lepanto," *PJS 9:* 465-529.

Rogers, Dolores M.
1959 *A history of American occupation and administration of the Sulu Archipelago, 1899-1920*, Master's thesis, University of San Francisco, Department of History.

Rosaldo, Michelle Z.
1971 "Context and metaphor in Ilongot oral tradition," unpublished Ph.D. dissertation, Cambridge, Harvard University.
1972 "Metaphors and folk classification," *SWJA 28:* 83-99.

Rosaldo, Renato
1970a "Ilongot society: the social organization of a non-Christian group in northern Luzon, Philippines," unpublished Ph.D. dissertation, Cambridge, Harvard University.

1970b "Ilongot kin terms: a bilateral system of northern Luzon, Philippines," *Proceedings VIIIth International Congress of Anthropological and Ethnological Sciences 2*: 81-4.

1970c "Descent without ancestors and discrete groups," paper read at the 69th Annual Meeting of the American Anthropological Association, November 1970 (mimeographed).

Ruey, Yih-fu, et al.
1955 "Ethnographical investigation of some aspects of the Atayal, Chin-shui ts'un, Miaoli hsien," *BDAA 5*: 113-27 (originally in Chinese, *BDAA 5*: 29-43; translated into English by C. L. Chen).

Saber, Mamitua
1961 "Darangan: the epic of the Maranaos," *PSR 11*: 42-48.
1963 "Some observations on Maranao social and cultural transition," *PSR 11*: 51-56.

Saito, Shiro
1972 "Philippine ethnography: a critically annotated and selected bibliography," Honolulu, University of Hawaii Press (*East-West Bibliographic Series 2*).

Saleeby, Najeeb
1905 "Studies in Moro history, law and religion," *Philippine Islands, Department of the Interior, Ethnological Survey Publication 4, pt. 1*, Manila, Bureau of Printing.
1908 "The history of Sulu," *Ethnological Survey Publication 4*, Manila, Bureau of Printing.

Santaren, Tomas
1956 "Bisayan accounts of early Bornean settlements in the Philippines," *SMJ 7*: 22-42 (translated from the Spanish by Enriqueta Fox, with introduction by Fred Eggan and notes by E. D. Hester).

Sather, Clifford
1967 "Social rank and marriage payments in an immigrant Moro community in Malaysia," *Ethnology 6*: 97-102.
1968 "Some notes concerning Bajau Laut phonology and grammar," *Sabah Society Journal 3*: 205-24.
1971 *Kinship and domestic relations among the Bajau Laut of Northern Borneo*, unpublished Ph.D. dissertation, Cambridge, Harvard University.

Sayama, Yukichi, ed.
1913-21 *Banzoku chosa hokokusho [Report of investigations on the aborigines]*, 8 vols., Taihoku, Formosa, Rinji Taiwan Kyukan Chosakai [Government General of Formosa, Special Research Committee on old Formosan Customs].

Schadenberg, Alex
1855 "Die Bewohner von Süd-Mindanao und der Insel Samal," *Zeitschrift für Ethnologie 17*: 8-37, 45-57.

Schafer, Edward H.
1963 *The golden peaches of Samarkand: a study of T'ang exotics*, Berkeley, University of California Press.
1967 *The vermilion bird: T'ang images of the south*, Berkeley, University of California Press.

Scheans, Daniel
1963 "Suban [Ilokan] society," *PSR 11*: 216-35.

Schebesta, Paul
1952-57 *Die Negrito Asiens*, 2 vols., Wien-Moedling.

Scheerer, Otto
1905 "The Nabaloi dialect," *Philippine Islands Department of the Interior, Ethnological Survey Publications 2, pt. 2*: 89-178.
1906 "Zur ethnologie der inselkette zwischen Luzon und Formosa," *Mitteilungen der Deutschen Gesellschaft für Natur- und Völkerkunde Ostasiens 11*: 1-31.

Schlegel, Stuart A.
1967 "Tiruray constellations: the agricultural astronomy of a Philippine hill people," *PJS 96*: 319-32.
1970 *Tiruray justice: traditional Tiruray law and morality*, Berkeley, University of California Press.

Schröder, Dominik
1967 "The Puyuma of Katipol (Taiwan) and their religion," *BDAA 29-30*: 11-39.

Scott, William Henry
1958a "Economic and material culture of the Kalingas of Madukayan," *SWJA 14*: 318-37.
1958b "A preliminary report on upland rice in northern Luzon," *SWJA 14*: 87-105.
1960 "Social and religious culture of the Kalingas of Madukayan," *SWJA 16*: 174-90.
1966 *On the Cordillera: a look at the peoples and cultures of the Mountain Province*, Manila, MCS Enterprises.
1967 "Some religious beliefs in Sagada Igorot," in Mario D. Zamora, ed., *Studies in Philippine Anthropology*, Quezon City, Alemar-Phoenix: 480-93.
1968 *A critical study of the prehistoric source materials for the study of Philippine history*, Manila, University of Santo Tomas Press.
1970 "Igorot responses to Spanish aims: 1576-1896," *PS 18*: 695-717.

Shih, Lei
1964 "Atayal-tsu Nan-ao ch'ün ti fang-chih kung-yeh [The handweaving industry of the Nanao Atayal]," *BIE 17*: 95-122.

Sicat, G. P., et al.
1964 *The Philippine economy in the 1960s*, Quezon City, University of the Philippines, Institute of Economic Development and Research.

Solheim, Wilhelm G., II
1959 "Notes on burial customs in and near Sagada," *PJS 88*: 123-33.
1960 "Jar burial in the Babuyan and Batanes islands and in central Philippines, and its relationship to jar burial elsewhere in the Far East," *PJS 89*: 115-48.
1971 "Research recommended on Batan and Sabtang," *Bulletin of the International Committee on Urgent Anthropological and Ethnological Research 13*: 115-16.

Sopher, David E.
1965 "The Sea Nomads: a study based on the literature of the maritime boat people of Southeast Asia," *Memoirs of the National Museum 5*, Singapore, National Museum.

Spencer, J. E.
1952 *Land and people in the Philippines: geographic problems in rural economy*, Berkeley, University of California Press.

Spencer, J. E., and G. A. Hale
1961 "The origin, nature and distribution of agricultural terracing," *Pacific Viewpoint 2*: 1-40.

Stokking, H. J.
1917 "Over het Oud-Talaoetsche huwelijk [On the old-time marriage of the Talaud]," *MNZ 61*: 342-48.
1919 "Gebruiken bij zwangerschap en geboorte op Talaoet [Customs during pregnancy and childbirth on Talaud]," *MNZ 63*: 219-29.
1920 "Gebruiken bij de naamgeving op Talaoet [Customs in connection with name-giving on Talaud]," *MNZ 64*: 70-74.
1922a "Gebruiken der Talaoerezen bij de Zeevaart [Customs of the Talaud-people in connection with navigation]," *MNZ 66*: 149-60.
1922b "Gebruiken bij den rijstbouw op Talaoet [Customs

in connection with rice-growing on Talaud]," *MNZ 66:* 242-54.

1923 "Geesten en vroegere geestenverering op Talaoet [Spirits and spirit-cult on Talaud]," *MNZ 67:* 108-21.

Stone, Richard L.
1962 "Intergroup relations among the Tausug, Samal, and Badjaw of Sulu," *PSR 10:* 107-33.
1967 "Some aspects of Muslim social organization," in Manuud, ed., *Brown Heritage,* Manila, Ateneo University Press.

Stone, Richard L., and Joy Marsella
1968 "Mahirap: a squatter community in a Manila suburb," in *Modernization: Its Impact in the Philippines vol. 3,* Manila, Institute of Philippine Culture, Ateneo de Manila: 64-91.

Struys, John
1684 *Account of the visit of John Struys to Formosa in 1650, done out of the Dutch by John Morrison,* London, 1684.

Sung, Lung-sheng
1964 "T'ai-tung p'ing-yüan ti Puyuma-tsu tiao-ch'a chien pao [Preliminary report on an ethnological investigation of the Puyuma tribe of Taitung plain, Formosa]," *BDAA 23-24:* 67-82.
1965 "Nan-wang ts'un Puyuma-tsu ti hui-so chih-tu [Men's house organization in Nanwang village of the Puyuma tribe]," *BDAA 25-26:* 112-44.

Suzuki, Sakutaro
1932 *Taiwan no banzoku kenkyu [Study of the aboriginal tribes of Formosa],* Taihoku, Formosa, Taiwan Shiseki Kankokai.

Svelmoe, Gordon, and Norman Abrams
1955 "A brief field trip among the Bukidnon Tigwa people and the Davao Salug people," *PSHR 18, no. 2:* 141-85.

Takaki, Michiko
1969 Review of Edward P. Dozier, *Mountain arbiters, AA 71:* 515-18.

Tang, Mei-chun
1955 "Miao-li hsien Nan-chuang hsiang Tung-ho ts'un Saisiat-tsu ai-jen-chi ts'an-kuan chi [A visit to the 'Pan-taai' in the Nan-chuang Saisiat, Miao-li county]," *Chu-yi Yü Kuo-ts'e 44:* 28-34.
1957 "Jih Yüeh T'an Thao-tsu ti tsung-chiao [Religion of the Thao, Sun-Moon Lake]," *BDAA 9-10:* 100-24.
1970 "Han and non-Han in Taiwan: a case of acculturation," *BIE 30:* 99-110.

Tangco, Marcelo
1951 "The Christian peoples of the Philippines," University of the Philippines, *Natural and Applied Science Bulletin 11:* 1-115.

Tarling, Nicholas
1963 *Piracy and politics in the Malay world,* Melbourne, F. W. Cheshire.

Taylor, C. N.
1933 "The sea gypsies of Sulu," *Asia 31:* 476-83, 534-35.

Teikoku Gakushiin
1941 *Takasagozoku kanshûhô goi [Dictionnaire de termes de droit coutumier des aborigènes de Formose],* Tokyo, Académie Impériale.

Tenorio, José
1892 *Costumbres de los Indios Tirurayes,* Manila.

Thomas, David, and Alan Healey
1962 "Some Philippine language subgroupings: a lexicostatistical study," *Anthropological Linguistics 4:* 21-33.

Torii, Ryuzo
1902 *Kotosho dozoku chosa hokoku [Report on investiga-tions of the aborigines of Botel Tobago],* Tokyo, Tokyo Imperial University.

Tu, Erh-wei
1959 "A contribution to the mythology of the Tsou, Formosa," *Anthropos 54:* 536-41.
1968 "Mähsi, the war ritual of the Tsou," *BDAA 31:* 98-103.

Tugby, Donald J.
1966 "A model of the social organization of the Ilongot of northeast Luzon," *Journal of Asian and African Studies 1:* 253-60.

Turnbull, Wilfred
1929 "Among the Ilongots twenty years ago," *Philippine Magazine 26:* 262-63, 307-10, 337-38, 374, 379, 416-17, 460-70.

Tweddell, Colin E.
1970 "The identity and distribution of the Mangyan tribes of Mindoro, Philippines," *Anthropological Linguistics 12:* 189-207.

Ullman, Edward L.
1960 "Trade centers and tributary areas of the Philippines," *Geographical Review 50:* 203-18.

Utsurikawa, Nenozo
1931 "Kotosho Yamizoku to nampo ni tsuranaru Philippin Batan no shimajima-kohi densho to jijitsu [Natives of Botel Tobago Island and their relationship with those of the Batan Archipelago in the Philippines—tradition and fact]," *ND 1:* 15-37.

Utsurikawa, Nenozo, et al.
1935 *Taiwan takasagozoku keito shozoku no kenkyu [The Formosan native tribes: a genealogical and classificatory study],* 2 vols., Tokyo, Toko Shoin (with N. Miyamoto and T. Mabuchi).

Valentyn, F.
1724-26 *Oud en Nieuw Oost-Indien ...,* 8 vols., Dordrecht (see esp. *Vol. 6:* 33-93 on Formosa, trans. in Campbell 1903: 1-9, 26-88).

Vanoverbergh, Morice
1925 "Negritos of northern Luzon," *Anthropos 20:* 148-99, 399-443.
1929-30 "Negritos of northern Luzon again," *Anthropos 24:* 1-75, 897-911; *25:* 25-71, 527-65.
1932 "The Isneg," *Publications of the Catholic Anthropological Conference 3:* 1-80.
1936-38 "The Isneg life cycle," *Publications of the Catholic Anthropological Conference 3:* 81-280.
1937-38 "Negritos of eastern Luzon," *Anthropos 32:* 905-28; *33:* 119-64.
1941 "The Isneg farmer," *Publications of the Catholic Anthropological Conference 3:* 281-386.
1950 "The Isneg body and its ailments," *Annali Lateranensi 14:* 193-293.
1952 "Tales in Lepanto Igorot or Kankanay as it is spoken at Bauko," *JEAS 1:* 1-42, 61-108.
1953a "Isneg buildings," *PJS 82:* 77-108.
1953b "Prayers in Lepanto Igorot or Kankanay as it is spoken at Bauco," *JEAS 2:* 1-28, 69-107.
1953-55 "Religion and magic among the Isneg," *Anthropos 48:* 71-104, 557-68; *49:* 233-75, 1004-12; *50:* 212-75.
1954a "Isneg domestic economy," *Annali Lateranensi 18:* 119-256.
1954b "Songs in Lepanto Igorot as it is spoken at Bauko," *Studia Instituti Anthropos 7:* 1-141.
1960 "Isneg songs," *Anthropos 55:* 463-504.

Venturello, M. H.
1907 "Manners and customs of the Tagbanuas and other tribes of the island of Palawan, Philippines" (translated from the original Spanish by Mrs. Ed-

ward Y. Miller), *Smithsonian Miscellaneous Collections 48:* 514-58.

1908 "The 'Batacs' of the island of Palawan, Philippine Islands" (translated from the Spanish by Mrs. Edward Y. Miller), *Internationales Archiv für Ethnographie 18:* 137-44.

Verschuer, F. H. van
1883 "De Badjos," *TNAG 7:* 1-7.

Villaluz, Dom. K.
1966 *The Lake Lanao fisheries and their conservation,* Manila, Bureau of Printing.

Villaverde, Fr. Juan Fernandez
1909 "The Ifugaos of Quiangan and vicinity," *PJS 4-A:* 237-62.

Volkstelling 1930. See Dutch East Indies.

Walkup, Orie S.
1919 "The Bagobo-Japanese land troubles in Davao Province," in H. Otley Beyer, comp., *Philippine Ethnographic Series, Pagan Peoples of Mindanao 6,* Papers 60 and 61.

Wallace, Ben J.
1967 *Gaddang agriculture: the focus of ecological and cultural change,* Ph.D. dissertation, Madison, University of Wisconsin [UM 67-17,043].
1969 "Pagan Gaddang spouse exchange," *Ethnology 8:* 183-89.

Wang, Gung-wu
1958 "The Nanhai trade: a study of the early history of Chinese trade in the South China Sea," *JRASMB 31:* 3-135.

Wang, Jen-ying
1966 "T'ai-wan kao-shan-tsu ti k'ung-chien fen-pu [The spatial distribution of the Formosan aborigines]," *BDAA 27:* 1-28.
1967 "T'ai-wan kao-shan-tsu chien-lüeh sheng-ming piao [Abridged life tables for Formosan Aborigines]," *BIE 24:* 41-79.

Wang, Sung-hsing
1961 "Ma-t'ai-an (Vataan) Ami-tsu chih tsung-chiao chi shen-hua [Religion and myth among the Vataan Ami]," *BIE 12:* 107-78.

Warren, Charles P.
1953 "Marriage and associated customs among the Batak of Palawan (Philippines)," *Eighth Pacific Science Congress, Abstracts of Papers Supplement,* Quezon City: 87.
1956 "Dream interpretation of the Tagbanuwa," *Anthropology Tomorrow 4:* 50-61.
1959 "A vocabulary of the Batak of Palawan," *Transcript No. 7,* Philippine Studies Program, University of Chicago.
1964 "The Batak of Palawan: a culture in transition," *Research Series No. 3,* Philippine Studies Program, University of Chicago.

Warriner, C. K.
1964 "Traditional authority and the modern state: the case of the Maranao of the Philippines," *Social Problems 12:* 51-56.

Wei, Hwei-lin
1950 "Tsou-tsu san tsu-ch'ün ti shih-tsu tsu-chih [The clan system of three ethnic groups of Tsou people, central Taiwan]," *Tai-wan Wen-hsien 1:* 1-11.
1955 "P'ing-tung hsien Lai-i hsiang Lai-i ts'un Paiwan-tsu min-tsu-hsüeh tiao-ch'a chien-pao [Investigation of social organization of the Chala'abus Paiwan, Pingtung Hsien]," *BDAA 5:* 20-28.
1956 "T'ai-wan t'u-chu she-hui ti erh-pu tsu-chih [Dual organization among the Formosan tribes]," *BIE 2:* 1-30.

1957 "Pei-pu Bunun-tsu ti erh-pu tsu-chih [Dual organization of the northern Bunun, central Formosa]," *BDAA 9:* 21-37.
1958a "Atayal-tsu ti pu-lo chih-tu [The tribal system among the Atayal]," *TW 9:* 33-41.
1958b "Saisiat-tsu ti shih-tsu tsu-chih yü ti-yü she-hui [Clan system and local grouping of the Saisiat]," *BIE 2:* 15-24.
1958c "T'ai-wan t'u-chu she-hui ti shih-hsi chih-tu [Lineage system among the Formosan tribes]," *BIE 5:* 1-44.
1960 "Paiwan-tsu ti tsung-tsu tsu-chih yü chieh-chi chih-tu [Ambilateral lineage and class system of the Paiwan]," *BIE 9:* 71-108.
1961 "Ami-tsu ti mu-hsi-shih-tsu yü mu-hsi-shih-hsi-ch'ün [Matriclan and lineage system of the Ami]," *BIE 12:* 1-40.
1962 "Pei-ma-tsu ti mu-hsi shih-hsi tsu yü shih-hsi chih-tu [Matrilineal clan-lineage system of the Puyuma]," *BDAA 19-20:* 65-82.
1963 "Atayal-tsu ti fu-hsi shih-hsi-chün yü shuang-hsi hsüeh-chin chün [Patrilineages and bilateral corporate groups of the Atayal]," *TW 14:* 20-27.
1965 "T'ai-wan t'u-chu she-hui ti pu-lo tsu-chih yü ch'üan-wei chih-tu [Tribal organization and authority system of the Formosan aboriginal societies]," *BDAA 25-26:* 71-92.

Wei, Hwei-lin, and Pin-hsiung Liu
1962 "Lan-yü Yami-tsu ti she-hui tsu-chih [Social structure of the Yami of Botel Tobago]," *MIE 1:* 1-284.

Wei, Hwei-lin, and Jen-ying Wang
1966 "T'ai-wan t'u-chu ko tsu chin nien jen-k'ou tseng-chia yü chü-lo i-tung tiao-ch'a pao-kao [A survey of population growth and migration patterns among Formosan aborigines]," *OPDAA 3:* 1-122.

Wei, Hwei-lin, Chi-lu Chen, and Ting-jui Ho
1954 "T'ai-tung hsien Pei-nan hsiang Nan-wang ts'un min-tsu-hsüeh tiao-ch'a chien-pao [Preliminary report of ethnological fieldwork with the Puyuma tribe, Taitung]," *BDAA 3:* 14-26.

Wei, Hwei-lin, Chin-chuan Yu, and Heng-li Lin
1952 "Ts'ao-tsu p'ien [Ethnography of the ethnic group Tsou]," *Taiwan Sheng T'ung Chih Kao 8:* 1-253. [Published by the Commission of Historical Research of Taiwan.]

Wernstedt, Frederick L., and P. D. Simkins
1965 "Migrations and the settlement of Mindanao," *Journal of Asian Studies 29:* 83-103.

Wernstedt, Frederick L., and J. E. Spencer
1967 *The Philippine Island world: a physical, cultural, and regional geography,* Berkeley, University of California Press.

Whinnom, Keith
1954 "Spanish in the Philippines," *Journal of Oriental Studies 1:* 129-94.

Wickberg, Edgar B.
1965 *The Chinese in Philippine life, 1850-1898,* New Haven, Yale University Press.

Wilson, Lawrence L.
1947a *Apayao life and legends,* Baguio, n.p.
1947b *Ilongot life and legends,* Baguio, n.p.
1953a "Nabaloi shamanism and sympathetic magic," *PSHR 18:* 187-93.
1953b *The skyland of the Philippines,* Baguio, Baguio Publishing Company.

Wolf, Margery
1968 *The House of Lim,* New York, Appleton-Century-Crofts.
1972 *Women and the family in rural Taiwan,* Stanford, Stanford University Press.

Wood, Grace
  1957 "The Tiruray," *PSR 5:* 12-39.
Wu, Yen-ho
  1964 "T'ai-ma-li ch'i liu-yü Paiwan-tsu t'ien-yeh tiao-ch'a chien-pao [Fieldnotes on the eastern Paiwan along the Taimali River]," *BDAA 24:* 83-93.
  1965 "Paiwan-tsu tung-Paiwan ch'ün ti wu-i yü wu-shu [Shamanism and other beliefs among the eastern Paiwan]," *BIE 20:* 105-53.
  1968 "Paiwan erh-t'ung ti yang-yü [Child training among the eastern Paiwan]," *BIE 25:* 55-107.
Wulff, Inger
  1964 "Features of Yakan culture," *Folk 6:* 53-72.
Wurfel, David
  1959 "The Philippines," in George McT. Kahin, ed., *Government and Politics of Southeast Asia,* Ithaca, Cornell University Press: 421-508.

Yamada, Yukihiro
  1965 "Phonology of Itbayaten," *PJS 94:* 373-93.
  1967 "Fishing economy of the Itbayat, Batanes, Philippines, with special reference to its vocabulary," *Asian Studies 5:* 137-219.
Yang, Hsi-mei
  1956 "Taiwan Saisiat-tsu ti ko-jen ming-ming chih [An analytical study on the naming system of the Saisiat tribe, Taiwan]," *Annals of Academia Sinica 3:* 311-40.
Yengoyan, Aram A.
  1964 *Environment, shifting cultivation, and social organization among the Mandaya of Eastern Mindanao, Philippines,* Ph.D. dissertation, Chicago, University of Chicago.

  1965 "Aspects of ecological succession among Mandaya populations in eastern Davao Province, Philippines," *Papers of the Michigan Academy of Science, Arts, and Letters 50:* 437-43.
  1966a "Baptism and 'Bisayanization' among the Mandaya of eastern Mindanao," *Asian Studies 10:* 324-27.
  1966b "Marketing networks and economic processes among the abaca cultivating Mandaya of eastern Mindanao, Philippines," *Report to the Agricultural Development Council.*
  1966c "Marketing networks and economic processes among the abaca cultivating Mandaya of eastern Mindanao, Philippines," in R. Borton, ed., *Getting Agriculture Moving,* New York, Agricultural Development Council: 689-701.
  1967 "The initial populating of the Philippines: some problems and interpretations," in Mario D. Zamora, ed., *Studies in Philippine Anthropology,* Quezon City, Alemar-Phoenix: 175-85.
  1971 "The Philippines: the effects of cash cropping on Mandaya land tenure," in Ron Crocombe, ed., *Land Tenure in the Pacific,* Melbourne, Oxford University Press: 362-74.
Yuan, Chang-rue
  1964 "Nan-ao Atayal-tsu ti nung-yeh [Agriculture of the Nanao Atayal]," *BIE 17:* 123-200.

Zaide, Gregorio F.
  1957 *Philippine political and cultural history,* Manila, Philippine Educational Company.
Zamora, Mario D., ed.
  1967 *Studies in Philippine Anthropology (in honor of H. Otley Beyer),* Quezon City, Alemar-Phoenix.

INDEX OF ETHNIC NAMES

Abaka—ILONGOT, 103
Aeta—NORTHERN GROUPS, 25; ZAM-
    BALES NEGRITOS, 26. See also
    Western Aeta
Agta—NEGRITOS, 24
AGUSAN MANOBO, 55; MINDANAO,
    31
Agutayano—PALAWAN, 64
Agutaynon—PALAWAN, 64
Aita—NEGRITOS, 24
Aklan—CHRISTIAN FILIPINOS, 16;
    BISAYAS, 70
Aklanon—BISAYAS, 70
Alangan—MINDORO, 73
Alishan—TSOU, 138
Amamanua—MAMANUA, 29
AMI, 117
Amia—AMI, 117
Antiqueño—BISAYAS, 70; SOUTHERN
    GROUPS (NEGRITOS), 87
APAYAO, 97
Apayaw—APAYAO, 97
Arikun—WESTERN LOWLAND
    GROUPS, 126
Arisan—TSOU, 138
ATA, 63; NEGRITOS, 24; NORTHERN
    GROUPS, 25; SOUTHERN GROUPS,
    28; MINDANAO, 31; CENTRAL
    HIGHLANDS, 46
Ataas—ATA, 63
Atag—ATA, 63
Atas—ATA, 63
ATAYAL, 142
Atazan—ATAYAL, 142
Ati—NEGRITOS, 24; NORTHERN
    GROUPS, 25; SOUTHERN GROUPS
    (NEGRITOS), 28; BISAYAS, 70
Attaw—CENTRAL HIGHLANDS, 46
Ayta—NEGRITOS, 24; ZAMBALES NE-
    GRITOS, 26

Babuza—WESTERN LOWLAND
    GROUPS, 126
Badjaw—BAJAU LAUT, 9
Badjo—BAJAU LAUT, 9
Bagobo—MINDANAO, 31; CENTRAL
    HIGHLANDS, 46. See also COAST-
    AL BAGOBO; UPLAND BAGOBO
    [MANUVU]
Bajau—JAMA MAPUN, 12
BAJAU LAUT, 9
Bajo—BAJAU LAUT, 9
Bakun—KANKANAI, 90
BALANGINGI, 6
Balangingi Samal—BALANGINGI, 6
Balanguingui—BALANGINGI, 6
Balanini—BALANGINGI, 6
Balbalan—KALINGA, 92
Balbalasan—KALINGA, 92
Balud—BILAAN, 61
Baluga—NORTHERN GROUPS (NE-
    GRITOS), 25
Banaran—JAMA MAPUN, 12
Banaue—IFUGAO, 78
Banawi—IFUGAO, 78
Bangon—MINDORO, 73
Banton—BISAYAS, 70
Banuanon—BUKIDNON, 39

Banuaon—BUKIDNON, 39
Baraan—BILAAN, 61
Baran—AMI, 117
Basai—EASTERN LOWLAND GROUPS,
    116
Batac—PALAWAN, 64; BATAK, 68
BATAK, 68
Batak—PALAWAN, 64
BATAN-BOTEL TOBAGO, 107
Batanese—BATAN-BOTEL TOBAGO,
    107
Batangan—MINDORO, 73
Bauko—LEPANTO (SAGADA), 86
Benauwe—IFUGAO, 78
Benguetano—IBALOI, 88
Benguet Igorot—IBALOI, 88
Bicolano—CHRISTIAN FILIPINOS, 16
Bikolan—CHRISTIAN FILIPINOS, 16
BILAAN, 61
Bilaan—SOUTHWEST HIGHLANDS, 40
Bilanes—BILAAN, 61
Binokid—MINDANAO, 31; BUKIDNON,
    39
Binukid—BUKIDNON, 39
Binukidnon—BISAYAS, 70
Biraan—BILAAN, 61
Bisayans—CHRISTIAN FILIPINOS, 16;
    BISAYAS, 70
BISAYAS, 70
Blaan—BILAAN, 61
Bontoc—BONTOK, 82
Bontoc Igorot—BONTOK, 82
BONTOK, 82
BOTEL TABAGO. See BATAN-BOTEL
    TOBAGO
Buchoru—PAIWAN-RUKAI, 129
Budai—PAIWAN-RUKAI, 129
Buhid—MINDORO, 73
Buhil—MINDORO, 73
Bu'id—MINDORO, 73
Buki—SULOD, 71
Bukid—MINDORO, 73
BUKIDNON, 39
Bukidnon—SULOD, 71; MAGAHAT, 72
Bukidnon Manobo—MINDANAO, 31;
    BUKIDNON, 39. See also *Southern
    Bukidnon Manobo; Western Bukidnon
    Manobo*
BUKIDNON PLATEAU, 39
Bulalakao—HANUNÓO, 74
Buluan—BILAAN, 61
Buluanes—BILAAN, 61
Bungian—IFUGAO, 78
Bunhian—IFUGAO, 78
Bunum—BUNUN, 134
BUNUN, 134
Buquil—MINDORO, 73
Buquitnon—MAGAHAT, 72
Butsul—PAIWAN-RUKAI, 129

Cagayan. See *Orang Cagayan; Samal
    Cagayan; Tao Cagayan*
Cagayanes—CHRISTIAN FILIPINOS, 16
Cagayano—JAMA MAPUN, 12; PALA-
    WAN, 64
Calaganes—TAGAKAOLO, 62
Calamian—PALAWAN, 64
Calinga—KALINGA, 92

Cebuan—CHRISTIAN FILIPINOS, 16
Cebuano—CHRISTIAN FILIPINOS, 16;
    BISAYAS, 70
CENTRAL GROUPS (LUZON), 78
CENTRAL HIGHLANDS, 46
Central Manobo—MINDANAO, 31
Central Mindanao Manobo—BUKID-
    NON, 39
CENTRAL MOUNTAIN GROUPS, 128
Chakobokoboji—PAIWAN-RUKAI, 129
Chaobobol—PAIWAN-RUKAI, 129
Chibora—TSOU, 138
CHINESE, 116. See also *Overseas Chi-
    nese*
Chipon—PUYUMA, 122
CHRISTIAN FILIPINOS, 16
Ci'uli—ATAYAL, 142
COASTAL BAGOBO, 58
Congking—MAMANUA, 29
Conquista—MAMANUA, 29
COTABATO. See LANAO-COTABATO
COTABATO MANOBO, 45
Cotabato Manobo—MINDANAO, 31
Culaman—KULAMAN, 62
Culamanes—KULAMAN, 62
Cuyono—PALAWAN, 64

Dainan—PAIWAN-RUKAI, 129
Daundung—SAMAL, 5
DAVAO GULF, 50
Dibabaon—MANDAYA, 51; AGUSAN
    MANOBO, 55
Dibabawon—MINDANAO, 31
Divavaoan—MANDAYA, 51
Dolatok—EASTERN LOWLAND
    GROUPS, 116
Dufutu—TSOU, 138
Dugbatang—ATA, 63
Dugbatung—ATA, 63
Dulangan—COTABATO MANOBO, 45
Dumaga—NORTHERN GROUPS (NE-
    GRITOS), 25
Dumagat—NORTHERN GROUPS (NE-
    GRITOS), 25

EASTERN LOWLAND GROUPS, 116
Eastern Samal—SAMAL, 5
Egongut—ILONGOT, 103
Eta—NEGRITOS, 24
Etall—ATAYAL, 142

Falanao—AMI, 117
Favorlang—WESTERN LOWLAND
    GROUPS, 126
FILIPINOS. See CHRISTIAN FILI-
    PINOS
FORMOSA, 115

Gadan—PAGAN GADDANG, 100
Gaddanes—PAGAN GADDANG, 100
Gaddang—CHRISTIAN FILIPINOS, 16;
    PAGAN GADDANG, 100
Gaogan—ATAYAL, 142
Guianes—BONTOK, 82
Guianga—CENTRAL HIGHLANDS, 46;
    COASTAL BAGOBO, 58
Guiangan—CENTRAL HIGHLANDS, 46

Haian—AMI, 117
Haisen—TSOU, 138
Hakka—CHINESE, 116
Halipan—IFUGAO, 78
Hambal—NORTHERN GROUPS, 25; ZAMBALES NEGRITOS, 26
Hampangan—HANUNÓO, 74
Hamtikanon—BISAYAS, 70
Hanglulu—IFUGAO, 78
Hanono-o—HANUNÓO, 74
Hantik—CHRISTIAN FILIPINOS, 16; BISAYAS, 70
HANUNÓO, 74
Hanunóo—MINDORO, 73
Hanya—WESTERN LOWLAND GROUPS, 126
Hapao—IFUGAO, 78
Hapaw—IFUGAO, 78
Hasshaban—PUYUMA, 122
Hataas—ATA, 63
Hengchun—AMI, 117
Higaonan—BUKIDNON, 39
Higaunen—BUKIDNON, 39
HIGHLANDS. See CENTRAL HIGHLANDS; SOUTHWEST HIGHLANDS
Hiligaynon—CHRISTIAN FILIPINOS, 16; BISAYAS, 70
Hiloona—MARANAO, 36
Hinan—AMI, 117; PUYUMA, 122
Hiniraya—BISAYAS, 70
Hoanya—WESTERN LOWLAND GROUPS, 126
Hokkien—CHINESE, 116
Hsiukulan—AMI, 117
Hsiukuluan—AMI, 117

Ibaho—BUNUN, 134
IBALOI, 88
Ibaloy—IBALOI, 88
Ibanag—CHRISTIAN FILIPINOS, 16
Ibilao—ILONGOT, 103
Ibilaw—ILONGOT, 103
IFUGAO, 78
Ifugaw—IFUGAO, 78
Igolotes—LUZON, 76
Igorot—LUZON, 76; BONTOK, 82; KANKANAI, 90. See also Benguet Igorot, Bontoc Igorot, Lepanto Igorot, Sagada Igorot
Iimutsu—TSOU, 138
Ilano—ILANON, 35
ILANON, 35
Ilanum—ILANON, 35
Ilanun—ILANON, 35
Ilianen—MINDANAO, 31; CENTRAL HIGHLANDS, 46
Illanun—ILANON, 35
Ilocano—CHRISTIAN FILIPINOS, 16
Ilokan—CHRISTIAN FILIPINOS, 16
Ilongo—CHRISTIAN FILIPINOS, 16; BISAYAS, 70
ILONGOT, 103
Ilungut—ILONGOT, 103
Imutsu—TSOU, 138
Inibaloi—IBALOI, 88
Inibaloy—IBALOI, 88
Inibiloi—IBALOI, 88
Ipagi Egongot—ILONGOT, 103
Ipugao—IFUGAO, 78
Iranon—ILANON, 35; MARANAO, 36

Iraya—MINDORO, 73; PAGAN GADDANG, 100
Isbukun—BUNUN, 134
Isinai—CHRISTIAN FILIPINOS, 16
Isinay—CHRISTIAN FILIPINOS, 16
Isnag—APAYAO, 97
Isned—APAYAO, 97
Isneg—APAYAO, 97
Ita—NEGRITOS, 24
Itall—ATAYAL, 142
Italon—ILONGOT, 103
Itavi—CHRISTIAN FILIPINOS, 16
Itawes—CHRISTIAN FILIPINOS, 16
Itbayaten—BATAN-BOTEL TOBAGO, 107
Itneg—TINGGIAN, 95; APAYAO, 97
Ituy—SOUTHEASTERN GROUPS, 102
Ivatan—CHRISTIAN FILIPINOS, 16; BATAN-BOTEL TOBAGO, 107
Ivaxo—BUNUN, 134
Iyongut—ILONGOT, 103

JAMA MAPUN, 12
Jangan—CENTRAL HIGHLANDS, 46
Japao—IFUGAO, 78
Joloanos—TAUSUG, 2
Jolo Moros—TAUSUG, 2

Kabinga'an—SAMAL, 5
Kachirai—PAIWAN-RUKAI, 129
Kagan—TAGAKAOLO, 62
Kagayan—CHRISTIAN FILIPINOS, 16
Kagayano—PALAWAN, 64
Kakanay—KANKANAI, 90
Kalagan—SANGIR, 13; TAGAKAOLO, 62
Kalaisan—ATAYAL, 142
Kalamian—PALAWAN, 64
Kalanguyya—IFUGAO, 78
Kalasan—IFUGAO, 78
Kale-whan—PUYUMA, 122
Kalibugan—SUBANUN, 32
Kalina'—APAYAO, 97
KALINGA, 92. See also Southern Kalinga
Kalingga—KALINGA, 92
Kallahan—IFUGAO, 78
Kanabu—TSOU, 138
Kanakanabu—FORMOSA, 115; TSOU, 138
Kanay—PALAWAN, 64
KANKANAI, 90. See also Northern Kankanai; Southern Kankanai
Kankanai—LEPANTO (SAGADA), 86. See also Northern Kankanai; Southern Kankanai
Kankanay—KANKANAI, 90
Kaoshantsu—FORMOSA, 115
Ka-paiwan-an—PAIWAN-RUKAI, 129
Kapampangan—CHRISTIAN FILIPINOS, 16
Kapiyan—PAIWAN-RUKAI, 129
Katalangan—PAGAN GADDANG, 100
Katangnang—LEPANTO (SAGADA), 86
Kata-tipol—PUYUMA, 122
Katoguran—BUNUN, 134
Katongulan—BUNUN, 134
Katsausan—PUYUMA, 122
Kaulungan—SAMAL, 5
Kavalan—EASTERN LOWLAND GROUPS, 116

Kaviangan—PAIWAN-RUKAI, 129
Kenei—PALAWAN, 64
Kenne—PALAWAN, 64
Kenoy—PALAWAN, 64
Ketagalan—EASTERN LOWLAND GROUPS, 116
Ketangalan—EASTERN LOWLAND GROUPS, 116
Ketanganau—BUNUN, 134
Kiangan—IFUGAO, 78
Kibi—AMI, 117
Kiniraya—BISAYAS, 70
Kipiyan—PAIWAN-RUKAI, 129
Kiwarawa—EASTERN LOWLAND GROUPS, 116
Kiwit—AMI, 117
Kongadavanu—PAIWAN-RUKAI, 129
Kongking—MAMANUA, 29
Koshun—AMI, 117
Kuamanon—UPLAND BAGOBO (MANUVU), 47
Kulalau—PAIWAN-RUKAI, 129
KULAMAN, 62
Kulamanen—MINDANAO, 31; CENTRAL HIGHLANDS, 46
Kulavan—EASTERN LOWLAND GROUPS, 116
Kunanau—PAIWAN-RUKAI, 129
Kuvalan—EASTERN LOWLAND GROUPS, 116
Kuwarawan—EASTERN LOWLAND GROUPS, 116
Kuyono—PALAWAN, 64
Kuyonon—CHRISTIAN FILIPINOS, 16; PALAWAN, 64

La'aluwa—TSOU, 138
La'aroa—TSOU, 138
Laliklik—PAIWAN-RUKAI, 129
Lanon—ILANON, 35; MARANAO, 36
LANAO-COTABATO, 34
Laoc—TAGAKAOLO, 62
LAUT. See BAJAU LAUT; Orang Laut; Sama Laut
Lepanto Igorot—LEPANTO (SAGADA), 86
LEPANTO (SAGADA), 86
Lilisha—PAIWAN-RUKAI, 129
Linau—EASTERN LOWLAND GROUPS, 116
Lingotes—ILONGOT, 103
Lloa—WESTERN LOWLAND GROUPS, 126
Loncjou—EASTERN LOWLAND GROUPS, 116
Longkiau—EASTERN LOWLAND GROUPS, 116
LOWLAND GROUPS. See EASTERN LOWLAND GROUPS; WESTERN LOWLAND GROUPS
Lua'an—BAJAU LAUT, 9
Lubuagan—KALINGA, 92
Lufutu—TSOU, 138
Luhtu—TSOU, 138
Luilang—WESTERN LOWLAND GROUPS, 126
Luwaqan—BAJAU LAUT, 9
LUZON, 76

Maddukayang–PAGAN GADDANG, 100
Madukayan–KALINGA, 92
Maga–PAIWAN-RUKAI, 129
MAGAHAT, 72
MAGINDANAO, 35
Magosan–MANDAYA, 51
Maguindanao–MAGINDANAO, 35
Makatau–EASTERN LOWLAND
  GROUPS, 116
MAMANUA, 29
Mamanwa–MAMANUA, 29
Mamaua–MAMANUA, 29
Mamaw–MAMANUA, 29
Managosan–MANDAYA, 51
MANDAYA, 51
Mandaya–APAYAO, 97
Mandelaut. See *Sama Mandelaut*
Mangguangan–MANDAYA, 51; AGU-
  SAN MANOBO, 55
Manghianis–MINDORO, 73
Mangianes–MINDORO, 73
Mangrangan–MANDAYA, 51
Manguianes–MINDORO, 73
Mangwanga–MANDAYA, 51
Mangyan–HANUNÓO, 44; MINDORO,
  73
Manidé–NORTHERN GROUPS (NE-
  GRITOS), 25
Manmanua–MAMANUA, 29
Manobo–MINDANAO, 31; UPLAND
  BAGOBO, 47; KULAMAN, 62. See
  also AGUSAN MANOBO; *Bukidnon
  Manobo; Central Manobo; Central
  Mindanao Manobo;* COTABATO MA-
  NOBO; *Sarangani Manobo; Western
  Bukidnon Manobo*
Mansaka–MANDAYA, 51
Mantauran–PAIWAN-RUKAI, 129
MANUVU. See UPLAND BAGOBO
  (MANUVU)
Manuvu–CENTRAL HIGHLANDS, 46;
  UPLAND BAGOBO (MANUVU), 47
MAPUN. See JAMA MAPUN
Maran–AMI, 117
MARANAO, 36
Maranaw–MARANAO, 36
Matidsa'ug–CENTRAL HIGHLANDS,
  46
Matigsalug–CENTRAL HIGHLANDS,
  46
Mayaoyao–IFUGAO, 78
Mayawyaw–IFUGAO, 78
Mayoyao–IFUGAO, 78
Mayoyo–IFUGAO, 78
Melebuganon–MUSLIMS, 23; PALA-
  WAN, 64
Melebugnan–MUSLIMS, 23
Melipa–ATAYAL, 142
Melqoan–ATAYAL, 142
MINDANAO, 31
Mindanao Manobo. See *Central Mindanao
  Manobo*
Mindanao Muslims–LANAO-COTA-
  BATO, 34
MINDORO, 73
Mo-amiami–AMI, 117
Molbog–PALAWAN, 64
Mo-qami–AMI, 117
Moro–MUSLIMS, 23
MOUNTAIN GROUPS. See CENTRAL
  MOUNTAIN GROUPS

"Mountain" Tinggian–TINGGIAN, 95
Mundo–SULOD, 71
MUSLIMS, 23. See also *Mindanao
  Muslims*

Nabaloi–IBALOI, 88
Nagisaran–TSOU, 138
Nagisaru–TSOU, 138
Naibun–PAIWAN-RUKAI, 129
Namahabana–TSOU, 138
Namakaban–TSOU, 138
Namakabau–TSOU, 138
Nanao–ATAYAL, 142
Nansei–AMI, 117
Nanshih–AMI, 117
Nanwang–PUYUMA, 122
Nataoran–AMI, 117
Nauhan–MINDORO, 73
NEGRITOS, 24. See also *Pinatubo Ne-
  gritos,* ZAMBALES NEGRITOS
NORTHERN GROUPS (LUZON), 91
NORTHERN GROUPS (NEGRITOS),
  25
Northern Kankanai–LEPANTO (SAGA-
  DA), 86
Northern Tsou–TSOU, 138

Obbo–UPLAND BAGOBO (MANUVU),
  47
Obo–UPLAND BAGOBO (MANUVU),
  47; COASTAL BAGOBO, 58
Oboobojan–PAIWAN-RUKAI, 129
Opunoho–PAIWAN-RUKAI, 129
Orang Cagayan–JAMA MAPUN, 12
Orang Laut–BAJAU LAUT, 9
Overseas Chinese–PHILIPPINES, 15

PAGAN GADDANG, 100
Pagsupan–MANDAYA, 51
Paitsiana–TSOU, 138
Paiwan–PAIWAN-RUKAI, 129
PAIWAN-RUKAI, 129
Pakarokaro–PAIWAN-RUKAI, 129
Palaqau–BAJAU LAUT, 9. See also
  Sama Palaqau
Pala'u–BAJAU LAUT, 9
PALAWAN, 64
Palawanin–PALAWAN, 64
Palawano–PALAWAN, 64
Palaweño–PALAWAN, 64
Palilalilao–PAIWAN-RUKAI, 129
Paluanes–PALAWAN, 64
Pampangan–CHRISTIAN FILIPINOS,
  16
Panapanayan–PUYUMA, 122
Panayan–CHRISTIAN FILIPINOS, 16
Panayano–BISAYAS, 70
Pangasinan–CHRISTIAN FILIPINOS,
  16
Pangsoia–EASTERN LOWLAND
  GROUPS, 116
Pangtsah–AMI, 117
Pantikanon–BISAYAS, 70
Papora–WESTERN LOWLAND
  GROUPS, 126
Paposa–WESTERN LOWLAND
  GROUPS, 126
Paridarijao–PAIWAN-RUKAI, 129

Pa-she-fan–PUYUMA, 122
Patsaval–PAIWAN-RUKAI, 129
Patsavan–PAIWAN-RUKAI, 129
Payao–APAYAO, 97
Payeo–LEPANTO (SAGADA), 86
Pazeh–WESTERN LOWLAND
  GROUPS, 126
Peinan–AMI, 117
Pelam–PUYUMA, 122
PHILIPPINES, 15
Pilam–PUYUMA, 122
Pinam–AMI, 117
Pinan–PUYUMA, 122
Pinatubo Negritos–ZABALES NEGRI-
  TOS, 26
P'ingp'ufan–FORMOSA, 115
Piuma–PUYUMA, 122
Poavosa–WESTERN LOWLAND
  GROUPS, 126
Pu'angi'on–UPLAND BAGOBO (MA-
  NUVU), 47
Pula–MINDORO, 73
Putian–SULOD, 71
PUYUMA, 122
Pyuma–PUYUMA, 122

Qauqaut–EASTERN LOWLAND
  GROUPS, 116
Queney–PALAWAN, 64
Quiangan–IFUGAO, 78

Rabaru–PAIWAN-RUKAI, 129
Raisha–PAIWAN-RUKAI, 129
Ranao–MARANAO, 36
Raokrik–PAIWAN-RUKAI, 129
Ratagnon–MINDORO, 73
Raval–PAIWAN-RUKAI, 129
Ravar–PAIWAN-RUKAI, 129
Rikiriki–PAIWAN-RUKAI, 129
Ruftu–TSOU, 138
Rukai–PAIWAN-RUKAI, 129

Sa'aroa–TSOU, 138
Sabari–AMI, 117
SAGADA. See LEPANTO (SAGADA)
Sagada Igorot–LEPANTO (SAGADA),
  86
Saiset–SAISIAT, 127
SAISIAT, 127
Saisiat–WESTERN LOWLAND
  GROUPS, 126
Saisirat–SAISIAT, 127
Saisiyat–SAISIAT, 127
Saka–TAGAKAOLO, 62
Salipan–IFUGAO, 78
Salug. See *Tigwa-Salug*
Sama–BALANGINGI, 6; BAJAU LAUT,
  9
Sama Balangingi–BALANGINGI, 6
SAMAL, 5. See also *Balangini Samal;
  Eastern Samal; Western Samal*
Samal–BALANGINGI, 6
Sama Laut–BAJAU LAUT, 9
Samal Cagayan–JAMA MAPUN, 12
Sama Mandelaut–BAJAU LAUT, 9
Sama Palaqau–BAJAU LAUT, 9
Samaran–CHRISTIAN FILIPINOS, 16
Samareño–CHRISTIAN FILIPINOS, 16;
  BISAYAS, 70

Samar-Leyte—BISAYAS, 70
Samarnon—CHRISTIAN FILIPINOS, 16
Sambal—CHRISTIAN FILIPINOS, 16;
    ZAMBALES NEGRITOS, 26
Sambali—CHRISTIAN FILIPINOS, 16
SANGIHE. See SULU-SANGIHE
Sangil—SANGIR, 13
SANGIR, 13
Sangirezen—SANGIR, 13
Sanwhai—PUYUMA, 122
Sao—WESTERN LOWLAND GROUPS,
    126
Sapao—IFUGAO, 78
Saprek—PUYUMA, 122
Sarangani Manobo—MINDANAO, 31;
    KULAMAN, 62
Sazek—ATAYAL, 142
Sedeq—ATAYAL, 142
Sediq—ATAYAL, 142
Sejeq—ATAYAL, 142
Se'ole'—ATAYAL, 142
Seqoleq—ATAYAL, 142
Shao—WESTERN LOWLAND
    GROUPS, 126
Shimopaiwan—PAIWAN-RUKAI, 129
Shukoran—AMI, 117
Shukuoluan—AMI, 117
Sibutu—JAMA MAPUN, 12
Sideia—EASTERN LOWLAND
    GROUPS, 116
Silanganen—TAGBANUWA, 64
Silipan—IFUGAO, 78
Sinkan—EASTERN LOWLAND
    GROUPS, 116
Siraya—EASTERN LOWLAND
    GROUPS, 116
Siukuluan—AMI, 117
SOUTHEASTERN GROUPS (LUZON),
    102
Southern Bukidnon Manobo—BUKID-
    NON, 39
SOUTHERN GROUPS (LUZON), 87
SOUTHERN GROUPS (NEGRITOS), 28
Southern Kalinga—KALINGA, 92
Southern Kankanai—KANKANAI, 90
SOUTHWEST HIGHLANDS, 40
Sqolyeq—ATAYAL, 142
Squliq—ATAYAL, 142
Subanen—SUBANUN, 32
Suban'on—SUBANUN, 32
SUBANUN, 32
Sug. See Taw Sug
Sugbuhanon—CHRISTIAN FILIPINOS,
    16; BISAYANS, 70
SULOD, 71
Suluk—TAUSUG, 2. See also Taw Suluk
Sulus—TAUSUG, 2
SULU-SANGIHE, 1

Taboli—SOUTHWEST HIGHLANDS, 40
Tachaban—PAIWAN-RUKAI, 129
Tadyawan—MINDORO, 73
Tagabawa—CENTRAL HIGHLANDS,
    46
Tagabili—SOUTHWEST HIGHLANDS,
    40
Tagaidan—MINDORO, 73
TAGAKAOLO, 62
Tagal—CHRISTIAN FILIPINOS, 16

Tagalagad—BILAAN, 61
Tagalog—CHRISTIAN FILIPINOS, 16
Tagaydan—MINDORO, 73
Tagbanoua—PALAWAN, 64; TAGBA-
    NUWA, 64
Tagbanua—PALAWAN, 64; TAGBA-
    NUWA, 64
TAGBANUWA, 64
Tagbanwa—PALAWAN, 64; TAGBA-
    NUWA, 64
Taha'urug—UPLAND BAGOBO (MA-
    NUVU), 47
Tahavawa—CENTRAL HIGHLANDS, 46
Taivuan—EASTERN LOWLAND
    GROUPS, 116
Taiwanese—CHINESE, 116
Taiyal—ATAYAL, 142
Takamakau—PAIWAN-RUKAI, 129
Tak'banuath—BUNUN, 134
Takebaka—BUNUN, 134
Taketodo—BUNUN, 134
Takevatan—BUNUN, 134
Takogan—BILAAN, 61
Talamakau—PAIWAN-RUKAI, 129
Talaoerezen—SANGIR, 13
Tamado'wan—BUNUN, 134
Tamari—PAIWAN-RUKAI, 129
Tamaroan—BUNUN, 134
Tamaroau—BUNUN, 134
Tamsui—EASTERN LOWLAND
    GROUPS, 116
Tangdulanen—TAGBANUWA, 64
Tao Cagayan—JAMA MAPUN, 12
Taokas—WESTERN LOWLAND
    GROUPS, 126
Tapangu—TSOU, 138
Taparon—AMI, 117
Taramakau—PAIWAN-RUKAI, 129
Taromak—PAIWAN-RUKAI, 129
Tasaday—SOUTHWEST HIGHLANDS,
    40
Tauran—AMI, 117
TAUSUG, 2
Tavalon—AMI, 117
Tavarong—AMI, 117
Taw Sug—TAUSUG, 2
Taw Suluk—TAUSUG, 2
Tayal—ATAYAL, 142
T'boli—SOUTHWEST HIGHLANDS, 40
Teduray—TIRURAY, 41
Teguray—TIRURAY, 41
Tevorang—EASTERN LOWLAND
    GROUPS, 116
Tfuea—TSOU, 138
Thao—WESTERN LOWLAND
    GROUPS, 126
Tidulay—TIRURAY, 41
Tigwa-Salug—MINDANAO, 31; BUKID-
    NON, 39; CENTRAL HIGHLANDS,
    46
Tinananon—UPLAND BAGOBO (MA-
    NUVU), 47
TINGGIAN, 95. See also "Mountain"
    Tinggian; "Valley" Tinggian
Tinggian—CHRISTIAN FILIPINOS, 16.
    See also "Mountain" Tinggian; "Val-
    ley" Tinggian
Tinglayan—KALINGA, 92
Tinguian—TINGGIAN, 95
Tinguianes—TINGGIAN, 95
Tinitianes—BATAK, 68

TIRURAY, 41
TOBAGO. See BATAN-BOTEL
    TOBAGO
Tokovul—PAIWAN-RUKAI, 129
Tokubun—PAIWAN-RUKAI, 129
Tokuvul—PAIWAN-RUKAI, 129
Tona—PAIWAN-RUKAI, 129
Tordukana—PAIWAN-RUKAI, 129
Tsala'avus—PAIWAN-RUKAI, 129
Tsalisen—PUYUMA, 122
Tsaovali—PAIWAN-RUKAI, 129
Tsa'ovo'ovol—PAIWAN-RUKAI, 129
Tsarisen—PUYUMA, 122; PAIWAN-
    RUKAI, 129
Tse'ole'—ATAYAL, 142
Tsoa-qatsilai—PAIWAN-RUKAI, 129
TSOU, 138. See also Northern Tsou
Tsuihwan—TSOU, 138
Tsuou—TSOU, 138
Tsu'u—TSOU, 138
Tudag—COTABATO MANOBO, 45
Tufuja—TSOU, 138
Tufuya—TSOU, 138
Tugauanum—ATA, 63
Tumanao—BILAAN, 61
Turijene—BAJAU LAUT, 9
Turubiawan—EASTERN LOWLAND
    GROUPS, 116
Tzo—TSOU, 138

Ubian—JAMA MAPUN, 12
Ubo—SOUTHWEST HIGHLANDS, 40
UPLAND BAGOBO (MANUVU), 47
Upunuhu—PAIWAN-RUKAI, 129

"Valley" Tinggian—TINGGIAN, 95
Vataan—AMI, 117
Vilanes—BILAAN, 61
Visayan—CHRISTIAN FILIPINOS, 16
Vonum—BUNUN, 134
Vunun—BUNUN, 134
Vupuran—WESTERN LOWLAND
    GROUPS, 126

Waray-waray—CHRISTIAN FILIPINOS,
    16; BISAYAS, 70
Western Aeta—ZAMBALES NEGRITOS,
    26
Western Bukidnon Manobo—MINDA-
    NAO, 31
WESTERN LOWLAND GROUPS, 126
Western Samal—SAMAL, 5

Xaqul—ATAYAL, 142

Yacanes—YAKAN, 13
YAKAN, 13
YAMI, 108
Yfugao—IFUGAO, 78
Ygolotes—LUZON, 76
Yogad—PAGAN GADDANG, 100
Yrraya—PAGAN GADDANG, 100

ZAMBALES NEGRITOS, 26
ZAMBOANGA, 32

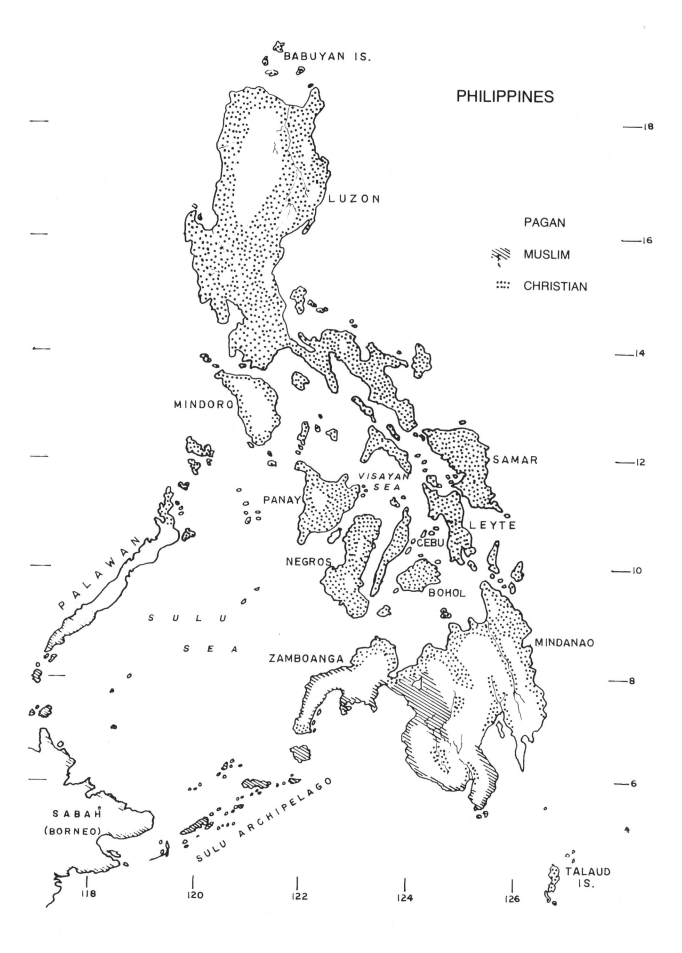

PHILIPPINES

BABUYAN IS.

LUZON

PAGAN

MUSLIM

CHRISTIAN

MINDORO

SAMAR

VISAYAN SEA

PANAY

LEYTE

CEBU

NEGROS

BOHOL

PALAWAN

SULU

SEA

ZAMBOANGA

MINDANAO

SABAH
(BORNEO)

SULU ARCHIPELAGO

TALAUD
IS.

118   120   122   124   126

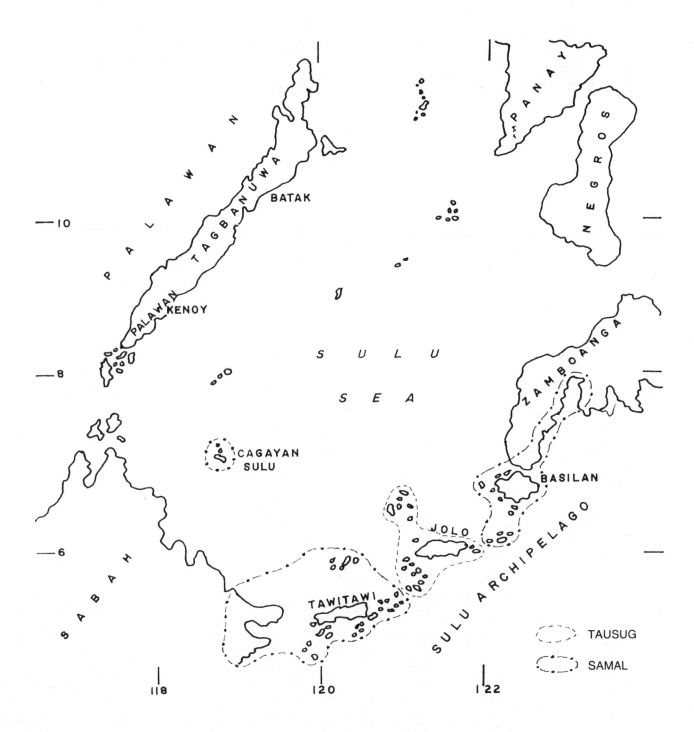

SULU SEA

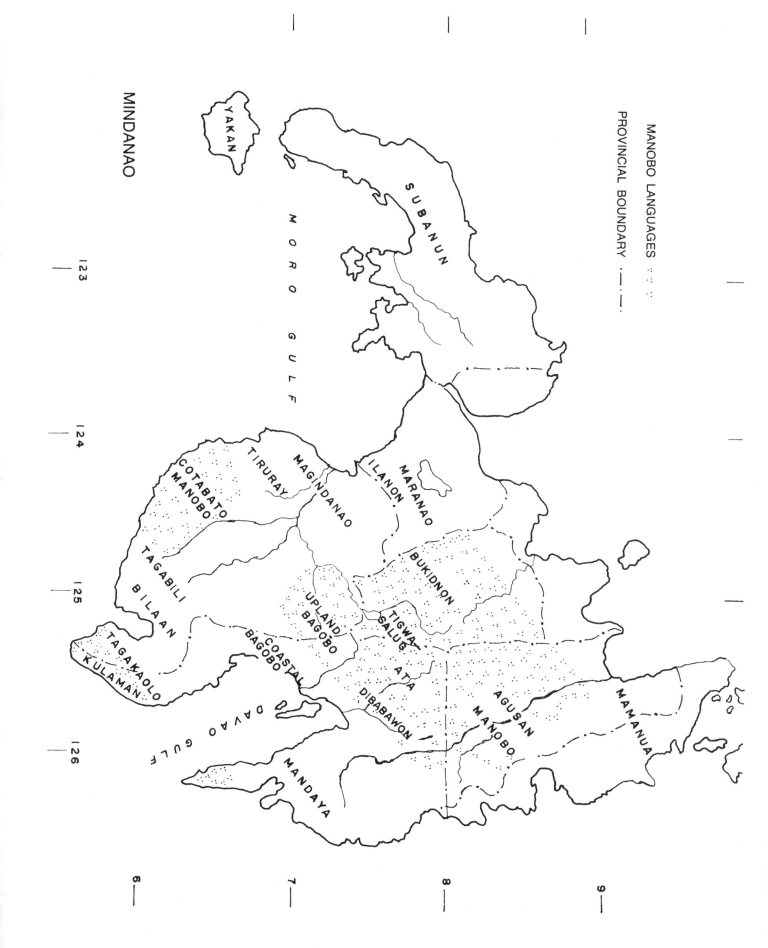

MANOBO LANGUAGES :::::
PROVINCIAL BOUNDARY —·—·—

MINDANAO

123

124

125

126

6

7

8

9

YAKAN

SUBANUN

MORO GULF

TIRURAY

COTABATO
MANOBO

MAGINDANAO

ILANON

MARANAO

BUKIDNON

TAGABILI

BILAAN

UPLAND
BAGOBO

TIGWA
SALUG

ATA

DIBABAWON

AGUSAN
MANOBO

MAMANUA

TAGAKAOLO
KULAMAN

COASTAL
BAGOBO

DAVAO GULF

MANDAYA

LUZON

IRAYA

TADYAWAN

ALANGAN

BATANGAN

13

BUHID

HANUNOO

CHRISTIAN FILIPINOS

RATAGNON

121

MINDORO

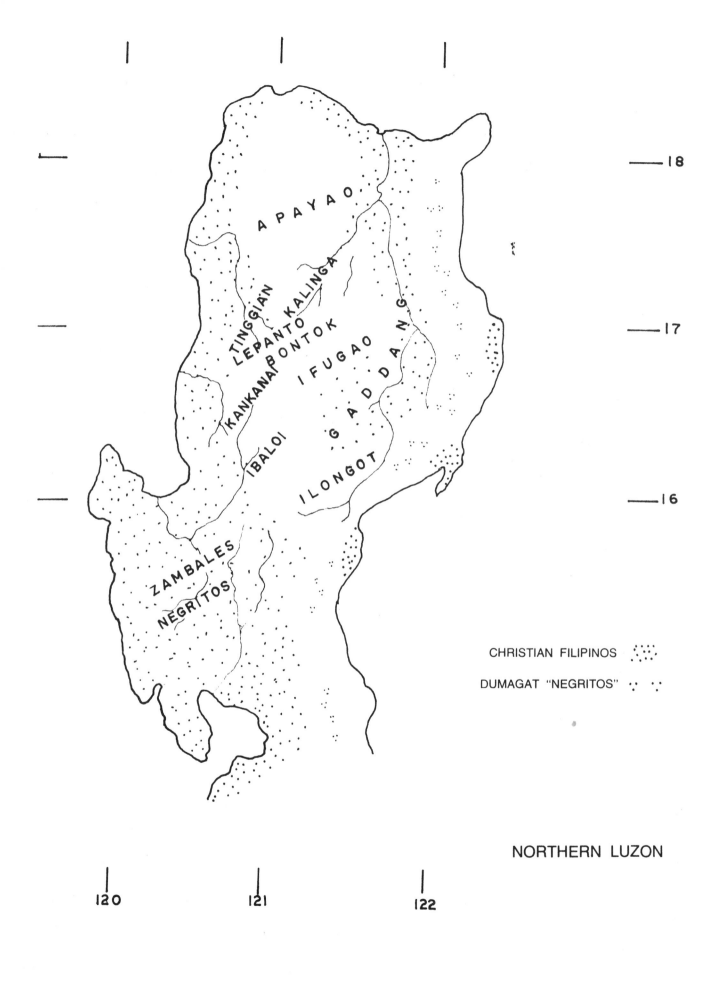

18

17

16

A P A Y A O

TINGGIAN
LEPANTO KALINGA
KANKANAI BONTOK
IFUGAO
IBALOI G A D D A N G
ILONGOT

ZAMBALES
NEGRITOS

CHRISTIAN FILIPINOS

DUMAGAT "NEGRITOS"

120   121   122

NORTHERN LUZON

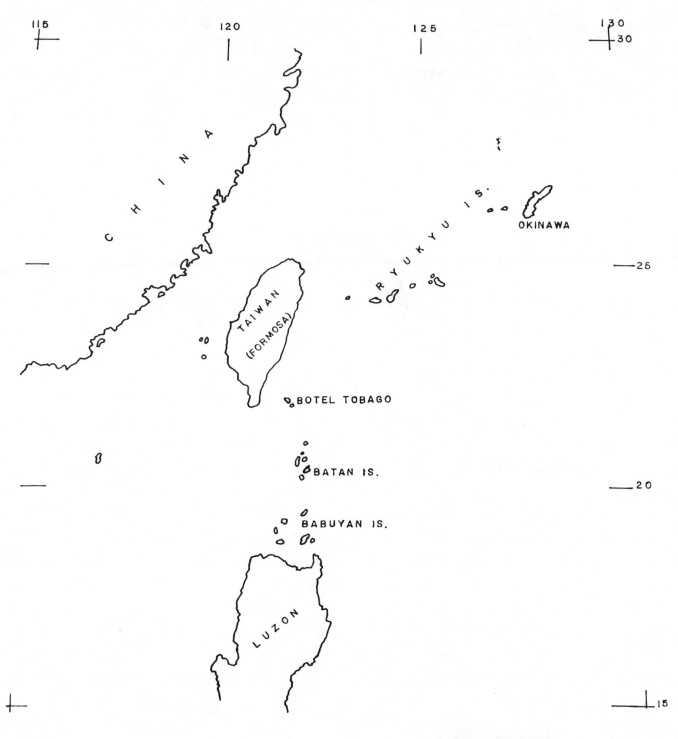

115

120

125

130
30

CHINA

RYUKYU IS.

OKINAWA

TAIWAN
(FORMOSA)

25

BOTEL TOBAGO

BATAN IS.

20

BABUYAN IS.

LUZON

15

BATAN ISLANDS

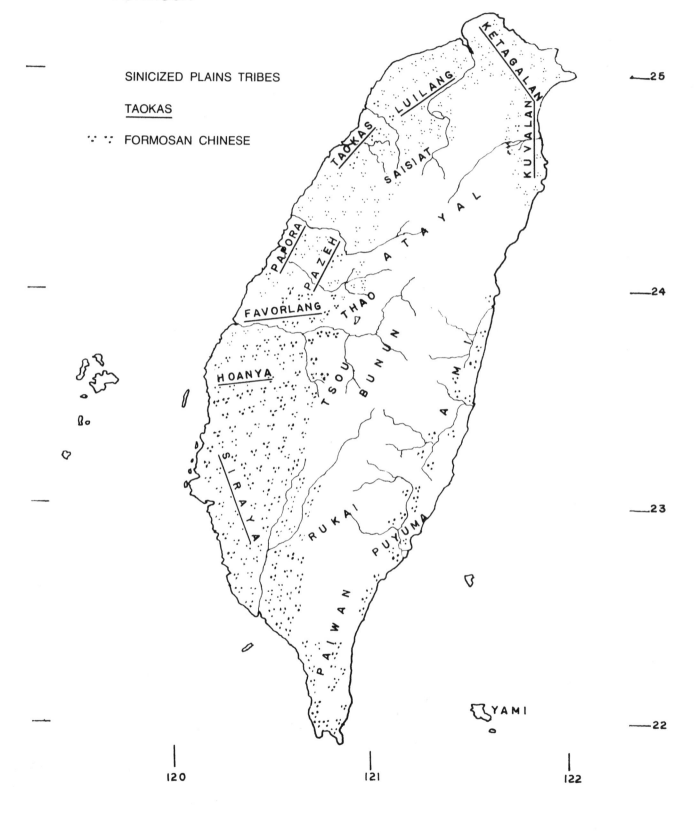

FORMOSA

SINICIZED PLAINS TRIBES

TAOKAS

:·: ·: FORMOSAN CHINESE

KETAGALAN

LUILANG

TAOKAS

SAISIAT

KUVALAN

PAPORA

PAZEH

A T A Y A L

FAVORLANG

THAO

HOANYA

TSOU

BUNUN

A M I

SIRAYA

RUKAI

PUYUMA

PAIWAN

YAMI

25

24

23

22

120

121

122